RAWALPINDI CEMETERIES & CHURCHES

PUNJAB, PAKISTAN

by

Susan Maria Farrington

BACSA
PUTNEY, LONDON
1995

Published by the British Association
for Cemeteries in South Asia (BACSA)

Secretary: Theon Wilkinson, MBE
76 1/2 Chartfield Avenue
LONDON SW15 6HQ

Copyright **Susan Maria Farrington, 1995**

*All rights reserved. No part of this publication
may be reproduced, stored in a retrieval system, or
transmitted, in any form or by any means, electronic,
mechanical, photocopying, recording or otherwise,
without the prior permission of the copyright owner.*

ISBN 0 907799 55 8

Printed by
The Chameleon Press Ltd
5-25 Burr Road
Wandsworth
LONDON SW18 4SG

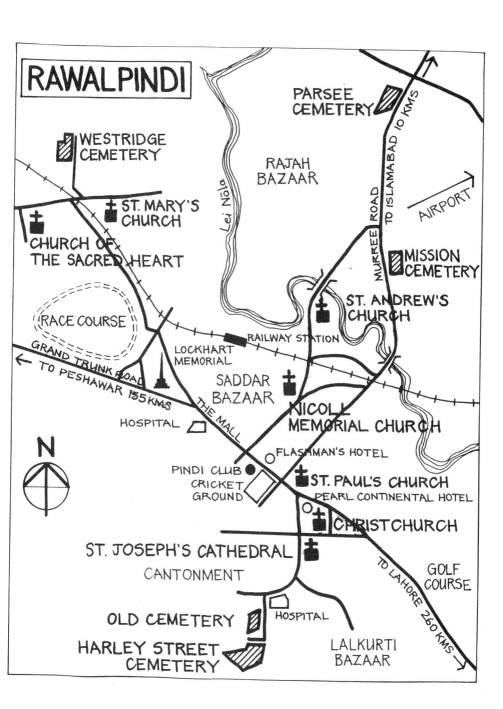

FOR

A and C
and
An Old Lady

CONTENTS

Rawalpindi Map	- i -
Illustrations	- iv -
Introduction	1
Rawalpindi Cemeteries and Churches	2
Analysis of Deaths	4
INSCRIPTIONS	**5**
PART I Harley Street Cemetery Inscriptions	7
Harley Street Regimental Inscriptions	194
Notes on Harley Street Cemetery Maps	211
Harley Street Cemetery Map	212
Harley Street Cemetery - Individual Maps	213
PART II Additional Inscriptions	228
Westridge Cemetery Map	282
Appendix A Regimental Lists	283
Appendix B Chaplains of Christchurch	289
Appendix C Missing & Additional Inscriptions	290
Sources	292
Acknowledgements	293

ILLUSTRATIONS

David ARCHIBALD headstone		Drawing	27
Barracks	Cambridge	PC	279
	Cavalry	PC	236
	Margalla	PC	255
	Westridge	PC	239,250
James BORTHWICK headstone		Photo	21
Maj Gen H F CALEY headstone		Photo	28
Coffin Carrier		Photo	268
Churches	Christchurch	PCs/Photo	257,281
	St Mary's Westridge	Photo	265
	Sacred Heart, Westridge	PC	241
Ellen CLEARY headstone		Drawing	94
Maxine, Princess di CARIATI headstone		Photo	44
June Margaret DUTTON headstone		Photo	53
Elizabeth ENRIGHT headstone		Drawing	3
Alice Owen GANNON headstone		Photo	129
"Growing Stone"		Photo x 2	186
Cemeteries	Harley Street (general view)	Photo	16,58,139
	Harley Street (Lychgate)	Drawing	6
	Old Cemetery (general view)	Photo	280
	Westridge (Chapel)	Drawing	228
Sir Henry HAVELOCK-ALLAN headstone		Photo	76
Leonard HILL headstone		Photo	80
General LOCKHART's Memorial		PC/Photo	100
" "		Drawing	86
Mother Mary I MacDERMOT headstone		Photo	105
Lt John W MAFFETT headstone		Photo	109
The Mall, Rawalpindi		PC	48
Maps	Harley Street Cemetery	Drawing	212-227
	Harley Street Cemetery Plan	Photo	193
	Rawalpindi	Drawing	- i -
	Westridge Cemetery	Drawing	282
Military Band outside the Club		PC	275
Post Office, Rawalpindi		PC	116
Queen Victoria Memorial		PCs x 2	177
Roadsign - Grand Trunk Road		Photo	142
Royal Artillery Monument		Drawing	137
Royal Horse Artillery Monument		Photo	204
" "		Drawing	206
Private C J SKELLY headstone		Photo	157
Soldiers Home, Rawalpindi		PC	291
Somerset Light Infantry Memorial		Photo	207
Frederic Augustus TALBOT headstone		Photo	120
Private J TIPTON headstone		Drawing	172
Clara WILD headstone		Photo x 2	186
Ann WRIGHT headstone		Photo	192

Postcards on pps. 48,116,177,236,239,241,255,257,275
and 279 have kindly been loaned by Michael Stokes
The cover, maps and drawings on
pps. -i-,3,6,7,27,72,86,94,137,172,206,228, and 294
are by my sister-in-law Diana Farrington
Other photos and postcards are from the author's collection

INTRODUCTION

In the last decade of the 20th Century, Rawalpindi is all but united with Islamabad, Pakistan's new capital city built in the 1960's and located some 10 miles distant. With the airport part way between the two, the "Twin Cities" are creeping closer together, but they still maintain their totally different identities.

One hundred years ago a few tiny villages existed where now Islamabad stands, tucked under the Margalla Hills. Rawalpindi, on the other hand, was the largest cantonment in the Punjab, having been founded in 1849 following the annexation of the Punjab at the end of the Second Sikh War. Two years later it was decided that a permanent garrison should be established there and the first troops to be based in Rawalpindi were the 53rd Regiment.

Amidst all the new building, you can see glimpses of the British influence: the cricket ground with its pavilion; the wide streets (now even more necessary with the increase in traffic); trees; the remains of old bungalows, barracks and Government buildings; and last but definitely not least the fine spires of the churches, and the tombs and lych gates of the cemeteries.

Although Islamabad is the main seat of Government, Pindi, as it is still affectionately known, is the District and Divisional headquarters, and where the Army General Headquarters is located. As with the majority of the nearly two hundred cantonments in British India, the city was divided and it is still easy to determine how Pindi must have looked in the 19th Century, with the "native city" on one bank of the Lei stream, and the civil station and cantonments on the other. About a mile to the west lies the Railway Colony, just to the north of Westridge along which runs the Grand Trunk Road to Peshawar. The railway had reached Pindi in 1879, and substantial workshops were soon established and to this day many of older bungalows still survive in this part of the city. Being slightly elevated, barracks were also built here for the soldiers (see pages 239 and 250).

RAWALPINDI CEMETERIES AND CHURCHES

There was no Christian presence in the Punjab when annexation took place in March 1849 following the Second Sikh War. The nearest was an American Presbyterian Mission in Ludhiana, but it was not until 1856 that a church was established in Rajah Bazaar, in the "native city" of Rawalpindi. The army chaplain, however, had arrived shortly after the first troops in 1850, and it was some time later that a Roman Catholic chaplain was appointed, after there were the requisite 100 RC's in the service of the government.

Cemeteries

The earliest surviving grave dates from 1852 in the Old Cemetery, which is located within a couple of hundred yards of the main Harley Street cemetery. In the mid 1980's, about a third of this Old Cemetery was acquired by the nearby military hospital, which explains its unusual shape and the current lack of a main entrance gate. Harley Street is the main cemetery, which make up the bulk of the following inscriptions. The far end of this cemetery is now run by the Commonwealth War Graves Commission (see Map, page 212). There are three other cemeteries:- Westridge (near the Railway Colony), the old Mission cemetery to the east of the Murree Road, and the Parsee cemetery, dating from 1884, which contains some 100 inscriptions and is in excellent condition.

Churches

Christchurch
Less than three years after the arrival of the first troops in Rawalpindi, the foundation stone for the Garrison Church (Christchurch) was laid on 12 March 1852. Until that time services had been conducted in a tent, by the first Chaplain, Rev J M Shaw, who had arrived on 10 February 1850 (see page 289). Consecration took place on 13 February 1856 by Dr Dealtry, the Bishop of Madras and the church seated 450. It was restored in 1879, with its capacity increased to 730, but the Punjab Gazetteer of 1893-4 may be a little harsh when it describes it as being "a large but most unpicturesque building". It has no elegant spire, and the planned tower was never added, but it is bright and airy inside, and contains many commemorative plaques, which can be found at page 229.

St Mary's, Westridge
The foundation stone for this church was laid on 24 September 1882, and completed in two years, consecration taking place on 30 November 1884. It was built for the railway employees, and Rev A A Storr was appointed "Railway Chaplain" in 1883. It contains only one plaque.

St Paul's
Built in red brick, this Gothic Church of Scotland dates from 1909, although a Presbyterian Chaplain had been appointed as early as 1886. It has a fine spire, and pretty brass lights.

St Andrew's
This Anglican mission church was built by SPG in 1910. It is situated in the Gawalmundi district of the Old City. A plaque reads: "Rev Isaac Bert Paul. To the Glory of God this stone was laid on St Andrew's Day AD 1910".

Nicoll Memorial Church
Situated in Saddar Bazaar, this United Presbytarian church was built in 1927.

Weslyan Church
This church is marked on a 1954 map of Rawalpindi, just behind the Pindi Club. A new building now stands on the site.

St Joseph's Catholic Cathedral
The exterior of St Joseph's has altered considerably since 1947 with the addition of a new facade. However a plaque inside reads: "The celebration of the Centenary of the Catholic Mission of Islamabad/Rawalpindi on 11 September 1987. Since 14 September 1887, the following Mill Hill Missionaries were sent here to proclaim the good news and to minister to God's people".... there follow 137 names.

Sacred Heart Church, Westridge
Situated on Connaught Road, this Catholic church was erected in 1890, although it was added to later (?1905). It has a large and intricate marble altar dedicated to "The Royal Munster Fusiliers who died at Shabkadar - in memory of their comrades May 1908. RIP.". The Stations of the Cross were erected by the Royal Irish Fusiliers in 1907.

Detail from Elizabeth ENRIGHT headstone

Appendix A (page 283)
The names of all those buried in the cemeteries are listed under their respective Regiments.

Appendix B (page 289)
Chaplains of Christchurch, Rawalpindi.

Appendix C (page 290)
Two lists of: - headstones which were recorded in 1982, but no longer survive, and
- headstones recorded for the first time during the 1993 survey.

ANALYSIS OF DEATHS

The following graph has been drawn up from the dates of death in the Harley Street cemetery. 15% of the inscriptions gave no month of death, but the following reflects the dates given on the remaining 85%. It should, therefore, give a fairly accurate picture of which part of the year resulted in the majority of casualties.

The graph appears to indicate that there were more fatalities in the colder winter months. It is difficult to know whether this might have been caused by the onset of sickness or debility after the heat of the summer or by suffering from the comparitive cold of winter, especially as the deaths seem to pick up again when the temperatures start to rise. It should also be remembered, however, that during the hot summer months the families moved up to the hill stations of the Murree Hills, and from April to September far fewer people would have been in Rawalpindi. Therefore it would be necessary to analyse the pattern of deaths in the Murree cemeteries and compare these with the Rawalpindi figures in order to draw a totally accurate conclusion.

ANALYSIS OF FATALITIES BY MONTH

INSCRIPTIONS

**NOTES AND KEY
TO THE INSCRIPTION CATALOGUE**

Some explanation is necessary on the presentation of the inscription lists. The layout of the engraving on each headstone varies considerably, both in spelling, style and content. For example, Rawalpindi may be spelt Rawul Pindee, regimental names can be drastically shortened or written out in full, and there are many variations on the way dates and ages have been recorded. As a result, these have all been standardised here, with Rawalpindi spelt as it is recognised today, no abbreviations for the majority of ranks and regiments, and dates typed as day/month/year. The only exception is *yrs* and *mths* for ages.

Likewise, poems and epitaphs have not been reproduced in the format in which they were engraved, but simply follow after the biographical details. The information given on a typical inscription is therefore:

<u>BAKE, James Walter Henry</u>   *(X/791)*
James Walter Henry BAKE. Staff Sergeant Indian Army Corps of Clerks who died at Rawalpindi 1 Mar 1936. For 3 mths the dearly loved husband of Freda BAKE.
                                           (82)(93)(WM)(end)

   X/791 = *The plot letter and number as indicated on the maps*
   (82) = *Recorded in 1982*
   (93) = *Recorded again in 1993*
   (WM) = *The headstone is made of White Marble*
   (end) = *The grave was endowed*
Additional information may be given, such as:
   (BS) = *The headstone is made of Black Slate*
   (PS) = *The headstone is made of Pink Stone*
   (mb) = *The headstone is surrounded by a metal railing box*

A name in capital letters at the end of an inscription is the monumental mason or engraver who prepared the headstone.

Headstones which date from post-Partition (ie. August 1947) have not been recorded in full, but only the name, dates and any specific family information are given.

The cross referenced REGIMENTAL inscriptions will be found in the section immediately following the main list (page 194).

Little biographical information is given. Two good sources for such material are listed at page 292:
   <u>Soldiers of the Raj</u> and <u>Supplementary List of Inscriptions on Tombs or Monuments in the Punjab, etc etc</u>.

The inscriptions have been split into two sections, followed by their respective maps:

PART I
HARLEY STREET CEMETERY inscriptions

PART II
ADDITIONAL INSCRIPTIONS from the other four cemeteries and the plaques from the churches, viz:

Murree Road Cemetery	*Old Cemetery*	*Parsee Cemetery*
Westridge Cemetery	*Christchurch*	*St Andrew's Church*
St Joseph's Cathedral	*St Mary's Church*	*St Paul's Church*
Sacred Heart Church	*Nicholl Memorial Church*	

PART I

H A R L E Y   S T R E E T   C E M E T E R Y

Two surveys have been undertaken in Harley Street cemetery: the first in 1982, with a further study in 1993. During this latter survey, all graves were added to a map (see page 212).

THE LYCHGATE OF HARLEY STREET CEMETERY

ABLETT, Ida May   *(X/782)*
In loving memory of Ida May ABLETT. Dearly loved wife of A W ABLETT. Army Remount Department. Born 21 Nov 1886. Died 4 Nov 1931. Erected by her loving husband and children. Not dead not sleeping, not e'en gone, but present still, and waiting for the coming hour of God's sweet will. *(82)(93)(WM)*

ACTON, John   (see ROYAL FIELD ARTILLERY (2))
ADAMS, T   (see WEST RIDING REGIMENT (1))
ADAMSON, E V   (see ROYAL ARTILLERY (6))

AHL, Winnifred   *(M/1205)*
In loving memory of Winnifred. The little daughter of Armourer Staff Sergeant and F AHL. *(82)(93)*

AIKIN, Mary   *(L/1043)*
In loving memory of Mary (Mollie). The dearly loved wife of William W AIKIN, Military Accounts Department. Born 15 Sep 1870. Died 21 Jun 1902. A sincere friend, an affectionaate wife and devoted mother. They who are come are of great ..... washed their robes..... in the blood of the lamb.....
                                         (82)(93)

ALBERRY, R   *(Z/664)*
H Company. 1st Royal Sussex Regiment. Sacred to the memory of No 8112 Private R ALBERRY, who died at Rawalpindi 23 Jan 1910. Aged 26 yrs. The Lord gave and the Lord hath taken away. Blessed be the name of the Lord. AHMUD BUX, SCULPTOR, RAWALPINDI.   *(82)(93)*

ALBERT, Phoebe Frances   *(M/1159)*
Phoebe Frances. Dearly loved wife of W ALBERT. Sub Engineer, PWD. Born 13 Oct 1862. Died 25 Apr 1901. Aged 39 yrs 6 mths 12 days.   *(82)(93)(mb)*

ALDERTON, Daisy Lilly Grace   *(B/136)*
In loving memory of Daisy Lilly Grace. Daughter of Agnes (late) and William ALDERTON. Born 25 Nov 1889. Died 29 Apr 1891.   *(82)(93)*

ALGAR, Alfred William
Alfred William, the beloved infant son of Alice and Alfred ALGAR, who was taken away on 25 Jun 1872. Aged 3 mths.
                                         (82)(mb)

ALLAN, Henry Marshman Havelock (see HAVELOCK-ALLAN, Henry Marshman)

ALLAN, W (see ROYAL ARTILLERY (2))

ALLARD, Walter Cyril   (J/456)
Sacred to the memory of Walter Cyril ALLARD, F Troop 2nd
Dragoon Guards (Queen's Bays), who died at Rawalpindi after a
few days illness 5 Mar 1891. Aged 24 yrs 6 mths. This tablet
is erected by the officers, NCOs and men of his troop and also
the military signallers.......   (82)(93)

ALLEN, A   (BB/18)
Sacred to the memory of Surgeon Major A ALLEN. Late Rifle
Brigade who died at Rawalpindi 4 Dec 1876.
                                    (82)(93)(WM)

ALLEN, Isabella Eveline   (P/1249)
Isabella Eveline. In memory of the loved wife for 30 years of
T ALLEN, Telegraph Department. Born 11 Aug 1855. Died 6 Jul
1900.   (82)(93)

ALLEN, Isobel Gladys Florence   (W/969)
In loving memory of our little sunshine Isobel Gladys
Florence. Daughter of Sergeant and Mrs T ALLEN. Born 6 Dec
1934. Died 4 May 1935. Suffer little children to come unto
me.   (82)(93)

ALLEN, Lillian Florence Wilson (see WILSON-ALLEN, Lillian F)

ALLEN, William
To the memory of Gunner William ALLEN. 82nd Company RGA.
Died Rawalpindi 1 May 1908. Aged 31 yrs. Gone but not for-
gotten.   (82)

ALLEN, W. I. (see ROYAL HORSE ARTILLERY (2))

ALLMAN, S A   (N/1430)
Sacred to the memory of Private S A ALLMAN, B Squadron 4th
Dragoon Guards. Died Rawalpindi 8 Mar 1895. Aged 25 yrs.
                                    (82)(93)(PS)

ALLSEBROOK, A (see ROYAL ARTILLERY (6))

ALLSOP, Sadie   (S/302)
Sacred to the loving and undying memory of our Sadie. The beloved daughter of Mr and Mrs ALLSOP. Born 27 Apr 1889. Died
27 Aug 1922. RIP. Home at last thy labour done, safe and
blest the victory won, troubles passed, from pain set free,
angels now have welcomed thee. Never shall your memory fade,
sweetest thoughts will ever linger round the spot where our
darling's laid.   (82)(93)

ALWYN, Irene   (Y/722)
Mrs Irene ALWYN. Born 3 Mar 1896. Died 28 Sep 1979.
                                    (93)

AMES, W R   (X/783)
In loving memory of Lieutenant Colonel W R AMES, OBE. Late
4th Battalion 7th Rajput Regiment. Died Rawalpindi 22 Oct
1932. Aged 53 yrs.   (82)(93)(end)

ANDERSON
Child of Mr and Mrs A ANDERSON. Born 3 Feb 1937. Died 13 Dec
1942.   *(82)*

ANDERSON, A   *(C/95)*
Sergeant A ANDERSON,   31st Regiment, who died at Rawalpindi
on 28 Dec 1879. Aged 35 yrs. Deeply regretted by his brother
sergeants. This tomb is erected by his brother sergeants as a
mark of esteem and respect.   *(82)(93)(BS)*

ANDERSON, Agnes Georgina   *(X/812)*
In loving memory of our dear Ma. Agnes Georgina ANDERSON.
Born 14 Dec 1880. Died 6 Jan 1944. Gone but not forgotten.
                                         (82)(93)

ANDERSON, Arthur Sly   *(X/811)*
In loving memory of our dear Pa. Arthur Sly ANDERSON. Born 22
Dec 1862. Died 13 Jan 1946. Gone but not forgotten.
                                         (82)(93)

ANDERSON, Arthur Thomas   *(V/988)*
Thy will be done. In loving memory of Arthur Thomas ANDERSON.
Born 7 Nov 1900. Died 23 Jun 1930.   *(82)(93)*

ANDERSON, Mary   *(W/949)*
Mary. The dearly loved infant daughter of Mr and Mrs L R
ANDERSON. Died 6 Apr 1925.   *(82)(93)*

ANDERTON, L   (see ROYAL ARTILLERY (6))
ANDREWS, Clifford   (see ROYAL ARTILLERY (4))

ANDREWS, P D   *(X/861)*
P D ANDREWS who passed away on 22 Feb 1968. From his wife and
daughter.   *(93)*

ANDREWS, W (see GORDON HIGHLANDERS (2))

ANSCOMB, Charles   *(P/1257)*
Sacred to the memory of Sergeant Major Charles ANSCOMB who
departed this life 26 Dec 1901. Aged 50 yrs. Erected by his
comrades of F Battery, RHA, in which he served 31 years, as a
token of affection and esteem. Thy will be done.
                                         (82)(93)

ANTONINUS   *(JJ/351)*
IHS. To the sacred memory of the Very Reverend Father
ANTONINUS,   OSFC Catholic Chaplain who died at Rawalpindi 13
Mar 1886. This monument has been erected by the Catholic
congregation of Rawalpindi.   *(82)(93)*

APPLEYARD, C (see ROYAL ARTILLERY (3))

APPS, Edward Alfred   *(W/914)*
Edward Alfred APPS who died 1 Mar 1921. Aged 9 mths. We
loved him and no tongue can tell, how much we loved him, and
how well. God loved him too, and thought it best to take him
home with him to rest.   *(93)*

APTED, Oliver
Oliver. Beloved son of Sergeant and Rhoda APTED.   *(82)(mb)*

ARCHER, Herbert Stanley   *(H/596)*
In loving remembrance of my fond husband Herbert Stanley ARCHER who died 9 Aug 1888. Aged 29 yrs. I have loved thee with an everlasting love, therefore with loving kindness have I drawn thee. JER.31.3. This stone was erected by his disconsolate widow who mourns the loss of an affectionate husband and a tender father.   *(82)(93)(mb)*

ARCHIBALD, David   *(DD/74)*
Sacred to the memory of David ARCHIBALD, SMD, son of William & Ellen ARCHIBALD, 104th Bengal Fusiliers, who died at Rawalpindi 6 Nov 1869 from disease contracted during the epidemic at Peshawar. Aged 19 yrs 2 mths.   *(82)(93)(BS)*
    (For illustration, see Page 27)

ARMSTRONG, Emily Mary Anne   *(C/98)*
In memory of Emily Mary Anne. Wife of W F ARMSTRONG. Chaplain. Died 28 Jan 1880. Aged 25 yrs.   *(82)(93)(PS)*

ARMSTRONG, Norman Wright   *(IX/1012)*
In memory of No 7012281 Rifleman Norman Wright ARMSTRONG. A(S) Company 1st Battalion Royal Ulster Rifles. Died at Rawalpindi 10 Jan 1938. Aged 24. Erected by the officers, warrant officers, NCOs and men of the 1st Battalion.   *(82)(93)*

ASHBY, H   (see 1ST KING'S DRAGOON GUARDS (1))
ASHBY, Thomas (see ROYAL GARRISON ARTILLERY (3))

ASHLEY, F   *(P/1288)*
In loving memory of Private F ASHLEY, 1st Battalion Wiltshire Regiment, who departed this life at Rawalpindi 23 Dec 1903. Aged 22 yrs 3 mths. This stone was erected by his comrades.
                                      (82)(93)

ASPIN, Bertha Alice   *(N/1468)*
Bertha Alice ASPIN. B Battery, RHA, who died at Rawalpindi 1 Apr 1895. Aged 9 days. Jesus called this little child.
                                      (93)(BS)

ASPIN, Ruley (see ROYAL HORSE ARTILLERY (3))

ATHERLEY, Tom   *(LL/240)*
Tom. The beloved son of Cecil A and Mary E ATHERLEY. The Royal Irish Regiment. Sent 8 Jan 1903. Recalled 17 Dec 1905. Until the day break and the shadows flee away.
                                      (82)(93)(WM)(mb)

ATKIN, John Henry   *(A/118)*
Sacred to the memory of John Henry ATKIN. Son of Agnes and Richard ATKIN, Farrier Sergeant, D4RA, who died at Rawalpindi 3 Nov 1881. Aged 6 yrs. Go home dear parents and shed no tear, I am not dead, but sleeping here. Short was my stay, long is my rest. Jesus called me when He thought best. May the Lord bless him.   *(82)(93)(BS)*

AVIS, Sidney   (AA/1/253)
Sacred to the memory of No 4869 Private Sidney AVIS. B Squadron 9th Queen's Royal Lancers, who died on 8 Jun 1905. Aged 21 yrs 11 mths. Erected by the officers, NCOs and men of his squadron.   *(82)(93)(PS)*

BABBETT, Robert Jeramiah
Robert Jeramiah BABBETT.   Died Rawalpindi 30 Dec 1892.   Aged 43 yrs.   *(82)(mb)*

BACK, W (see SOMERSET LIGHT INFANTRY (1))

BAGLEY, John   *(AA/1/250)*
Sacred to the memory of No. 26100 Gunner John BAGLEY, 57th Battery RFA, who died on 18 Feb 1905. Aged 30 yrs 6 mths. Erected by the officers, NCOs and men of the battery.
                                    (82)(93)(PS)

BAILEY, John   *(N/1436)*
In loving memory of our late comrade Private John BAILEY. 1st Gordon Highlanders. Departed this life on 3 Nov 1895. Aged 25 yrs. Deeply regretted by his comrades. RIP. Erected by the officers, NCOs and men of G Company. *(82)(93)*

BAILEY, J (see GORDON HIGHLANDERS (2))

BAILEY, Walter James   *(E/197)*
Sacred to the memory of Private Walter James BAILEY. C Company, 2nd Royal Sussex Regiment. Died 31 Jul 1887. Aged 23 yrs. Thou wilt keep him in perfect peace.
                                    (82)(93)(WM)

BAILIE, Pamela Mary and Gertrude   *(W/922)*
Pamela Mary and Gertrude BAILIE.   13 Apr 1923.
                                    (93)

BAILY, F
No 6195 Private F BAILY. G Company. 1st Battalion Wiltshire Regiment.   Died 29 Dec 1904.   Aged 22 yrs.
                                    (82)

BAINBRIDGE, C   *(Y/705)*
In memory of No 3436611 Corporal C BAINBRIDGE. A Company 2nd Lancashire Fusiliers. Died at Rawalpindi 5 Sep 1923. Aged 22 yrs. Erected by all ranks of his company.
                                    (82)(93)

BAINBRIDGE, J M (see ARMY SERVICE CORPS (1))

BAKE, James Walter Henry (X/791)
James Walter Henry BAKE, Staff Sergeant Indian Army Corps of Clerks, who died at Rawalpindi 1 Mar 1936. For 3 mths the dearly loved husband of Freda BAKE. He lives for ever in my heart beloved and unforgotten. Erected by his comrades past and present of Headquarters Northern Command Rawalpindi District and Rawalpindi Brigade. Daddy from his unseen baby son. Mizpah.
(82)(93)(WM)(end)

BAKER, Beatrice (VII/1391)
Mother Beatrice BAKER. 13 Dec 1963. (93)

BAKER, Emily (Y/730)
Emily. The beloved wife of BSM BAKER, 126th Battery, Royal Field Artillery. Died 1 Feb 1922. Aged 25.
(82)(93)

BAKER, E (see GORDON HIGHLANDERS (4))

BAKER, May and Maud (D/160)
In loving memory of darling little May. Daughter of Sergeant and Mrs F C A BAKER. Born at Murree 10 Jun 1884. Died Rawalpindi 2 Jan 1886. In loving memory of little Maud. Infant daughter of Sergeant and Mrs F C A BAKER. Born at Murree 10 Jun 1884. Died at Murree 3 Jul 1884.
(82)(93)

BAKER, Robert Alfred (D/158)
Robert Alfred BAKER. 19th Bengal Lancers. Born 16 Apr 1856. Died 14 Feb 1884. (82)(93)(BS)

BALDWIN, S (see ROYAL GARRISON ARTILLERY (4))

BALFE, Josephine Marie Kate (R/284)
In loving memory of Josephine Marie Kate. The beloved wife of Patrick BALFE. Died 26 Dec 1938. Jesus grant her eternal rest.
(82)(93)

BALFOUR, Nigel Arnold (W/958)
In loving memory of Nigel Arnold BALFOUR. 23 Dec 1929. Aged 3 mths 1 day. (82)(93)(mb)

BALLINGALL, James (V/983)
In loving memory of our dear brother James BALLINGALL of Methill, Scotland, who was accidentally drowned while bathing 30 Aug 1927. (82)(93)

BAMBRICK, Richard (D/157)
Sacred to the memory of Private Richard BAMBRICK who died 11 Jan 1884. Aged 27 yrs. This stone is erected by the non com- missioned officers and men of his troop as a token of esteem.
(82)(93)(BS)

BAMBRICK, R (see 1ST KING'S DRAGOON GUARDS (1))

BANACH, Wladyslaw and Julian Michael   *(VII/1325)*
Wladyslaw BANACH. Born 15 Jun 1919. Aircraft pilot of the Attock Oil Co Ltd, who was killed on duty 12 Dec 1964. From his devoted wife and children. In loving memory of Julian Michael. Baby son of W and Mrs BANACH. Taken away from us 28 Dec 1960. Aged 2 mths 12 days.   *(93)(WM)*

BAND, Thomas (see 70TH REGIMENT (4))

BANKS
Infant son of Colour Sergeant and Mrs A BANKS of 2nd Battalion Gloucestershire Regiment, who died Rawalpindi 18 Mar 1921. Aged 9 mths.   *(82)*

BAPTIST, Richard Joseph Timothy   *(F/379)*
Richard Joseph Timothy. Beloved son of Lieutenant and Mrs BAPTIST. Born 14 Apr 1881. Died 9 Feb 1899. Very deeply regretted. The Lord gave and the Lord hath taken away, blessed by the name of the Lord.   *(93)(WM)*

BARBER, Herbert (see ROYAL HORSE ARTILLERY (1))

BARCLAY, Hone Charles   *(Z/673)*
In memory of No 2183. Private Hone Charles BARCLAY........
    (93)

BARGER, H (see 1ST KING'S DRAGOON GUARDS (1))

BARKER, F Anne   *(D/175)*
Sacred to the memory of F Anne, the wife of J BARKER, S M Department, who died 22 Sep 1880. Aged 30 yrs.
    (93)

BARKER, Jane Anne   *(X/819)*
Sacred to the memory of Jane Anne. The dearly beloved wife of H T BARKER who left for her heavenly home on 19 May 1942. Aged 52 yrs 8 mths. She said goodbye to no-one, she bade farewell to none, the gates of heaven flew open, and a gentle voice said come. Father who hast gathered my dear wife to rest, unto thee I yield her, sure thou knowest best.
    (82)(93)

BARKER, Mary Ann   *(HH/329)*
Sacred to the memory of Mary Ann BARKER. The dearly beloved wife of T J J BARKER, Supervisor PWD, who departed this life on 18 Nov 1878. Aged 18 yrs 10 1/2 mths.*(82)(93)*

BARLOW, Benjamin (see RIFLE BRIGADE (1))

BARNARD, A B   *(P/1252)*
IHS. To the sacred memory of Private A B BARNARD, H Company 3rd Battalion Rifle Brigade, who died Rawalpindi 26 Jan 1901. Aged 23 yrs 11 months. Erected by the officers, NCOs and men of H company 3rd Rifle Brigade as a mark of esteem.
    (82)(93)

BARNARD, J (see SOMERSET LIGHT INFANTRY(1))

BARNES, Barbara   (see ROYAL HORSE ARTILLERY (1))
BARNES, H   (see 1ST KING'S DRAGOON GUARDS (1))

BARNES, Shirley   (W/939)
In loving memory of darling daughter Shirley BARNES.   Died 22
Mar 1938. Aged 8 mths 12 days.   (93)

BARRETT, John   (D/171)
To the memory of Lieutenant General John BARRETT. Died 16 Dec
1880. Aged 70 yrs.   (82)(93)(PS)

BARRETT, Robert Jeremiah   (K/615)
In loving memory of Robert Jeremiah BARRETT who died at
Rawalpindi 30 Dec 1892. Aged 43 yrs. (93)(PS)

BARRETT, W (see ROYAL ARTILLERY (6))

BARRITT, Millicent Elizabeth   (O/1080)
Millicent Elizabeth BARRITT, the beloved daughter of Sergeant
and Mrs E BARRITT, who died at Rawalpindi 8 May 1908.   Aged
16 mths. RIP.   (93)

BARTLETT, Gertrude   (M/1197)
In memory of Gertrude. Beloved wife of Lieutenant Daniel F
BARTLETT, Leyland, and dearly loved daughter of Mr and Mrs S
SMAILS, Preston, England. Died 21 Nov 1917. Aged 24 yrs.
                                      (82)(93)(mb)

BARTLEY, Doris Margaret Dane   (Y/683)
In sweet memory of our darling Doris Margaret Dane BARTLEY.
                                      (82)(93)(WM)

BARTON, Charles   (IV/545)
Sacred to the memory of No 4104184 Private Charles BARTON.
2nd ACC Royal Tank Corps. Died 19 Sep 1932. Aged 23 yrs.
                                      (82)(93)

BARTON, Claude John   (M/1223)
In loving memory of Claude John BARTON. Son of Captain H J
BARTON, RE, and Mary his wife. Died 10 Nov 1901. Aged 3 1/2
mths.   (82)(93)

BATCHELOR, Alice Kathleen and John   (Y/694)
In loving memory of Alice Kathleen. The dearly beloved wife
of Corporal J BATCHELOR. No 9 MB RGA. Died 2 Apr 1913. Aged
31 yrs 4mths. And of John, the darling babe of the above, who
died on 4 Mar 1913. Aged 2 days.   (82)(93)

BATCHELOR, C (see 1ST KING'S DRAGOON GUARDS (1))

BATCHELOR, Patrick   (Z/638)
In memory of No 928 ...Patrick BATCHELOR.......   (93)

BATEMAN, Frankie   (M/1221)
Pet. Frankie. The beloved son of E J and M A BATEMAN.   Died
12 Apr 1901. Aged 8 mths.
                                      /cont........

BATEMAN, Frankie (cont)

He is gone but not forgotten, never shall his memory fade, sweetest thoughts shall ever linger, round the spot where Frankie's laid. Thy will be done. And now Lord what is my hope, truly my hope is even in thee.   *(82)(93)*

BATEMAN, George   *(N/1452)*
Sacred to the memory of George BATEMAN, Staff Armourer Sergeant, Ordnance Department who met his death from a trap accident at Rawalpindi 31 Jul 1896. Aged 32 yrs. Regretted by his sorrowing wife and children.   *(82)(93)*

BATES (see ROYAL HORSE ARTILLERY (2))

BATES, Henry   *(P/1254)*
In loving memory of Private Henry BATES, A Squadron, IX Lancers, who died 28 Jun 1903. Aged 25 yrs. Erected by the officers, NCOs and men of his squadron.   *(93)(PS)*

BATES, J (see ROYAL ARTILLERY (10))

BATTEN, J, Mary Elizabeth and Jane Eleanor
Sacred to the memory of Sergeant J BATTEN. 10th Hussars. Drowned in the River Cabul 31 Mar 1879. Aged 28 yrs. Also Mary Elizabeth BATTEN. Died 21 Oct 1878. Aged 2 yrs. Also Jane Eleanor BATTEN. Died 17 Feb 1879. Aged 9 days. Thy will be done.   *(82)*

BATTYE, Isabel Jane   *(H/602)*
IHS. In loving memory of Isabel Jane. Wife of Major F D BATTYE. Queen's Own Corps of Guides. Born 1 Sep 1858. Died 25 Nov 1888.   *(82)(93)(WM)*

BAXTER, William
No 2921083 Sergeant William BAXTER. 1st Battalion Cameron Highlanders. Died 15 Aug 1922. Aged 35 yrs.
(82)

BAYLY, A R   *(P/1258)*
In memory of Colonel A R BAYLY. Bengal Staff Corps. Died Rawalpindi 2 Jan 1902. Aged 70 yrs. They may rest from their labours.   *(82)(93)*

BAZELY, Percival Charles   *(M/1145)*
Sacred to the memory of Percival Charles BAZELY who entered into rest at Rawalpindi 14 Oct 1903. Aged 29 yrs 4 mths. Erected by his sorrowing mother, loving brothers and sisters, and Miss May JONES. Peace, perfect peace. He giveth his beloved sleep.   *(82)(93)*

BAZIN, Walter Childs   *(X/754)*
Walter Childs BAZIN, DDS, DMD. Born Montreal 15 Oct 1879. Killed in a railway accident 1 Sep 1919. Erected by his sorrowing family.   *(82)(93)*

BEAN, Emmeline Mary   (M/1139)
In loving memory of Emmeline Mary (Minna), the dearly beloved
wife of Richard BEAN, who died at Rawalpindi 20 Apr 1900.
Aged 37 yrs 2 mths 5 days. If thou shouldst call me to resign
what most I prize it ne'er was mine, I only yield thee what is
thine. Thy will be done.   (82)(93)

BEATTY, Edward Tyrell
Edward Tyrell BEATTY. Chaplain, Madras Presidency, who died
while on active service with the Tirah Expeditionary Force 31
Oct 1897. Aged 46.   (82)

BEATY, Francis Henry   (S/313)
In loving memory of our dear father Francis Henry BEATY.
Eldest son of Major Francis BEATY, European Regiment, Bengal
Establishment, HEICS. Died 14 May 1929. Aged 88 yrs.   Till
the day breaks.   (82)(93)

BECKETT, Elizabeth   (BB/28)
Sacred to the memory of Elizabeth, the beloved wife of G S
BECKETT, Assistant Supt, Department Public Works who departed
this life on 7 Oct 1863. Aged 25 yrs. In sure and steadfast
hope to rise and claim her mansion in the skies. A Christian
here her flesh laid down, the cross exchanging for a crown.
                                                 (93)(BS)

BEEBY, W (see WEST RIDING REGIMENT (1))

BEER, A   (Y/738)
In memory of No 10388889 Lance Sergeant A BEER. Died
Rawalpindi 25 Dec 1922. Aged 40 yrs.   (82)(93)

BEILBY, Mary Shirley   (VII/1359)
IHS. In loving memory of our darling mother Mary Shirley
BEILBY who died 23 Aug 1936. Aged 50 yrs. There is a link
death cannot sever, love and remembrance live forever.
                                                 (82)(93)

General View of Harley Street Cemetery

BELL, Alfred Richard (X/803)
Resting. In ever loving memory of my darling husband Alfred Richard BELL, Major MBE (Retd). Born 10 May 1877. Died 7 Dec 1941. God rest his dear soul in peace. *(82)(93)*

BELL, Catherine (F/382)
In loving memory of Catherine BELL, the beloved wife of Leonard BELL, FQMS, 4th Dragoon Guards, who died at Rawalpindi 18 Feb 1899. Aged 34 yrs. RIP. Blessed are the pure in heart for they shall see God. AHMAD BUX, SCULPTOR, RAWALPINDI. *(82)(93)*

BELL, J (see 1ST KING'S DRAGOON GUARDS (1))
BELL, J (see GORDON HIGHLANDERS (4))

BELL, M (O/1106)
In loving memory of Sergeant M BELL, C Company 2nd King's Royal Rifles, who died at Rawalpindi 25 May 1903. Aged 27 yrs 3 mths. Gone from us but not forgotten, never shall thy memory fade. Sweetest thoughts shall ever linger, round the spot where thou are laid. *(82)(93)*

BELL, M Gertrude (VII/1355)
Mother M Gertrude BELL. Died 24 Jul 1935. R.I.P.
(82)(93)

BELTON, John William (P/1242)
In loving memory of John William BELTON. Beloved son of Staff Sergeant W BELTON, SVD. Died 9 Oct 1901. Aged 15 yrs. In life he was loved and esteemed, in death he is mourned and lamented. Peace perfect peace. *(82)(93)(WM)*

BENHAM, E (O/1118)
Sacred to the memory of No 19540 Driver E BENHAM, 69th Battery RFA, who died at Rawalpindi 27 Jan 1906. Aged 23 yrs. Erected by the officers, NCOs and men of his battery.
(82)(93)(PS)

BENJAMIN, Charles Raymond (X/858)
Charles Raymond BENJAMIN. Priest. 21 Jun 1892. Died 5 Oct 1966. *(93)*

BENJAMIN, J (see ROYAL GARRISON ARTILLERY (4))

BENNETT, Frederick Garget (see GARGET-BENNETT, Frederick)

BENNETT, G (see ROYAL HORSE ARTILLERY (2))

BENT, Hugh
Sacred to the memory of Colonel Hugh BENT. RA. Died Rawalpindi 28 Oct 1875. Erected by the officers under his command. *(82)(mb)*

BENTLEY, W (Z/636)
In memory of Driver W BENTLEY. 18th Battery RFA. Died 22 Jan 1908. Aged 35 yrs. *(82)(93)(PS)*

BERNARD, William					(L/1048)
Sacred to the memory of No 4454 Private William BERNARD, A Company, 1st Battalion Royal Irish Regiment, who was killed by falling from the ramparts of the arsenal while on sentry duty on 30 Apr 1905. Aged 31 yrs. Erected as a token of esteem by his comrades in the company.		(82)(93)(PS)

BESTFORD, A E					(V/991)
Sacred to the memory of Lance Sergeant A E BESTFORD. 98th Field Battery Royal Artillery. Died at Rawalpindi 11 Nov 1932. Aged 27 yrs.			(82)(93)

BEVILLE, Eileen Cecil				(J/442)
In loving memory of Eileen Cecil. Twin daughter of Charles and May BEVILLE			(93)(SS)(mb)

BEVITT, Elizabeth				(DD/53)
Sacred to the memory of Elizabeth, the beloved wife of Private Thomas BEVITT, HM's 36th Regiment, who departed this life on the 30 Jul 1872. Aged 30 yrs. Mourn not for me my husband dear. I am not dead but sleeping here. I was not yours but Christ's alone. He loved me best and took me home.
					(82)(93)(BS)

BIGNELL, Hugh Glennie				(M/1168)
Sacred to the memory of Lieutenant Hugh Glennie BIGNELL 36th Sikhs. Rawalpindi 20 Apr 1907. Aged 24.
					(82)(93)(end)

BINGE, Edward Theophilus
Edward Theophilus BINGE who died 27 Jul 1920. Aged 53 yrs. AHMUD BUX AND SONS, RAWALPINDI.		(82)

BINGE, Stella					(W/910)
In loving memory of our darling Stella who fell asleep on her 9th birthday 27 Oct 1918. The beloved daughter of Mr and Mrs E T BINGE.					(93)

BIRCHELL, R (see ROYAL HORSE ARTILLERY (2))

BIRDWOOD, George Brodrick			(M/1182)
In loving memory of a beloved son and brother George Brodrick BIRDWOOD, "Eric", the Royal Sussex Regiment, who passed away at Rawalpindi 22 Nov 1910. Aged 22 years. He giveth his beloved sleep.				(82)(93)(mb)

BIRKS, J (see 5TH REGIMENT (1))

BIRTWISTLE, N L					(Y/735)
Sacred to the memory of No M/2745937 A/Sergeant N L BIRTWISTLE. No 21 MT Company RASC. Died 16 Jun 1922. Aged 25 yrs.					(82)(93)

BISHOP, F (see ROYAL GARRISON ARTILLERY (1))

BISHOP, John					(Z/675)
In memory of No 8896 Private John BISHOP.....   (93)

BLACKBURN, Edward   (J/437)
3rd Dragoon Guards.   Sacred to the memory of Private Edward
BLACKBURN who died at Rawalpindi 24 Sep 1891.   Aged 26 yrs 6
mths.   (82)(93)

BLACKBURN, Mary Kirkham   (D/152)
In loving memory of Mary Kirkham.   Relict of the late James
BLACKBURN, CE, of Calcutta. Died 3 Jan 1883.   Aged 41 yrs
                                             (82)(93)

BLACKMAN, Alfred Roy William   (W/954)
In loving memory of Alfred Roy William. Son of Mr and Mrs A P
BLACKMAN, RAOC.   Born 20 Mar 1926.   Died 18 Oct 1926.   The
Lord gave and the Lord hath taken away, blessed be the name of
the Lord.   (82)(93)

BLACKWELL, Emma Jane
Emma Jane.   The beloved wife of E W BLACKWELL.   4th Hussars.
Died Rawalpindi 28 Jun 1874. Aged 35.   (82)

BLAIR, G (see UNNAMED REGIMENT (1))
BLAKE, G (see 1ST KING'S DRAGOON GUARDS (1))

BLAKE, Herbert Stanley   (X/797)
In loving memory of Herbert Stanley BLAKE.   Punjab Police.
Born 28 Sep 1899.   Died at Jhelum 9 Mar 1939. Memories are
treasures no one can steal, death leaves a heartache no one
can heal, time may wear away the edge of grief, but memory
sadly turns back every leaf. Thy will be done.
                                             (82)(93)(WM)

BLAKER, George   (JJ/348)
George, infant son of H and M BLAKER. Died 5 Apr(?)   1887.
Aged 2 yrs. Thy will be done.   (82)(93)

BLAND, F   (Z/650)
No 9240 Private F BLAND, B Company 1st Battalion The
Connaught Rangers, who departed this life at Rawalpindi 4 Jun
1908. RIP. Erected by the officers, NCOs and men......
                                             (82)(93)

BLATCHLY, Jackie   (M/1201)
In loving memory of Jackie. Beloved son of John and Cathrine
BLATCHLY. Born 18 Oct 1904. Died 17 May 1905.   (82)(93)

BLEAKLEY, William, Anna Maria & William (DD/54)
Sacred to the memory of Sergeant William BLEAKLEY,   HM's 70th
Regiment, who departed this life on 12 Sep 1872.   Aged   32
yrs.   Also Anna Maria.   Died 22 Jan 1872.   Aged 32 yrs.
William.   Died 10 Sep 1872.   Aged 3 yrs. Wife and child of
the above. Erected by his brother sergeants as a mark of their
esteem and respect.   (82)(93)(BS)

BLEASE, Albert   (Y/692)
In loving memory of No 493 Sergeant Albert BLEASE. Q Squadron
21st E of I Lancers. Died 18 May 1913. Aged 26 yrs.
                                             (82)(93)(WM)

BLISSETT (see ROYAL ARTILLERY (7))
BOATWRIGHT, R (see 1ST KING'S DRAGOON GUARDS (1))

BOGG(?), Dorothy Lilian (X/748)
IHS. In loving memory of Dorothy Lilian. Beloved wife of George Arthur BOGG(?). Died 20 Nov 1929. Aged 27 yrs 6 mths 25 days. Rest in peace. (82)(93)

BOGGISS, H (see 1ST KING'S DRAGOON GUARDS (1))

BOILEAU, Neil Edmonston and Richard
The sons of Neil and Kate BOILEAU. Neil Edmonston born 13 Dec 1872. Died 10 Apr 1873. Richard ....ember 1870.
(82)

BOLLEY, M (see ROYAL ARTILLERY (6))

BOLTON, Charles H (D/176)
Sacred to the memory of Charles H BOLTON, 8th Hussars, who departed this life 25 Nov 188- Aged 34 yrs.
(93)(BS)

BOLTON John (N/1438)
IHS. Sacred to the memory of No 2402 Bandsman William SIMS, 2nd King's Own Scottish Borderers, who died during the Chitral Campaign at Jambatai Kotal on 22 Jun 1895. Aged 22 yrs. No 2109 Lance Corporal Bandsman John BOLTON, 2nd King's Own Scottish Borderers, who died at Rawalpindi 22 Feb 1896. Aged 23 yrs. Erected by their brother bandsmen as a token of respect. Thy will be done. (82)(93)

BOLTON, W (see 60TH ROYAL RIFLES (1))

BOND, Edwin Trevelyan (BB/9)
Sacred to the memory of Edwin Trevelyan. Only child of Captain E BOND, Bengal Staff Corps, who died on 29 May 1865(?) Aged 1 yr 9 days. The Lord gave and the Lord hath taken away, blessed be the name of the Lord. (82)(93)

BONHAM, A (see ROYAL ARTILLERY (2))

BOODRIE, Catherine (M/1142)
In loving memory of our darling Mamma who entered her rest on 9 Apr 1901. Aged 80 yrs 7 mths. Catherine BOODRIE.
(82)(93)

BOOKEY, Sylvia Brownrigg (N/1463)
Sylvia Brownrigg BOOKEY. Born 12 Aug 1893. Died 1 Nov 1894.
(93)(mb)

BOOTH, J (see ROYAL ARTILLERY (2))

BORTHWICK, Algie (M/1216)
In loving memory of Wee Algie. The darling son of E and M BORTHWICK. Born 8 Mar 1900. Died 11 May 1900. God is love.
(82)(93)

BORTHWICK, Anne Stewart   (X/879)
Anne Stewart BORTHWICK.   Beloved wife of James BORTHWICK.
Counsellor, British High Commission, Rawalpindi.   Died on 27
Dec 1969.   Aged 47 yrs.   In loving memory.   This memorial was
erected by her husband,   her children Frances,   James and John
and by members of the Protestant International congregation of
Islamabad.   Blest be the tie that binds our hearts in Jesus'
love.   (93)

BORTHWICK, James   (X/877)

James BORTHWICK.
Counsellor, British
High Commission,
Rawalpindi.
Beloved husband
of Anne Stewart
BORTHWICK.
Died on 25 Jul 1970.
Aged 57 yrs.
This memorial was
erected in loving
memory by his
children Frances,
James and John.
Oh Jesus I have
promised to serve
thee to the end.
He went to prepare a
place for us.

(93)

BOSLEY, J (see ROYAL ARTILLERY (8))

BOUGHTON, Elizabeth, Margaret Ann,
Charles Roger and Catherine Elizabeth
Elizabeth,   the beloved wife of Colour Sergeant BOUGHTON,   2nd
Battalion 9th Regiment,   who died at Rawalpindi on 9 Jun 1875.
Aged 29 yrs.   Her end was peace.   Also children of the above.
Margaret   Ann who died at Bombay 26 Nov 1874.   Aged 1 yr 5
mths.   Charles Roger who died at Jubbulpore 17 Dec 1874.   Aged
3 yrs 11 mths 17 days.   Catherine Elizabeth who died at
Rawalpindi 10 Jul 1875.   Aged 1 mth 17 days.   The Lord giveth,
and the Lord taketh away, blessed be the name of the Lord.
                                          (82)

BOULTER, Henry
In loving memory of Henry BOULTER. Sergeant. 4th Queen's Own
Hussars. Died 10 Jul..... *(82)*

BOURKE, Lawrence *(L/1064)*
Sacred to the memory of No RGA 23984 Gunner Lawrence BOURKE.
No 7 MB RGA. Died 25 Dec 1907. Aged 22 yrs. Erected by the
officers, NCOs and men of No 7 MB, RGA. NEYAZ ALI & CO,
RAWALPINDI. *(82)(93)(PS)*

BOURKE, L (see ROYAL GARRISON ARTILLERY (2))

BOUT, J *(S/296)*
Postal Service. Corporal J BOUT. 1 Dec 1919. RIP.
(82)(93)

BOUTCHER, Henry *(O/1098)*
In loving memory of Henry BOUTCHER. Store Sergeant Bengal
Ordnance Department. Died at Rawalpindi of disease contracted
on China field service on 13 Jun 1901. Aged 35 yrs 8 mths.
Let not your heart be troubled neither let it be afraid.
(82)(93)

BOWCHER, Clarice Irene *(M/1227)*
Clarice Irene BOWCHER (Mother's pet) Dearly loved child of
Frank and Lizzie BOWCHER. Died 12 Oct 1903. Aged 4 yrs 6
mths 29 days. At rest. *(82)(93)*

BOWDER, Walter Charles *(M/1171)*
In loving memory of Walter Charles BOWDER. Assistant Surgeon.
Called away 1 Feb 1908. Redeemed, restored, forgiven.
(82)(93)

BOWELL, Rowland (see ROYAL HORSE ARTILLERY (1))

BOWERS, W T *(Z/677)*
In memory of No 8627 Private W T BOWERS, 1st Battalion Royal
Sussex Regiment, who was accidentally drowned in the Sohan
River 18 Sep 1910. Aged 22 yrs. This stone was erected by
his comrades. *(82)(93)(PS)*

BOWLES *(P/1269)*
In memory of Private James HOMER. 2nd Battalion Kings Royal
Rifle Corps who died at Rawalpindi 8 Aug 1902. Aged 20 yrs.
Also Private BOWLES. This stone is erected by the officers,
NCOs and riflemen of G Company in remembrance of their lost
comrades. Gone but not forgotten. *(82)(93)*

BOWMAN *(A/107)*
.....BOWMAN .....sleeps in peace. *(93)*

BOWYER, Walter *(P/1271)*
Sacred to the memory of Gunner Walter BOWYER, F Battery RHA,
who died 26 Jan 1902. Aged 25 yrs. Erected by his comrades.
(82)(93)(PS)

BOYDELL, Violet   (D/161)
Violet. Born Jan 1886. Died 18(?) Feb 1886. Infant daughter
of James Edwards Neville and Jessie Murray BOYDELL. Suffer
little children to come unto me.   (93)

BOYLE, Moira Margaret   (W/951)
A little child shall lead them. Moira Margaret BOYLE. Born
27 Jan 1925. Died 31 Jan 1925.   (93)

BRADLEY   (W/905)
......Sergeant and Mrs BRADLEY. S & T Corps. Died 3 Mar
1916. Aged 8 days. Thy will be done.   (93)(BS)

BRADY, T   (see YORKSHIRE REGIMENT (1))
BRIDGLAND, F   (see ARMY SERVICE CORPS (1))

BRIEN, H   (R/275)
IHS. In memory of No 4031106 Private H BRIEN. 1st Battalion
King's Shropshire Light Infantry. Died 26 Jul 1933. Erected
by his comrades.   (82)(93)

BRIGGS, Elizabeth Sophia   (G/435)
In loving memory of Elizabeth Sophia BRIGGS. Wife of George
Howard BRIGGS. Died 26 Dec 1888. Aged 20 yrs 10 mths. Not
lost but gone before to be with Christ which is very far
better (sic).   (93)(mb)

BRIGGS, G (see WEST RIDING REGIMENT (1))

BRIGGS, Ruth Darwood   (A/122)
In loving memory of Ruth Darwood (Bunty). Beloved daughter of
G H and E S BRIGGS. Born 11 Jun 1888. Died 29 Jun 1891. Thy
will be done.   (93)(PS)(mb)

BRIGHT, Hector William   (UU/1018)
Hector William BRIGHT. 13 Oct 1911 - 12 Jul 1988. With love
from the wife, sons, daughter, daughter-in-laws, son-in-law
and grandchildren.   (93)(WM)

BRIMSON, J   (see ROYAL ARTILLERY (3))
BRINKLER, H   (see SOMERSET LIGHT INFANTRY (1))

BRISCOE, Stanley Bean   (W/903)
Stanley Bean BRISCOE. 19 Nov 1915. For in Him is no darkness
at all.   (93)

BRISTOW, Helen Aurelia   (III/482)
Peace. Helen Aurelia BRISTOW (nee KIRKHAM). In loving memory
of our darling Nell who left us on 11 Mar 1945. Sleep on
beloved, God give you rest.   (82)(93)(WM)

BRISTOW, Hilda Mary   (III/476)
In loving memory of Hilda Mary. The dearly beloved wife of
Sub Conductor C H BRISTOW, IAOC. Born 11 Nov 1896. Died 10
Feb 1938.   (82)(93)

BRITAIN, Margaret Elizabeth   (R/277)
In loving memory of Margaret Elizabeth, the beloved wife of Mr
E C BRITAIN of Karachi, who died at Rawalpindi on 23 Dec 1934.
Aged 71 yrs 9 mths. RIP.   (93)

BROADWAY, Noelle Evelyn
In loving memory of Noelle Evelyn, infant daughter of Alan
Brice and Agnes Mabel BROADWAY, who fell asleep 27 Apr 1906.
Aged 5 mths 12 days.   (82)(mb)

BROGAN, Daniel   (GG/213)
Sacred to the memory of Daniel, the beloved son of Thomas and
Ann BROGAN,   D Battery .... Horse Artillery,   who died 10
May 1869.......   (93)(BS)

BROMLEY, Fay   (W/968)
Fay. In loving memory of Fay. Daughter of Sergeant and Mrs F
BROMLEY. South Wales Borderers. Born 17 Jan 1928. To rest
24 Sep 1936(?) God has saved from weary strife, in its dawn
this fresh young life. Now it waits for us above, resting in
the Saviour's love. Thy will be done. (82)(93)

BROOKS, A   (Z/649)
Sacred to the memory of No 21297 Gunner A BROOKS. No 7 MB RGA
who died at Rawalpindi 5 Jun 1908.   (82)(93)(PS)

BROOKS, A (see ROYAL GARRISON ARTILLERY (2))

BROOKS, William   (P/1263)
Sacred to the memory of Driver William BROOKS. F Battery RHA.
Died 13 Jun 1902. Aged 27 yrs. Erected by his comrades.
                                     (82)(93)(PS)
BROOME, J
Rifleman J BROOME, G Company 4th Battalion King's Royal Rifle
Corps. Died Rawalpindi 3 Feb 1913.   (82)

BROWN, Alfred   (K/624)
Sacred to the memory of Private Alfred BROWN, B Troop, 3rd
Dragoon Guards, who died at Rawalpindi 19 Aug 1892. Aged 23
yrs.   (82)(93)(BS)

BROWN, Elizabeth   (V/976)
In loving memory of Elizabeth. Beloved wife of Rev Alex D
BROWN. Wesleyan Chaplain. Passed away 20 Jun 1927. Until
the day breaks and the shadows flee away. DHYAN SINGH & SONS,
SIMLA & LAHORE.   (82)(93)(end)

BROWN, J (see ROYAL ARTILLERY (3))
BROWN, J (see ROYAL HORSE ARTILLERY (2))

BROWN, Lucy
In memory of Lucy. The beloved wife of Corporal A F BROWN.
Band, 4th Dragoon Guards. Died Rawalpindi 7 Jan 1895. Aged
34 yrs.   (82)

BROWN, William (see ROYAL ARTILLERY (4))
BROWN, W   (see RIFLE BRIGADE (2))

BROWNBILL, Rebecca Alice   (L/1071)
Rebecca Alice BROWNBILL. Beloved wife of ARMT Staff Sergeant
BROWNBILL, AOC, attached V Battery, RHA, who departed this
life 20 May 1909. Aged 27 yrs. Erected by her sorrowing husband.
                                            (82)(93)

BROWNE, George Eddis   (IV/540)
Sacred to the memory of George Eddis BROWNE, late Sergeant
Royal Field Artillery, who died at Rawalpindi 9 Apr 1933.
Aged 62 yrs 8 mths. Erected by the Masonic fraternity of
Rawalpindi.   (82)(93)

BROWNLEE, Henry
Henry BROWNLEE. Died 5 Jul 1900. Aged 35 yrs 8 mths.   (82)

BRUCE, D W   (JJ/342)
D W BRUCE. Son of Driver J BRUCE, RA and Mary BRUCE. Born 14
Oct 1887. Died 14 Oct 1889.   (93)

BRUCE, George   (III/486)
In memory of No 845487 Gunner George BRUCE. 64th Field
Battery RA. Died at Rawalpindi 20 Oct 1937. (93)

BRUTON
Infant son of Sergeant E and Annie BRUTON. Born 30 Jan 1889.
Died 12 Jan 1890.   (82)

BRYANT, John   (DD/68)
Erected by his brother officers to the memory of John BRYANT,
Quartermaster 36th Foot, who died at Rawalpindi 1 Dec 1871.
Aged 41. Deeply regretted by all ranks of the regiment in
which he had served 25 years.   (82)(93)(PS)

BRYDONE, Mary Alice   (VII/1386)
Mary Alice BRYDONE. Died 26 Oct 1954. Erected by her
sorrowing husband, sons, daughter and grand-daughter.
                                            (93)

BRYDONE, Trevor Desmond   (VIII/1417)
Trevor Desmond BRYDONE. Born 2 Oct 1925. Died 19 Jun 1981.
Deeply mourned by wife Molly, children Irene, John and
Patrick, son-in-law and grandchildren.   (93)(WM)

BUCHANAN, W A M   (X/773)
W A M BUCHANAN (Bobby). Born 14 May 1897. Died 8 Sep 1959.
                                            (93)

BULLIMORE, Enid   (L/1026)
Sacred to the memory of Enid. Daughter of Arthur and Enid
BULLIMORE. Died 19 Mar 1903. Aged 2 days. She to us for a
time was given, a gem of true love's finding, & taken for the
brighter heaven, leaves a memory ever binding.
                                            (82)(93)

BURBIDGE, Elizabeth   (DD/73)
In memory of Elizabeth. Wife of William BURBIDGE. Sergeant.
A Battery. A Brigade.   (82)(93)(BS)

BURCHETT, Gertrude Anne				(Z/667W)
In loving memory of my dear wife Gertrude Anne BURCHETT who departed this life 20 Oct 1920. Aged 37 yrs 8 mths. Deeply regretted by her sorrowing husband and children. The cup was bitter, the sting severe, to part with one we loved so dear, the trial was hard, we'll not complain, but trust in God to meet again.				*(82)(93)(WM)*

BURDETT, George Derek				(W/913)
George Derek. Infant son of Sub Conductor and Mrs BURDETT. Died 30 Dec 1921.				*(93)*

BURKE, John				(L/1069a)
Sacred to the memory of No 8367 Private John BURKE, 1st Royal Sussex Regiment, who died at Rawalpindi 9 Feb 1909. Aged 22 yrs 8 mths. Erected by E Company.				*(82)(93)(PS)*

BURN, Minnie				(IV/553)
In loving memory of Minnie. The beloved wife of RSM G O BURN. 2nd Battalion The Welch Regiment. Died at Rawalpindi 24 Feb 1934. Aged 38 yrs. A noble and faithful wife, a good pal and a good mother. Peace perfect peace.				*(82)(93)*

BURNIDGE, Robert Edward
No 14626 Gunner Robert Edward BURNIDGE. 91st (Heavy Battery) RGA. Died Rawalpindi 23 Jun 1906.				*(82)*

BURNS, Robert David				(M/1222)
In loving memory of Robert David. Son of W T and A G BURNS. Died 25 Oct 1901. Aged 14 mths.				*(82)(93)*

BURNS, W T				(P/1274)
Quartermaster Sergeant W T BURNS who departed this life 16 Nov 1903. Aged 37 yrs. Erected by his comrades of F Battery, RHA.				*(82)(93)*

BURT, H				(P/1295)
Sacred to the memory of No 4941 Private H BURT, F Company 1st Wiltshire Regiment, who departed this life at Rawalpindi 3 Feb 1904. Aged 23 yrs.				*(82)(93)*

BURTON, Constantine				(K/625)
... of No 4491 Lance Corporal Constantine BURTON. 1st King's Royal Rifles. Died 1 Sep 1892. Aged 25 yrs.				*(93)(BS)(mb)*

BURWOOD, C				(IV/510)
In loving memory of No 6137612. Lance Corporal C BURWOOD. D(MG) Company. 1st Battalion East Surrey Regiment. Died Rawalpindi 13 Apr 1930. Aged 22 yrs. Erected by all ranks of D(MG) Company.				*(82)(93)*

BUTCHER, Gladys May				(N/1467)
In loving memory of Gladys May, infant daughter of Harry and Kate BUTCHER, who died 22 Feb 1897. Aged 1 yr 15 days. Suffer little children to come unto me. Forbid them not for of such is the kingdom of God. Thy will be done.
				(82)(93)

BUTLER, E   (Z/669)
1st Battalion Royal Sussex Regiment. In memory of No 9377
Private E BUTLER, aged 25 yrs, who was accidentally drowned
near Leh pumping station, Rawalpindi, whilst bathing 29 Mar
1912. This stone was erected by his comrades of "D" Company.
In the midst of life we are in death.   AHMUD BUX, SCULPTOR,
RAWALPINDI.   (82)(93)

BUTLER, John Eldridge   (M/1179)
Sacred to the memory of John Eldridge BUTLER, 2nd Lieutenant,
Indian Army, attached to the 35th (1st Battalion Royal Sussex
Regiment), who died at Baghra, near Rawalpindi 13 Mar 1911.
Aged 20 yrs. Whosoever therefore shall confess me before men
him will I confess also before my father which is in heaven.
                                         (82)(93)

BUTLER, R (see 1ST KING'S DRAGOON GUARDS (1))

BUXTON, Alastair Stuart
Alastair Stuart. The beloved son of PSM and Mrs BUXTON. 1st
Battalion Devonshire Regiment. Born 31 Mar 1939. Died 2 Apr
1939.   (82)

BYE, Gwendolyn Grace Agnes   (III/485)
In loving memory of Gwendolyn Grace Agnes BYE and infant son.
Dearly loved wife and son of Captain R E BYE, Royal Signals,
and daughter of Major and Mrs A E CLARKE. Born 2 July 1908.
Died 3 Aug 1941. Blessed are the dead which die in the Lord.
For us the quest but our beloved rest, among the blest who
have attained their quest, out of the darkness into God's
marvellous light.   (93)

BYRNE, Fredrick Keays   (X/832)
Lieutenant Colonel Fredrick Keays BYRNE. Born 26 Apr 1886.
Died 2 Apr 1950. Beloved husband of Kathleen. Tomorrow is
another day.   (93)

BYRNE, Martha   (S/289)
Martha BYRNE, the wife of Corporal BYRNE, who died at
Rawalpindi 13 May 1911. Erected by officers, NCOs and men of
4 Mountain Battery, RGA.   (82)(93)

BYRNE, P   (VII/1399)
Rev Fr. P BYRNE, MHM. Born 10 Nov 1918. Ordained 29 Jun
1944. Died at Rawalpindi, St Mary's Academy, on 24 Oct 1972.
                                         (93)

*Detail from
David ARCHIBALD
headstone*

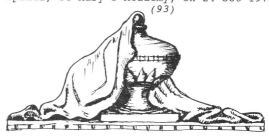

CABRAL, Joan Rita   (T/372)
In sweet memory of Joan Rita. Dearly beloved daughter of Harry and Freda(?) CABRAL. Died 21 Aug 1930. Aged 11 mths 20 days.   (82)(93)(WM)

CADMAN, W   (P/1246)
IHS. In memory of Gunner W CADMAN. 24th Company ED RGA who died on 8 Jun 1901. Aged 25. Erected by his comrades.
                                     (82)(93)(PS)

CADOGAN, T J   (S/293)
S & T Corps. Conductor T J CADOGAN. 22 Oct 1918. RIP. (82)(93)

CAHOON, Alex   (O/1126)
Sacred to the memory of No 4540 Private Alex CAHOON, B Squadron 9th (Queen's Royal) Lancers, who died 17 Dec 1904. Aged 25 and eight twelth years. Erected by the officers, NCOs and men of his squadron.   (82)(93)(PS)

CALDER, D (see 70TH REGIMENT (1))

CALDER, Ian   (W/934)
In sweet memory of Ian. Dearly beloved son of Staff Sergeant and Mrs A E CALDER, RIASC. Born 9 Apr 1934. Fell asleep in Jesus 15 Mar 1935.   (82)(93)

Major General H F CALEY (see page 29)

CALEY, H F   (DD/48)
Sacred to the memory of Major General H F CALEY. Late of the 64th Bengal Native Infantry. Born 15 May 1792. Died 21 Dec 1866. Aged 74 yrs 7 mths.   (82)(93)(BS)(mb)
(see previous page for illustration)

CALLINGHAM E (see 1ST KING'S DRAGOON GUARDS (1))

CALTRESS, Thomas   (IV/576)
Sacred to the memory of No 1860284. Sergeant Thomas CALTRESS. Royal Corps of Signals. Died Rawalpindi 29 March 1936. Erected by all ranks of A Corps Signals. (82)(93)

CAMP, H   (IV/507)
Sacred to the memory of No 598772 Signalman H CAMP. Royal Corps of Signals. Died Rawalpindi 8 Apr 1929. Aged 42 yrs. Erected by all ranks of 1st Indian Divisional Signals.
                                              (82)(93)

CAMP, Mary Ann
Mary Ann CAMP. The beloved wife of Sergeant CAMP. HM's 70th Regiment. Died at Rawalpindi 23 Sep 1872. Aged 19 yrs 11 mths.   (82)

CAMPBELL, Donald   (K/610)
In affectionate memory of Lance Corporal Donald CAMPBELL. 2nd Seaforth Highlanders. Died 21 Nov 1892. Aged 23 yrs 10 mths.
                                              (82)(93)(BS)

CAMPBELL, F W (see ROYAL HORSE ARTILLERY (3))

CAMPBELL, J H D Burgh   (DD/75)
Sacred to the beloved memory of J H D Burgh CAMPBELL. Died 21 Mar 1870. Aged 24 yrs. Not lost but gone before.
                                              (82)(93)

CAMPBELL, Mabel   (KK/267)
In loving memory of Mabel Campbell who fell asleep on 4 Feb 1931. Dulce cor Jesu miserere mei.   (82)(93)

CAMPBELL, Mildred
In loving memory of little baby Mildred CAMPBELL.
                                              (82)

CAMPBELL, Thomas (see 98TH REGIMENT (1))
CAMPION, W   (see 1ST KING'S DRAGOON GUARDS (1))

CANN, Beatrice Luxton   (M/1152)
Sacred to the memory of Beatrice Luxton CANN. Indian Army Nursing Service. Died Rawalpindi 9 Mar 1902. Requiescat in pace.   (82)(93)

CANN, Susie Phillipa   (Y/732)
In loving memory of Susie Phillipa, the beloved wife of CSM R J CANN, Royal Corps of Signals, who departed this life 4 May 1926. Aged 29 yrs 6 mths. Deeply mourned by her sorrowing husband.   (82)(93)

CARDY, Cissie   (IV/521)
In loving memory of Cissie. The beloved wife of Sergeant W A
CARDY, RA, who died at Rawalpindi on 19 Dec 1931. Aged 30
yrs. How I missed her, no one can tell, how much I loved her,
and how well. God loved her too and thought it best to take
her home with him to rest. Just sleeping. Peace perfect peace.
                                           (82)(93)

CARE, Betty   (W/884)
Our darling Betty. Daughter of Lance Sergeant and Mrs CARE.
1st Royal Sussex Regt who died at Rawalpindi 24 Dec 1909.
                                           (93)

CARIATI, Maxine   (see DI CARIATI, Maxine)

CARLYLE, Fannie Ellen Margaret (see HOUSDEN, Fannie Ellen
Margaret)

CARNEGY, Alexander Edward   (G/425)
Jesu Mercy. Alexander Edward CARNEGY. Eldest son of
Lieutenant General A CARNEGY, CB, Bombay Army. At rest 11 Feb
1890. Aged 34 yrs.   (82)(93)

CARR, Edgar Arthur Joseph   (W/957)
In loving memory of Edgar Arthur Joseph. Beloved son of Mr
and Mrs E J CARR. Born at BM Hospital 12 Mar 1921. Died at
Rawalpindi 24 Mar 1928.   (82)(93)

CARR, Frederick Schomberg   (G/423)
In loving memory of Frederick Schomberg CARR. Lieutenant
Colonel, 5th Punjab Cavalry. Born 8 Apr 1845. Died 29 Mar
1890.   (82)(93)

CARROLL, Dorothy Marguerite Prout   (X/753)
Sacred to the loving memory of Dorothy Marguerite Prout
CARROLL. Beloved wife of Sub Conductor H G CARROLL, IAOC.
Born 6 Nov 1900. Died 2 Sep 1927. God's will is best. She
lies before me still and pale. The roses that I prayed might
bloom along her path of life, are on her bosom laid. Crowned
with a strange rapt calm she lies, like one made dumb with
sweet surprise. Better than I can ask or dream this was my
prayer and now, that she is lying still and pale with God's
peace on her brow. I wonder sobbing sore dismayed if this be
that for which I prayed. Erected by her loving husband and
darling children.   (82)(93)

CARROLL, Maurice   (JJ/360)
No 6 Mountain Battery Royal Artillery. Sacred to the memory
of Sergeant Maurice CARROLL who departed this life on 31 Mar
1890. Erected by the officers and NC officers of the battery.
                                           (82)(93)(BS)

CARROLL, Patricia Mary   (X/753)
Patricia Mary (Patty) Daughter of Assistant Surgeon and Mrs
CARROLL.   (93)

CARSWELL, J (see GORDON HIGHLANDERS (2))

CARTER, C (IV/501)
Sacred to the memory of No 1070123 Driver C CARTER. 33rd Field Battery, Royal Artillery. Died Rawalpindi 17 Jul 1928. Aged 20 years. Erected by the NCOs and men of his battery.
(82)(93)

CARTER, F W A (Y/746)
Sacred to the memory of Captain F W A CARTER, MC, 1st Battalion The King's Shropshire Light Infantry, who died at Rawalpindi 10 Jan 1930. Aged 33 yrs. A good life hath but few days but a good name endureth forever.
(82)(93)

CARTER, Hugh Henry (W/926)
Our little boy Hugh Henry CARTER. Son of Mr and Mrs CARTER, IASC. Born 21 Oct 1931. Died 6 Jan 1932.
(82)(93)

CARTER, John (H/585)
Lodge Mayo No 1413 E. C. Sacred to the memory of John CARTER, schoolmaster 2nd Royal Sussex Regiment, who departed this life at Rawalpindi on 31 Jan 1888 leaving his dearly beloved wife to mourn his loss. He giveth his beloved sleep. This monument is erected by the sergeants of the regiment, NCOs and men of his company and brother masons in token of their deep regret at the loss of one who was known and esteemed by all.
(82)(93)(WM)

CARTER, Nina Ann (W/930)
Nina Ann. Beloved child of Conductor and Mrs J C CARTER. Headquarters Northern Command. Born Brighton 20 Feb 1930. Died 10 Jan 1931.
(82)(93)

CARTLEDGE, James (see ROYAL ARTILLERY (4))
CARVER, H (see ROYAL HORSE ARTILLERY (2))

CASEY, John (JJ/361)
IHS. 2/Devon Regiment. In memory of No 1362 Private John CASEY who departed this life on 22 Dec 1889. Aged 24 yrs. Life eternal here begins, these few years are but it's portal, earth it's clouds, it's joys, it's sins, is not home for soul's immortal. RIP. Erected by the officers, NCOs and men of G Company as a mark of respect. Devon Regiment.
(82)(93)(BS)

CATER, A (Y/721)
Sacred to the memory of No 1031750 Gunner A CATER. Died Rawalpindi 23 Feb 1925. Aged 24 yrs 4 mths. Erected by the officers, NCOs and men of the 33rd Field Battery, RA.
(82)(93)

CAVENDISH, Henry (N/1449)
In loving memory of Henry CAVENDISH, Rifle Brigade. Eldest son of 4th Baron WATERPARK. Born 3 Mar 1875. Died 22 Oct 1897. Underneath are the everlasting arms. DEUT. XXXIII.27.
(82)(93)

CAVES, R (O/1117)
In memory of No 7265 Private R CAVES, D Company 2nd Royal Irish Fusiliers, who drowned at Rawalpindi 10 Apr 1906. Erected by the officers, NC officer (sic) and men of his company. (82)(93)

CECIL, Mary (HH/339)
Mary CECIL. In peace. (82)(93)(WM)

CHADDOCK, Winifred Gladys (M/1226)
In loving memory of Winifred Gladys. Infant child of Quarter Master Sergeant W G and Mrs CHADDOCK. 1st Somerset Light Infantry. Aged 6 mths. Suffer little children to come unto me for of such is the kingdom of heaven. AHMUD BUX, RAWALPINDI.
 (82)(93)

CHALK, Muriel St Editha (S/306)
In loving memory of my beloved wife Muriel St Editha CHALK who died Rawalpindi 23 Apr 1927. Aged 34 yrs 5 mths. Thy will be done. Thine forever, God of love, hear me from thy throne above. There forever may we be, here and in eternity.
 (82)(93)

CHAMBERS (T/369)
The beloved youngest son of Corporal and Mrs CHAMBERS. Ox and Bucks Light Infantry. Born 15 Aug 1924. Died 17 Oct 1924. Look upon a little child. Pity my simplicity, suffer me to come to thee. Rest in peace my darling. (93)(WM)

CHANSEY, Maria
Sacred to the memory of Maria. Wife of Sergeant J CHANSEY. 2nd Battalion 9th Regiment. Born in the parish of Grange, Queens Country, who died 10 Nov 1877. Aged 30 yrs.
 (82)

CHAPMAN, Ivy and Elsie (O/1078)
Our darling Ivy. Born 16 Mar 1895. Died 13 Oct 1895. Aged 7 mths. Also Elsie. Born 23 Sep 1896. Died Jun 1898. Aged 1 yr 9 mths. The beloved children of Thomas and Elizabeth CHAPMAN. 4th Dragoon Guards, Rawalpindi.
 (82)(93)

CHARLES, Jimmie (J/441)
In loving memory of little Jimmie. Infant son of Henry and Matilda CHARLES, Queen's Bays, who died at Rawalpindi 13 May 1894. (93)

CHARLESWORTH, Sidney (AA/1/246)
Sacred to the memory of No 4757 Lance Corporal Sidney CHARLESWORTH, B Squadron 9th Queen's Royal Lancers, who died 20 Jun 1905. Aged 25 yrs. A precious one from us has gone, the voice we loved is still, a place is vacant in our ranks which never can be filled. Erected as a mark of esteem by his comrades through..... (82)(93)(WM)

CHARLTON, George   (AA/1/251)
No 2227 Colour Sergeant George CHARLTON, A Company, 1st Battalion Wiltshire Regiment, who departed this life at Rawalpindi 28 Feb 1905. Aged 35 yrs 3 mths. This stone was erected by the officers....   (82)(93)(WM)

CHATTERTON, Jack   (M/1193)
In loving memory of Colonel Jack CHATTERTON. Commandant 6th Gurkhas. Born 21 Dec 1864. Died 16 Mar 1914.
                                           (82)(93)

CHEESEMAN, Monica Patricia Morley (see MORLEY, Monica Patricia)

CHESTER, T (see ROYAL GARRISON ARTILLERY (1))

CHESTER, W N   (D/154)
In memory of Sergeant W N CHESTER, Royal Engineers, who died 2 Aug 1883. Aged 42 yrs. Let my sorrow cease to flow, God has recalled his own, let my heart in every way, still say "Thy will be done".   (93)(BS)

CHILCOTT, George (see ROYAL ARTILLERY (5))
CHILVERS, F   (see ROYAL HORSE ARTILLERY (2))

CHRISTIE, Lawrence   (M/1175)
In loving memory of Lawrence CHRISTIE who died at Rawalpindi 18 Dec 1911. Aged 57 years.   (82)(93)

CHRISTOPHER, Henry Ashington   (DD/76)
Sacred to the memory of Henry Ashington CHRISTOPHER. Ensign. 1st Battalion HM's 19th Regiment. Second son of Lieutenant Colonel E R CHRISTOPHER. Died Rawalpindi 20 Jun .... Aged 18 yrs 6 mths 14 days. His early death is deeply lamented by his brother officers.   (82)(93)(BS)

CHRISTOPHERSON, C F (see 1ST KING'S DRAGOON GUARDS (1))

CHRISTY, Edwin   (D/172)
Sacred to the memory of Edwin CHRISTY, 2nd Lieutenant 8th (King's Royal Irish) Hussars, who died at Rawalpindi 13 Dec 1880. Aged 25 yrs.   (82)(93)(WM)

CIVIL, A (see GORDON HIGHLANDERS (4))

CLAISH, Louise Mary   (VII/1332)
My dearly beloved wife and fond loving Mother Louise Mary CLAISH. Died 23 Apr 1959. Aged 78 yrs. (93)

CLAISH, Malcolm Joseph   (T/371)
In loving memory of Malcolm Joseph. The beloved and only son of Mr and Mrs W CLAISH. ITD. Born 3 Jul 1921. Died 29 Jul 1928. Weep not for me my parents dear, I am not dead but sleepeth here. I was not yours, but Christ's alone, He loved me best and took me home. Oh God, thy will be done.
                                           (82)(93)(WM)

CLAISH, Wilfred Anthony   (VII/1406)
Wilfred Anthony CLAISH. Died 8 Feb 1964. Aged 77. *(93)*

CLARIDGE, A (see SOMERSET LIGHT INFANTRY (1))

CLARK, W   (DD/62)
Sacred to the memory of Private W CLARK. F Company. HM's 70th Regiment. Died at Rawalpindi 25 Apr 1873. Aged 24 yrs. This stone was erected by the officers, NC officers and men of the above company as a tribute of respect.
                                           (82)(93)(BS)

CLARKE   (P/1250)
Sacred to the memory of Private CLARKE, C Squadron 4th Dragoon Guards, who died at Rawalpindi 27 Jun 1900. Aged 27 yrs. Erected by the NCOs and men of his squadron as a token of respect. Thou art O God, my lot is in thy hands.
                                           (82)(93)(PS)

CLARKE, Austin   (GG/211)
In sacred memory of Austin CLARKE. Beloved child of Margret (?) and Patrick CLARKE. HM's 70th Regiment. Born 8 Dec 1868. Died 20 Oct 1872. Aged 3 yrs 10 mths. *(82)(93)(BS)*

CLARKE, Bernadette   (VII/1377)
Sister Bernadette CLARKE. Died 12 Jan 1967. *(93)(WM)*

CLARKE, Emilie Marie
Emilie Marie CLARKE. Our dear Mother who was called to rest 24 Apr 1938. Aged 68 yrs.   *(82)*

CLARKE, G (see ROYAL GARRISON ARTILLERY (4))

CLARKE, Gwendolyn Grace Agnes (see BYE, Gwendolyn Grace Agnes)

CLARKE, H   (O/1097)
In memory of Gunner H CLARKE, 2nd Company ED RGA, who died through injuries on duty 8 May 1901. Aged 20 yrs. Erected by his comrades.   *(82)(93)(PS)*

CLARKE, John   (Z/647)
Sacred to the memory of No 22543 Driver John CLARKE who was drowned in the Sohan River aged 29 yrs on 30 May 1908.
                                           (82)(93)
      (see DAVIE, Archibald)

CLARKE, Ted   (B/134)
In loving memory of little Ted. Infant son of Edward and Emmeline CLARKE. Born 9 Jan 1891. Died 22 Dec 1891. He died in his kind arms. The Saviour bore away his own.
                                           (82)(93)

CLARKE, William   (D/173)
Sacred to the memory of Private William CLARKE, 8th Hussars, who departed this life at Rawalpindi 1 Dec 1880. Aged 25 yrs. Erected by the officers, NC officers and men of his troop.   *(82)(93)(BS)*

CLARKSON, Arthur James				(IV/555)
In loving memory of Arthur James CLARKSON.   Died 23 Apr 1934.
Aged 44 yrs.					(82)(93)

CLAYTON, Harry Swinton				(M/1163)
To the memory of Harry Swinton CLAYTON. Assistant District Superintendent Punjab Police. Born 27 Oct 1883. Died 26 Dec 1904. This stone is erected as a mark of respect and esteem by his brother officers.		(82)(93)(mb)

CLAYTON, William Francis
Sacred to the memory of William Francis CLAYTON. The beloved child of Quartermaster Sergeant and Anne CLAYTON. 3rd Battalion Rifle Brigade. Died 4 Jun 1866. Aged 16 mths. *(82)*

CLEARY, Ellen					(GG/227)
Sacred to the memory of Ellen CLEARY, the beloved wife of Drum Major John CLEARY, HM's 70th Regiment, who departed this life on 29 Aug 1872 at Rawalpindi. Aged 21 yrs.
						(82)(93)
	(For illustration, see Page 94)

CLEARY, Mary Helena				(L/1035)
Mary Helena. The dearly beloved daughter of Sergeant John and Alice CLEARY. No 8 MB RGA. Departed this life Rawalpindi 9 May 1905. Aged 1 yr 5 mths 10 days. Deeply lamented. Gone but not forgotten. We loved her, O no tongue can tell, how much we loved her, and how well. God loved her too and thought it best to take her home with him to rest. *(82)(93)*

CLEMENTS, Mami
Our darling Mami. Beloved daughter of F and H S CLEMENTS. O.D. Born 26 Jun 1906. Died 11 Apr 1908. Aged 1 yr 9 mths 15 days.			(82)(mb)

CLEMMETT, Robert				(GG/228)
In memory of Robert CLEMMETT and John SHEAHAN of B Company, HM's 36th Regiment, who departed this life at Rawalpindi 6 Sep and 21 Nov 1870, respectively 31 and 27 yrs.
						(82)(93)(BS)

CLEMO, William					(P/1278)
In memory of No 13259 Gunner William CLEMO. No 3 MB RGA. Died Rawalpindi 8 Jan 1903. Aged 25 yrs 10 mths.
						(82)(93)

CLIFFORD, Robert (see ROYAL HORSE ARTILLERY (1))

CLOSE, Edward					(C/102)
Sacred to the memory of Lance Corporal Edward CLOSE, 1st Battalion, 17th Regiment, who departed this life at Rawalpindi on the 4 Apr 1880. Aged 28 yrs. Erected by his comrades as a token				(82)(93)(BS)

CLOTHIER, Charles				(Z/662)
In memory of No 4700 Private Charles CLOTHIER, 10th Royal Hussars who died at Rawalpindi..... (82)(93)

COATES, Charles W
In memory of Charles W COATES who died Rawalpindi 8 Dec 1886.
(82)

COATSWORTH, Mary Evangelist *(L/1067)*
Sacred to the memory of Mother Mary Evangelist COATSWORTH of the Presentation Convent. Died 7 Jun 1908. Let my mouth be filled with praise that I may sing thy glory. Thy greatness all the day long. ES.LXX. Erected by the Presentation nuns with the help of kind friends. RIP. *(93)(WM)(end)*

COBB, Guy Harold Humphrey *(W/897)*
Guy Harold Humphrey. Infant son of Captain and Mrs C COBB. S & T Corps. *(82)(93)*

COLDICOTT, Sheelagh *(W/940)*
In loving memory of Sheelagh COLDICOTT. Died 24 Jan 1937.
(93)

COLDWELL, Eric H V *(X/833)*
Eric H V COLDWELL. Died 17 Jun 1950. *(93)*

COLE, Timothy Charles *(VV/537)*
In memory of Timothy Charles (Tittle Mouse). Beloved son of CQMS and Mrs L C COLE. Royal Signals. Born 2 Nov 1941. Died 15 Jan 1942. Safe in the arms of Jesus. *(82)(93)*

COLE, W (see 60TH ROYAL RIFLES (1))

COLEMAN, C *(EE/195)*
Sacred to the memory of Sergeant C COLEMAN. Died Rawalpindi 8 Jan 1888. Also G WRIGHT, who died at Rawalpindi 16 Nov 1887. This stone is erected by their brother sergeants.
(82)(93)(BS)

COLEY, J T *(L/1062)*
IHS. In loving memory of Captain J T COLEY. Died 20 Jun 1906. Aged 36. Erected by his brother officers.
(82)(93)

COLLINS, Alicia Clara Campbell *(L/1033)*
Our darling Alicia Clara Campbell. Daughter of Sergeant and Matilda COLLINS. 1st RMF. Died 18 Oct 1905. Aged 2 yrs.
(82)(93)(mb)

COLLINS, A   (see 1ST KING'S DRAGOON GUARDS (1))
COLLINS, D   (see 1ST KING'S DRAGOON GUARDS (1))
COLLINS, Mrs   (see ROYAL FIELD ARTILLERY (2))

COLLINS, Dora Elizabeth *(B/144)*
In loving memory Dora Elizabeth COLLINS. Born 20 Sep 1887. Died 12 Oct 1888. Faultless before the throne of God.
(82)(93)(BS)

COLLINSON, John *(O/1121)*
In memory of No 2505 Private John COLLINSON, 10th Royal Hussars, who died at Rawalpindi. *(82)(93)*

COLLIS, Eric   (N/1479)
Our little pet, Eric. Infant son of Harry and Grace COLLIS.
Ordnance Department. Born 3 Jun 1895. Died 23 May 1896.
                                              (82)(93)

COLLISTER   (see ROYAL ARTILLERY (7))

COLLYER, R W (see 1ST KING'S DRAGOON GUARDS (1))

COLYER, Walter Henry
Private Walter Henry COLYER.   A Troop.   1st Dragoon Guards.
Died Rawalpindi 22 Sep 1884. Not lost but gone before.
                                              (82)

CONNELL, Miles Joseph   (HH/332)
Miles Joseph. The eldest son of Miles and Ellen CONNELL. Armourer Sergeant. 2/8th Regiment. Born at Ashton under Lyme on 6 Apr 1869. Died 19 Dec 1877. Accidentally drowned.
                                              (82)(93)(BS)(mb)

CONNICALE, Robert Alfred   (Y/723)
Sacred to the memory of Rifleman Robert Alfred CONNICALE, HQ Wing, 1st Battalion The King's Royal Rifle Corps, who died at Rawalpindi 1 Mar 1925. Aged 22 yrs. O for the touch of a vanished hand and the sound of a voice that is still.
                                              (82)(93)

CONNOLLY, Josephine   (S/319)
In ever loving memory of Josephine. The dearly beloved wife of Conductor E T CONNOLLY, IAOC who departed this life 11 Jan 1928. Aged 46 yrs. Deeply mourned by her devoted husband and children.   Not as I will but as thou wilt, O Lord.
                                              (82)(93)(WM)

CONNON, C (see GORDON HIGHLANDERS (3))

CONNOR, Bridget and John James   (GG/215)
Sacred to the memory of Bridget and John James CONNOR. The beloved wife and child of Corporal J CONNOR. HM's 70th Regiment, who died on 10 Jul 1872. Child on the 20th same month.   Wife aged 20 yrs.   Child 17 days.   Erected by her beloved husband as a mark of esteem and respect.
                                              (82)(93)(BS)

CONNOR, M (see ROYAL HORSE ARTILLERY (2))

CONNORS, Albert   (L/1025)
In sweet memory of Albert. The son of Mabel and Henry CONNORS. Died Rawalpindi 15 Jan 1903. Age 2 years.
                                              (82)(93)

CONSTABLE, T (see ROYAL ARTILLERY (6))

CONTES, Cornelius   (W/938)
In loving sweet memory of Cornelius CONTES. Born 12 Sep 1938. Died 21 Apr 1939. God's will be done. (82)(93)

CONWAY, J (Z/635)
In memory of Sergeant J CONWAY, RE who died Rawalpindi 18 Oct 1907. Aged 32 yrs. Rest in peace. (82)(93)(PS)

CONWAY, M Peter (VII/1376)
Sister M Peter CONWAY. Died 10 Dec 1969. (93)(WM)

COOK, A (IV/581)
Sacred to the memory of No 5495640. Pte A COOK. C Company 1st Battalion The Hampshire Regt. 19 May 1937.
 (82)(93)

COOK, George (see ROYAL FIELD ARTILLERY (2))
COOK, James (see ROYAL FIELD ARTILLERY (2))
COOK, William (see ROYAL ARTILLERY (1))

COOK, William
In memory of John EVANS. Gunner 15/9th Battery. Died at Rawalpindi 15 Nov 1877. Aged 33. Also William COOK. Gunner 15/9th Battery. Accidentally killed at Rawalpindi 15 Jan 1877. Aged 51. (82)

COOKE, James McLellan (IV/561)
In fond memory of a devoted son James McLellan COOKE. RAF. Died at Rawalpindi 15 Jul 1935. Aged 24.
 (82)(93)

COOKE, William (see ROYAL HORSE ARTILLERY (1))

COOKES, George R (H/595)
To the glory of God and in loving memory of George R COOKES. Lieutenant M/B Royal Horse Artillery. The only and beloved son of General COOKES, who died 9 Aug 1888, aged 26 yrs, to the inexpressible grief of his father and all who knew him.
 (82)(93)(WM)

COOKES, G R (see ROYAL HORSE ARTILLERY (2))

COOMBES, C (IV/550)
In memory of No 4030616 Private C COOMBES. 1st Battalion King's Shropshire Light Infantry. Died 25 Jan 1932. Erected by his comrades. (82)(93)

COOMBES, T (see 1ST KING'S DRAGOON GUARDS (1))

COOMBS, Margaret (HH/333)
2/9th Regiment. Sacred to the memory of Margaret COOMBS. Born in Dublin. Died Rawalpindi 11 Feb 1877. Aged 35 yrs. Often think of death and death will not surprise you. Erected by her husband Lance Corporal G COOMBS. (82)(93)(BS)

COOPER, Alfred (see ROYAL HORSE ARTILLERY (1))

COOPER, Charles William (III/475)
In memory of No 6008960. Private Charles William COOPER. 1st Battalion The Royal Norfolk Regiment. Died on active service rank on 18 Aug 1937. Aged 23 yrs. (93)

COOPER, Charlotte   (K/619)
In loving memory of dear Mother Charlotte COOPER. Born 13 Mar
1838. Died 5 Dec 1898.   (93)(PS)

COOPER, M (see ROYAL HORSE ARTILLERY (2))

COOPER, Thomas   (E/189)
Sacred to the memory of Private Thomas COOPER. Aged 25 yrs 8
mths. F or Major L F B CAREY's Company. 4th Battalion, Rifle
Brigade, who departed this life 4 Apr 1885. RIP. This stone
was erected by the officers, NC officers and men of his
company as a token of respect.   (82)(93)(BS)

COOTES, E   (IV/515)
In loving memory of No 3443972 Private E COOTES of HQ wing
2nd Battalion Border Regiment. Died Rawalpindi 6 Aug 1931.
Aged 23 yrs 9 mths. Erected by all ranks of HQ wing.
                                         (82)(93)

COPLESTONE, W E   (E/181)
Sacred to the memory of Sergeant W E COPLESTONE, RA, Ordnance
Department, who lost his life by the bursting of a shell in
the Rawalpindi Arsenal. 23 May 1884. Aged 27 yrs 7 mths.
                                         (82)(93)(BS)

COPPINGER, Edward John   (HH/335)
Edward John. Dearly loved child of Major COPPINGER, APD.
Died 28 Apr 1885. Aged 1 yr 3 mths.   (82)(93)(WM)

CORLEY, James   (P/1237)
Sacred to the memory of No 3598 Private James CORLEY, D
Company The Queen's Regiment, who died at Rawalpindi 29 May
1900. Erected by the officers, NCOs and men of D Company.
Father in thy gracious keeping, leave we now thy servant
sleeping.   (82)(93)

CORNFORD, Winifred and CORNFORD, H   (III/481)
In loving memory of Winifred. Wife of Lieutenant Colonel H
CORNFORD, RAOC. Died May 1939. Also in memory of Lieutenant
Colonel H CORNFORD, RAOC, who left this life when SS Yorkshire
was sunk by enemy action on 17 Oct 1939. (82)(93)(WM)

CORNISH, Francis Thackeray Warre (see WARRE-CORNISH, Francis
Thackeray)

CORRIGAN, John (see ROYAL GARRISON ARTILLERY (3))

CORRY, Beryl   (S/299)
In loving memory of Beryl. Wife of Lieutenant Colonel M
CORRY, IMS, who died 11 Nov 1927. RIP. (82)(93)

CORRY, Lilian   (X/757)
In loving memory of Lilian. The beloved wife of Lieutenant
Colonel M CORRY, IMS, who died at Rawalpindi 26 Apr 1925. Love
is strong as death.   (82)(93)

CORWOOD, Norah Esme (see GORWOOD, Norah Esme)

COSTELLO, Lorna Phyllis
Lorna Phyllis. Dearly beloved child of Richard and Anne COSTELLO. Died at Rawalpindi 24 Apr 1915. Aged 1 yr 2 mths 2 days. *(82)*

COTTER, Ma Pu   *(X/859)*
In ever loving memory of Mother Mrs Ma Pu COTTER. Aged 84 yrs who died on 10 Feb 1967. Thy will be done. Erected by her loved ones. *(93)*

COUGHLAN, Patrick (see ROYAL FIELD ARTILLERY (2))
COWBOROUGH, G   (see GORDON HIGHLANDERS (2))
COWEN, Hurst   (see ROYAL ARTILLERY (5))

COWER, Florence   *(Y/701)*
In loving memory of Florence COWER who died 5 Nov 1918. Peace perfect peace. *(82)(93)*

COWTON, Dudley Alfred Christopher   *(B/132)*
To the loving memory of Dudley Alfred Christopher. The darling child of Ben and Mabel COWTON. Born 18 Feb 1893. Died 22 Mar 1894. *(82)(93)(WM)*

COX, F   (see SOMERSET LIGHT INFANTRY (1))
COX, Henry (see ROYAL ARTILLERY (5))
COX, H   (see 60TH ROYAL RIFLES (1))

COX, Joanna Hester   *(W/964)*
In loving memory of Joanna Hester COX. Died 19 Jan 1933.
(82)(93)

COX, Louie   *(N/1455)*
IHS. In loving memory of Louie, the beloved wife of George COX, who departed this life 8 Jan 1896. Aged 31.
(82)(93)

COX, William   *(P/1241)*
Sacred to the memory of Private William COX, K Company 1st Battalion The Queen's, who died at Rawalpindi 14 Nov 1901. Aged 27 yrs 11 mths. Erected as a token of respect by the officers, NCOs and men of his company. Gone but not forgotten. *(82)(93)*

COYLE, J   *(F/380)*
Sacred to the memory of Private J COYLE, A Company, Royal Scots Fusiliers, who died at Rawalpindi 10 May 1898. Erected as a mark of respect by the officers, NCOs and men of A company, Royal Scots Fusiliers. *(82)(93)*

COYNE, David   *(Y/711)*
In ever loving memory of our darling David. Son of Sergeant and Mrs COYNE. 2nd Oxfordshire and Bucks Light Infantry. Born 2 Jun 1914. Died 28 Mar 1924. Jesus loves......
(82)(93)

CRAEER, A E   (O/1119)
Sacred to the memory of No 8727 Private A E CRAEER, H Company 1st Royal Sussex Regiment, who died at Rawalpindi 30 Jul 1911. Aged 28 yrs 8 mths. Erected by the officers, NCO and men of H company as a token of respect. RIP.
                                                 (82)(93)

CRAGG, W A (see ARMY SERVICE CORPS (1))

CRAUFURD, Mildred Mary   (S/311)
In loving memory of Mildred Mary. The dear wife of Lieutenant Colonel R Q CRAUFURD. Royal Scots Fusiliers. Died Rawalpindi 2 Nov 1929.   (82)(93)

CRAWFORD, Anthony Brabazon Charles Godsell (K/607)
In loving memory of Anthony Brabazon Charles Godsell CRAWFORD. 2nd Lieutenant Devonshire Regiment. Only son of Captain Charles Robert CRAWFORD. He died at Rawalpindi 3 Jun 1893.
                                                     (93)

CRAWLEY, H   (F/388)
Sacred to the memory of Lance Sergeant H CRAWLEY, 1st Battalion The Queen's, who died at Rawalpindi 10 May 1900. Aged 26 yrs. Erected as a token of respect by the members of the Sergeants mess 1st Battalion The Queen's. AHMUD BUX & SONS, RAWALPINDI AND UMBALLA.   (82)(93)

CREES, George
No 5021 Private George CREES, D Company 1st Battalion The Queen's, who died at Rawalpindi on 5 Feb 1902. Aged 24 yrs.
                                                     (82)

CRESSWELL, Mabel   (O/1079)
In ever loving memory of our little Mabel. Only daughter of Farrier Quartermaster Sergeant and Mrs CRESSWELL who died at Clifden 22 Apr 1906. Aged 1 yr 8 mths. (82)(93)

CROCE, Catherine Jarman (see HOLMES, Catherine Jarman)

CROCKER, Gladys   (VII/1338)
Gladys. Beloved wife of Major J C CROCKER. Died 2 Jan 1943.
                                                 (82)(93)

CROMPTON, Evelyn
Evelyn CROMPTON.   (82)(mb)

CROSBIE, Charles   (M/1132)
In loving memory of Charles CROSBIE. Lieutenant 4th Dragoon Guards. Died Rawalpindi 12 Jan 1898. Aged 24 yrs. Blessed are the pure in heart.   (82)(93)

CROSBY, A G   (P/1286)
Sacred to the memory of No 4543 Private A G CROSBY, C Squadron 9th (Queen's Royal) Lancers, who died on 13 May 1903. Aged 24 yrs. Erected by his squadron.   (82)(93)(PS)

CROSSE, Mary Violet   (VIII/1408)
Mary Violet CROSSE.   3 Apr 1901 - 22 Apr 1986.   By children
and grandchildren.   (93)(WM)

CRUNDEN, Edward George   (AA/1/257)
Conductor Edward George CRUNDEN.   MWS (Retired list) who died
at Rawalpindi 31 Oct 1906. Aged 62 yrs 5 mths. Rest in peace.
Had he asked us well we know, we would cry Oh spare this blow.
Yes with streaming tears should pray, Lord we love him, let
him stay.   But the Lord doth naught amiss and since he hath
ordered this, we have naught to do but still rest in silence
on his will.   (82)(93)(WM)

CRUTCHLEY, A J (see GORDON HIGHLANDERS (4))

CUDDY, J W   (R/271)
In memory of No 1423951 Gunner J W CUDDY,   21st Medium Battery
RA, who died at Rawalpindi 26 Feb 1932. Aged 36 yrs.   Gone
from us but not forgotten, never shall thy memory fade.
                                       (82)(93)

CULBARD, Wallace   (O/1099)
In memory of Wallace CULBARD of Palumpur Kangra who died 10
Feb 1902. Aged 55 yrs 1 1/2 mths. Thy will be done.
                                       (82)(93)

CULLETON, M   (L/1060)
In loving memory of No 7659 Private M CULLETON,   1st Battalion
The Royal Irish Regiment,   who died at Rawalpindi 22 Jan
1908.   Aged 26 yrs. Erected by his sorrowful brother Patrick
and the NCOs and men of F Company as a token of respect.
                                       (82)(93)

CULLIMORE, Eleanor
In loving memory of Eleanor.   Beloved wife of Sergeant J R
CULLIMORE.   1st Battalion East Surrey Regiment.   Died 13 Jan
1929.   Aged 30 yrs. Deeply mourned by her husband and children.
                                       (82)

CUMMING, J (see ROYAL HORSE ARTILLERY (2))

CUMPER, Annie   (M/1150)
In loving memory of Annie, beloved wife of Alfred C CUMPER,
who departed this life 7 Jan 1903. Aged 37 yrs.   Mourned for
by her sorrowing husband and children. Not as I will but as
thou will. Thy will be done.   (82)(93)(mb)

CUNLIFF, Lottie   (D/153)
Lottie. The beloved wife of Sam F CUNLIFF. Died 25 Jun 1881.
                                       (82)(93)

CUNNINGHAM, George and Ivy   (L/1032)
George.   Aged 5 yrs. The dearly loved son of late Private
Albert Gurney, X Hussars, and Elsie, his wife. Ivy.   Dearly
loved child of ...... and Elsie CUNNINGHAM.
                                       (93)

CUPIT, A E   (P/1267)
Sacred to the memory of Gunner A E CUPIT.   F Battery RHA who
died 17 Jul 1902.   Aged 20 yrs.   Erected by his comrades.
                                        (82)(93)(PS)

CURLEY, Elizabeth Mary   (N/1441)
In loving memory of Elizabeth Mary CURLEY.   Wife of Sergeant
Major J CURLEY.   RA.   Born 1 Jun 1854.   Entered into rest 9
Jan 1894.   (82)(93)

CURLEY, Ellen Christina
Ellen Christina.   Beloved wife of Mr J CURLEY, Kashmir, India.
Died 21 Feb 1910.   Aged 34 yrs.   (82)

CURRY, G
Private G CURRY,   L Company 1st Battalion Somerset Light In-
fantry, who was accidentally drowned while bathing at Rawal
Camp on 4 Nov 1900.   Aged 23 yrs.   (82)

CURTIS, Alice Maud   (X/808)
In loving memory of our dear mother Alice Maud CURTIS who left
us on 7 Aug 1944.   Aged 69 yrs 11 mths.   To live in hearts we
leave behind is not to die.   (82)(93)

CURTIS, D   (K/611)
Sacred to the memory of Gunner D CURTIS.   B Battery, RHA who
died at Rawalpindi 24 Jan 1893.   Aged 24 yrs.   Erected by the
officers, NCOs and men of the battery. (82)(93)(BS)

CURTIS, D (see ROYAL HORSE ARTILLERY (3))

CUYLENBURG, Elsie Evelyn Van (see VAN CUYLENBURG, Elsie E)

de ...., Walter and de........Mary Emma
Sacred to the memory of Walter de .....   Died 1871.   Aged 10
mths.   Also Mary Emma.   Died Jun 1875.   Aged 13 mths.   Children of Walter .....   (82)

D'AGUILAR, Charles Swainson   (M/1174)
In loving memory of Charles Swainson D'AGUILAR.   Captain.
84th Punjabis.   Born 16 Sep 1880.   Died 21 Mar 1912.   In
peaceful hope.   (82)(93)(mb)

d'AUVERGNE, Alice Maude Clara   (Z/672)
In loving memory of our loving mother Alice Maude Clara
D'AUVERGNE.   Born 26 Oct 1875.   Died 7 Oct 1911.   Aged 37 yrs.
When on my aching burdened heart, my sins lie heavily, my
pardon speak, new peace impart, in love redeemable.
                                        (82)(93)

di CARIATI, Maxine　　　　　　　　　　(IV/505)

In loving memory of
my wife Maxine
Princess di CARIATI.
9 Mar 1929. RIP.

(82)(93)(WM)

DE COSTA, Charles William　　　　　　(IV/1335)
Charles William de COSTA.   Died 9 Feb 1959.
　　　　　　　　　　　　　　　　　　　(93)(WM)

de CRUZ, J　　　　　　　　　　　　　　(S/295)
12th E & M. Private J de CRUZ. 9 Oct 1919. RIP.
　　　　　　　　　　　　　　　　　　　(82)(93)

d'CUNHA, Amelia　　　　　　　　　　　(S/316)
In loving memory of Amelia. Beloved wife of Ernest d'CUNHA.
Telegraph Master. Died 6 Jul 1928. RIP.
　　　　　　　　　　　　　　　　　　　(82)(93)(WM)

d'CUNHA, Pansy Margaret
Pansy Margaret d'CUNHA. Died Rawalpindi 19 Jan 1947. Aged
54. My wife.　　　　　　　　　　　　*(82)*

de FREITAS, Mary Isabel　　　　　　　(R/266)
In loving memory of Mary Isabel. Beloved wife of Captain D A
de FREITAS. Died 22 Jan 1931. RIP. *(82)(93)(WM)*

DE MARS, Louis and Eugine　　　　　　(N/1471)
In memory of our little Louis. Born 20 Jul 1890. Died 3 Nov
1897.   Eugine. Born 15 Aug 1892. Died 3 Nov 1892. Beloved
children of Auguste and Evelyne de MARS. *(93)(PS)*

de MONTE, Mary Theresa   (T/365)
In ever loving memory of our darling Mary Theresa. Infant daughter of Assistant Surgeon A N de MONTE. Died 1 Jan 1926. Aged 3 mths.   Sweet that memory which never can fade of her we loved but could not save.   *(82)(93)(WM)*

de PENNING, Gerald Albert Maurice   (W/906)
In ever loving memory of Gerald Albert Maurice, the dearly beloved son of Hubert and Amy de PENNING, who died 9 May 1915. Aged 6 mths 5 days. If thou shouldst call me to resign what most I prize, it ne'er was mine. I only yield thee what is thine. Thy will be done.   *(82)(93)*

de RUYTER, B   (VII/1343)
IHS. Jesus mercy Mary help. Of your charity pray for the soul of the Very Revd B de RUYTER of St Joseph's Foreign Missionary Society. Ordained at Mill Hill 1908. Died 14 May 1945. Aged 64 yrs. RIP.   *(82)(93)*

de SILVA, Margaret   (I/410)
IHS. In loving memory of Margaret de SILVA, the beloved wife of J W de SILVA, who died at Rawalpindi 8 Oct 1893. Aged 50 yrs leaving a husband, children and grandchildren to mourn her loss. The voice that was loving in the house is still now.
                                        (82)(93)(mb)

D'SOUZA   (J/439)
.... beloved son of Thomas and Estelle D'SOUZA. Died at Rawalpindi 21 May 1894.   *(93)*

D'VAZ, Millicent   (VII/1342)
Millicent D'VAZ. Died 6 Nov 1959. Aged 77 yrs.   *(93)*

De VREEDE, Piet   (UU/1019)
Father Piet de VREEDE. Born 6 Jul 1893 (?) Ordained Mill Hill 1937. Died Rawalpindi 19 Sep 1987. *(93)(WM)*

DAER, Joshua Valentine   (E/203)
In memory of Joshua Valentine DAER who was born on 27 Dec 1844 and departed this life on 11 Nov 1887. Aged 42 yrs 10 mths 15 days. Believe in the communion of saints, the forgiveness of sins, the resurrection of the body and life everlasting.
                                        (82)(93)(WM)

DALEY, Patrick   (L/1069)
Thy will be done. Sacred to the memory of Sergeant Patrick DALEY. 2nd Royal Irish Fusiliers. Died at Murree 12 Oct 1905. Aged 36 yrs. Erected by his comrades of the Sergeants Mess, 2nd Royal Irish Fusiliers.   *(82)(93)*

DALRYMPLE HAY, Mary Emily (see HAY, Mary Emily Dalrymple)

DANIEL, Anthony
In loving memory of loving brother Anthony DANIEL, BA Hons. Born 31 Oct 1919. Died 12 Dec 1942. *(82)*

DARBY, Alfred (see ROYAL HORSE ARTILLERY (1))

DARLING, Jessica   (DD/72)
Jessica DARLING. Daughter of Lord LOW of the Laws, Berwick-
shire, and wife of Malcolm DARLING, ICS. 23 Nov 1879 - 18 Dec
1932.   Love, beauty and joy, these were the secrets she
mastered.   (82)(93)(WM)

DAVID, Dora   (X/872)
Mrs Dora DAVID.   Born 7 Aug 1914. Died 4 Jan 1973.   Erected
by her husband, children and sister.   (93)

DAVID, Henry Taylor   (AA/5)
In memory of Henry Taylor DAVID, the beloved child of Mr and
Mrs James DAVID, who died on the 9 Dec 1860.   7 yrs of age.
Farewell my child, but not farewell for ever: we shall meet
when sounds creations dooming knell before the judgement
seat.....   (93)(PS)

DAVID, Joseph   (VII/1341)
Joseph DAVID (photographer). Died 19 May 1974. Age 66.
                                             (93)(WM)

DAVIDSON, Charles   (O/1096)
Erected by his comrades of H company to the memory of Private
Charles DAVIDSON,   1st Gordon Highlanders, who died at
Rawalpindi 11 Dec 1897. Aged 21 yrs.   (82)(93)(PS)

DAVIDSON, Ethel Beatrice May Cavell   (IV/579)
IHS.   Sacred to the memory of Ethel Beatrice May Cavell.
Beloved daughter of Colonel and Mrs J S DAVIDSON.   Died at
Rawalpindi 1 Apr 1936.   She said goodbye to no one, she bade
farewell to none, the gates of heaven flew open, and a gentle
voice said come. Father who hast gathered our dear one to
rest, unto thee we yield her, sure thou knowest best. Deeply
mourned by her husband, children, sisters and brother.
                                             (82)(93)

DAVIE, Archibald   (Z/646)
Sacred to the memory of No 35270 Acting Bombadier Archibald
DAVIE who was drowned in the Sohan River 30 May 1908. Aged 26
1/2 yrs. Erected by the officers, NCOs ...... of the
battery......   (82)(93)
       (see CLARKE, John)

DAVIE, J (see GORDON HIGHLANDERS (4))
DAVIES   (see ROYAL ARTILLERY (7))

DAVIES, Annie Marie   (X/821)
In loving memory of my darling Granny Annie Maria DAVIES who
left me on 6 Oct 1945.   Aged 77 yrs 3 mths. She said goodbye
to no one, she bade farewell to none, the gates of heaven flew
open, and a gentle voice said come.   (82)(93)

DAVIES, Gordon John   (W/943)
Gordon John. The dearly loved infant son of Captain and Mrs S
C DAVIES. Military Accounts Department.   Died 28 Nov 1922.
Aged 5 mths 22 days.   (82)(93)

DAVIES, John (see ROYAL ARTILLERY (9))

DAVIES, Percy William   (X/747)
In loving memory of our darling Daddy Percy William DAVIES who
was called away on 9 Dec 1919. Aged 50 yrs 6 mths.
                                         (82)(93)

DAVIES, Thomas John   (Q/1299)
Sacred to the memory of Bombadier Thomas John DAVIES, 24th
Company, Southern Division, Heavy Battery, Royal Garrison
Artillery, who died at Rawalpindi 28 Feb 1899. Aged 27 yrs.
Erected by the officers, NCOs and men of the battery.
                                         (82)(93)(PS)

DAVIN, Hubert Henry   (IV/564)
In loving memory of my beloved husband Hubert Henry DAVIN.
Born Dublin 4 Jul 1878. Died Rawalpindi 12 Aug 1934. Rest in
peace.   (93)

DAVIS, E H (see ROYAL HORSE ARTILLERY (3))

DAVIS, Ena   (IV/562)
IHS. In loving memory of Ena. Wife of S Condt A E DAVIS.
RAOC who died at Rawalpindi 4 Jul 1935. Aged 27 yrs.
                                         (82)(93)

DAVIS, Ernest Horace   (J/444)
Sacred to the memory of Ernest Horace DAVIS. Lieutenant. B
Battery, RHA. Eldest son of Henry William Banks DAVIS, Esq.,
RA. Born 18 Jul 1865. Died of fever at Rawalpindi 20 Dec
1897(?).   (93)(BS)

DAVIS, I (see 1ST KING'S DRAGOON GUARDS (1))

DAVIS, W   (IV/500)
Sacred to the memory of No 752232 Private W DAVIS, 2nd
Battalion The Royal Sussex Regiment, who died at Rawalpindi
31 Mar 1927. Erected by the officer, NCOs and men of his
regiment.   (93)

DAVIS, William (see 9TH REGIMENT (1))

DAVISON, Ethel Ann   (X/827)
In ever loving memory of Ethel Ann DAVISON. Beloved wife of
Major D H DAVISON, RIASC, who died at Rawalpindi 3 Jul 1947.
                                         (82)(93)

DAVY, P (see SOMERSET LIGHT INFANTRY (1))

DAWES, W (see RIFLE BRIGADE (2))

DAWKINS, Leslie Harry   (R/287)
In loving memory of my dear husband Leslie Harry DAWKINS who
departed this life on 15 Jun 1939. Aged 39 yrs. Deeply
mourned by his sad wife and baby son. Rest in peace.
                                         (82)(93)(WM)

DAWSON, Annie Kathleen Maud   (L/1023)
Annie Kathleen Maud. The beloved daughter of Henry and
Elizabeth DAWSON who died 13 Oct 1902 aged 2 yrs 11 mths. Had
he asked us well we know, we should cry, O spare this blow.
As with streaming tears should cry, Lord we loved..........
                                      (82)(93)(mb)

DAWSON, James (see ROYAL ARTILLERY (6))
DAY, D   (see WEST RIDING REGIMENT (1))
DAY, E   (see ROYAL GARRISON ARTILLERY (4))

DAY, Mary   (Y/698)
Mary. The beloved wife of Sub Conductor R E DAY.   IM List.
Died 25 Jun 1915. Aged 45 yrs.   (82)(93)

DEAN, George (see 70TH REGIMENT (4))

DEAN, Magdalene   (VIII/1418)
Mrs Magdalene DEAN. Died 25 Aug 1981. (93)(WM)

DEAN, R   (R/283)
In memory of No 5249921 Private R DEAN, HQ Company 2nd Bat-
talion the Worcestershire Regiment, who died at Rawalpindi 19
Feb 1939. Aged 27 yrs. Erected by the officers, Warrant
Officers, NCOs and men of the regiment. (82)(93)

THE MALL, RAWALPINDI

DEARLOVE, W J C   (Y/703)
In loving memory of Major W J C DEARLOVE. Aged 72 yrs.   Died
27 Oct 1976. RIP.   (93)(WM)

DELANEY, Anne   (HH/323)
Anne DELANEY. Widow of the late Sergeant John DELANEY, RE,
and Supervisor DPW. Died of cholera at Rawalpindi on 10 May
1879. Aged 30. She has left four young children to bewail
her early death.   (82)(93)

DELANEY, Mary and Edmund   (GG/223)
Sacred to the memory of Mary DELANEY, the beloved wife of Sergeant J DELANEY, HM's 70th Regiment, who departed this life on 23 Dec 1873 at the age of 30 yrs 10 mths. Also Edmund, infant son of the above. Born 12 Dec 1873. Died 14 Jan 1874. Aged 21 days. May they rest in peace. *(82)(93)(BS)*

DELM....., Louisa Anne   (EE/89)
Sacred to the memory of Louisa Anne. The beloved daughter of James and Isabell DELM...... Born 25 Jun 1862. Died 25 Mar 1864. *(93)*

DENLEY, Blanchette   (B/133)
In loving memory of Blanchette. The beloved child of Quartermaster E DENLEY who died at Rawalpindi 8 Jun 1893. Aged 6 yrs 4 mths. *(82)(93)*

DERING, Edgar William Wallace   (N/1460)
IHS. Sacred to the memory of Lieutenant Colonel Edgar William Wallace DERING, Commanding 2nd Battalion The Kings Own Scottish Borderers, who died at Rawalpindi 2 Dec 1894. Erected to his memory by his brother officers.
(82)(93)

DEVANNEY, Peter   (L/1039)
In loving memory of Peter. Son of Sergeant Major DEVANNEY and Nellie his wife. Died 24 Oct 1906. Aged 9 mths 2 days.
(82)(93)

DEW, William George   (P/1280)
In loving memory of Quartermaster Sergeant William George DEW, Sappers and Miners, who departed this life 2 Nov 1902. Aged 67 yrs. If thou shouldst call me to resign, what most I prize, it ne'er was mine, I only yield thee what was thine. Thy will be done. Erected by his loving wife.
(82)(93)

DIBETT, A T   (R/276)
In loving memory of A T DIBETT of Cochin. C.H., H.R.S.(MT) Chaklala. Died 19 Jan 1936. Aged 34 yrs. He is not dead but sleepeth. Erected by his sorrowing wife and brother-in-law K V JOCKIM. *(82)(93)*

DICK, Ellen   (M/1138)
IHS. In loving memory of our mother Ellen DICK, wife of the late John George DICK, who died at Rawalpindi 3 Nov 1899. Aged 74 yrs. Peace perfect peace. *(82)(93)*

DICK, Georgina Florence   (M/1166)
IHS. Sacred to the memory of Georgina Florence. The dearly loved wife of Albert William DICK. Died 13 Dec 1905. Aged 38 yrs. These are they which came out of great tribulation and have washed their robes and made them white in the blood of the lamb. REV VII.14. *(82)(93)*

DICKENS, J   (see RIFLE BRIGADE (2))

DICKENSON, Thomas (see RIFLE BRIGADE (1))

DICKINSON, Biddy   (T/367)
In loving memory of Biddy. The beloved child of Mr and Mrs N
DICKINSON, IOD. Born 12 Aug 1917. Died 5 Mar 1920. Lord,
she was thine and not our own, thou hast not done us wrong.
We thank thee for the precious loan afforded us so long. Thy
will be done.   *(82)(93)(WM)*

DICKS, J (see 60TH ROYAL RIFLES (1))

DIPPLE   *(W/933)*
Baby DIPPLE. Unseen but not forgotten.   26 Mar 1934.
                                          (82)(93)

DISNEY, Leslie Clarence   *(VII/1381)*
Leslie Clarence DISNEY. Loved husband and devoted father.
Born 31 Jul 1898. Died 9 Apr 1950.   *(93)*

DIXON, Robert   *(J/449)*
In loving memory of Sergeant Robert DIXON, D Company 2nd Battalion Seaforth Highlanders, who died Rawalpindi on 29 Oct
1890.   *(82)(93)*

DOBSON, D (see ROYAL ARTILLERY (6))

DOBSON, John and Minnie
To the memory of Gunner John DOBSON, RHA, who died 15 Jan
1885. Aged 36 yrs. Also of Minnie, daughter of the above,
who died 13 May 1884. Aged 8 mths.   *(82)*

DODD, Maud Mary   *(M/1191)*
Maud Mary. The beloved wife of W R DODD. Deputy Superintendent Telegraphs. Born 10 Aug 1862. Died 28 Jan 1913.
                                          (82)(93)
DOHERTY, James
James DOHERTY. Gunner. 15/9th Battery. Died at Umballa 1
Jan 1876. Aged 28 yrs.   *(82)*

DOHERTY, James (see ROYAL ARTILLERY (1))
DOHERTY, P   (see 70TH REGIMENT (5))
DOLAN, Patrick (see ROYAL ARTILLERY (4))

DONALDSON, Lionel   *(M/1194)*
In loving memory of Lionel DONALDSON. Indian Police. Died 12
Jun 1915. Beloved son of J H and G M DONALDSON. Grandson of
the late Lieutenant General W OSBORN, Indian Army.
                                          (82)(93)

DONALDSON, S   *(III/473)*
In memory of No 1055154. Lance Sergeant Saddler S DONALDSON
.......RA. Died at Rawalpindi 22 Jun 1937. Aged 34. Erected
by widow, officers, NCOs and men of the battery.
                                          (93)(WM)

DONALDSON, T (see GORDON HIGHLANDERS (2))

DONN, W R   (see 1ST KING'S DRAGOON GUARDS (1))

DONOGHUE, Michael   (L/1044)
Of your charity pray for the repose of the soul of No 6938 Private Michael DONOGHUE, C Company 2nd Royal Irish Fusiliers, who departed this life 28 Aug 1904. Aged 24 yrs. RIP. Erected by the officers, NCOs and men of his company as a token of their esteem.   (82)(93)(PS)

DONOGHUE, P   (S/298)
Sacred to the memory of No. 7144887 Private P DONOGHUE. 1st Battalion The Connaught Rangers. Died 1 Sep 1921.
                                     (93)

DONOVAN, J   (see 60TH ROYAL RIFLES (1))
DORAN, P   (see 70TH REGIMENT (2))
DOREY, Albert   (see RIFLE BRIGADE (1))
DOREY, E   (see RIFLE BRIGADE (2))

DOREY, Leonard Frank   (M/1199)
In loving memory of Leonard Frank. The dearly loved child of Sergeant and Mrs DOREY. 69th..... Died 19 Nov 1905. Aged 6 mths.   (82)(93)

DORTON, Ada J   (X/820)
In loving memory of our dear sister Ada J DORTON who passed away 6 Jan 1942. Born 4 Jan 1870. Father in thy gracious keeping, leave we now our loved one sleeping. Only dead to earthly sorrows, sleeping till the shadows cease, living thro the endless ages, God's fair life of rest and peace.
                                     (82)(93)(end)

DORTON, William Morris   (X/787)
In loving memory of William Morris DORTON. Born 9 Oct 1870. Died 23 Jun 1934. Erected by his sorrowing wife and children. On the resurrection morning, soul and body meet again, no more sorrow, no more weeping, no more pain.
                                     (82)(93)(end)

DOUDWELL, John (see ROYAL GARRISON ARTILLERY (3))

DOUGLAS, Emily Helen   (S/315)
In loving memory of Emily Helen DOUGLAS. Died 19 Dec 1928. RIP.   (82)(93)

DOUGLASS, John   (G/422)
Erected in loving memory by his comrades. Sacred to the memory of Corporal Piper John DOUGLASS. 2nd Battalion Seaforth Highlanders (late 78th) who departed this life 1 Apr 1890 at Rawalpindi. Aged 29 yrs.   (82)(93)

DOUTHWAITE, E   (see RIFLE BRIGADE (2))
DOWDALL, Patrick (see ROYAL ARTILLERY (5))

DOWDING, H C   (Y/690)
Sacred to the memory of our late brother H C DOWDING. ....
1848.....   (82)(93)(PS)

DOWNEY, Patrick   (I/402)
IHS. Sacred to the memory of Private Patrick DOWNEY, 2nd
Battalion Argyll & Sutherland Highlanders, who died at
Rawalpindi 30 Dec 1895. Aged 22 yrs 7 mths. This stone is
erected by the NCOs and men of C Company as a mark of esteem.
                                           (82)(93)(PS)

DOWNS, Arthur (see ROYAL HORSE ARTILLERY (1))

DOWNS, Wallace Jacoby   (V/1008)
In loving memory of Wallace Jacoby DOWNS. 1894-1941.
Missionary Professor, Gordon College 1920-1941.
                                           (82)(93)

DRAPER, William Ernest   (W/945)
Darling baby William Ernest. Son of CQM & Mrs DRAPER. B Corps
Signals. Died at Rawalpindi 8 Nov 1922. Aged 15 mths. The
Lord gave and the Lord hath taken away. (82)(93)

DRISCOLL, W (see WEST RIDING REGIMENT (1))

DRUMMOND, George Richard   (Y/736)
In ever loving memory of George Richard DRUMMOND. Died
Rawalpindi 12 Jul 1926. Aged 49 yrs. Blessed are the pure in
heart for they shall see God. O for the touch of a vanished
hand, and for the sound of a voice that is stilled.
                                           (82)(93)

DRUMMOND, Thomas   (V/1005)
To the glory of God and in memory of Private Thomas DRUMMOND.
.. Rest in peace.   (93)

DUCKWORTH, A H   (IV/504)
IHS. In loving memory of our dear father Sergeant A H
DUCKWORTH, MD, who died on 24 Dec 1928. Aged 47 yrs. Erected
by his sorrowing wife and children. Forget no, nor never
will, we love him here, we love him still, nor love him less
although he's gone from us to his eternal home.
                                           (82)(93)

DUCKWORTH, James Wilfred   (R/280)
IHS. In loving memory of James Wilfred DUCKWORTH. Died 6 May
1936. Aged 25 yrs 5 mths. The cup is bitter, the sting
severe, to part with one we loved so dear, the trial is hard,
we will not complain but trust in God till we meet again.
Erected by his heartbroken brothers and sisters.
                                           (82)(93)

DUFFEY, M   (GG/216)
In memory of Private M DUFFEY. F Company. HM's 70th
Regiment. Died 28 Dec 1871. Aged 25 yrs. Erected by the of-
ficers, NC officers and men of the above as a mark of respect.
                                           (82)(93)(BS)

DUFFY, M (see WEST RIDING REGIMENT (1))

DUGGAN, J (see ROYAL ARTILLERY (3))

DUN, Ann (X/851)
IHS. Ann. Beloved wife of Bill DUN. Died 6 Sep 1956.
(93)

DUNCAN, Netta (O/1073)
In loving memory of darling wee lassie Netta. Darling daughter of Sergeant T and E DUNCAN. 1st Battalion Gordon Highlanders. Born 18 Nov 1895. Died 13 Nov 1896. The reapers are the angels, and the angels echoed around the throne. Rejoice for the Lord brings back his own.
(82)(93)

DUNFORD, G
In memory of No 1022950 Staff Sergeant G DUNFORD. RIASC. Died Rawalpindi 30 Jan 1935. (82)

DUTTON, June Margaret (V/531)
Rest in peace. In loving memory of June Margaret. Beloved eldest daughter of Tom and Marjorie DUTTON. Born Hythe 21 Feb 1932. Died Rawalpindi 26 Dec 1944. This flower conceived by God and nurtured to perfection, then gathered he himself to save her from the world's infection, leaving an empty barren space in life's big garden with only precious memories of all her loveliness and grace. Free of sorrows, sins and petty meanness with a fearless face. LORD. Give her for light the sunshine of thy sorrow, give her for shelter shadow of thy Cross, give her a share of thy glorious tomorrow, take from our hearts the bitterness of loss. (82)(93)

JUNE MARGARET DUTTON

EAGLE, Mave Eileen   (Y/688)
Mave Eileen EAGLE. Beloved wife of William Styles EAGLE who
departed this life Rawalpindi 5 Oct 1913. Aged 36 yrs 9 mths.
Out of pain into bliss.   (82)(93)

EARLE, J (see ROYAL ARTILLERY (2))

EARP, Edward Arthur   (P/1240)
Sacred to the memory of Gunner Edward Arthur EARP, 3rd
Battery, Royal Field Artillery, who died 17 Oct 1900.
Erected as a token of respect and esteem by his comrades of
the battery. RIP.   (82)(93)

EASTLAND, W   (K/620)
To the memory of No. ....93 Private W EASTLAND. (82)(93)(BS)

ECKERT, H C M   (K/608)
Sergeant H C M ECKERT. 1st King's Royal Rifles. Died
Rawalpindi 26 Mar 1893.   (82)(93)(PS)

EDDEN, William   (D/150)
Sacred to the memory of Private William EDDEN, 8th Hussars,
who departed this life at Rawalpindi on 15 Jun 1881. Aged 27
yrs. Erected by the officers and men of his troop. (93)(BS)

EDMONDS, J   (see 1ST KING'S DRAGOON GUARDS (1))
EDWARDS, E H (see 1ST KING'S DRAGOON GUARDS (1))

EDWARDS, Ernest   (Z/654)
In memory of No 929 Private Ernest EDWARDS. 10th Royal Hussars.   (82)(93)(WM)

EGAN, Charles
Private Charles EGAN. D Company 2nd Royal Sussex Regiment.
Died Rawalpindi 27 Sep 1887. Aged 32 yrs. Also Albert Edward
IRVING who died at Meerut 17 Sep 1887. Aged 22 yrs.   (82)

EGGERS, W (see ROYAL ARTILLERY (6))

ELDER, Rosalie Eugenie   (VI/464)
In loving memory of Rosalie Eugenie. Infant daughter of John
and Lucy ELDER. Born 21 Aug 1945. Died 31 Aug 1945. (82)(93)

ELDRED, E   (Z/676)
Sacred to the memory of No 8185 Drummer E ELDRED who died at
Rawalpindi 10 Oct 1910. Erected as a token of respect by his
brother drummers & comrades of H Company.   (82)(93)

ELDRIDGE, H   (Z/655)
In loving memory of No 8327 Private H ELDRIDGE, F Company 1st
Royal Sussex Regiment, who died at Rawalpindi 14 Jan 1909.
Aged 22 yrs. Erected by his comrades.   (82)(93)(PS)

ELIOT, Belle   (M/1140)
In sweet memory of Belle. The beloved wife of Ernest E M
ELIOT. Died Rawalpindi 23 Oct 1900.   (82)(93)(PS)

ELLIS, C (see ROYAL HORSE ARTILLERY (2))

ELLIS, John William   (Y/733)
In memory of No. 2310326 Corporal John William ELLIS. No 2
(Wireless) Company. B Corps Signals. Died at Rawalpindi on 12
Jul 1926. Aged 33 yrs. Erected by the officers, warrant
officers, NCOs and men of No 2 (Wireless) Company, B Corps
Signals.   (93)

ELLIS, L S   (see ROYAL HORSE ARTILLERY (2))
ELLIS, S   (see ROYAL HORSE ARTILLERY (2))
ELLIS, W   (see 70TH REGIMENT (1))
ELSON, H B   (see ROYAL GARRISON ARTILLERY (4))

EMERSON, Elizabeth Rosa   (M/1156)
IHS. In loving memory of Elizabeth Rosa EMERSON who died at
Rawalpindi 9 Nov 1901.   (82)(93)

ENGLAND, John Henry   (X/835)
In ever loving memory of John Henry ENGLAND. Born 1 Aug 1897.
Died 4 Nov 1950. Erected by his loving wife Noreen.
                                           (93)

ENNIS, George   (M/1192)
Sacred to the memory of Wor. Bro. George ENNIS, PM, and past
President of DC Board of General Purposes, Punjab. Died 16
Feb 1914 at the age of 75 yrs. Erected by the Masonic
Fraternity. Had he asked us, well we know, we should cry, O
spare this blow. Yes, with streaming tears should pray, Lord,
we love him, let him stay.   (82)(93)

ENNIS, Harriet   (M/1187)
In loving memory of Harriet ENNIS. Beloved wife of G ENNIS.
Called to rest 4 Dec 1908. Aged 68 yrs. Deeply mourned by
her sorrowing husband and children. Farewell darling, rest in
peace.   (82)(93)

ENRIGHT, Elizabeth   (CC/35)
Sacred to the memory of Elizabeth, the beloved wife of
Sergeant John ENRIGHT, 2/8 The Kings Regiment, who departed
this life on the third day of July 1878. Aged 32 yrs. How
sweet the scene when virtue dies, when seeks a righteous soul
to rest. How mildly beam the closing eyes, how gently heaves
the expiring breast. Erected by her sorrowing husband.
                                           (82)(93)(BS)(mb)
     (See Page 3 for illustration)

ENSOR   (A/126)
... The dearly loved child of J & L ENSOR. Aged 6 mths. Died
21 Jan 1888....   (93)

ERRINGTON, James (see GORDON HIGHLANDERS (1))

EVANS, James Symond   (X/759)
James Symond EVANS who died 16 May 1919. Aged 53 yrs 7 mths.
Thy will be done.   (82)(93)

EVANS, John (see ROYAL ARTILLERY (1))

EVANS, John
In memory of John EVANS. Gunner 15/9th Battery. Died at Rawalpindi 15 Nov 1877. Aged 33. Also William COOK. Gunner 15/9th Battery. Accidentally killed at Rawalpindi 15 Jan 1877. Aged 51.   (82)

EVANS, Lucy   (H/600)
In loving memory of Lucy. The beloved wife of Sergeant J R P EVANS. Died 10 Aug 1888. Aged 19 yrs 6 mths. I saw her fade and waste away, I saw her gasp for breath, I saw upon her sunken cheeks, the fatal sign of death. This stone was erected by her sorrowing husband, relations and friends as a small token of their last respect.   (82)(93)(mb)

EVANS, William David   (V/994)
In loving memory of No 3955186 Lance Corporal William David EVANS. 2nd Battalion The Welch Regiment. Died at Rawalpindi 11 Feb 1933. Aged 24 yrs 6 mths. (82)(93)

EVATT, Harriet   (G/427)
Sacred to the memory of Harriet, the beloved wife of C A EVATT, who departed this life 11 Jan 1890 in the 49th year of her age. Here let me wait with patience, wait till the night is o'er, wait till I see the morning, break on the golden shore.   (82)(93)(BS)

EVEREST, F   (K/622)
Sacred to the memory of Private F EVEREST who died 19 Feb 1892. 3rd Dragoon Guards. Aged 27 yrs.
                                        (82)(93)(BS)

EWART, C C E   (M/1131)
In memory of C C E EWART. Lieutenant. 5th Bengal Cavalry. Son of R W EWART, Esq of Ellerslie, Moffat, NB, who died at Rawalpindi of disease contracted on service on 7 Jan 1898. Erected by his brother officers. AHMUD BUX.
                                        (82)(93)(mb)

FAGAN, Joseph   (L/1052)
In loving memory of No 3321 Lance Corporal Joseph FAGAN, 2nd Battalion Royal Irish Fusiliers, who departed this life at Rawalpindi 12 Dec 1903. Aged 36 yrs. RIP. Erected by his wife.   (82)(93)

FALLON, Ernest Stanhope					(GG/221)
In ever loving remembrance of Ernest Stanhope. Son of Mr FALLON. 17th Regiment who died 22 ... 1874 ....
					(82)(93)(BS)(mb)

FANCE, C (see ROYAL ARTILLERY (3))

FARMER, C (see 60TH ROYAL RIFLES (1))

FARMER, J					(Y/710)
Sacred to the memory of No 4966099 Private J FARMER. HQ Wing 2nd Battalion The Sherwood Forresters. Died 18 Jan 1924. Aged 20 yrs 6 mths.			(82)(93)

FARMER, Mary Jill				(T/376)
In loving memory of Mary Jill FARMER who left us 1 Oct 1933. Aged 2 days.				(82)(93)(WM)

FARMER, W					(AA/1/633)
In memory of Private W FARMER. 2nd North Staffordshire Regiment. Died Rawalpindi 13 Jun 1906. Aged 20 yrs 3 mths. This stone is erected by NCOs and men of B company. In the land of strangers our son doth lie, no father or mother to bid him goodbye, but the angels of heaven will guard his soul until we meet again at the call of the roll.
					(82)(93)(WM)

FARNON, Norman					(VIII/1421)
Our beloved son. "Chippy" Norman FARNON. Died 3 Feb 1980. Mum, Dad, John, Godfrey, Errol.		(93)(WM)

FARRELL, Eleaor (sic) Jane			(M/1164)
In loving memory of Eleaor (sic) Jane FARRELL. Died 29 Oct 1934. Aged 71 yrs. Widow of the late T P FARRELL. Indian Finance Department.				(82)(93)

FARRELL, Kathleen Ruth				(L/1037)
In loving memory of little Nooky Kathleen Ruth FARRELL. Dearly loved child of Sub Conductor and Mrs FARRELL. MWS. 3 yrs 3 mths. A lovely bud so sweet and fair, in paradise does bloom.					(93)

FARRINGTON, Mary Ann
Sacred to the memory of Mary Ann, the beloved child of Ann and George FARRINGTON, Sergeant 1st Battalion 6th Royal Regiment, who departed this life at Rawalpindi 22 Feb 1871. Aged 11 mths 28 days.				(82)

FAULKNER, Alfred (see RIFLE BRIGADE (1))

FEELEY, Frank					(L/1068a)
Sacred to the memory of No 6580 Acting Bombadier Frank FEELEY, No 3 MB RGA, who died at Rawalpindi 29 Dec 1908. Aged 35 yrs 1 mth. RIP.				(82)(93)(PS)

FEHILY, Jeramiah (see ROYAL ARTILLERY (5))

FENCOTT, George Ernest   (X/874)
To the treasured memory of a dearly beloved husband, father
and grandfather George Ernest FENCOTT, aged 56 yrs, who left
us for his heavenly home on 10 May 1972. Mourned by his wife
and 2 daughters. RIP. The blow was hard, the shock severe,
to part with one we loved so dear. Our loss is great, we'll
not complain, but trust in God to meet again.
                                                  (93)(WM)

FENDALL, Patrick George   (L/1021)
In loving memory of Patrick George. Youngest son of Major and
Mrs C P FENDALL. Born at Kirkee 11 Nov 1898. Died at
Rawalpindi 1 Feb 1900.   (93)

FERNS, W R (see ARMY SERVICE CORPS (1))

FERRIER, Peter   (VV/526)
Peter. Son of Captain and Mrs P FERRIER. Died 16 Nov 1942.
                                                  (93)

FIELDER, C   (see ROYAL ARTILLERY (6))
FINCKE, H R   (see ROYAL ARTILLERY (6))
FINDLATER, J   (see ARMY SERVICE CORPS (1))
FINDLAY, R   (see 1ST KING'S DRAGOON GUARDS (1))

FINK, Lisette Isabella Falkland   (K/614)
In loving memory of Lisette Isabella Falkland FINK who fell
asleep in Jesus on 1 Jan 1893. Aged 24 yrs 2 mths 21 days.
She is not dead but sleepeth. Thy will be done. A light is
from our household gone, a voice we loved is stilled. A place
is vacant on our hearth, which never can be filled.
                                              (82)(93)(mb)

SECTION OF OLDER GRAVES, HARLEY STREET CEMETERY

FINLEY, Grace Cowdy (V/1003)
Grace Cowdy FINLEY. 12 Apr 1871 - 11 Feb 1936. An inspiration and partner to her husband for 43 yrs. Dutiful and honoured, loving and loved, Christlike in service, a mother to many. (82)(93)

FINLEY, Harry Lincoln (V/1004)
Harry Lincoln FINLEY. 19 Feb 1855 - 12 Mar 1936. Served as a medical missionary in Egypt for 30 yrs. A physician, a friend, a Christian, loved by little children, the confidant of many, respected and honoured by all. (82)(93)

FINNER, Eliza
Eliza FINNER. Died 27 Dec 1883. (93)

FINNERTY (DD/49)
FINNERTY. Assistant Apothecary who died 21 Apr 1872. Aged 25 yrs. (82)(93)(BS)

FINNIS, Henry John Steriker (CC/33)
In loving memory of Henry John Steriker. Son of Henry and Mary FINNIS. Born 23 Nov 1878. Taken home 28 Dec 1878. Of such is the kingdom of heaven. I know that thou hast gone to the home of thy rest, then why should my soul be so sad? I know thou hast gone where the weary .... and the mourner looks up and ... (82)(93)(WM)

FIRTH (III/492)
.... FIRTH. 1894 .... 1947. (93)

FIRTH, Christopher John (T/373)
In sweet memory of Christopher John. The beloved son of Henry Raywood and Norah FIRTH. Born 10 Jun 1929. Died 3 Mar 1930. (82)(93)(WM)

FITT, Cecil (see ROYAL HORSE ARTILLERY (1))

FITT, Jessie (see ROYAL HORSE ARTILLERY (1))

FITZPATRICK, Thomas (I/399)
IHS. In loving memory of Thomas FITZPATRICK who departed this life on 26 Sep 1897. Aged 55 yrs 4 mths 18 days. Fortified by the sacrament of the Holy Church. (93)

FLANAGAN, Dorothea (VII/1365)
Mother Dorothea FLANAGAN. 5 Jun 1949. (93)

FLANAGAN, Harold (VII/1367)
Harold FLANAGAN. Husband and father. 5 Feb 1949. Aged 68 yrs. (93)

FLANAGAN, T P (see ROYAL HORSE ARTILLERY (2))

FLEMING, Ernest (E/200)
Sacred to the memory of Bombadier Ernest FLEMING, J Battery 2nd Brigade RA, who died at Rawalpindi on 3 Mar 1887. Aged 21 yrs. (82)(93)(PS)

FLINDAL, Richard (see ROYAL FIELD ARTILLERY (2))

FLOWER, Margaret (IV/571)
In loving memory of Margaret. The beloved and loving wife of James FLOWER. 7 Jan 1937. With thy Saints, O Lord.
(93)

FLOYED, Louisa Elizabeth (X/800)
In ever loving memory of Louisa Elizabeth FLOYED. Born 16 Jan 1858. Died 7 Feb 1938. Blessed are the dead that die in the Lord. Father in thy gracious keeping leave we now our loved one sleeping. Erected by her daughter, relations and friends.
(82)(93)

FLOYED, Tom (X/750)
In ever loving memory of my darling husband Tom FLOYED who died 26 Dec 1928. Aged 50 yrs. (82)(93)(end)

FLYNN, P (see ROYAL HORSE ARTILLERY (2))

FOLEY, C (L/1056)
In loving memory of No 5246 Private C FOLEY. E Company 1st Battalion Royal Irish. Died Rawalpindi 24 May 1908. Aged 32 yrs. RIP. Erected by the officers, NCOs and men of his company. (82)(93)

FOLEY, Eveline (HH/322)
Sacred to the memory of Eveline. The beloved wife of J FOLEY, 2nd/9th Regiment. Died Rawalpindi 26 Jan 1879. Aged 27 yrs. Requiescat in pace. (82)(93)

FORBES, Alice Mary (X/848)
Alice Mary FORBES (nee MACKECHINE). Born 2 Jul 1905. Died 18 Dec 1954. (93)(WM)

FORBES, Robert (G/415)
Sacred to the memory of No 2997 Private Robert FORBES who died at Rawalpindi 16 Jun 1890. Aged 23 yrs 4 mths. 3rd Dragoon Guards. "Ich Dien". (82)(93)(BS)

FORBES, Walter Scott (EE/83)
Sacred to the memory of Walter Scott FORBES. Quartermaster Sergeant HM's 70th Regiment. Died 26 Jun 1872. Aged 33 yrs. I am the resurrection and the life. (82)(93)(BS)

FORCE, Emma
Sacred to the memory of Emma, the beloved wife of Alfred FORCE, who died at Murree 10 Jun 1876. Aged 44. (82)

FORD, H R K (J/448)
In memory of H R K FORD, 2nd Lieutenant Bedfordshire Regiment, who died 3 Jun 1891. Aged 21 yrs 10 mths. I thank my God upon every remembrance of you. (82)(93)

FORD, Michael John (W/937)
Michael John. Son of Mr and Mrs C FORD. South Wales Borderers. Died 26 Dec 1937. Aged 9 mths. (82)(93)

FORDYCE, John Frederick Dingwall (B/146)
In loving memory of John Frederick Dingwall FORDYCE. Born 20 Apr 1887. Died 15 Dec 1887. (93)

FORSYTH, Ellen Louisa (CC/32)
Ellen Louisa. Beloved infant child of Andrew and Mary FORSYTH who died 11 Jun 1878. (82)(93)(WM)

FORSYTH, Fanny Elizabeth (CC/31)
Fanny Elizabeth. Infant child of Andrew and Maria FORSYTH. Born 17 Mar 1875. Died 1 Jun 1878. (82)(93)(WM)

FOSTER, W (see ROYAL HORSE ARTILLERY (3))

FOWLER, A E (see ROYAL HORSE ARTILLERY (2))

FOWLER, Clara and George (AA/1/252)
Sacred to the memory of Clara, wife of Corporal S S G FOWLER, No 5 Ammunition Column RFA, late of 57th Battery RFA, who departed this life 12 Mar 1905. Aged 35 yrs. Deeply regretted by all. Also George. Son of the above who died on 12 Jan 1902. Aged 6 yrs 6 mths. Suffer little children to come unto me. Erected by the officers, NCOs and men of the battery. (82)(93)(PS)

FOX, Reginald James (X/761)
In memory of Reginald James FOX. Lately Captain ....
(93)

FOY, John and Gertrude (JJ/343)
In loving memory of John. Aged 8 yrs 10 mths and Gertrude. Aged 1 yr 10 mths. Children of Sergeant and Mrs FOY, KOSB, who both died at Rawalpindi on 12th day of April 1895. Also child of the above who died at Murree on 27 May 1895. Aged 4 yrs 7 mths. Not lost but gone before. (82)(93)(WM)

FRANCES, A (see GORDON HIGHLANDERS (3))

FRANCIS, Dominic (VII/1326)
Dominic FRANCIS. Born 13 Oct 1913. Died 2 Jul 1974.
(93)(WM)

FRANCIS, Henry Joseph (VII/1358)
Henry Joseph FRANCIS. Died New Year's Day 1948. Aged 63 yrs.
(93)

FRANCIS, William (see 70TH REGIMENT (4))

FRANKLIN, G (P/1245)
Acting Corporal G FRANKLIN. 3rd Battalion Rifle Brigade. Died Rawalpindi 17 Aug 1900. Aged 23 yrs 11 mths. Also of Acting Corporal A E RUTTER of the same battalion who died at Rawalpindi 28 Aug 1900. Aged 28 yrs. Erected by the corporals of the 3rd Battalion Rifle Brigade as a mark of esteem.
(82)(93)

FRANKLIN, John Robert   (Q/1318)
Sacred to the memory of John Robert FRANKLIN. 4th Royal
(Irish) Dragoon Guards. Died at Rawalpindi 18 Sep 1896. Aged
23. Erected by his sorrowing brother and comrades in A
Squadron. Jesus saith thy brother shall rise again. AHMUD
BUX, SCULPTOR, RAWALPINDI.   *(82)(93)(PS)*

FRANKLIN, William Henry   (Y/727)
Sacred to the memory of Rifleman William Henry FRANKLIN, B
Company The King's Royal Rifle Corps, who was accidentally
drowned at Rawalpindi 17 Apr 1925. Aged 22 yrs.
                                         (82)(93)

FRANKLINE, Charlie   (M/1215)
In affectionate memory of Charlie. Beloved son of Sergeant
and Annie FRANKLINE, 3rd Battalion Rifle Brigade, who died on
11 Mar 1900. Aged 13 mths. Suffer little children to come
unto me.   *(82)(93)*

FRANKS, Theresa   (JJ/359)
Sacred to the memory of Theresa. Beloved wife of William
FRANKS, 1st King's Royal Rifles, who died at Rawalpindi 17
Feb 1892. Aged 28 yrs 9 mths.   *(82)(93)(WM)(mb)*

FRASER, Arthur Herbert   (M/1195)
In loving memory of Arthur Herbert FRASER who died at
Rawalpindi 27 Mar 1916. Now the labourer's task is o'er, now
the battle day is past, now upon the further shore, lands the
voyager at last. Father in thy gracious keeping, leave we now
thy servant sleeping.   *(82)(93)*

FRASER, James   (K/612)
In memory of No 1864 James FRASER. E Company. 2nd Seaforth
Highlanders. Died Rawalpindi 13 Jan 1893. Aged 25 yrs.
Erected by the officers, NCOs and men of his company.
                                         (82)(93)(BS)

FRASER, Margaret   (DD/44)
Sacred to the memory of Margaret FRASER. Beloved wife of
Private Thomas FRASER, HM's 79th Highlanders, who departed
this life at Rawalpindi 12 Nov 1865. Aged 33 yrs. Erected by
her husband who regrets the loss of a tender mother and an
affectionate wife. In the midst of life we are in death.
                                      (82)(93)(BS)(mb)

FRASER, Phoebe Sylvia and Donald Walter (J/455)
Sacred to the memory of Phoebe Sylvia, the beloved wife of
Sergeant Piper FRASER, 2nd Seaforth Highlanders, who died 7
Mar 1891. Aged 31 yrs. Also of Donald Walter, beloved son,
who died 10 Jun 1891. Aged 3 mths. Until the day breaks and
the shadows flee away.   *(82)(93)*

FRAY, Arthur O   (IV/557)
Sacred to the memory of Arthur O FRAY. Died 16 Jun 1934.
Aged 47.   *(82)(93)*

FREEMAN, B
Private B FREEMAN. H Company 4th Battalion Rifle Brigade. Died 11 Apr 1880. Aged 23 yrs.   *(82)*

FRENCH, J A   *(P/1281)*
Sacred to the memory of No 4837 Private J A FRENCH, C Squadron 9th Queen's Royal Lancers, who died 23 Jun 1903. Aged 25 and 3/12th yrs. Erected by his Squadron.
(82)(93)

FROOME, Sheilah   *(LL/238)*
In loving memory of Little Sheilah, the dear daughter of George William and Matilda FROOME, 3rd King's Own Hussars.
(82)(93)(WM)(mb)

FROST, Charles G   *(E/190)*
In memory of Lance Corporal George TODD, Bandsmen Henry MOORE and Charles G FROST, The 2nd Battalion The Royal Irish Regiment, who were killed in a railway accident on 15 Mar 1885.   *(82)(93)(BS)*

FRY, Sarah Ann   *(E/199)*
To my darling Mother Sarah Ann FRY who died Jun 1887. AHMUD BUCSH, RAWALPINDI AND UMBALLA.   *(82)(93)(WM)*

FRYER, E (see SOMERSET LIGHT INFANTRY (1))

FULFORD, Arthur Wickes   *(LL/233)*
In loving memory of Arthur Wickes FULFORD, the beloved child of Sybil A FULFORD, who died 25 May 1908. Had he asked me, well I know, I should cry, Oh spare this blow. Yes, with streaming tears should pray, Lord, I love him, let him stay.
(82)(93)(WM)

FULLER, Abraham Richard   *(DD/77)*
Sacred to the memory of Abraham Richard FULLER. Major Royal Artillery and Director of Public Instruction in the Punjab. He was drowned in crossing the Bungreel River near Rawalpindi 20 Aug 1867. Aged 39 yrs. God is love and he that dwelleth in love dwelleth in God and God in him. 1.JOHN.IV.19.
(82)(93)(PS)

FULTON, Deborah Susan   *(VII/1330)*
IHS. Deborah Susan FULTON. In loving memory of my darling wife Suey who died 30 Jan 1942. Aged 21. Be happy until we are together again my beloved and comfort me in my anguish. RIP.   *(82)(93)*

FUNNELL   *(W/883)*
.... who died 15 Feb 1912. Born 10 Aug 1907. Child of Colour Sergeant W FUNNELL. 1st Royal Sussex Regt.
(93)

FURR, Dorothy
Dorothy. Darling daughter of Corporal and Mrs FURR, No 9 MB, RGA. Died 11 Nov 1914. Aged 14 yrs.   *(82)*

G....., Joseph
In memory of Joseph G..... G Company. HM's 1/19th Regiment. Died Rawalpindi 23 Jun 18.. Aged 20 yrs.
(82)

GABRIEL, Margaret   *(UU/1017)*
Margaret. The beloved daughter of Henry and Ivy GABRIEL.
(93)

GAGLIARDI, Peter   *(S/314)*
In loving memory of my beloved husband Peter GAGLIARDI. Born Naples 29 Jun 1855. Died Rawalpindi 19 Jan 1929. Requiescat in pace. No sin, no grief, no pain, safe in my happy home, my fears all fled, my doubts all slain, my hour of triumph come.   *(82)(93)*

GAGLIARDI, Pudentia Mary   *(R/273)*
In loving memory of our beloved mother Pudentia Mary GAGLIARDI who died on 1 Aug 1933. Aged 74 yrs 3 mths. No sin, no grief, no pain, safe in my happy home, my fears all fled, my doubts all slain, my hour of triumph come. *(82)(93)*

GALE, F (see ROYAL GARRISON ARTILLERY (1))

GALLAGHER, Mina   *(X/802)*
Resting. Sacred to the memory of Mina. Dearly loved wife of Lieutenant Colonel L S GALLAGHER, RA. Born 9 Aug 1894. Passed away 23 Oct 1941. Gentle and self sacrificing, she considered others.   *(82)(93)*

GALLOWAY, H R
H R GALLOWAY.   *(82)*

GAME, P O (see SOMERSET LIGHT INFANTRY (1))

GANNON, Alice Owen and Eliza Christina   *(GG/207)*
Sacred to the memory of Alice Owen who died at Rawalpindi 10 Aug 1874. Aged 1 yr 9 mths. Also Eliza Christina who died at Shadra 7 Dec 1872. Aged 5 yrs. The beloved children of Sergeant John and Eliza GANNON. 4th.....
                                     (93)(BS)(mb)
        (see page 129 for photograph)

GARDENER, Ronald A   *(UU/1016)*
Ronald A GARDENER. Born 26 Apr 1921. Died 11 Dec 1988. From your wife, children and grandchildren. *(93)(WM)*

GARDINER, Jane
In memory of Jane GARDINER. The beloved wife of Sergeant Major R GARDINER, RHA. Died 3 Oct .... Aged 38 yrs.
(82)

GARDINER, M J					(N/1454)
Sacred to the memory of Private M J GARDINER. A Squadron 2nd Dragoon Guards. Died 29 Sep 1893. Aged 20 yrs 8 mths. If thou shouldst call me to resign what most I prize, it ne'er was mine, I only yield thee what was thine. Thy will be done.
					(82)(93)(PS)

GARDNER, William				(G/432)
Sacred to the memory of Gunner William GARDNER, J Battery, 2nd Brigade RA, who died at Rawalpindi 7 Mar 1889. Aged 31 yrs. This stone was erected by the officers, NCOs and men ....
					(82)(93)(PS)

GARGET-BENNETT, Frederick			(X/799)
In loving memory of our darling Daddy Frederick GARGET-BENNETT. Died 21 Apr 1941. Aged 70 yrs.
					(82)(93)

GARLTON, H (see RIFLE BRIGADE (2))

GAUDOIN, Victoria Annie			(X/825)
In loving memory of our dear aunt Victoria Annie GAUDOIN. Died 28 Jan 1947. Aged 83 yrs 11 mths. Father in thy gracious keeping, here we leave our loved one sleeping.
					(82)(93)

GAWKRODGER, Robert (see ROYAL FIELD ARTILLERY (2))
GEDDES, A A		(see ARMY SERVICE CORPS (1))

GELDER, E
No 2762 Acting Sergeant E GELDER. 2nd Battalion Rifle Brigade. Died Rawalpindi 14 Mar 1913. Aged 27. *(82)*

GEMMELL, J					(V/989)
In memory of No 2815758 Private J GEMMELL. Machine Gun Company 2nd Battalion Seaforth Highlanders. Died Rawalpindi 1 Sep 1930. Aged 25 yrs. Erected by his comrades.
					(82)(93)

GEORGE, M Magdalen				(VII/1347)
Mother M Magdalen GEORGE. Died 1 Sep 1945. RIP.
					(82)(93)(WM)

GERARD, Frederick George William		(A/116)
Sacred to the memory of Frederick George William. The infant son of William and Georgina GERARD. *(82)(93)(PS)*

GERRING, Peter					(P/1293)
In loving memory of Pioneer Peter GERRING, B Company, 1st Wiltshire Regiment, who died 16 Jan 1904. Aged 25 yrs. Erected by the officers, NC officers and men of No 3 Section. Gone but not forgotten. *(82)(93)*

GHOSH, B G					(X/818)
Resting. Sacred to the memory of Captain B G GHOSH (FRCSE, IMS) Civil Surgeon (Retd). Born 24 Apr 1868. Left for his heavenly home 18 Aug 1942. *(93)*

GIBBONS, Kathleen *(F/391)*
In loving memory of Kathleen. Infant daughter of James and Margaret GIBBONS. Born 9 Feb 1897. Died 10 Nov 1897. An angel took our flower away, yet we will not repine, for Jesus in his bosom wears, the flower that once was ours.
(82)(93)(WM)

GIBBS, J (see ROYAL ARTILLERY (3))

GIBSON, Charles Henry Blundell *(M/1151)*
In loving memory of Charles Henry Blundell GIBSON who fell asleep in Jesus 3 Nov 1902. Aged 30 yrs 11 mths. For so he giveth his beloved sleep. Thy word is true, thy will is just.
(82)(93)

GIBSON, J (see 60TH ROYAL RIFLES (1))

GILBERT, W (see UNNAMED REGIMENT (1))

GILL, Amy *(X/794)*
In loving memory of Amy. Widow of Major George GILL. Aged 70 yrs 8 mths 17 days. Born 25 Apr 1868. Died 11 Jan 1938. Deeply mourned by her only daughter and stepchildren. Hold thou thy cross before my closed eyes, shine through the gloom and join me in the skies. Heaven's morning breaks and earth's vain shadows flee, in life, in death, O Lord, abide with me.
(82)(93)(WM)

GILL, George *(X/786)*
Sacred to the memory of Major George GILL, retired, Indian Medical Department, who died Rawalpindi at midnight 30/31 Dec 1933. Aged 82 yrs 3 mths 7 days. Deeply mourned by his sorrowing wife and children. Earth to earth, and dust to dust, calmly now the words we say. Leaving him to sleep in trust, till the resurrection day. Saviour in thy gracious keeping, leave we now thy servant sleeping. *(82)(93)(WM)(end)*

GILL, Hannah *(M/1162)*
Sacred to the memory of Hannah, the dearly beloved wife of Captain George GILL, ISMD, Resident Medical Officer, NW Railway, who departed this life Rawalpindi 30 Sep 1904. Aged 47 yrs 5 mths 21 days. Deeply mourned by her sorrowing husband and children. Earth to earth, and dust to dust, calmly now the words we say, leaving her to sleep in trust, till the resurrection day. Father in thy gracious keeping leave we now thy servant sleeping. *(82)(93)*

GILL, Mary Frances *(VII/1403)*
Mary Frances GILL. Born 25 Mar 1923. Died 9 Mar 1971.
(93)

GILLESPIE, Muriel Eleanor (see HOWARD, Muriel Eleanor)

GILLICK, Maria de Lourdes *(VII/1352)*
Sister Maria de Lourdes GILLICK. PBVM. Born Cavan, Ireland 21 Jul 1907. Died Rawalpindi 11 Apr 1977.
(93)

GILLOIT(?), Pam Elizabeth   (X/769)
Pam Elizabeth GILLOIT (?).   Aged 8 yrs.   Born 24 Sep 1951.
Passed away 26 Jan 1960. Deeply missed by Mummy, Daddy, Diana
and Peter.   (93)

GILMORE, Robert   (DD/47)
IHS.   Sacred to the memory of Robert GILMORE.   Farrier
Sergeant 4th Company 2nd Battalion Bengal Artillery.   Died 5
Jan 1861.   Aged 42 yrs.   This tomb is erected by his brother
noncommissioned officers in token of their deepest regret at
his sudden removal from them. Prepare to meet thy God.
                                          (82)(93)(BS)(mb)

GITTINGS, George Aleck   (W/893)
In loving memory of George Aleck (Scout) GITTINGS. 1st
Rawalpindi Troop, B.P. Boy Scouts and the eldest son of BQMS
and Mrs Gwen GITTINGS.   78th Battery RFA.   Born 20 Apr 1905.
Died 4 Mar 1914.   Gone but not forgotten.   Short was thy life
my darling son, and sudden was thy call. He had a kindly word
for each, and died beloved of all.   (93)

GIUSEPPINA, Casabianca   (VII/1389)
Casabianca GIUSEPPINA. Born at Palermo 17 Jan 1918.   Died at
Rawalpindi 14 Oct 1975. Beloved wife of Iqbal.
                                          (93)

GLADSTONE, Ronald Dick   (D/162)
In memory of Ronald Dick. Only son of C E and F E GLADSTONE.
Born 4 Jun 1881. Died 4 May 1885. Aged 3 yrs 11 mths. And he
took them in his arms, put his hands upon them and blessed
them.   (82)(93)

GLASBY, Ivy Violet   (M/1225)
Ivy Violet, the beloved daughter of Corporal and Beatrice
GLASBY, 104 Company RGA, who died on 1 Nov 1902. Aged 4 mths
8 days. Safe in the arms of Jesus.   (82)(93)

GLASSPOOL, W   (V/1006)
Sacred to the memory of No 4740129 Sergeant W GLASSPOOL.   C
Company 1st Battalion Hampshire Regiment.   Died at Rawalpindi
22 Jul 1936.   Aged 30 yrs.   Erected by all ranks of his
company.   (82)(93)

GLAZIER, Frederick
No 4570 Private Frederick GLAZIER, 10th Royal Hussars, who
accidentally drowned in the Sohan River 22 May 1908. Aged 27
yrs.   (82)

GLEN, W   (S/300)
Sacred to the memory of No 7143056 Colour Quartermaster
Sergeant W GLEN.   1st Battalion The Connaught Rangers.   Died
30 Jan 1922.   (82)(93)

GLOVER, William Louis Percival   (X/807)
William (Billy) Louis Percival GLOVER.   6 Jan 1944 - 15 Apr
1962. (poem)   (93)

GODFREY, J (IV/506)
In loving memory of No 3702261 Drummer J GODFREY of HQ Wing, 2nd Battalion The King's Own Royal Regiment. Died Rawalpindi 1 Apr 1929. Aged 26 yrs. Erected by all ranks of the company. (82)(93)

GODWIN, Charles Henry Young (K/616)
In loving memory of Charles Henry Young GODWIN. Surgeon Colonel Medical Staff, P.M.O. Rawalpindi District. Born 22 Oct 1838. Died..... (82)(93)

GOLDNEY, Philip (Y/682)
Philip GOLDNEY. Indian Police. Dearly loved husband of Nina GOLDNEY who died Rawalpindi 2 Sep 1917. (82)(93)(WM)

GOLDSTEIN, Jessie McIntyre von (see VON GOLDSTEIN, Jessie)
GOLLAGHY, F (see 1ST KING'S DRAGOON GUARDS (1))

GOMES (AA/1/255)
... Beloved son of Daniel and Petronilla GOMES. Died 14 Apr 1966. Aged 1 yr 5 mths. (93)(WM)

GONNESBY, A (see RIFLE BRIGADE (2))

GOODALL, Thomas (Q/1323)
IHS. Sacred to the memory of No 2645 Bandsman Thomas GOODALL, 2nd Kings Own Scottish Borderers, who died at Rawalpindi 1 Jan 1897. Aged 23 yrs. Thy will be done. (82)(93)

GOODWIN, Eric Robert Carlyle (VIII/1413)
Lieutenant Colonel Eric Robert Carlyle GOODWIN. Indian Army. Died at Rawalpindi 25 Oct 1980. This stone is placed here by his many friends. (93)(WM)

GOODWIN, Florence Henrietta (X/845)
Florence Henrietta GOODWIN. Wife of Fredrick Hickie GOODWIN. Born 13 Aug 1878. Died 24 Dec 1953. A kind and gracious lady. (93)

GOODWIN, Peter (X/847)
Peter GOODWIN. A lovable and a courageous man. 3 Sep 1901. (93)(WM)

GOODWIN, William Ernest (X/846)
William Ernest GOODWIN. Age 79. Son of Florence and Fredrick GOODWIN. Born 30 Sep 1898. Died 24 May 1978. Mourned by his sisters and brothers. (93)(WM)

GORDEN (see UNNAMED REGIMENT (1))

GORDON, Grace Williamson (V/1002)
In loving memory of Grace Williamson. Wife of Reverend David R GORDON, DD. Born 19 May 1871 at Xenia, Ohio, USA. Died 5 Feb 1936 at Rawalpindi, India. For 40 yrs 6 mths she was the faithful and loving companion of her husband in his missionary life and work in the Punjab. This memorial is erected by her sorrowing husband. (82)(93)

GORDON, James   (O/1100)
Sacred to the memory of Private James GORDON, B Squadron 4th Royal Irish Dragoon Guards, who died at Rawalpindi 14 Feb 1902. Aged 23 yrs. Erected by his sorrowing comrades. Thy will be done.   (82)(93)(PS)

GORDON, James Robert   (VI/462)
James Robert. Infant son of Captain and Mrs J L GORDON. Born 16 Sep 1945. Died 17 Jun 1946. RIP.   (82)(93)(end)

GORDON, Leonard   (N/1453)
Major Leonard GORDON. 2nd King's Own Scottish Borderers. Died at Rawalpindi 5 Feb 1896. Aged 41. Erected by his brother officers.   (82)(93)

GORDON, Michael   (JJ/356)
Northumberland Fusiliers. Sacred to the memory of Sergeant Michael GORDON who died at Rawalpindi 15 Jan 1889. Aged 34 yrs. And Sergeant Charles WELDON, who died at Rawalpindi 15 Jan 1889.   (82)(93)(BS)

GORWOOD (?CORWOOD), Norah Esme   (W/944)
Norah Esme. The beloved little daughter of Sergeant and Mrs GORWOOD (CORWOOD?). 2nd Battalion Gloucestershire Regiment, West Ridge, Rawalpindi. Born 4 Dec 1921. Died 12 Nov 1922.
                                        (82)(93)

GOSS, Harrold A   (VIII/1412)
Harrold A GOSS. Born 19 Apr 1911. Died 3 Feb 1984.
                                        (93)(WM)

GOSSE, Sheila   (see SHIER, Sheila)
GOULD, G   (see ROYAL HORSE ARTILLERY (3))

GOVIER, Edward
In loving memory of Edward. The beloved son of Sergeant H GOVIER. 3rd Rifle Brigade who died at Rawalpindi 17 Nov 1899. Aged 6 mths 17 days. RIP.   (82)(93)(PS)

GOWER, Florence (see COWER, Florence)
GOWTON, G   (see ROYAL ARTILLERY (6))

GRACIAS, Lavinia Constance   (L/1068)
In loving memory of Lavinia Constance GRACIAS, relict of the late Henry Dominic GRACIAS, who died at Rawalpindi 13 Jan 1906. Aged 64 yrs 2 mths 2 days.   (82)(93)(mb)

GRAHAM C (see WEST RIDING REGIMENT (1))

GRAHAM, Kenneth   (W/894)
Kenneth. The beloved son of Robert and Katherine GRAHAM. S & T Corps. Died 5 Dec 1913. Aged 7 mths 7 days. Safe in the arms of Jesus.   (82)(93)(mb)

GRAY, Edward
Lance Corporal Edward GRAY. 1st Wiltshire Regiment. Died Rawalpindi 22 Dec 1903.   (82)

GRAY, W (Q/1306)
In memory of Gunner W GRAY, 50th Field Battery, RA, who died at Rawalpindi 20 Dec 1897. Aged 22 yrs. *(82)(93)(PS)*

GRAY, William Henry (Z/674)
In memory of No 2953 Private William Henry GRAY, 10th Royal Hussars, who was accidentally drowned. *(82)(93)*

GRE..., W A (IV/497)
In memory of Saddler W A GRE... 32nd Field Batt..... Died 24 Dec.. Aged 34 yrs. Erected by his comrades.
(93)

GREEN, Barbara Isobel (W/909)
In loving memory of our darling daughter Barbara Isobel GREEN who passed away 28 Jan 1919. *(82)(93)*

GREEN, Eileen (O/1085)
In loving memory of our darling Eileen. Dearly loved child of W E and A GREEN. Aged 1 yr 2 mths 27 days. She to us for a time was given, ... leave a memory ever binding.
(82)(93)(mb)

GREEN, F (AA/8)
To the memory of Sergeant F GREEN, 10th Royal Hussars, who was drowned whilst crossing the Cabul River 31 Mar 1879. Aged 35 yrs. In the midst of life we are in death. Erected by his sorrowing widow. *(82)(93)(W)*

GREEN, George
Gunner George GREEN. Died 10 Apr 1911. Aged 28. *(82)*

GREEN, Joseph (I/397)
Sacred to the memory of Bombadier Collar Maker Joseph GREEN, B Battery RHA, who died at Rawalpindi 4 Nov 1895. Aged 27 yrs.
(82)(93)(BS)

GREEN, Vera and Kenneth (O/1074)
In loving memory of little Vera who died at Ferozepure 17 Jan 1893. Also little Kenneth who died at Rawalpindi 27 Oct 1894. Dearly beloved children of Edward and Annie GREEN. And the parents came in tears and pain, the flowers they most did love. They knew they would find them both again in the fields of light above. *(82)(93)(mb)*

GREEN, W (P/1247)
In memory of Gunner W GREEN. 24 Company ED RGA. Died 11 Apr 1901. Aged 26 yrs. Erected by his comrades. AHMUD BUX AND SON, RAWALPINDI AND PESHAWAR. *(82)(93)(PS)*

GREEN, William James (O/1109)
In memory of No 7565 Private William James GREEN, 1st Battalion Royal Sussex Regiment, who was accidentally drowned in the Sohan River, Rawalpindi 9 Mar 1909. Aged 23 yrs. Erected by his comrades of B Company as a token of respect. Truly my hope is ever in thee. P.S.XXXI.7.
(82)(93)(PS)

GREENE (see ROYAL HORSE ARTILLERY (3))

GREENSHIELDS, Hugh   (A/123)
Sacred to the memory of Private Hugh GREENSHIELDS, H Company 4th Battalion Rifle Brigade, who was killed by Wazirs at Reznai on 8 May 1881. This stone was erected as a mark of regard by his comrades.   (82)(93)(W)

GREGORY, Vera   (L/1025a)
In loving memory of our bonnie Vera. Beloved child of T and B GREGORY. Born 3 Jun 1899. Died 15 May 1900.
                                            (82)(93)

GRIFFEN, William
No 4418 Driver William GRIFFEN. 57th Battery RFA. Died Rawalpindi 15 May 1903. Aged 25 yrs 3 mths.
                                            (82)

GRIFFIN, Hilda Elizabeth   (T/368)
Sacred to the memory of Hilda Elizabeth GRIFFIN. (Wee Betty) Beloved daughter of Sub Conductor and Mrs GRIFFIN, IASC who went to Jesus 3 Nov 1924. She was only lent to us a little while.   (82)(93)(WM)

GRIFFITHS, J H   (N/1432)
Sacred to the memory of Corporal J H GRIFFITHS, C Squadron, 4th (Royal Irish) Dragoon Guards, who died at Rawalpindi 1 Jan 1896. Aged 22 yrs. A crown for me. Erected as a token of respect by the officers of the regiment and his comrades in C Squadron.   (82)(93)

GRIFFITHS, William   (P/1260)
Corporal William GRIFFITHS, 104 Company RGA, who died at Rawalpindi 4 Jun 1902. Aged 34 yrs. Erected by the officers, NCOs and men of 104 company. Requiescat in pace.
                                            (82)(93)(PS)

GRIMES, Sybil Marion   (M/1228)
In loving memory of Sybil Marion. Daughter of Arthur and Florence GRIMES. Died 8 Apr 1902. (82)(93)

GRIMES, W (see 1ST KING'S DRAGOON GUARDS (1))

GRIMLEY, Edythe F   (VII/1368)
RIP. In loving memory of Edythe F GRIMLEY. Died 10 Dec 1946. Sweet Jesus mercy.   (82)(93)

GROSE   (EE/86)
Sacred to the memory of ...... The wife of Assistant Apothecary S GROSE. ... yrs 7 mths. Died on 17th .... Also ...... Aged 7 mths ....   (93)

GROSE, Francis John   (H/601)
In loving memory of Francis John GROSE, MRCS, IMS who died 30 Nov 1888. Aged 59 yrs. His soul rests in peace. Thy throne O God is forever and ever.   (82)(93)

- 71 -

GROSE, George Edward Silva *(K/617)*
In loving memory of George Edward Silva, only son of Mrs F J GROSE, who died 24 Dec 1892. Aged 24 yrs 7 mths. In the midst of life we are in death. *(82)(93)*

GROVER, J (see WEST RIDING REGIMENT (1))

GUAZZARONI, E H *(BB/19)*
Sacred to the memory of Drummer E H GUAZZARONI. 2/9th Regiment. Died Rawalpindi 17 Sep 1877. Aged 24 yrs. Look on me as you pass by, as you are now, so once was I, as I am now, so you must be, prepare yourself to follow me. Erected by his Corps de Drummers of the regiment as a mark of respect.
(82)(93)(BS)

GUEST, J A (see ROYAL ARTILLERY (6))

GUEST, Percy *(M/1204)*
In loving memory of our dear little Percy. ... son of .....GUEST. ..1904. *(93)*

GUNSCH, Lucas Josef *(VII/1360)*
Rev Brother Lucas Josef GUNSCH. Died 11 Apr 1960 at Sargodha.
(93)

GUPPY, C *(M/1239)*
Private C GUPPY, L Company, 1st Battalion Somerset Light Infantry, who was accidentally drowned whilst bathing at Rawalpindi Camp 4 Nov 1900. Aged 23 yrs. Erected by the officers, NCOs and men of his company. *(93)(PS)*

GURNEY, George (see CUNNINGHAM, George)

GUTHRIE, Henry Gibb *(EE/82)*
Sacred to the memory of Sergeant Henry Gibb GUTHRIE, HM's 70th Regiment, who died on 27 Jun 1872. Aged 22 yrs. Erected by his brother sergeants. *(82)(93)(BS)*

GUTTERIDGE (see RIFLE BRIGADE (2))

GWATKIN, Louisa Helen Fraser *(A/129)*
In loving memory of Louisa Helen Fraser. Daughter of Captain and Mrs F S GWATKIN. 18th (DC) Bengal Lancers.
(93)

GWILLIAM C (see 1ST KING'S DRAGOON GUARDS (1))

HADDON (see ROYAL ARTILLERY 7))

HAGLUND, Magnus *(Y/718)*
Magnus HAGLUND. 23 Jul 1946 - 27 Apr 1979. *(93)*

HAGYARD, William (see ROYAL HORSE ARTILLERY (1))

HAILSTONE, Ernest Frank *(III/490)*
In memory of Ernest Frank HAILSTONE, MC. Rawalpindi 31 Mar 1946. *(93)*

HALES, H *(IV/514)*
In loving memory of No 3594511 Private H HALES of D(MG) Company 2nd Battalion The Border Regiment. Died Rawalpindi 1 Feb 1931. Aged 24 yrs. Erected by all ranks of D(MG) Company. *(82)(93)*

HALKETT, Duncan Cragie *(G/431)*
Erected by his brother officers in memory of Duncan Cragie HALKETT. Captain 2nd Seaforth Highlanders (Rothshire Buffs, the Duke of Albany's) late 78th Highlanders. Died 9 Mar 1889. Aged 31 yrs 6 mths. *(82)(93)(mb)*

HALL, George *(D/178)*
Sacred to the memory of Sergeant Instructor in Fencing George HALL, The Carbiniers, who died at Rawalpindi whilst en route from Afghanistan on 17 Oct 1880. Aged 32 yrs 10 mths. Deeply regretted. *(82)(93)(BS)*

HALL, W (see 70TH REGIMENT (2))
HALL, W (see ROYAL ARTILLERY (8))

HALLIDAY, W *(D/168)*
Sacred to the memory of Corporal W HALLIDAY, 8th Hussars, who departed this life at Rawalpindi on 18 May 1881. Aged 32 yrs. *(82)(93)*

HALLIGAN, Richard (see ROYAL ARTILLERY (5))

HAMILTON, D (see ROYAL ARTILLERY (2))

HAMILTON, Henry Cope *(IV/509)*
In loving memory of Henry Cope HAMILTON. 2nd Lieutenant. RA. Died 7 Oct 1930. *(82)(93)(mb)*

HAMMILL, Viva *(F/385)*
In loving memory of Viva. Infant daughter of Patrick and Clara HAMMILL. Aged 3 mths 18 days. NYAZ ALLY, RAWALPINDI. *(82)(93)*

HAMMOND, Fred W   (IV/499)
In loving memory of our darling Fred. F W HAMMOND, MES, who
left us on 3 Apr 1927. Aged 42 yrs. RIP. O for the touch of
a vanished ......, and the sound of a voice that is stilled.
                                         (93)

HANCOCK, A (see 1ST KING'S DRAGOON GUARDS (1))

HAND, Alfred   (P/1268)
In memory of No 512 Lance Corporal Alfred HAND, 2nd Battalion
King's Royal Rifle Corps, who died at Rawalpindi 8 Aug 1902.
This stone is erected by the corporals and lance corporals 2nd
King's Royal Rifles as a token of deep regard and respect.
                                         (82)(93)

HANDLEY, Frederick William   (L/1024)
Frederick William. Dearly loved son of Frederick and Kate
HANDLEY. Ordnance Department. Born 27 Dec 1901. Died 24 Oct
1902. We loved him, O no tongue can tell, how much we loved
him and how well, God loved him too and thought it best to
take him home with him to rest. God's will be done.
                                         (82)(93)

HANKERS, G (see ROYAL GARRISON ARTILLERY (1))

HANN, Robert John   (W/915)
Robert John HANN. Darling son of Robert and Florence HANN.
2nd Battalion Gloucestershire Regiment, Rawalpindi. Born 24
Dec 1920. Died 25 Nov 1921. Aged 11 mths.
                                         (82)(93)

HANNANT, W (see ROYAL ARTILLERY (3))
HANNEN, J   (see ROYAL ARTILLERY (6))
HANNON, M   (see ROYAL ARTILLERY (6))

HANSEN, Clara   (X/758)
Mother Clara HANSEN. Born 11 Apr 1888. Died 17 Oct 1962. In
this land she loved so much.   (93)

HARDING, Brian   (X/793)
In loving memory of our darling Brian. Only son of Mr and Mrs
A W HARDING. Born 17 Aug 1928. Died 17(?) May 1937. The
Lord gave and the Lord hath taken away, blessed be the name of
the Lord. Brian's angel nature was not made for sorrow or for
care, he was too gentle and too good for heaven long to
spare. He was but lent a little while to soothe and to
sustain, Christ Jesus missed him from his band & took him home
again. Gentle Jesus meek and mild look upon our little child.
                                         (82)(93)(mb)

HARDING, L H   (see SOMERSET LIGHT INFANTRY (1))
HARMER, Annie (see ROYAL HORSE ARTILLERY (3))

HARRADINE, Valerie Eunice   (VV/532)
In ever loving memory of our darling baby Valerie Eunice
HARRADINE. Aged 1 yr 11 mths. Born 9 Dec 1924. Died 12 Nov
1926.   /cont..........

HARRADINE, Valerie Eunice (cont)

We mourn for you in silence, no eyes shall see us weeping darling, but in our aching hearts your memory we shall keep. From Mummy, Daddy and sister Lorna. *(82)(93)*

HARRIS *(W/961)*
... Daughter of Sergeant and Mrs HARRIS. 1st Battalion The East Surrey Regiment who died 23 Mar 1931. Aged 1 yr 3 mths. Suffer little children to come unto me. *(93)(BS)*

HARRIS, F *(O/1107)*
Sacred to the memory of No 7507 Lance Corporal F HARRIS, D Company 2nd Gordon Highlanders, who died 15 Dec 1903. Aged 21 yrs. Erected by the officers, NCOs and men of his company. *(82)(93)(PS)*

HARRIS, H M *(O/1112)*
In loving memory of No 3459 Private H M HARRIS, A Squadron 21st Empress of India Lancers, who died 19 Nov 1913. Aged 21 yrs. *(82)(93)*

HARRIS, William *(BB/7)*
Sacred to the memory of William HARRIS, Lieutenant 21st Regiment Punjab Infantry, who was shot dead by a sepoy of his regiment at Rawalpindi on 28 Nov 1876. In the midst of life we are in death. *(82)(93)(WM)*

HARRISON, Hettie *(Y/699)*
In loving memory of Hettie, the beloved wife of Sergeant Fred M K HARRISON, 2nd North Staffs Regiment, who departed this life 25 Dec 1916. *(93)*

HARRISON, James (see ROYAL ARTILLERY (4))

HARRISON, T (see 1ST KING'S DRAGOON GUARDS (1))

HART, Florence Ruth *(X/878)*
Florence Ruth HART. Beloved Christian doctor, Multan and Clarkabad 1933-1970. Died 19 Jul 1970. *(93)*

HART, Mary P *(AA/1/254)*
Sacred to the memory of my dear wife Mary P HART who passed this life on 28 Nov 1905. Aged 28 yrs. Erected by her sorrowing husband. *(82)(93)(WM)*

HARTLEY, Edward *(Z/653)*
Lance Corporal Edward HARTLEY, 10th Royal Hussars, who died Rawalpindi....... *(82)(93)(WM)*

HARTNETT, Jane Ann Wallace *(L/1029)*
Of your charity pray for the soul of Jane Ann Wallace, the dearly beloved wife of George HARTNETT, who died at Rawalpindi 10 Dec 1908. Aged 25 yrs. *(82)(93)*

HARVEY, Eleanor (see McGOWN, Eleanor Harvey)

HARVEY, I   (IV/552)
In remembrance of No 4031210 Private I HARVEY. 1st Battalion
K S L I. Died 7 Sep 1933. Erected by his comrades.
                                           (82)(93)

HASTINGS   (W/962)
... of Archibald and Beatrice HASTINGS. Military Accounts
Department.... Born 25 Aug 1929. Died 11 Apr 1930.
                                           (82)(93)

HASWELL, William
William HASWELL. Ordnance Department. Died 16 Nov 1897.
Aged 33 yrs.   (82)

HATHERILL, J (see RIFLE BRIGADE (2))

HAUGH, P
No 8577 Corporal P HAUGH. No 8 MB RGA. Died Rawalpindi 6 Mar
1910. Aged 31.   (82)

HAVELOCK-ALLAN, Henry Marshman   (M/1130)

In memory of Lieutenant General Sir Henry Marshman HAVELOCK-ALLAN Bart, VC, GCB, MP. Son of Major General Sir Henry HAVELOCK of Lucknow, Bart, KCB. Born 6 Aug 1830. Killed by Afridis in the Khyber Pass 30 Dec 1897 whilst watching military operations. Fought in Persia, the Indian Mutiny and New Zealand. A true soldier, fearless and heroic and devoted to his country's service. Buried in Rawalpindi by brave soldiers in a soldiers grave. "My times are in thy hand". This monument is erected by his sorrowing widow and family.

(82)(93)(end)

<u>Lieutenant General Sir Henry Marshman HAVELOCK-ALLAN</u>

HAWKINS, Alfred (see KING'S OWN SCOTTISH BORDERERS (1))

HAWKINS, J (P/1285)
Sacred to the memory of No 4553 Private J HAWKINS, B Squadron (QR) 9th Lancers, who died on 16 May 1903. Aged 33 yrs. Erected by his Squadron. (93)(PS)

HAWKINS, John (see ROYAL ARTILLERY (9))
HAWTIN, J (see SOMERSET LIGHT INFANTRY (1))

HAY, G (N/1445)
In memory of Gunner G HAY. MB RA. Died Rawalpindi 25 May 1896. Aged 27 yrs. (82)(93)(PS)

HAY, Lorna Daphne (W/935)
Peace. In ever loving memory of Lorna Daphne. Dearly loved daughter of Hugh and Marjorie HAY. Born at Murree 17 Aug 1927. Died at Rawalpindi 27 Apr 1939. A BUX, SCULPTOR, RAWALPINDI. (82)(93)(mb)(end)

HAY, Mary Emily
Mary Emily. Daughter of Major and Mrs Dalrymple HAY. Born 12 Oct 1867. Died 1 May 1870. (82)(mb)

HAYES, Denis (see ROYAL HORSE ARTILLERY (1))

HAYES, E E (N/1437)
Sacred to the memory of Driver E E HAYES. B Battery, RHA. Died Rawalpindi 6 Feb 1896. Aged 25 yrs 7 mths. Erected by the officers, NCOs and men of B Battery. RIP.
(82)(93)(BS)

HAYES, E E (see ROYAL HORSE ARTILLERY (3))

HAYMAN, Mabel (HH/325)
Sacred to the memory of Mabel HAYMAN. Wife of Colour Sergeant W HAYMAN. Died on 29 Jun 1883. Aged 30 yrs. Erected by a dear friend. (82)(93)(BS)

HEALY, John (see ROYAL ARTILLERY (5))

HEARD, Robert Anthony (W/897)
In ever loving memory of Robert Anthony. The very dearly loved younger twin son of Edward S and Freda HEARD. Born 29 Jul 1916. Died 12 Sep 1919. Father in thy gracious keeping leave we now our darling sleeping. Bobby sleeping. (93)(mb)

HEARNDON, M (Y/696)
Sacred to the memory of No 9215 Private M HEARNDON. H Company 1st Royal Sussex Regiment. Died Rawalpindi 13 Jan 1913. Aged 29 yrs 5 mths. (82)(93)

HEATH, E (Y/704)
No 1039064 BSM E HEATH, DCM, 70th Battery, RFA. Killed at Rawalpindi 25 Jun 1923. From his sorrowing wife, children and comrades. I have lost my life companion, none can tell the pain that is felt in not saying farewell.(82)(93)

HEBERLEIN, Adalbert George   (M/1198)
In ever loving memory of our Adalbert George HEBERLEIN. 24 Nov 1917. The peace that passeth all understanding.
                                    (82)(93)

HEELING, J   (see WEST RIDING REGIMENT (1))
HEHIR, D   (see 1ST KING'S DRAGOON GUARDS (1))
HEHIR, H   (see 70TH REGIMENT (5))

HELLABY, Evelyn Anne   (X/829)
Sacred to the memory of Evelyn Anne HELLABY. Born 7 Jun 1892. Died 8 Feb 1948. Dearly beloved wife of Ralph Gordon HELLABY. God rest her soul in peace.   (93)

HELLABY, Ralph Gordon   (X/865)
Ralph Gordon HELLABY. Born 24 May 1891. Died 25 May 1970.
                                    (93)

HENDERSON, Georgie   (W/891)
Our darling Georgie. The son of Corporal and Mrs HENDERSON, 94 Company, Royal Garrison Artillery, who died 18 Apr 1914. Aged 5 and 1/2 mths. Safe in the arms of Jesus.
                                    (82)(93)

HENDERSON, J   (see GORDON HIGHLANDERS (3))
HENDERSON, James   (see GORDON HIGHLANDERS (3))

HENDRICKS, Grace   (VII/1329)
Grace HENDRICKS. A sweet and beloved mother, wife and sister. Died 10 Feb 1942. Aged 48 yrs 4 mths. (82)(93)

HENLEY, J S
J S HENLEY. The Royal Irish Regiment. Died Rawalpindi 6 Apr 1908. Aged 29.   (82)

HENNESSY, Ada Mary   (VII/1385)
Ada Mary HENNESSY. Wife of Thomas Francis HENNESSY. 21 Dec 1950.   (93)

HENNING, Carl Ferdinand Von (see VON HENNING, Carl Ferdinand)

HENRY, Robert   (AA/3)
Also Robert HENRY who died 12 Jun 1866. Aged 8 mths 28 days and .... Born 1866. Died 11 Oct 1866. Aged 1 yr.
                                    (93)(BS)

HERBERT, William (see ROYAL ARTILLERY (6))

HERING, Ingrid   (Y/706)
Ingrid HERING. 28 Sep 1949 - 7 Mar 1978. (poem)   (93)(WM)

HERRING, J (see 5th REGIMENT (1))

HERSEY, A
No 4230 Private A HERSEY, C Squadron 9th Queen's Royal Lancers, who died 9 Dec 1903. Aged 26 and 8/12th yrs.
                                    (82)

- 78 -

HERSEY, Frederick John   (Z/656)
Sacred to the memory of No 26506 Gunner Frederick John HERSEY,
No 3 MB RGA, who died Rawalpindi 16 Feb 1909. Aged 22 yrs 1
mth.   (82)(93)(PS)

HETHERINGTON, Jeffery Cyril   (W/896)
In always loving memory of Jeffery Cyril, the dearly loved
child of Sergeant and Mrs HETHERINGTON, 4th King's Royal
Rifles, who fell asleep 1 Dec 1912. Aged 5 mths.
                                        (82)(93)

HEWITT, Ann   (DD/64)
Sacred to the memory of Ann, the beloved wife of Bombadier G
HEWITT, E Battery 19th Brigade Royal Artillery, who departed
this life 29 Jun 1870(?) Aged 39 yrs 6 mths. This stone is
erected by her husband as a token of affection who deeply
regretted her loss. Brethren live so that you may die happy,
for in this life we are in death.   (82)(93)(BS)

HEXT, John Edward   (X/772)
In memory of John Edward HEXT. Major S & T Corps. Died 2 Nov
1921. Until the day breaks.   (82)(93)

HEYMERDINGNER, William Ernest   (X/842)
In ever loving memory of my beloved husband and our darling
father and grandfather William Ernest HEYMERDINGNER. Born 7
Oct 1883. Died 19 Feb 1953.   (93)

HICKIE, Gladys Estelle   (N/1465)
Gladys Estelle. The infant daughter of Mr and Mrs W B HICKIE.
Died 5 Jan 1896. Aged 8 days.   (82)(93)

HICKMAN, Charles (see ROYAL HORSE ARTILLERY (1))
HICKMAN, J   (see 1ST KING'S DRAGOON GUARDS (1))

HICKMOTT, Hartridge Edward   (L/1055)
In loving memory of Hartridge Edward HICKMOTT who died at the
station hospital Rawalpindi 26 Nov 1905. Aged 19 yrs. Jesus
the very thought of thee, with sweetness fills my breast. But
sweeter far thy face to see, and in thy presence rest. RIP.
                                        (82)(93)

HICKMOTT, J F   (M/1147)
J F HICKMOTT who departed this life 7 Jun 1903 at Rawalpindi
hospital after a long and painful illness. O Lord my God I
have cried unto thee and thou hast healed me.
                                        (82)(93)

HILEY, T P   (R/281)
IHS. In memory of No 3907934 Lance Corporal T P HILEY. 1st
Battalion South Wales Borderers who died at Rawalpindi on 14
Jul 1936. RIP.   (82)(93)

HILL, Annie   (EE/85)
In fond remembrance of Annie. The beloved wife of Captain
Percy Graham HILL. Rifle Brigade. To thou that hearest
prayer, to thee shall all flesh come. (93)(BS)(mb)

HILL, Daphne Maude   (W/892)
In loving memory of our darling Daphne Maude (Dumpty) The beloved daughter of QMS and Mrs HILL. No 1 Mountain Battery. Born 6 Nov 1912. Died 31 Mar 1914.   *(82)(93)*

HILL, Herbert Lawrence   (X/849)
Major General Herbert Lawrence HILL, CBE. Born 4 Aug 1899. Died 5 Apr 1955. Aged 55 yrs 8 mths. A man of faith.
                                            (93)(WM)

HILL, Josiah   (DD/58)
Sacred to the memory of Private Josiah HILL, 2nd/60th Royal Rifles, who was drowned while bathing at Rawalpindi 24 Apr 1873. Aged 33 yrs.   *(82)(93)(BS)*

HILL, Leo   (W/899)
In loving memory of our darling Leo. The beloved son of SSM and Mrs HILL. Punjab Light Horse. Born 25 Sep 1912. Died on the Jhelum River 29 Mar 1915. Lord in thy gracious keeping here we leave our darling sleeping.   *(82)(93)*

HILL, Leonard   (J/454)

"Independent Order of Good Templars".

In loving memory of
Leonard HILL.
CD Chaplain of the
Grand Lodge of India,
IOGT, who died at
Rawalpindi 19 Mar
1891. They that
turn many to
righteousness shall
shine as the stars
for ever and ever.
Erected by the
Grand Lodge of
India, Independent
Order of Good
Templars, in
token of the regard
in which he was
held by the members
of the order, he
being the founder
of the same in this
country.

(82)(93)

HILLMAN W (see 1ST KING'S DRAGOON GUARDS (1))

HILLMAN W J (H/586)
..... Dragoon ..... Sacred to the memory of Trooper W J HILLMAN. Died 23 Jan 1888. Aged 20 yrs. Like as the hart desireth the water brooks: so longeth my soul after thee O God. *(82)(93)(BS)*

HILLYER, James (see ROYAL ARTILLERY (10))

HINGE, Joan Marian Theresa (T/374)
In loving memory of Joan Marian Theresa. Dear daughter of Battery Sergeant and Mrs W E HINGE, IAOC. Born 16 Aug 1927. Died 25 Oct 1931. *(82)(93)(WM)*

HINGSTON, Alfred Bose (IV/569)
In loving memory of Alfred Bose HINGSTON. Only son of Lieutenant Colonel G B HINGSTON, RE. Killed by an avalanche at Killanmarg with two companions 1 Mar 1936. Aged 26 yrs. Blessed are the pure in heart. *(93)*

(see NOLAN, John Luke)

HIRD, Annie Mary Kathleen (L/1034)
In loving memory of Annie Mary Kathleen. Only child of Sergeant and Julia HIRD. 9th Queen's Royal Lancers.....
(82)(93)

HITCHCOCK, H (see ROYAL ARTILLERY (2))

HOARE, Edith Emily
Edith Emily. The beloved daughter of James and Minnie HOARE. Died 16 Apr 1902. Aged 13 mths. *(82)*

HODDER, Charles (see ROYAL ARTILLERY (4))

HODGES, G H (E/198)
In loving memory of Farrier Sergeant G H HODGES, RHA, Station Veterinary Hospital, Rawalpindi, who departed this life 11 Jul 1887. Aged 29 yrs. Thy will be done. *(82)(93)*

HODGKINS(?), Agnes Ellen (BB/21)
..... Agnes Ellen HODGKINS(?) Died 25 Apr 1877. Aged 17 months. He shall gather the lambs with his arm and carry them in his bosom. *(93)*

HODGSON, H (Q/1310)
In memory of Corporal H HODGSON, RE, who died at Rawalpindi 24 Dec 1897 from sickness contracted while serving with the Tirah Field Force. Aged 24 yrs. AHMUD BUX. *(82)(93)(PS)*

HOLDEN, Jacky
Jacky. The beloved little son of Sergeant and Mrs HOLDEN. 2nd Royal Sussex Regiment. Born 7 Jul 1925 at S...... Died 18 Apr 1926. Aged 9 mths. *(82)*

HOLDWAY, Harold Blake   (IV/559)
In loving memory of Captain Harold Blake HOLDWAY, RIASC. Born 10 Feb 1901. Died 11 Oct 1935. Erected by his wife and brother officers.   (82)(93)

HOLLAND, Charlie
Little Charlie. The loved son of J and I HOLLAND. Born 26 Feb 1892. Died 18 Aug 1892.   (82)

HOLLAND, Henry (see RIFLE BRIGADE (1))

HOLLAND, Kate   (S/291)
In loving memory of Kate HOLLAND. Wife of Private HOLLAND. Died 2 Aug 1913. Aged 32 yrs. 21st (Empress of India's) Lancers.   (82)(93)

HOLMES, Catherine Jarman   (III/493)
Sacred to the memory of Catherine Jarman. Dearly beloved wife of Major J T HOLMES, IAOC, and widow of Conductor T S CROCE, IAOC. Born 20 Sep 1888. Died 29 Aug 1945.
                                         (82)(93)

HOLMES, Ellen Josephine   (VII/1369)
Ellen Josephine. Wife of Major R HOLMES, IA. Born 1 Aug 1876. Died 23 Feb 1948.   (93)

HOLT, J   (IV/546)
In loving memory of No 3593969 Private J HOLT of D(MG) Company 2nd Battalion The Border Regiment. Died Rawalpindi 13 Sep 1932. Aged 28 yrs. Erected by all ranks of D(MG) Company.
                                         (82)(93)

HOME, Phylis E (see ROYAL FIELD ARTILLERY (2))

HOMER, James   (P/1269)
In memory of Private James HOMER, 2nd Battalion King's Royal Rifle Corps, who died at Rawalpindi 8 Aug 1902. Aged 20 yrs. Also Private BOWLES. This stone is erected by the officers, NCOs and riflemen of G Company in remembrance of their lost comrades. Gone but not forgotten.   (82)(93)

HOOK, Ellen Mary   (F/381)
In sacred memory of Ellen Mary HOOK. Wife of Corporal George HOOK. 4th Dragoon Guards who died at Rawalpindi on 10 Oct 1898. Aged 32. Erected by her sorrowing husband. RIP.
                                         (82)(93)

HOOKER, W (see ROYAL HORSE ARTILLERY (2))

HOPCRAFT, Samuel   (J/445)
Sacred to the memory of Sergeant Farrier Samuel HOPCROFT who died at Rawalpindi 29 Nov 1891. Aged 29 yrs.
                                         (82)(93)(BS)

HOPE, John Haden   (M/1188)
In loving memory of John Haden HOPE. Born 23 Mar 1864. Died 16 Nov 1908. He here awaits the resurrection. (82)(93)

HOPKINS, Fredrick Bradshaw   (M/1141)
Thy will be done.   Sacred to the memory of Fredrick Bradshaw
HOPKINS who died in Rawalpindi 22 Dec 1900. Aged 79 yrs.
                                     (82)(93)

HOPPER, W E (see ROYAL GARRISON ARTILLERY (4))

HORNER, Mary   (W/950)
Mary.   Daughter of NS Sergeant and Mrs A H HORNER, RASC, who
died 18 Feb 1925.   Aged 3 days.   Suffer little children to
come unto me.   (82)(93)

HORNER, Ralph   (Z/642)
Sacred to the memory of No 5078 Private Ralph HORNER, D
Squadron Queen's Royal Lancers, who died of enteric fever 14
May 1906. Aged 22 1/4 yrs. Erected by the officers, NCOs and
men of his squadron.   (82)(93)

HORSINGTON, H R   (V/979)
In loving memory of H R HORSINGTON, who departed this life 16
Aug 1922. Greatly missed by his wife and family. No mother's
kiss in sad goodbye, no wife's last fond farewell, but in our
hearts a memory lives that nought on earth can quell.
                                     (82)(93)

HOSFORD, John (see ROYAL ARTILLERY (5))

HOSS, Peter A   (VII/1405)
Peter A HOSS.   23 Jun 1949. 17 Dec 1970.   In tieffer trauer
deine Eltern Bruder, Freund Winfried.   (93)

HOULDSWORTH, W (see 1ST KING'S DRAGOON GUARDS (1))

HOUSDEN, Fannie Ellen Margaret   (O/1129)
In loving memory of Fannie Ellen Margaret, widow of the late
Frederick George HOUSDEN, Inspector of Government Schools,
United Provinces and elder daughter of the late Archibald
Campbell CARLYLE, Archaeological Department of India, who died
at Rawalpindi 16 Dec 1915.   (82)(93)

HOUSTO...   (BB/16)
.... HOUSTO ... Royal Horse Artillery.   Born 28 Feb 1872.
Died 11 Oct 1872. Of such is the kingdom of heaven.
                                     (93)(BS)

HOWARD, J (see ROYAL HORSE ARTILLERY (2))

HOWARD, Muriel Eleanor   (X/776)
Muriel Eleanor HOWARD.   Beloved wife of Captain H J HOWARD,
RASC, and 2nd daughter of the Very Reverend Henry J GILLESPIE,
DD, Dean of Killaloe and Mrs GILLESPIE, of Clonlora, Co Clare,
Ireland who died from typhoid fever at Rawalpindi on 26 Mar
1921 in her 22nd year.   Erected by her sorrowing husband and
parents. I will not fail thee nor forsake thee. JOSHUA 1.5.
                                     (82)(93)

HOWARD, Samuel (see 9th REGIMENT (1))

- 83 -

HOWARTH   (I/406)
.... Beloved son of Colour Sergeant and Emily HOWARTH. 2nd
Battalion Seaforth Highlanders, who died on 18 Dec 1892.
Aged 2 yrs 5 mths.   (93)(WM)

HOWELLS, G   (IX/1013)
In memory of No 3908015 G HOWELLS, 1st Battalion The South
Wales Borderers, who died at Rawalpindi 18 Oct 1937. Erected
by the officers, warrant officers, NCOs and men of his
regiment. Most worthy of remembrance.   (82)(93)

HOWIE, Gerald Theodore   (III/495)
In loving memory of Gerald Theodore HOWIE. Born 12 Jan 1902.
Died 4 Jan 1957.   (93)(WM)

HOYES, A T   (P/1284)
Sacred to the memory of No 4552 Lance Corporal A T HOYES,
....9th (QR) Lancers, who died on 16 May 1903. Aged 23 yrs.
Erected by his Squadron.   (93)

HUDSON, Laurence   (VV/524)
In loving memory of Laurence HUDSON. Born 29 Oct 1940. Died
25 Mar 1941. And a little child shall lead them.
                                         (82)(93)

HUGHES, Christopher Joseph   (GG/205)
In loving memory of Christopher Joseph, the beloved son of
Robert and Jessie HUGHES, 70th Regiment, who fell asleep 3 Jan
1875.   Aged 2 yrs 3 mths.   (82)(93)(PS)

HUGHES, Delacy Frank   (B/141)
Delacy Frank HUGHES. Born 30 Jan 1889. Died 18 Nov 1889.
                                         (82)(93)

HUGHES, F (see GORDON HIGHLANDERS (2))

HUGHES, T   (IV/568)
In memory of No 3907617 Private T HUGHES, 1st Battalion South
Wales Borderers, who died at West Ridge on 28 Feb 1936.
Erected by the officers, WOs, NCOs and men of his regiment.
                                         (82)(93)

HULME, J S   (O/1108)
Sacred to the memory of No 4164, Corporal J S HULME, D
Squadron 9th Lancers, who was accidentally killed at
Rawalpindi 2 Dec 1904. Aged 29 yrs. Erected by his Squadron
as a....   (82)(93)(PS)

HUMPHRIES, Hester Annie   (Q/1305)
IHS. Sacred to the memory of Hester Annie HUMPHRIES, the
beloved wife of SSM R R HUMPHRIES, 4th Dragoon Guards, who
died at Rawalpindi 1 Jan 1899. Thy will be done. (82)(93)

HUNT, M   (IV/519)
In memory of No 1424987 Gunner M HUNT. 4th Light Battery RA.
Died at Rawalpindi 9 Nov 1931. Aged 26 yrs. Erected by all
ranks of the battery.   (82)(93)

HUNTER, Andrew *(C/101)*
I am the resurrection and the life. Love is strong as death. Death is swallowed up in victory. To the dearly loved memory of Sergeant Major Andrew HUNTER, RHA and late of the Convalescent Depot, Murree, who died on 26 Apr 1880. Aged 50 years. *(82)(93)(PS)*

HUNTER, John (see GORDON HIGHLANDERS (5))
HUNTER, John (see KING'S OWN SCOTTISH BORDERERS (2))

HUNTER, John Charles *(M/1161)*
Here rest in the Lord John Charles HUNTER. Second son of Henry Lannoy and Anna HUNTER of Beech Hill, Reading, England. Born 24 Jun 1884. Attached 2nd Royal Irish Fusiliers Nov 1903. Died 11 Jun 1904. He shall give his angels charge over thee. The eternal God is thy refuge and underneath are the everlasting arms. *(82)(93)*

HURRELL, C (see ROYAL HORSE ARTILLERY (2))

HURRELL, Timothy John *(CC/30)*
For Timothy John HURRELL who died on 20 Jul 1982. Aged 28 in an avalanche on Mt Kuksar near the Batura Glacier, Hunza. With love from his friends. *(93)*

HURSEY, A *(P/1273)*
Sacred to the memory of No 4230 Private A HURSEY, C Squadron 9th (QR) Lancers, who died on 9 Dec 1903. Aged 26 8/12 years. Erected by his Squadron. *(93)(PS)*

HURST, Jessie Marion *(N/1442)*
Sacred to the memory of Jessie Marion HURST, the dearly beloved wife of Schoolmaster James HURST, 1st Gordon Highlanders, who departed this life 10 Mar 1894. Aged 24 yrs 4 mths. I know that my redeemer liveth and that he shall stand..... *(82)(93)*

HURST, W (see RIFLE BRIGADE (2))

HUSSEY, R O *(IV/512)*
In loving memory No 6081614 Private R O HUSSEY of C Company 1st Battalion East Surrey Regiment. Died Rawalpindi 3 Dec 1929. Aged 25 yrs. Erected by all ranks of C Company. *(82)(93)*

HYDE *(W/920)*
The beloved daughter of Mr and Mrs B C HYDE who died at Rawalpindi 20 Aug 1921. Aged 2 mths 29 days. *(82)(93)*

HYDE, Bertram Charles *(W/946)*
Bertram Charles. Beloved son of Mr and Mrs B C HYDE who died at Rawalpindi on 16 Apr 1925. Aged 8 mths. *(82)(93)*

HYDE, Richard *(GG/224)*
Pray for the repose of the soul of Richard HYDE. 2/60th Rifles. Born at Macclesfield, Cheshire, England. Died at Rawalpindi 19 Jan 1876. Aged 39 yrs. /continued.........

HYDE, Richard (continued)
As there is but one Lord, one Faith, one Baptism, one God and Father of all, so there is but one true Church. Beware of false teachers. This tomb was erected by his wife Hannah.
(82)(93)(BS)

HYLAND, W (see GORDON HIGHLANDERS (2))

HYNDS, Ethel   *(JJ/345)*
In memory of Ethel. Beloved daughter of J and E HYNDS. Died 28 Jan 1888. Aged 21 days. O God thou hast taken back what but for a time was given.   *(82)(93)(WM)(mb)*

HYNES, M (see 5TH REGIMENT (1))

HYNES, Margaret
In memory of Margaret. The beloved daughter of Patrick and Ann HYNES. HM's 38th Regiment. Died 14 Jun 1871. Aged 1 yr 10 mths.   *(82)*

INGRAM, George   *(Z/644)*
To the memory of No 8533 Private George INGRAM. Died Rawalpindi 28 Jan 1914. Erected by the officers, NCOs and men of G Company 2nd North Staffordshire Regiment. Thy will be done.   *(82)(93)*

IRVING, Albert Edward
Private Charles EGAN. D Company 2nd Royal Sussex Regiment. Died Rawalpindi 27 Sep 1887. Aged 32 yrs. Also Albert Edward IRVING who died at Meerut 17 Sep 1887. Aged 22 yrs. *(82)*

ISABELLA   *(VII/1396)*
Sr ISABELLA F.M.M. Born 21 Jan 1892. Died 25 Sep 1973.
(93)

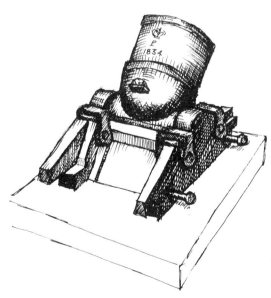

One of the cannons from the base of the Lockhart Memorial. (See Page 100).

JACKSON, C (see ROYAL HORSE ARTILLERY (2))

JACKSON, Charles
Private Charles JACKSON. Died 3 Jul 1885. Aged 22(?21) yrs.
(82)

JACKSON, G (see 1ST KING'S DRAGOON GUARDS (1))

JACKSON, John   *(F/386)*
Sacred to the memory of Bombadier John JACKSON. 50th Field Battery Royal Artillery. Died Rawalpindi 1 Jan 1898. Aged 40. Watch and pray. Mourned deeply by his sorrowing wife and family.   *(82)(93)(PS)*

JACKSON, Mary Cecilia   *(S/292)*
To the memory of my sister Mary Cecilia JACKSON. Wife of George JACKSON, PWD, who died on 27 Oct 1918 in the 26th year of her life.   *(93)*

JACOBS   *(X/857)*
Mrs JACOBS. 2 Apr 1965. Aged 64 yrs. Erected by her son, daughters and grandchildren.   *(93)*

JAMES, Alfred (see ROYAL GARRISON ARTILLERY (3))

JAMES, Alfred   *(Z/640)*
Sacred to the memory of No 4550 Private Alfred JAMES. D Squadron. 3rd King's Own Hussars. Died Rawalpindi 25 Dec 1905 of pneumonia. Aged 23 yrs 9 mths.   *(82)(93)(PS)*

JAMES, Charles   *(Z/665)*
Sacred to the memory of Gunner Charles JAMES, No 2 Ammunition Column Royal Field Artillery, who died 23 Jun 1908. Aged 23 yrs 4 mths. This stone was erected by the officer, NCOs and men of 2 AC, RFA as a mark of their esteem and sorrow.
                                                 (82)(93)(PS)(W)

JAMES, Charles   *(Y/689)*
Gunner Charles JAMES. ......   *(93)*
    (JAMES may be a Christian name with the surname missing)

JARMAIN, Georgie   *(F/389)*
In loving memory of our darling little Georgie. Beloved son of Sergeant William and N M JARMAIN. 4th Royal Irish Dragoon Guards. Died Rawalpindi 16 Dec 1897. Aged 2 yrs 3 mths 9 days. If thou shouldst call me to resign what most I prize, it ne'er was mine, I only yield thee what is thine. Thy will be done.   *(82)(93)(WM)*

JARRETT, R E (see ROYAL ARTILLERY (10))

JARRETT-KERR, John   *(EE/204)*
John.   The eldest son of H J and G M JARRETT-KERR.   Died   26
Mar 1910. Aged 17 days.   *(82)(93)(PS)*

JARVIS, Mark   *(VV/539)*
Mark. Darling son of Lieutenant Colonel and Mrs JARVIS. Born
29 Sep 1947. Died 20 Oct 1947.   *(82)(93)*

JELLY, Verna Noreen   *(X/781)*
Verna Noreen JELLY who left us for her heavenly rest 12 Jun
1931. Aged 26. Forever with the Lord. Mums, Edna and Rod.
                                      (82)(93)

JENKINS, Richard   *(C/100)*
Sacred to the memory of Colonel Richard JENKINS.   Commandant
1st Bengal Cavalry.   Eldest son of Sir Richard JENKINS, GCB,
of Becton Hall, Salop. Died at Rawalpindi on 9 Sep 1880. Aged
52 yrs.   This tablet is erected as a mark of respect by his
brother officers.   *(82)(93)(PS)*

JENKINSON, J (see 70TH REGIMENT (3))

JENNER, William   *(AA/1/247)*
Sacred to the memory of No 6878 Private William JENNER,   1st
Battalion The Queen's Regiment, who died at Rawalpindi 26 Oct
1904. Aged 21 yrs 11 mths. Erected by the officers, NCOs and
men of A Company.   *(82)(93)*

JEPHSON, Robert Dalkeith   *(M/1144)*
Sacred to the memory of Captain Robert Dalkeith JEPHSON, RAMC,
who died 9 Jan 1904. Aged 32 yrs. Son of R H JEPHSON, JP of
Dublin.   *(82)(93)*

JEPSON, J (see ROYAL ARTILLERY (2))

JOBSON, Violet Esther Colborne   *(IV/575)*
In loving memory of Violet Esther Colborne. Wife of Lieutenant
Colonel T S JOBSON.   Army Remount Department.   Died 4 Mar
1937. Aged 48 yrs.   *(82)(93)*

JOCKIM, K V (see DIBETT, A T)

JOHNSON   (see ROYAL ARTILLERY (7))

JOHNSON, A   (see 1ST KING'S DRAGOON GUARDS (1))

JOHNSON, Adelaine   *(N/1470)*
In loving memory of Adelaine. The darling infant daughter of
Major and Mrs F O JOHNSON. SMD. Died 25 Apr 1897. Aged 6
mths 20 days. Thy will be done. Gone to our father's home
our dear child.   *(93)*

JOHNSON, Annie   *(B/134)*
In loving memory of Annie. Second daughter of Sergeant E and
G JOHNSON, Bedfordshire Regiment. Born 22 Sep 1883.   Died
Rawalpindi 4 Jan 1893. Aged 9 yrs 3 mths.
                                      (82)(93)(BS)

JOHNSON, Arthur   (VII/1384)
Rev Fr Arthur JOHNSON, MHM. Born 19 Sep 1917. Ordained Jul
1944. Died Burn Hall, Abbottabad 3 Jan 1974.
                                  (93)

JOHNSON, Dorothy Marie   (VII/1362)
IHS. In memory of Dorothy Marie. Beloved wife of Major C E
JOHNSON. RIE. Died at Rawalpindi 14 Aug 1947. Aged 51 yrs.
RIP.   (93)

JOHNSON, Harold (see GORDON HIGHLANDERS (1))
JOHNSON, Henry   (see ROYAL GARRISON ARTILLERY (3))
JOHNSON, J   (see ROYAL ARTILLERY (6))
JOHNSON, J W   (see UNNAMED REGIMENT (1))

JOHNSON, J W
Sacred to the memory of Private T ROBINSON who died of cholera
on the march from Mianmir to Rawalpindi 4 Nov 1887. Aged 24
and 1/2 yrs.   Also Private J W JOHNSON who was drowned while
bathing in the park at Rawalpindi 18 Mar 1888. Aged 21 yrs.
                                  (82)

JOHNSON, John   (Q/1301)
In loving memory of John JOHNSON who departed this life at
Rawalpindi on 26 May 1898. Aged 25 yrs 3 mths. This stone was
erected by his sorrowing brother.   (82)(93)(PS)

JOHNSON, Samuel (see ROYAL FIELD ARTILLERY (2))

JOHNSON, Walter
Walter. Son of William and Alice JOHNSON. Died 4 Aug 1904.
Aged 1 yr 9 mths.   (82)

JOHNSTON, Daniel   (D/156)
Sacred to the memory of Daniel JOHNSTON, Pensioned Quarter
Master Sergeant, RHA, who died 24 Dec 1883. Now the labourers
task is o'er, now the battle day is past; now upon the further
shore lands the voyager at last. Father in thy gracious
keeping, leave we now thy servant sleeping.
                                  (82)(93)(PS)

JOHNSTON, Ethel Ellen Stella   (X/777)
Ethel Ellen Stella JOHNSTON. Born 22 Sep 1871. Died 2 Sep
1964. Erected by her sorrowing sons and daughter.
                                  (93)

JOHNSTON, Florence   (K/618)
In loving memory of Florence. The dearly loved daughter of
Daniel and Rebecca Margaret JOHNSTON. Born 23 Dec 1870. Died
14 Dec 1892. She sleeps in Jesus.   (82)(93)

JOHNSTON, G F   (O/1090)
Sacred to the memory of No 4371 Lance Corporal G F JOHNSTON,
A Squadron,   4th Dragoon Guards, who died at Rawalpindi 26
Dec 1900. Aged 26 yrs. Erected as a token of respect by the
NCOs and comrades of his Squadron.   (82)(93)(PS)

JOHNSTON, Rebekah Margaret *(M/1134)*
In affectionate memory of our dear Mother Rebekah Margaret JOHNSTON who fell asleep 7 Jun 1898. Lord we know it was thy will and so Lord Jesus, be it still, we consign her to thy care. *(82)(93)(End)*

JOHNSTON, Roland Arthur Percival *(X/778)*
Roland Arthur Percival JOHNSTON. Born 8 Nov 1866. Died 31 Jan 1959. Erected by his widow, Ethel, sons and daughter.
(93)

JOHNSTONE, James *(IV/574)*
In loving memory of Lieutenant James (Jay) JOHNSTONE, OBE, IMD, who passed away on 3 Mar 1937. Aged 54 yrs. Father in thy precious keeping leave we now our loved one sleeping. Thy will be done. *(93)(WM)*

JOHNSTONE, James Henry *(B/147)*
In loving memory of James Henry. Son of James and Alice JOHNSTONE who fell asleep 12 Nov 1888. Aged 22 days. Our treasure is with God. *(93)*

JOHNSTONE, William
William. Infant son of Captain H C JOHNSTONE. Died 7 Jan 1861. Aged 1 mth 18 days. *(82)(mb)*

JONES *(C/105)*
Sacred to the memory of Sergeant JONES, 10th Hussars, who died 23 Jun 1879. Aged 27 and 6/12 yrs. Erected by the Sergeants 10th Hussars as a token of respect.
(82)(93)

JONES, A (see 1ST KING'S DRAGOON GUARDS (1))

JONES, E R
No 5249769 Private E R JONES. HQ Company, Worcestershire Regiment. Died(?) 20 Mar 1939(?). Aged 25 yrs.
(82)

JONES, Florence Mary *(Y/713)*
Florence Mary, Beloved wife of Sergeant J JONES, 125th Battery RFA, who departed this life 16 Jun 1921. Aged 41.
(82)(93)

JONES, Frederick (see 9TH REGIMENT (1))

JONES, H M *(G/428)*
H Troop. King's Dragoon Guards. Sacred to the memory of Private H M JONES, who died at Rawalpindi 22 Nov 1889. Aged 26 yrs. ... erected by .... *(82)(93)(BS)*

JONES, John *(G/434)*
Sacred to the memory of Driver John JONES, 2nd Brigade Royal Artillery, who died at Rawalpindi 20 Dec 1888.
(82)(93)(PS)

JONES, May (see BAZELY, Percival Charles)

JONES, Nell Margaret					(X/840)
In loving memory of our beloved mother Nell Margaret JONES.
Born 14 Feb 1882. Called to rest 13 Oct 1951.
					(93)

JONES, Olive Beatrice				(IV/560)
In loving memory of Olive Beatrice. Widow of Major JONES.
Died 23 Aug 1935. Aged 36 yrs. Erected by her sorrowing
adopted son Shushal. Was employed as lady doctor, Indian Welfare Centre, Chaklala, from Feb 1933 to Aug 1935.
					(82)(93)

JONES, Percy					(A/112)
Little Percy. Born 10 Dec 1879. Died 1 Feb 1880. Infant son
of W.C. Nigel JONES. Without fault before the throne of God.
					(82)(93)

JONES, Victor Douglas				(W/924)
In memory of Victor Douglas JONES. Born 29 Oct and died 5 Nov
1927.					(82)(93)

JONES, William					(Z/657)
In memory of No 3848 Corporal William JONES. 10th Royal Hussars. Died Rawalpindi 24 Mar 1909.	(82)(93)(WM)

JOSIAH, Patrick Philip				(VV/534)
In loving memory of Patrick Philip JOSIAH. Born 20 Apr 1942.
Died 26 Jul 1950.				(93)

JOWETT, Tom					(J/451)
In loving memory of Tom JOWETT, late of Jubulpur, who died
22 Oct 1890. Aged 48 yrs. Have mercy Lord on me, as thou wert
ever kind, let me opprest with loads of guilt, thy wonted
mercy find.					(82)(93)

JOYCE, Ann					(P/1289)
Ann JOYCE, the beloved wife of Sergeant W E JOYCE, who
departed this life 28 Dec 1903 at Rawalpindi. Aged 29 yrs 3
mths 6 days. Her end was peace. Thy will be done.
					(82)(93)

JOYCE, James
Gunner James JOYCE. Died 26 Sep 1908. Aged 23.	(82)

JUPP, Charles					(N/1469)
In loving memory of our darling Charles, the beloved son of
Charles and Minnis JUPP, who died 20 Apr 1897. Aged 7 mths.
Gone but not forgotten.			(93)

JUPP, G H W (see ROYAL ARTILLERY (6))

JUPP..., R G					(AA/2)
Sacred to the memory of Lance Corporal R G JUPP... HM's 70th
Regiment who died 25 May 1873. Aged 22 yrs. This stone was
erected by the officers, NC officers and men of H company as a
token of their regard.			(93)(BS)

KANE (see RIFLE BRIGADE (2))

KANE, T (see 1ST KING'S DRAGOON GUARDS (1))

KEANE, Mary   *(DD/67)*
Sacred to the memory of Mary, the beloved wife of Sergeant John KEANE, HM's 36th Regiment, who died at Rawalpindi 18 Sep 1872. Aged 22 yrs.   *(82)(93)(BS)*

KEATING, John   *(L/1054)*
Sacred to the memory of No 7572 Private John KEATING. 1st Battalion The Royal Irish Regiment. Departed this life at Rawalpindi 10 Sep 1905. Aged 23 yrs. Erected as a token of esteem by the NCOs and men of his company. *(82)(93)*

KEDDA, Cara   *(T/377)*
Vivi nel cuore dei tuoi Cari alla Cara KEDDA. I Genitori.
                                                     (93)(WM)

KEEFE, Michael (see 9TH REGIMENT (1))

KEELAN, Robert Luke   *(X/762)*
In loving memory of Robert Luke KEELAN. Late Postmaster who died at Rawalpindi 22 Apr 1924. Born 11 Feb 1855. Hard though his course in all his latter life was run, deprived of sight for twenty years he ran his race and won. Sleep on beloved, terror now has taken flight, calm has followed storm, and after darkness light.   *(82)(93)*

KELLY, Agnes   *(GG/222)*
Sacred to the memory of Agnes KELLY. Died 30 Oct 1875. Aged 16 yrs.   *(93)(BS)*

KELLY, F C (see ROYAL ARTILLERY (5))
KELLY, John (see KING'S OWN SCOTTISH BORDERERS (1))

KELLY, Lily Every   *(K/631)*
In loving memory of Lily Every. Wife of Lieutenant H E T KELLY, RA. Only daughter of W B LEGGATT, Esq. Born 30 Nov 1865. Died at Rawalpindi 10 Mar 1898. *(82)(93)(WM)*

KEMP, Patty   *(N/1434)*
Sacred to the memory of Patty. The beloved wife of Sergeant W J KEMP who died Dec 1895. Aged 21 yrs. *(82)(93)(PS)*

KENNEDY   *(LL/234)*
... The beloved son of Albert and Lilian Edith KENNEDY. Born 26 Mar 1907. Died 28 Mar 1908.   *(93)(WM)*

KENNEDY, P   (see GORDON HIGHLANDERS (2))
KENNEDY, Thomas (see ROYAL ARTILLERY (5))

KENNEDY, Thomas John   (M/1186)
In memory of Thomas John KENNEDY, ICS. 1857-1908.   (82)(93)

KENNEY, Andre   (VV/529)
Andre KENNEY. In life a day, but memory forever. 7 Sep 1943.
                                        (93)

KENT, A   (see GORDON HIGHLANDERS (2))
KENT, A   (see GORDON HIGHLANDERS (5))
KENT, Alex   (see KING'S OWN SCOTTISH BORDERERS (2))
KEOUGH, C   (see 1ST KING'S DRAGOON GUARDS (1))

KEOUGH, C
Sacred to the memory of Private C KEOUGH. Died 15 Apr 1887.
Aged 22 yrs.   (82)

KERR, John Jarrett (see JARRETT-KERR, John)
KERRY, A L   (see ROYAL HORSE ARTILLERY (2))

KIERNAN, Margaret Mary   (VII/1374)
Sister Margaret Mary KIERNAN. Presentation Sister. Born in
Dublin, Ireland 25 Dec 1884. Died at Peshawar 24 Jan 1974.
                                        (93)(WM)

KILBY, Robert   (E/193)
Sacred to the memory of Driver Robert KILBY. J Battery 2nd
Brigade RA. Died Rawalpindi 13 Jan 1887. Aged 29 yrs. This
stone was erected by the officer, NCOs and men of his battery
as a token of esteem.   (82)(93)(PS)

KILCOYNE, Josephine   (VII/1372)
Sister Josephine KILCOYNE, PBVM. Born 13 Feb 1897. Died
Rawalpindi 27 Apr 1983.   (93)(WM)

KILCULLEN, J (see 1ST KING'S DRAGOON GUARDS (1))

KING, Arthur Edward   (AA/1/261)
Private Arthur Edward KING. 10th Royal Hussars. (93)

KING, Cyril Arthur   (X/752)
In loving memory of Cyril Arthur KING who died 1 Apr 1928.
Aged 25 yrs. Until the day breaks and the shadows flee away.
                                        (82)(93)

KING, Mary Elizabeth   (CC/39)
Mary Elizabeth. Daughter of Mary Hannah and W KING. 10th
Hussars. Died Jun 1878.   (82)(93)(BS)(mb)

KING, Michael   (VV/533)
In loving memory of our baby Michael. Aged 18 hours. Son of
Ernest and Beatrice KING. Safe in the arms of Jesus.
                                        (82)(93)

KING, Patricia Mavis   (VI/466)
In loving memory of Patricia Mavis. Infant daughter of Mr and
Mrs Byrne KING. Born 6 Feb 1941. Died 7 Mar 1941. Suffer
little children to come unto me.   (93)

KING, Rita Marie   (VI/467)
In loving memory of Rita Marie. Infant daughter of Mr and Mrs
Byrne KING. Born 6 Feb 1941. Died 2 Mar 1941. Suffer little
children to come unto me.   (82)(93)(WM)

KIRBY, F   (Y/693)
Sacred to the memory of Sergeant F KIRBY, Royal Engineers,
who departed this life 23 May 1913. ... dear ones divided
here ....   (82)(93)(PS)

KIRKHAM, Helen Aurelia (see BRISTOW, Helen Aurelia)

KIRKWOOD, Nellie   (F/393)
In loving memory of Nellie, The beloved daughter of Colour
Sergeant J W and A M KIRKWOOD, King's Own Scottish Borderers,
who died Rawalpindi 26 Jan 1896. Aged 2 yrs 12 days. RIP.
                                        (82)(93)(mb)

KLEIN, Alden M   (VII/1363)
Alden M KLEIN. Born USA 1909. Died 1974.   (93)

KNIGHT, Samuel   (M/1146)
In loving memory of our beloved son Samuel KNIGHT who died 4
Jul 1903. Aged 20 yrs 6 mths 25 days. Peace perfect peace.
Deeply mourned.   Saviour in thy tender keeping, we leave here
now our loved one sleeping. The starting tear check, and
kiss the rod and not to earth resign him, but to God. (82)(93)

KNOWLES, H (see ROYAL HORSE ARTILLERY (3))

KOCH, Hildegard   (X/863)
Hildegard KOCH.   Born 17 Jan 1906.   Died 14 Mar 1969.   Our
beloved mother and grandmother.   Der Herr ist mein hirte mir
wird nichts mangeln.   (93)

KOSSAKOWSKI, Zbigniew   (VII/1331)
RIP. Squadron Leader
Zbigniew KOSSAKOWSKI, PAF.
Born 24 Sep 1923 in Poland. Died
in a flying accident 29 Jan 1959 at
Rawalpindi.   (93)

KUNHARDT, Edith May   (X/766)
In loving memory of Edith May,
the wife of Major F G
KUNHARDT, 2nd Punjab Regiment,
who died at Rawalpindi ....
                         (93)

KYLE, George
(see ROYAL ARTILLERY (6))

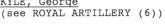
Ellen CLEARY's headstone

LA....., Nicholas and Mary   (A/125)
In memory of Nicholas and Mary. Beloved son and daughter of
Alfred and Mary LA..... who departed this life 29 Dec ... Aged
1 mth 10 days. Also 9 Dec 1888. Aged 2 days. Suffer little
children to come unto me.   (93)(BS)

LACEY, C   (P/1283)
Sacred to the memory of No 4459 Private C LACEY, F Company
The Queen's Regiment, who died on 9 Oct 1920. Aged 31 yrs 6
mths. This stone was erected by the officers, NCOs and men of
his company.   (82)(93)

LACY, John
Sacred to the memory of No 177 Private John LACY, B Company
1st Battalion Royal Irish Fusiliers, who departed this life
30 Jul 1885 at Rawalpindi. Aged 26 yrs. (82)

LA FRENAIS, Iris Kathleen   (R/269)
Iris Kathleen. Beloved wife of R M La FRENAIS, Indian Telegraphs. Born 29 Sep 1900. Died 12 Oct 1931.
                                    (82)(93)

LALOR, Edward Joseph and Arthur Charles O'Rourke   (L/1022)
Edward Joseph LALOR, the dearly beloved son of Sub Conductor J
LALOR, Ordnance Department, who died Rawalpindi 9 Aug 1902.
Aged 2 yrs 10 mths 3 days. Also his brother Arthur Charles
O'Rourke LALOR. Died Rawalpindi 17 Feb 1902. Aged 1 yr 6
mths. Lively and comely in their life. Even in death they
were not divided. II.Kings.1.25.   (82)(93)

LAMB, Charles   (JJ/352)
Sacred to the memory of Lance Corporal Charles LAMB, E Company 2nd Royal Sussex Regiment, who died at Rawalpindi 28 Jun
1887. Aged 22 yrs. O ... think of death and death will not
surprise you. Erected by the officers ....
                                    (82)(93)(BS)

LAMB, Ruth Christine   (X/869)
Ruth Christine LAMB. Born at Enfield, Middlesex 11 Sep 1964.
Died near Murree 23 Aug 1973.   (93)

LAMMAS, W (see 1ST KING'S DRAGOON GUARDS (1))

LANCASTER, T   (IV/542)
In loving memory of No 3595095 Private T LANCASTER of D(MG)
Company 2nd Battalion The Border Regiment. Died Rawalpindi 9
Feb 1933. Aged 22 yrs. Erected by all ranks of D(MG) Com-
pany.   (82)(93)

LANCE, W J (see ROYAL ARTILLERY (6))
LANE, A   (see ROYAL HORSE ARTILLERY (2))

LANE, Doris Audrey Conyers (IV/556)
In loving memory of Doris Audrey Conyers. Beloved wife of Lieutenant Colonel F R LANE. Died at Rawalpindi 31 May 1934. Rest in peace. (82)(93)

LANGFIELD, C B (N/1448)
Erected by his loving wife in memory of Corporal C B LANGFIELD. Died Rawalpindi 21 Jun 1896. Aged 38. Queen's Bays. (82)(93)(PS)

LANGFORD, Eliza (X/749)
In ever loving memory of Eliza LANGFORD (Bouie) Daughter of Captain John LANGFORD. Ballintoher, Menagh, Tipperary, Ireland and Leicestershire Regiment. Died 28 Apr 1929.
(82)(93)(End)

LANGSTON, Ada (B/140)
In loving memory of Ada. The beloved daughter of D and F LANGSTON. Died Camp Sohan 23 Sep 1888. Aged 5 days. (82)(93)

LANGSTON, Lottie (B/140)
In loving memory of Lottie, beloved daughter of D and F LANGSTON, who died at Rawalpindi 25 Sep 1888. Aged 1 yr 8 mths. Suffer little children. (82)(93)

LANGTON, W (Q/1302)
Sacred to the memory of No 5147 Private W LANGTON, F Company The Queen's Regiment, who died on 25 Aug 1898. Aged 20 yrs 6 mths. This stone was erected by the officers, NCOs and men of his company. (82)(93)

LAPPIN, J (see 70TH REGIMENT (5))

LARGE (W/941)
In loving memory of the dearly beloved son of Sergeant and Mrs LARGE. 17th Pack Battery, Royal Garrison Artillery. Died Rawalpindi 3 Apr 1921. Aged 16 mths. (82)(93)

LATIMER, John (see ROYAL ARTILLERY (4))
LAWRENCE, F (see RIFLE BRIGADE (2))

LAWRENCE, G (Y/726)
Sacred to the memory of No 49066115 Private G LAWRENCE. LRB Company. 2nd Battalion Sherwood Forresters. Died 2 Jul 1925. Aged 20 yrs 11 mths. (82)(93)

LAWRENCE, J (D/169)
To the sacred memory of Colour Sergeant J LAWRENCE, D Company 1st Battalion, The Royal Irish, who departed this life 9 Jun 1881. Aged 26 yrs. This is erected by the officers, NC officers and men of his company as a token of respect.
(82)(93)(BS)

LAWRENCE, John
John LAWRENCE. Gunner 15/9th Battery. Died at Khyra Gully 3 Aug 1877. Aged 26. Erected as a token of respect by the officers, NCOs and men 15/9th Battery, Royal Artillery.
(82)

LAWRENCE, John   (see ROYAL ARTILLERY (1))
LAWRENCE, R H   (see 1ST KING'S DRAGOON GUARDS (1))
LAWRIE, W   (see KING'S OWN SCOTTISH BORDERERS (2))

LAWRIE, William   (O/1094)
In memory of William LAWRIE, Colour Sergeant of A Company, 2nd Battalion King's Own Scottish Borderers, who died at Rawalpindi 18 Aug 1897. Aged 33. Erected by his company and brother non commissioned officers. *(82)(93)*

LEARMOUTH, A (see ROYAL ARTILLERY (2))

LEARY, Cornelius   *(GG/220)*
Sacred to the memory of Private Cornelius LEARY, D Company, HM's 70th Regiment, who departed this life on 20 Aug 1873. Aged 22 yrs. This stone was erected by his beloved friends as a mark of their respect and esteem. *(82)(93)(BS)*

LEARY, P   *(GG/219)*
Sacred to the memory of Private P LEARY. F Company HM's 70th Regiment. Died 1 Dec 1872. Aged 31 yrs. Erected by the officers, NC officers and men of the above as a tribute of respect. RIP. *(82)(93)(BS)*

LEDLIE, Elizabeth   *(VII/1397)*
Elizabeth. Beloved wife of Major F B LEDLIE. Born Baku 9 May 1904. Died 4 Apr 1969. *(93)*

LEDLIE, Franklin Burbridge   *(VIII/1419)*
Franklin Burbridge LEDLIE. Born 15 Aug 1895. Died 27 May 1982. Devoted wife Josie LEDLIE. *(93)*

LEDLIE, Josephine Angelo   *(VIII/1420)*
Mrs Josephine Angelo LEDLIE. Born 25 Aug 1915. Died 10 Jul 1983. *(93)(WM)*

LEE, Elizabeth   *(S/307)*
In fond memory of our darling mother Elizabeth LEE, who left us on 23 Jun 1927. Aged 55 yrs. Gone but not forgotten. RIP. *(82)(93)*

LEE, Ethel Gertrude
Sacred to the memory of Miss Ethel Gertrude LEE. Born 14 Aug 1896. Died 10 Jul 1919. *(82)*

LEE, G   *(IV/522)*
In memory of No 4030958 Private G LEE. 1st Battalion King's Shropshire Light Infantry. Died 3 Jan 1932. Erected by his comrades. *(82)(93)*

LEEDER, E C   *(IV/572)*
Sacred to the memory of No 2321 Signalman E C LEEDER, Royal Corps of Signals, who died at Rawalpindi on 21 Jan 1937. Aged 26 yrs. Erected by his comrades, Indian Divisional Signals.
(93)

LEEDS, Lionel Nelson   (Q/1314)
Lionel Nelson LEEDS. Lieutenant 5th Punjab Cavalry. Died 13
Jul 1896. Erected in affectionate memory by his brother
officers.   (82)(93)

LEGGATT, Lily Every (see KELLY, Lily Every)

LEICESTER, J H   (L/1047)
Sacred to the memory of Bombadier J H LEICESTER, F Battery,
RHA, who died 19 Oct 1902. Aged 25 yrs. Erected by his comrades.   (82)(93)

LENDON, Elizabeth Teague   (O/1123)
In loving memory of Elizabeth Teague LENDON, beloved wife of
Quartermaster Sergeant A E LENDON, 1st Battalion
Northumberland Fusiliers, who died at Rawalpindi 15 Mar 1910.
                                        (82)(93)

LEONARD, Richard (see ROYAL ARTILLERY (5))
LEWCOCK, R   (see 1ST KING'S DRAGOON GUARDS (1))
LEWINGTON, A   (see ROYAL FIELD ARTILLERY (1))
LEWINS, F   (see RIFLE BRIGADE (2))

LEWIS, Frances Robert   (M/1207)
Frances Robert. Infant son of Sergeant and Mrs LEWIS. 9th
Queen's Royal Lancers. Died Rawalpindi 18 Apr 1904. Aged 3
mths 18 days. Suffer little children to come unto me.
                                        (82)(93)

LEWIS, Stanley Reginald   (VIII/1416)
Stanley Reginald LEWIS. Born 19 Oct 1895. Died 17 May 1981.
                                        (93)(WM)

LEYDEN, Elizabeth Margaret Watson Carter (S/290)
IHS. Sacred to the memory of Elizabeth Margaret Watson
Carter. Beloved wife of Farrier Staff Sergeant J LEYDEN. No
1 Mountain Battery. Died 19 Jan 1913. Aged 25 yrs 3 mths.
Mothers of sorrows, pray for her. Blessed are the clean of
heart for they shall see God.   (82)(93)

L'FLEUR, Percival Joseph   (R/268)
Sacred to the memory of Percival Joseph L'FLEUR, IMD, who died
at Rawalpindi on 16 Mar 1931. Aged 38 yrs and 1 mth. Erected
by his sorrowing brothers and sisters. Keep him O Father in
thine arms and let him henceforth be a messenger of love
between our bleeding heart and thee.   (82)(93)

LILLEY, R (see ROYAL ARTILLERY (2))

LIMOND, Mary Harriet   (BB/15)
In loving remembrance of Mary Harriet. The wife of Lieutenant
Colonel D LIMOND, RE. Died Rawalpindi 20 Dec 1875. Aged 34
yrs.   (82)(93)

LINDSELL, Guy Vivian   (M/1178)
Sacred to the memory of Lieutenant Guy Vivian LINDSELL. 37th
Dogras. Born 19 Feb 1886. Died 13 May 1911. (82)(93)

LINK, Janet   (M/1165)
In affectionate remembrance of Janet LINK. Wife of Lieutenant
W C LINK. Died Rawalpindi 2 Dec 1905. Aged 45 yrs.
                                         (82)(93)

LINTOTT, Arthur William   (W/904)
Arthur William LINTOTT. Dearly beloved son of William Charles
and Constance Catherine LINTOTT...   (93)

LINTOTT, Constance Catherine   (X/788)
In loving memory of Mother Constance Catherine LINTOTT. Died
at Murree on 26 Sep 1934. Aged 51 yrs.   (82)(93)

LINTOTT, William Charles   (X/814)
In loving memory of Daddy. William Charles LINTOTT, OBE.
Died at Rawalpindi 16 Dec 1942. Aged 76 yrs.
                                         (82)(93)

LIPSHAM, Fredrick Charles   (Y/728)
In loving memory of Staff Sergeant Fredrick Charles LIPSHAM.
Army Remount Department. Died Rawalpindi 17 Mar 1925. Aged
35.   (82)(93)

LITTLE, Daphne   (VI/460)
In loving memory of Daphne. The infant daughter of Mr and Mrs
J M LITTLE. Born 3 Jul 1948. Died 21 Nov 1950.
                                         (93)

LITTLE, Joseph Melvyn   (VII/1382)
Joseph Melvyn LITTLE. Died 24 Nov 1950. Aged 29.   (93)

LIVINGSTONE, Colin Pritchard   (Y/720)
Sacred to the memory of Private Colin Pritchard LIVINGSTONE,
RAMC, who died at the BSH, Rawalpindi on 23 Jan 1925. Aged 22
yrs 8 mths. In arduis fidelis.   (82)(93)

LLOYD, Trevor John Home   (M/1220)
In loving memory of Trevor John Home. Beloved son of Captain
C T LLOYD, ASC, and Ethel his wife.   (82)(93)

LLOYD, W (see SOMERSET LIGHT INFANTRY (1))

LLOYDE, George   (P/1262)
No 5863 Private George LLOYDE, 2nd Battalion, North Staffordshire Regiment, who died Rawalpindi 3 Apr 1902. Aged 22
yrs. Erected as a token of respect of his services with the
battalion during the South African War by the officers, NCOs
and men of the 2nd Battalion North Staffordshire Regiment.
Gone but not forgotten.   (82)(93)

LOANE, Alice Florence Muriel   (N/1466)
Alice Florence Muriel. The darling child of Sarah and Hope
LOANE. Commst Department.   (93)(BS)

LOBO, Felix
Felix LOBO. Beloved son of Mr and Mrs S X L LOBO. Born 20
Nov 1934. Died 1937.   (82)

LOCKHART MEMORIAL

The monument survives, on a junction north of the Grand Trunk Road as you leave the centre of Rawalpindi heading towards Peshawar. The guns, dated 1834 and seen in the illustrations, have been removed within the past ten years. (see page 86)

The inscription on the monument reads:

General Sir William Stephen Alexander LOCKHART, GCB, KCSI, who died in Calcutta 18 March 1900 when Commander-in-Chief in India. Erected to his memory by the Army in India and many friends 1903.

LOFTHOUSE, J (see GORDON HIGHLANDERS (4))
LOMAX, A   (see ROYAL ARTILLERY (6))

LOONAM, W J   (L/1070)
IHS. Sacred to the memory of W J LOONAM, Sergeant of the Old Bengal Royal Horse Artillery, who departed this life on 3 Mar 1909 at Rawalpindi. Aged 74 yrs. RIP. Peace perfect peace. Erected by his sorrowing widow.   (82)(93)

LOUDEN   (see ROYAL FIELD ARTILLERY (1))
LOUDWELL, John (see ROYAL GARRISON ARTILLERY (3))

LOUND, Cynthia Mary   (T/264)
In ever loving memory of our darling little Cynthia Mary. Born 6 Dec 1923. Died 21 Nov 1925. The daughter of Colour Sergeant E LOUND and Alice Marian his wife. 2nd Sherwood Forresters. Suffer little children to come unto me and forbid them not for of such is the kingdom of heaven.   (82)(93)(WM)

LOVETT, Ronald Oscar   (X/871)
To the treasured memory of a dearly beloved husband, father and grandfather Ronald Oscar LOVETT, born 17 Aug 1909, who left us for his heavenly home 21 Mar 1973. Mourned by his wife, sons, daughter, grandsons and granddaughters. RIP. (93)

LOW, Jessica (see DARLING, Jessica)

LOW, Rodney John   (W/967)
In ever lasting memory of Rodney John. Dearly beloved son of Colour Sergeant and Mrs H J LOW. 1st Battalion Hampshire Regiment. Born 18 Oct 1934. Died 17 Nov 1935. It is well with the child, it is well. For our loss we must not weep, nor our loved one long to keep.   (82)(93)

LOWING, A A (see 1ST KING'S DRAGOON GUARDS (1))
LUBY, J   (see WEST RIDING REGIMENT (1))

LUCAS, Clare   (VIII/1415)
Clare LUCAS. Born 13 Apr 1920. Died 24 Feb 1981. Erected by John LUCAS and grandchildren.   (93)(WM)

LUCAS, James   (H/593)
Sacred to the memory of Corporal James LUCAS. 1st Battalion Suffolk Regiment. Died at Rawalpindi 4 Jul 1888. Aged 23 yrs. This stone was erected by his friends in the above regiment as a token of respect.   (82)(93)

LUCAS, John   (VIII/1410)
Mr John LUCAS (Johnny) From his son and grandchildren. Born 5 Jan 1908 Madras, India. Died 26 Oct 1984 Rawalpindi, Pakistan.   (93)(WM)

LUCAS, Richard   (AA/1/249)
Sacred to the memory of Saddler Bombadier Richard LUCAS, 57th Battery, Royal Field Artillery, who died Rawalpindi 15 Sep 1904. Aged 28 1/2 yrs. Erected by the officers, NCOs and men of the battery.   (82)(93)

LUCIEN, Adeline   (X/864)
In loving memory of beloved mother and grandmother Adeline
LUCIEN. Born 30 Apr 1896. Died 6 Jun 1969.
                                         (93)

LUCKETT, H   (see SOMERSET LIGHT INFANTRY (1))

LUDKIN, Alfred (see ROYAL HORSE ARTILLERY (1))

LUFF
In memory of Private LUFF. 2nd Dragoon Guards. Died
Rawalpindi 7 May 1893. Aged 23.   (82)

LUIF, Gerard   (VII/1393)
Rev Father Gerard LUIF. MHM. Born 22 Apr 1909. Ordained Mill
Hill 1934. Died Rawalpindi 6 Aug 1970. (93)

LUKE, Douglas Alfred   (VV/530)
Our beloved child Douglas Alfred LUKE, who died 26 Oct
194.... Aged 4 yrs 9 mths.   (82)(93)

LUMSDAIN, J (see ROYAL ARTILLERY (3))

LUMSDEN, Norrine H M D T   (VII/1339)
Sacred to the memory of Norrine H M D T LUMSDEN, wife of
Lieutenant Colonel J M LUMSDEN, RIASC, who departed this life
8 May 1944. Aged 46 yrs 9 mths. The Lord gave and the Lord
hath taken away, blessed be the name of the Lord. Job.1.21.
Dear is this spot where my loved one is laid. Dear is the
memory that never can fade. Sweet are the hopes that again we
shall meet, kneeling together at Jesus' feet.
                                         (82)(93)(end)

LUNN   (see RIFLE BRIGADE (2))

LUNNY, J (see 1ST KING'S DRAGOON GUARDS (1))

LUSH, Herbert George   (VII/1361)
Herbert George LUSH. Born 21 Oct 1887. Died 9 Jan 1948. Aged
60 yrs 2 mths 10 days.   (93)

LUTHER, W F   (Z/666)
Sacred to the memory of No 4381 Private W F LUTHER. D Squadron, 9th Queen's Royal Lancers. Died 15 Oct 1905. Aged 27
yrs. Erected by his Squadron as a token of esteem.
                                         (82)(93)(PS)(W)

LYNCH, John   (S/303)
In memory of No 1017547 Driver John LYNCH. 105th Battery RFA.
Died Rawalpindi 1 Jun 1923. Aged 36 yrs. Erected by all
ranks of the Battery.   (82)(93)

LYNCH, Lilian Gertrude Blanche   (X/831)
In loving memory of Lilian Gertrude Blanche LYNCH who entered
into rest 2 Nov 1948.   (93)

McARTHUR, John Campbell　　　　　　　(E/188)
In affectionate remembrance of my dear husband John Campbell McARTHUR, who died on 18 Apr 1885. Aged 48 yrs. Blessed are the dead who die in the Lord.　　　(82)(93)(PS)

McARTHUR, Joseph　　　　　　　　　　(A/126)
In memory of Joseph. Son of John and Catherine McARTHUR. Born 7 and died 9 Oct 1882. A flower too frail to bloom on earth, now sweetheart blooms in heaven. (82)(93)

MacBEAN, Jessie May Ida and Elizabeth Grace Margaret Cecilia
Jessie May Ida. Aged 1 mth 15 days and Elizabeth Grace Margaret Cecilia. Aged 1 yr 6 mths 18 days. Departed this life in May and June 1860. Children of Elizabeth and Duncan MacBEAN.　　　　　　　　　　　　(82)

McCAIN, Ingrid　　　　　　　　　　(VV/536)
In loving memory of Ingrid. Beloved daughter of Leslie and Lillimore McCAIN. Sister of Michael and Eric.
　　　　　　　　　　　　　　　(93)

McCANN, Francis (see 9TH REGIMENT (1))

McCARTHY, Edmund　　　　　　　　　(L/1045)
Sacred to the memory of No 4322 Gunner Edmund McCARTHY. 57th Battery Royal Field Artillery. Died Rawalpindi 1 Sep 1902. Aged 21 yrs 2 mths. Erected by the officers, NCOs and men of the battery. AHMUD BUX, SCULPTOR, RAWALPINDI.
　　　　　　　　　　　　　　　(82)(93)

McCARTHY, William Ogle
William Ogle McCARTHY. 7 June 1922. (82)

McCAULEY, Joseph Campbell　　　　　　(T/370)
In loving memory of Joseph Campbell. Dearly beloved son of CSM and Mrs McCAULEY. 55th Field Battery, Royal Artillery. Died 11 Jan 1927. Aged 6 weeks. The Lord gave and the Lord hath taken away.　　　　　　(82)(93)(WM)

McCAUSLAND, T (see ROYAL ARTILLERY (5))

McCAW, Violet Annie　　　　　　　　(Z/661)
In loving memory of Violet Annie, beloved wife of Sergeant McCAW, X Battery, RHA, who departed this life .....
　　　　　　　　　　　　　　　(82)(93)

McCAY, Betty　　　　　　　　　　　(V/982)
In memory of Betty. Beloved wife of Captain Ross McCAY. 17 Cavalry. 21 Mar 1921.　　　(82)(93)

MACLEOD, Eric Olaf (O/1120)
Sacred to the memory of Lieutenant Eric Olaf MACLEOD. 11th (KEO) Lancers. Born 8 Jan 1882. Died ......
(82)(93)

McCONNELL, H (AA/1/248)
Ubique. Sacred to the memory of Gunner H McCONNELL. 104 Company (HB) Royal Garrison Artillery. He died doing his duty. Erected by his friends, the officers, NCOs and men of his battery.
(82)(93)(PS)

McCONNELL, J (see ROYAL ARTILLERY (2))

McCORMACK, Samuel (G/426)
IHS. Sacred to the memory of No 581 Private Samuel McCORMACK. 2nd Battalion Royal Scots Fusiliers. Died Rawalpindi 25 Jan 1890. Erected by the officers, NC officers and men of D company as a token of respect.
(82)(93)

McCORMICK, Annunciata (UU/1015)
Sr. Annunciata McCORMICK, PBVM. Born in Glasgow 22 Dec 1899. Died at Rawalpindi 9 Dec 1989. May she rest in peace.
(93)(WM)

McCOURT, James (L/1050)
Sacred to the memory of No 4505 Lance Corporal James McCOURT, 1st Battalion, Royal Munster Fusiliers, who departed this life 9 Jul 1905 at Rawalpindi. Aged 26 yrs.
(82)(93)

McCOURT, Patrick (see ROYAL ARTILLERY (5))

McCREA, J (O/1125)
In affectionate remembrance of No 4267 Lance Sergeant J McCREA, D Squadron 9th Queen's Royal Lancers, who died from injuries 30 Mar 1905. Aged 28 yrs. Erected by his officers, brother NCOs and his Squadron.
(82)(93)

MacCUTCHAN, Maurice John Robert (X/795)
Sacred to the memory of Maurice John Robert MacCUTCHAN. Born 15 Oct 1901. Died 22 Jan 1938. Heavenly Father in thy gracious keeping leave I now my loved one sleeping.
(82)(93)(WM)

McCUTCHEON, W (see 1ST KING'S DRAGOON GUARDS (1))

MacDERMOT, Mary Ignatius (F/384)
Sacred to the memory of Mother. Mother Mary Ignatius MacDERMOT. Foundress of the Presentation Convent. Died 13 Jun 1899. I have loved O Lord the beauty of thy house: and the place where thy glory dwelleth. Ps.XXV.V.8. Erected by the Presentation nuns with the help of kind friends. RIP.
(82)(93)(WM)

(for illustration, see following page)

MOTHER MARY IGNATIUS MACDERMOT HEADSTONE

McDERMOTT, Evelyn Blanche   (HH/334)
Evelyn Blanche. Born 29 Dec 1872. Died 7 Nov 1879. Beloved child of Michael and Martha T McDERMOTT. *(93)(PS)*

McDERMOTT, Frederick James Parry   (HH/336)
In loving memory of Frederick James Parry. The beloved son of Mr and Mrs M T McDERMOTT. Died 29 Feb 1886. Aged 1 yr 7 mths. God thou hast taken back what but for a time was given, Teach us to bow to thy will on earth for our darling is safe in heaven.   *(82)(93)*

McDERMOTT, Michael William Bernard   (R/272)
Sacred to the memory of our dearly loved husband and father Michael (Barney) William Bernard McDERMOTT, who departed this life on 6 Oct 1932. Aged 56 yrs. Erected by his loving wife and children. He sleeps the sleep of peace. We miss him and mourn him in silence unseen, and dwell in the memories of days that have been. Unknown to the world he is still by our side, and lovingly whispers "death cannot divide". From us thou are gone, but glad memories live long years shall we strengthen the bond of our love, and offerings of prayer shall we daily give, may God in his goodness unite us above. A husband and father so true and so kind, on this earth his equal no one can find. Oh, Jesus and Mary give heed to our prayer, obtain for our loved one that treasure so rare. Eternal rest with God.   *(82)(93)(end)*

McDONALD, Florence Beatrice (A/109)
In loving memory of Florence Beatrice. The beloved child of
Henry Francis & Susan McDONALD. Aged 3 mths 24 days. *(82)(93)*

MacDONALD, G J   (see ROYAL HORSE ARTILLERY (2))

MacDONALD, George (O/1115)
In loving memory of my beloved husband George MacDONALD, who
died from the result of an accident. Born 23 Feb 1884.   Died
10 May 1913. Thy will be done. *(82)(93)(PS)*

McDONALD, Henry Donald (D/177)
In loving memory of Henry Donald, son of Henry Francis and
Susan McDONALD, who fell asleep on 9 Oct 1880. Aged 18 yrs.
He that believeth in me though he were dead yet shall be live.
St John XI.2.5. *(82)(93)(PS)*

McDONALD, Henry Francis (D/151)
In loving memory of Henry Francis McDONALD, Apothecary, who
fell asleep on 7 Dec 1882. Aged 46 yrs. He that believeth in
me though he were dead yet shall he live. *(82)(93)*

MacDONALD, John Duncan (III/478)
Sacred to the memory of No 828049 Bombardier John Duncan
MacDONALD. 73rd Field Battery, RA. Died 5 Aug 1938. Aged 28
yrs. Erected by his comrades. *(82)(93)*

McDONALD, M (see 60TH ROYAL RIFLES))

McDONALD, Norman Charles Rodric (X/872)
Norman Charles Rodric MacDONALD. Age 50. Born 21 Apr 1922.
Died 26 Oct 1972. *(93)*

McDONOUGH, Daniel (K/621)
In loving memory of my dear husband Daniel McDONOUGH who died
at Rawalpindi 31 Jul 1892. Himself hath done it, then I fain
would say, "Thy will in all things ever more be done".   E'en
though that will remove whom best I love, while Jesus lives I
cannot be alone. Father thy will be done. *(82)(93)(WM)*

McDONOUGH, Leonard (LL/235)
In ever loving memory of our darling Leonard.   Beloved infant
son of A and J A McDONOUGH, MWS. Born 25 Nov 1897.   Fell
asleep 28 Dec 1906. Aged 9 yrs 1 mth 3 days. He is gone, but
not forgotten. Never shall his memory fade. Sweetest thoughts
shall ever linger, around the tomb where Leonard's laid in
Christ's kingdom of peace. *(93)*

McEWAN, Mildred Rose (III/479)
Our beloved sister Mildred Rose McEWAN,   who died   at
Rawalpindi 17 Aug 1938. *(82)(93)*

McFARLAND, R (O/1092)
Sacred to the memory of Private R McFARLAND, who died at
Rawalpindi 26 Dec 1895. Aged 24 yrs. Erected by the
officers, NCOs and men of C Squadron as a mark of respect.
(82)(93)

MacFARLANE, Eugene Clayton (? Seayton)   (X/836)
Eugene Clayton (Seayton?) MacFARLANE.   Retired NWR Telegraph Engineer.   .... to sleep on his birthday 2 Jan 1951 after a full complete life of devotion, love and sacrifice.   Ever cheerful.   (93)

McFARLANE, Jessie Sinclair   (O/1095)
Jessie Sinclair. Wife of Quartermaster Sergeant D MacFARLANE. 2nd Battalion King's Own Scottish Borderers. Born 6 Mar 1859. Died 2 Nov 1897. If thou shouldst call me to resign what most I prize, it ne'er was mine, I only yield thee what is thine. Thy will be done.   (82)(93)

McFARLANE, R   (see 1ST KING'S DRAGOON GUARDS (1))
McGILL, E   (see 1ST KING'S DRAGOON GUARDS (1))

McGOWN, Eleanor Harvey   (O/1091)
Sacred to the memory of Eleanor Harvey. Schoolmistress. King's Own Scottish Borderers and the beloved wife of Sergeant J McGOWN, King's Own Scottish Borderers, who died at Rawalpindi 29 Feb 1898. Aged 35 yrs. Full many a gem of purest ray serene, the dark unfathomed caves of ocean hear. Full many a flower of purest ray serene, and waste its sweetness on the desert ...   (82)(93)

McGRATH, W   (see ROYAL ARTILLERY (2))

MacGREGOR, Donald Cameron   (W/881)
Donald Cameron. The beloved son of Barrack Sergeant and Mrs MacGREGOR, MWS. Born 9 Nov 1909. Died 27 Apr 1911. Suffer little children to come unto me.   (82)(93)

McGREGOR, J   (see ROYAL ARTILLERY (3))

McGREGOR, John   (H/599)
Sacred to the memory of Gunner John McGREGOR, 7/1 Easter Division, Royal Artillery, who died of cholera at Rawalpindi 11th Aug 1888. Aged 28 yrs. Looking for the blessed hope. This stone is erected by a few comrades.   (82)(93)(BS)

McGUINESS, Ursula   (VII/1375)
Sister M Ursula McGUINESS. Died 25 Feb 1970.   (93)(WM)

MacKAY, James Currie
In memory of James Currie. Infant son of Mr M MacKAY, who died Rawalpindi 17 Aug 1861. Aged 9 mths. (82)

McKELVIE, Minnie S and Mary R   (O/1075)
In loving memory of Minnie S McKELVIE, aged 2 yrs, and Mary R McKELVIE, aged 8 mths, the beloved children of Reverend G McKELVIE, who died Nov 1894. Jesus said suffer little children to come unto me.   (82)(93)(mb)

McKENNA, Cornelius Hugh   (VII/1346)
In loving memory of Cornelius Hugh McKENNA. Superintending Engineer who died 11 Nov 1944. Aged 48 yrs. RIP.   (82)(93)

MacKENZIE, Annie Adeline   (M/1169)
In loving memory of Annie Adeline MacKENZIE, QAMNSI.   Born 3
Apr 1878. Died 28 Mar 1907.   (82)(93)(end)

MacKENZIE, Harriet Mary   (O/1122)
In loving memory of Harriet Mary MacKENZIE, youngest daughter
of the late James MacKENZIE, Honourable Hudsons Bay Company,
Quebec, Canada, who died at Rawalpindi 4 or 5th (sic) Feb
1913.   (82)(93)

McKEON, Hugh O'B   (L/1038)
In loving memory of Hugh O'B. Son of Colour Sergeant and
Martha McKEON. 2nd Royal Irish Fusiliers. Died 25 Oct 1904.
Aged 9 mths.   (82)(93)

McKERNEY, John   (HH/338)
Sacred to the memory of Private John McKERNEY. H Company 1st
Royal Irish Fusiliers. Died Rawalpindi 15 Jul 1885. Aged 22
yrs. This stone was erected by ...... (82)(93)(BS)

McKNIGHT, M G   (see 1ST KING'S DRAGOON GUARDS (1))

McKNIGHT, T   (see 1ST KING'S DRAGOON GUARDS (1))

McLEOD, Richard   (see ROYAL HORSE ARTILLERY (1))

McLOUGHLIN, V   (S/309)
In loving memory of No 3594138 Private V McLOUGHLIN of C Company 2nd Battalion Border Regiment. Died Rawalpindi 27 Mar
1930. Aged 26 yrs. Erected by all ranks of C Company.
                                   (82)(93)

McMAHON, Francis Lionel   (Q/1320)
In memory of Francis Lionel McMAHON. 2nd Lieutenant. ISC.
Attached 3rd Battalion Rifle Brigade. Beloved son of Lieuten-
ant General and Mrs McMAHON. Died 11 Nov 1896. Aged 20 yrs.
                                   (82)(93)

McMANN..., M   (I/412)
Sacred to the memory of Private M McMANN... who died at
Rawalpindi ......   (93)(BS)

McMANUS, Irene Maude   (Y/741)
Resting. In affectionate memory of Irene Maude (Ivy), the
dearly beloved sister of Sybil McMANUS, who fell asleep 6 Feb
1923. The eternal God is thy refuge and underneath are the
everlasting arms. Deut.33.27.   (82)(93)(WM)

McMURRAY, Ellen Adelaide   (JJ/358)
Requiescat in pace. In loving memory of Ellen Adelaide, the
beloved wife of Assistant Apothecary P E A McMURRAY,
Superintendent Medical Department, who died at Rawalpindi 15
Jun 1889. Aged 24 yrs. The Lord gave and the Lord hath taken
away. Blessed be the name of the Lord. Deeply and sincerely
regretted.   (82)(93)(WM)

<u>McNABO, J</u> *(L/1041)*
Of your charity pray for the soul of No 6969 Private J McNABO, D Company Royal Irish Fusiliers, who died at Rawalpindi 28 Mar 1904. RIP.   Erected by the officers, NCOs and men of his company. *(82)(93)*

<u>MacPHERSON, Herbert Hamilton Gordon</u> *(EE/79)*
To the memory of Herbert Hamilton Gordon. The beloved son of Herbert and Maria MacPHERSON. Born 7 Dec 1863. Died 24 Sep 1865. *(82)(93)(mb)*

<u>McROBB, A</u> *(O/1102)*
Sacred to the memory of No 6164 Private A McROBB. B Company, 2nd Gordon Highlanders, who died at Baracoa on 14 Jul 1902. Erected by the officers, NCOs and men of B company.
(82)(93)

<u>MACKEN, M Brendan</u> *(VII/1354)*
Sister M Brendan MACKEN. Died 12 Dec 1948. RIP.   *(93)(WM)*

<u>MACKECHINE, Alice Mary</u> (see FORBES, Alice Mary)

<u>MAFFETT, John William</u> *(Z/643)*

Sacred to the memory of Lieutenant John William MAFFETT. 8th Connaught Rangers. Born 1 Mar 1841. Died 6 Oct 1867. Aged 26 yrs.
For I know that my redeemer liveth and that he shall stand at the latter day upon the earth and though after my skin, worms destroy this body yet in my flesh shall I see God.
Job 19.25-26.

(82)(93)(WM)(W)

There are several headstones set into the wall around the cemetery which had fallen in earlier times. They are marked (W) in the inscription lists.

MAGEE, Dan (see ROYAL ARTILLERY (5))

MAGUIRE, R (J/447)
Sacred to the memory of Private R MAGUIRE who died at Rawalpindi 6 Jun 1891. Aged 25 yrs. 3rd Dragoon Guards. Erected by NC officers and men of G Troop as a mark of respect. (82)(93)(BS)

MAHER, M Brigid (VII/1349)
Mother M Brigid MAHER. 11 Oct 1944. RIP.
(82)(93)(WM)

MAHON, A J (see YORKSHIRE REGIMENT (1))

MAILYER, Joseph Charles (I/408)
In memory of Joseph Charles MAILYER of 50th Field Battery Royal Artillery. Died Rawalpindi 10 Sep 1897. Aged 23 yrs 6 mths. This stone is erected by his sorrowing comrades.
(82)(93)(PS)

MAINPRICE, Frederick Paul (X/834)
In loving memory of Frederick Paul MAINPRICE, ICS. Late Indian Political Service. Eldest son of the Rev William Horace Briscoe and Constance MAINPRICE. Born at Leconfield 22 Aug 1915. Died 28 Oct 1950. (93)

MALLAM, J (Q/1305)
In memory of No 4032 Private J MALLAM, C Company 1st Battalion The Queen's RWS Regiment, who died at Rawalpindi 2 Jun 1898. Aged 23 yrs 11 mths. Erected by the officers, NCOs and men of his company. (82)(93)(PS)

MALLETT, Gerard (VII/1395)
Rev Father Gerard MALLETT, MHM. Born 4 Feb 1913. Ordained Mill Hill 1938. Died 28 Jun 1970. (93)

MALLON (see ROYAL ARTILLERY (7))

MALONE, Annie Louisa (L/1040)
Annie Louisa MALONE, the dearly beloved child of Sergeant J and Mary MALONE, 1st Battalion The Royal Irish Regiment, who fell asleep 17 Mar 1907. Aged 1 yr 8 mths. Deeply mourned by her loving parents. (82)(93)(PS)

MALONE, P
No 4336 Sergeant P MALONE. C Squadron 9th Queen's Royal Lancers. Died 23 Apr 1903. Aged 38 yrs. (82)

MANDITT, Teddy (M/1229)
Our darling Teddy. The beloved son of W and K MANDITT. 1st Battalion The Queen's Regiment. Died Rawalpindi 12 Apr 1902. Aged 9 mths 10 days. God has taken home our darling, placed our child among his flowers. Taken back the babe he lent us, to a better world than ours. (82)(93)

MANLEY, W (see ROYAL HORSE ARTILLERY (2))

MANNING, Jack   (X/771)
In memory of Captain Jack MANNING of the Indian Army and late
of the 3rd Battalion, AIF, who was accidentally killed at
Rawalpindi 22 Oct 1922.   (82)(93)

MANNION, J (see ROYAL HORSE ARTILLERY (3))

MANUALS, T A   (X/852)
Mr T A MANUALS. Beloved husband of Mrs E A MANUALS.   17 Oct
1963. Aged 53 yrs.   (93)

MANUEL (see ROYAL ARTILLERY (7))

MAPLE, Gemma   (VI/472)
In loving memory of Gemma (Bobby). The beloved daughter of Mr
and Mrs L B MAPLE. Born 1 Aug 1932. Died 22 May 1934.
                                        (82)(93)

MARCH, W (see ROYAL HORSE ARTILLERY (2))

MARIDIN(?), Cecil Colville   (X/784)
In hoc signo Vinges. Colonel Cecil Colvitte MARIDIN(?), CBE,
DSO. Royal Regiment of Artillery. Died 22 Oct 1932. Aged 53
yrs.   (82)(93)

MARK, John   (X/779)
In loving memory of John MARK, Military Accounts Department,
who died 30 Nov 1920. Aged 80 yrs. Erected by his sorrowful
wife Jessie MARK.   Thou are gone, but not forgotten.   Never
will thy memory fade. Sweetest thoughts will ever linger,
round the spot where thou art laid.   (82)(93)

MARKS, John Frank   (X/866)
John Frank MARKS. Died 24 Sep 1975. From daughter and
son-in-law.   (93)(WM)

MARSHALL, Gerald
Our baby boy Gerald MARSHALL .....   (82)

MARSHALL, S (see ROYAL GARRISON ARTILLERY (4))
MARSTON, A   (see ROYAL HORSE ARTILLERY (2))
MARTIN, F   (see GORDON HIGHLANDERS (4))

MARTIN, Fredrick
Sacred to the memory of No 4601 Lance Corporal Fredrick MAR-
TIN. C Company 1st Battalion Wiltshire Regiment. Died
Rawalpindi 1 Dec 1904.   (82)

MARTIN, John (see 9TH REGIMENT (1))

MARTIN, R   (VII/1357)
Mrs R MARTIN. Died 21 Apr 1946. Aged 82.
                                        (93)

MASCARENHA, Maryannie
In memory of Maryannie. The beloved daughter of Manuel
MASCARENHA. Died 7 Oct 1895.   (82)

MASKELL, J   (P/1279)
In memory No 5593 Private J MASKELL. C Company 1st Battalion
The Queen's RWS Regiment. Died Rawalpindi 12 Nov 1902. Aged
23 yrs. Erected by the officers, NCOs and men of his company.
                                        (82)(93)(PS)

MASON, A R (see 1ST KING'S DRAGOON GUARDS (1))

MASON, Fredrick John   (X/767)
Darling Fredrick John MASON who departed this life 5 Aug
1923. Aged 50 yrs. Erected by his sorrowing wife and
children.   Trust God in all you undertake, he never fails
his own.   Just do the best and leave the rest, You'll reap
where you are sown.   (82)(93)

MASON, William (see 98TH REGIMENT (1))

MASTER, Augustus Coventry Neville   (X/839)
In ever cherished memory of Augustus Coventry Neville MASTER.
Beloved husband of Norah. Born 25 Oct 1900. Died 28 Jun
1951.   (93)

MASTERSON, Ernest George   (X/780)
In loving memory of our dear Ernest George MASTERSON. The beloved husband of Maud MASTERSON. Died 30 Mar 1931. Aged 44
yrs 10 mths.   (82)(93)

MATHESON, T (see ROYAL ARTILLERY (6))

MATHUS, Louisa   (Y/702)
Louisa. The beloved daughter of R and M MATHUS. Died 3 Nov
1918. Aged 25 yrs. Gone but not forgotten. Deeply regretted
by her sorrowful parents.   (82)(93)

MATTHEWS, Audrey May   (IX/981)
Audrey May. The dearly loved infant daughter of Sergeant and
Mrs J MATTHEWS, 33rd Field Battery, Royal Artillery. Born 3
Nov 1926. Died 8 Dec 1926. Thy will be done. (93)

MATTHEWS, Patrick (see ROYAL ARTILLERY (10))
MATTHEWS, T   (see 70TH REGIMENT (2))

MAUGHAN, Cecil   (N/1476)
In loving memory of little Cecil, son of John and Laura
MAUGHAN, 4th Dragoon Guards, who died 28 Apr 1898. Aged 3
weeks. Suffer little children to come unto me. (82)(93)(PS)

MAXWELL, James   (P/1265)
Gunner James MAXWELL. F Battery Royal Horse Artillery. Died
2 Mar 1902. Aged 23 and 2/12th years. Erected by his
comrades.   (82)(93)(PS)

MAYBURY, Andrew and Elizabeth   (GG/209)
In memory of Andrew. Born 27 Nov 186? Died 4 Oct 186? Also
Elizabeth. Born 8 Jul 1868. Died 16 Oct 1869. The beloved
children of M and E MAYBURY. 19th Regiment. Thy will be
done.   (82)(93)(BS)

MAYR, Thomas S
Thomas S MAYR. Beloved child of Colour Sergeant and Emma
......1st Battalion 6th Regiment. Died 8 May 1869. Aged 9
mths. *(82)*

MEALE, Frederick (see 9TH REGIMENT (1))

MEALING, Caroline *(IV/566)*
IHS. Sacred to the memory of our beloved mother Caroline
MEALING, who died at Rawalpindi on 6 Jan 1936. Aged 60 yrs.
Rest in peace. *(93)*

MEDLEY, Charlotte E *(O/1116)*
In loving memory of Charlotte E MEDLEY, beloved wife of
Sergeant H MEDLEY, Royal Engineers, who died 2 Jun 1912. Aged
26 yrs. Thy will be done. *(82)(93)*

MEEK, Gladys Leslie *(W/907)*
Gladys Leslie. Little daughter of Major and Mrs MEEK. Born 3
Dec 1918. Died 4 Apr 1919. *(93)*

MENDHAM, C D *(M/1256)*
Sacred to the memory of Sergeant C D MENDHAM. 4th Dragoon
Guards. Died at Rawalpindi on 20 Dec 1901. Aged 27 yrs.
Erected by the NCOs and men of his Squadron. Asleep in Jesus,
blessed sleep, from which none ever wake to weep.
(93)(PS)

MERCHANT, Hilda May *(O/1084)*
In loving memory of Hilda May, the infant daughter of Sergeant
Major and Mrs MERCHANT, RFA, who died 27 May 1900. Aged 2
mths 7 days. And Jesus said forbid them not for of such is
the kingdom of heaven. *(82)(93)(mb)*

MERRY, T (see SOMERSET LIGHT INFANTRY (1))
MEYERS, Frederick (see ROYAL HORSE ARTILLERY (1))

MICHAEL *(JJ/350)*
IHS. To the sacred memory of the Reverend Father MICHAEL,
OSFC, Late Rector of St Thomas' College, Murree, who died 17
Mar 1886. This monument has been erected by the Catholic
congregation of Rawalpindi. *(82)(93)*

MICHAEL, Harold George *(VII/1351)*
Harold George MICHAEL. Beloved father of Linley and Dulcie.
Died 15 Feb 1971. *(93)(WM)*

MICHAEL, Violet May *(VII/1350)*
Violet May MICHAEL. Wife of Harold and mother of Linley and
Dulcie. Born 19 Jul 1898. Died 24 Apr 1958.
(93)(WM)

MIERS, Catherine Elizabeth *(I/401)*
In loving memory of Catherine Elizabeth MIERS, the beloved
wife of Sergeant MIERS, who died at Rawalpindi 29 Nov 1895.
(82)(93)

MILES, George   (E/184)
Sacred to the memory of Private George MILES,   C Company 2nd Battalion Wiltshire Regiment, who died at Rawalpindi 13 Jul 1884. Aged 21 yrs 3 mths. Erected by the officers, NC officers and men of his company.   (82)(93)(BS)

MILLARD, Ruth   (IV/567)
In loving memory of Ruth. Beloved wife of Captain L N MILLARD, RAOC. Died 21 Jan 1936. Aged 32 yrs. And of their infant son. Yet in these ears the hearing dies, one set slow bell will seem to toll. The passing of the sweetest soul that ever looked with human eyes.   (93)

MILLER (see ROYAL ARTILLERY (6))

MILLER   (W/890)
The beloved son of Sergeant Major P P and Margaret MILLER, who died on 6 May 1914.   (82)(93)

MILLER, Emmie and Jackie   (Y/697)
Emmie. Dearly loved wife of Sergeant J MILLER.   4th Battery Royal Field Artillery. Died 5 Nov 1912. Aged 22 yrs. And of Jackie. Darling baby of the above who joined his sweet mother 12 Nov 1912. Aged 7 mths.   (82)(93)

MILLER, Eric Owen   (Y/734)
In loving memory of Eric Owen. Dearly loved son of William and Clara MILLER ......   (93)

MILLER, Mabel   (M/1196)
Mabel MILLER, the beloved wife of 2nd Lieutenant Edward Cyril MILLER, who died at Rawalpindi 5 Oct 1917. Aged 27 yrs 9 mths. Erected by her sorrowing husband and daughter. How we missed her, no tongue can tell, how much we loved her and how well. God loved her too and thought it best to take her home with him to rest.   (82)(93)

MILLS, Florence E O   (M/1219)
IHS. In loving memory of Florence E O MILLS. Daughter of G T and F A MILLS. Chief Warder, Miscellaneous List. Died Rawalpindi 8 Apr 1901. Aged 8 mths.   (82)(93)

MILLS, W (see RIFLE BRIGADE (2))

MILMAN, Robert   (CC/36)
In loving memory of Robert MILMAN, DD.   Bishop of Calcutta. Born 25 Jan 1816. Died 15 Mar 1876. Be thou faithful unto death and I will give thee a crown of life. Revelations 2.10.
                                       (82)(93)(WM)

MILROY, C W   (IV/558)
14th/20th Hussars. To the memory of Trooper C W MILROY, 14/20th Hussars, who died at Rawalpindi 10 Nov 1935. Aged 23 yrs. This stone was erected by his comrades.
                                       (82)(93)

MINCHER, E (see 1ST KING'S DRAGOON GUARDS (1))

MINCHER, Edward   *(E/187)*
Sacred to the memory of Private Edward MINCHER, who was killed by his horse falling at General's Inspection on 24 Mar 1886. Aged 28 yrs.   *(82)(93)(BS)*

MISSON, Alice   *(Y/725)*
In loving memory of Alice, the beloved wife of Major W MISSON, IOD, who died at Rawalpindi 29 Jan 1922. Aged 50 yrs.
                                           (82)(93)

MISSON, Maude   *(LL/239)*
Maude, infant child of W and A MISSON, who died at Rawalpindi 14 Feb 1905. Aged 26 days.   *(82)(93)(WM)*

MITCHELL, Annie Gertrude   *(Y/724)*
In loving memory of Annie Gertrude. Beloved wife of S. Sergeant A C MITCHELL. MWS. Died 18 Nov 1921. Aged 32. Deeply mourned by her sorrowing husband. *(93)*

MITCHELL, Nancy Gertrude   *(W/919)*
In loving memory of Nancy Gertrude. Beloved daughter of Arthur and Annie Gertrude MITCHELL. Died 20 Nov 1921. Aged 8 days.   *(93)*

MITCHELL, William (see RIFLE BRIGADE (1))

MITTELBERGER, Thomas   *(VII/1398)*
Rev Thomas MITTELBERGER. MHM. Born 22 Sep 1938 Tirol. Ordained Mill Hill 1964. Died in accident 4 Jul 1967 Jhelum.
                                           (93)

MODGET, G A S (see ROYAL ARTILLERY (9))

MOFFAT, John (see ROYAL ARTILLERY (4))

MONEY, Arthur Peter   *(X/868)*
Arthur Peter MONEY. Died 6 Sep 1973. Erected by his sorrowing wife and children.   *(93)*

MONEY, E E   *(N/1459)*
IHS. Sacred to the memory of Lieutenant Colonel E E MONEY, Commandant 9th Bengal Lancers, who died at Camp Muridki on 20 Dec 1894. Erected by his brother officers as a token of esteem and regard. He is able to keep that which I have committed unto him against that day.   *(82)(93)(mb)*

MONK, Eileen Travers   *(S/317)*
In cherished memory of our sweet and gentle mother Eileen Travers MONK. Died 9 Mar 1928. This cross is put up by her sorrowful husband and her little children George, Gemma, Tony and Ann.   *(82)(93)(WM)*

MONKS, F (see ROYAL ARTILLERY (6))

MONKTON, J (see ROYAL ARTILLERY (6))

MONRO, Eric Alfred Russell   (R/282)
Jesus Mercy, Mary help. Of your charity pray for the repose
of the soul of Lieutenant Eric Alfred Russell MONRO, 6th
Gurkha Rifles, who died at Rawalpindi 18 Jan 1937. Aged 28
yrs. RIP.   (82)(93)

MONTGOMERY, Trina Mary
In memory of Trina Mary. Daughter of Frederick and Catherine
Lyons MONTGOMERY.   (82)

MONTGOMERY, W   (L/1059)
Sacred to the memory of No 7702 Corporal W MONTGOMERY, who
died at Rawalpindi on 26 Feb 1908. Erected as a token of
esteem by the corporals of the 1st Battalion, The Royal Irish.
                                          (82)(93)

MOON, G (see ROYAL HORSE ARTILLERY (2))

MOON, John   (CC/41)
In memory of John MOON. Late Color Sergeant ... (82)(93)(BS)

MOORE, A (see ROYAL HORSE ARTILLERY (2))

MOORE, A G E   (V/993)
In memory of No 5614799 Driver A G E MOORE. 14th Field Battery Royal Artillery. Died Rawalpindi 23 Dec 1932. Aged 25
yrs.   (82)(93)

MOORE, Elizabeth and Lawrence   (I/411)
In loving memory of Elizabeth, wife of Sergeant A MOORE, 3rd
Dragoon Guards, who died 19 Sep 1892. Aged 18 yrs 6 mths.
Also ... Lawrence ....son .... who died 16 Dec 1892.
                                          (82)(93)(BS)(mb)

POST OFFICE, RAWALPINDI

MOORE, Henry   (E/190)
In memory of Lance Corporal George TODD, Bandsmen Henry MOORE
and Charles G FROST, the 2nd Battalion The Royal Irish
Regiment, who were killed in a railway accident on 15 Mar
1885.   (82)(93)

MOORE, J (see 1ST KING'S DRAGOON GUARDS (1))

MOORE, Maude Frances   (N/1429)
In loving memory of Maude Frances. Beloved wife of Sergeant J
MOORE, RA. Died Rawalpindi 4 Feb 1895. (82)(93)

MOORE, Samuel William   (N/1477)
Samuel William MOORE, beloved son of Samuel and Sarah Ann
MOORE, who died Rawalpindi 11 Apr 1898. Aged 1 yr 6 mths.
                                       (82)(93)

MOORE, William (see ROYAL HORSE ARTILLERY (1))

MORANT, James Lushington   (M/1154)
In loving memory of James Lushington MORANT, Lieutenant 3rd
Punjab Cavalry, only son of the late Lieutenant Colonel
MORANT, RE, who died 1 Feb 1902. Aged 24. God so loved the
world that he gave his only begotten son that whosoever
believeth in him will not perish but have everlasting life.
AHMUD BUX, RAWALPINDI.   (82)(93)(end)

MORAY, Alan Bruce Dawson   (V/980)
Sacred to the memory of Alan Bruce Dawson MORAY, who died
Rawalpindi 24 Dec 1920. Also of ..... (82)(93)(mb)

MOREL   (N/1475)
The dearly loved little daughter of James and Sarah MOREL.
Died Rawalpindi 2 Apr 1897. Aged 4 yrs 1 mth. I shall go to
her, but she will not return to me.   (82)(93)

MOREL, Sarah Elizabeth   (X/743)
In loving memory of our dear mother Sarah Elizabeth MOREL.
Died 21 Jun 1920. Aged 69 yrs. Safely, safely gathered in,
far from sorrow, far from sin. Passed beyond all grief and
pain, death for thee is surest gain. For our loss we must
not weep, nor our loved one long to keep, from the home of
rest and peace, where all sin and sorrow cease.
                                       (82)(93)

MORGAN, A
Sacred to the memory of No 4863 Lance Corporal A MORGAN. 10th
Royal Hussars. Died Rawalpindi 12 Dec 1906. (82)

MORGAN, Charles Edward Hope   (A/130)
In loving memory of Charles Edward Hope. Infant son of
Lieutenant Colonel A MORGAN. Died 29 Apr 1885. Aged 9 mths.
                                       (82)(93)

MORGAN, Charles Henry
No 4021 Sergeant Charles Henry MORGAN. 10th Royal Hussars.
Died Rawalpindi...   (82)

MORGAN, J (see ROYAL HORSE ARTILLERY (2))

MORLEY, Monica Patricia
Monica Patricia MORLEY. Youngest daughter of the late Mr and Mrs J MORLEY. Step-daughter of Major E J CHEESEMAN, RIASC retired. Born 4 May 1924. Entered her heavenly home 29 Jun 1935. Erected by her parents, brother and sisters.
(82)

MORLEY, William (see 70TH REGIMENT (3))
MORRIS, C (see 1ST KING'S DRAGOON GUARDS (1))

MORRIS, Edith *(I/403)*
In sweet memory of Edith. The beloved wife of Surgeon Major W A MORRIS, AMS. Died Rawalpindi.... *(82)(93)*

MORRIS, G *(G/436)*
Dragoon Guards. Sacred to the memory of Private G MORRIS, who died 18 Apr 1889. Aged 22 yrs. *(82)(93)(BS)*

MORRIS, J *(K/628)*
To the memory of Private J MORRIS. E Company King's Royal Rifles. Died Rawalpindi 5 May 1892. *(82)(93)(BS)*

MORRISON, Arthur *(V/1007)*
To the glory of God and in memory of Corporal Arthur MORRISON. Sutherland Highlanders. ...... *(93)(BS)*

MORTIMER, Ivy *(A/127)*
To the memory of Ivy. Infant daughter of Clara Mary Anne and Major F J MORTIMER, RA. Born 24 Apr 1883. Died 14 May 1883.
(82)(93)(WM)

MORTON, William (see KING'S OWN SCOTTISH BORDERERS (1))
MOTT, Edward (see ROYAL ARTILLERY (4))
MOUNSEY, Samuel (see RIFLE BRIGADE (1))

MOUNTFORD, Emily Florence *(A/113)*
In loving memory of Emily Florence. The beloved daughter of William and Eliza MOUNTFORD. Sergeant 8th Hussars. Died 20 Feb 1881. Aged 2 yrs 5 mths. *(82)(93)(BS)*

MUFFETT, Terrence Henry *(UA/973)*
In loving memory of Terrence Henry. The beloved son of Mr and Mrs L Z MUFFETT. Born 3 Aug 1930. Died 12 May 1931. Suffer little children to come unto me. *(93)*

MUMFORD, Louise Ethel *(N/1474)*
In loving memory of Louise Ethel. Beloved daughter of Sergeant Major Edward and L A MUMFORD. .... *(93)(mb)*

MUNDAY, M G (see SOMERSET LIGHT INFANTRY (1))

MUNN, James
Private James MUNN. B Troop. 3rd Dragoon Guards. Died Rawalpindi 8 Jul 1892. Aged 21 yrs. *(82)*

MUNRO, William Nash and Mary Louisa   (EE/93)
Sacred to the memory of William Nash. Died 8 Jun 1866. Aged 3 yrs 10 mths. Also Mary Louisa. Died 24 May 1866. Aged 15 mths. The dearly beloved and deeply regretted children of ?William and Eliza MUNRO.   (93)(BS)

MURPHY, J   (R/274)
IHS. In memory of No 4031053 Private J MURPHY. 1st Battalion King's Shropshire Light Infantry. Died 2 Jul 1933. Erected by his comrades.   (82)(93)

MURPHY, J   (HH/324)
In memory of Lance Sergeant J MURPHY, 81st Regiment, who died at Rawalpindi on 20 Nov 1879. Aged 32 yrs. Deeply regretted by his brother sergeants. This tomb is erected by his brother sergeants as a mark of .... and respect.
    (82)(93)(BS)

MURPHY, Patrick Aidan   (JJ/344)
In loving memory of Patrick Aidan. Infant son of Conductor P MURPHY, Ordnance Department, and Edith his wife. Born 15 Nov 1893. Died 7 Nov 1894. RIP. This lovely bud so young and fair, called hence by early doom, just came to show how sweet a flower in paradise would bloom.   (82)(93)(WM)

MURPHY, W H and Elizabeth   (N/1439)
In sacred memory of Army Schoolmaster W H MURPHY, 2nd King's Own Scottish Borderers, who died at Rawalpindi 27 Apr 1896. Aged 25 yrs 11 mths. Also of Elizabeth MURPHY. Acting Schoolmistress, King's Own Scottish Borderers. His sister.
    (82)(93)(PS)

MURPHY, William   (L/1058)
Sacred to the memory of No 4123 Private William MURPHY, 1st Battalion Royal Irish Regiment, who departed this life Rawalpindi 18 Jan 1907. Aged 34 yrs. Erected as a token of esteem by the NCOs and men of his company.   (82)(93)

MURRAY, Archibald Ross   (C/94)
To the dearly loved memory of Archibald Ross MURRAY. Bengal Staff Corps. Born 5 Mar 1855. Died 18 Jul 1879. Love is strong as death. Death is swallowed up in victory.
    (82)(93)(PS)

MURRAY, James   (N/1451)
Sacred to the memory of Sergeant James MURRAY. Born 13 Jul 1842. Died 4 Sep 1897. During 18 years Conservancy Sergeant and Church Clerk at Rawalpindi.   (82)(93)(mb)

MURRAY, Michael   (VII/1353)
Sister M Michael MURRAY. Died 3 Jun 1948. RIP.   (93)(WM)

MUSSELWHITE, G   (P/1298)
Private G MUSSELWHITE, C Company, 1st Battalion Wiltshire Regiment, who departed this life at Rawalpindi 8 Mar 1904. Aged 24 yrs 8 mths. This stone was erected by the officers, NCOs and men of his company.   (82)(93)

MYERS, John William   (EE/84)
In memory of John William MYERS. Gas engineer. Died 6 Apr 1879. Aged 43 yrs. Thy will be done. (93)(PS)

MYLNE, Edgar Cunningham Monnier   (J/452)
Sacred to the memory of Edgar Cunningham Monnier MYLNE. Born 18 Jan 1864. Died 24 Jun 1891. Come for all things are now ready.   (82)(93)(BS)

Frederic Augustus Talbot Headstone
HARLEY STREET CEMETERY

NAISBETT, N (see 1ST KING'S DRAGOON GUARDS (1))

NASH, Berte Amelia (K/630)
Berte Amelia NASH. The beloved and only child of Edward and Bertha Alice NASH. B Battery, RHA .... *(93)(BS)*

NASH, Bertha (see ROYAL HORSE ARTILLERY (3))

NASH, Yvonne (W/959)
In loving memory of Yvonne. The beloved daughter of Henry and Lillian NASH.... *(82)(93)*

NAYLERRIN, Dennis Ian
Sacred to the memory of our beloved Dennis Ian NAYLERRIN. Born 21 Jan 1926. Died 11 Dec 1946. *(82)*

NEALE, A (D/119)
Sergeant A NEALE, 10th Hussars, who died 21 Oct 1880. Aged 28 yrs. Erected by the Sergeants, 10th Hussars, as a token of respect. *(82)(93)*

NEALE, Robert (see ROYAL HORSE ARTILLERY (1))

NEESAM, Marlene Theresa (VII/1333)
Marlene Theresa NEESAM. Aged 32 yrs. Died 24 Mar 1961 as a result of an accident at Kotri. *(93)(WM)*

NEEVES (W/916)
The beloved son of Reuben and Grace NEEVES. Born 6 Oct 1921. Died 27 Nov 1921. In his arms forever leaning on his breast. *(82)(93)*

NEIL, Frederick (see ROYAL ARTILLERY (4))

NELSON, Doris Mabel (W/963)
Doris Mabel. The beloved daughter of BSM and Mrs J NELSON. 66th Battery, 4th F Brigade, Royal Artillery. Born at Rawalpindi on the 15 Feb 1929. Died 25 Nov 1929. God has our cherished babe. Safe in the arms of Jesus. *(82)(93)*

NELSON, John Smyth (DD/69)
Sacred to the memory of John Smyth NELSON, Lieutenant and local Captain 38th Regiment, who died at Rawalpindi 9 Sep 1871. Aged 30 yrs 4 mths. Erected by his brother officers.
(82)(93)(BS)(mb)

NETSCHER, Pamela St Clair (X/823)
Sacred to the memory of Pamela St Clair. The dearly beloved wife of Major E G NETSCHER. Born 31 Jan 1902. Died 30 May 1946. Father in thy gracious keeping leave we now our loved one sleeping. *(82)(93)*

NEVILLE, Violet (see BOYDELL, Violet)

NEWBURY, Irene Rebecca (VII/1380)
Irene Rebecca NEWBURY. Died 8 May 1953. Aged 54 yrs.
(93)

NEWBY, D (see YORKSHIRE REGIMENT (1))

NEWELL, Sidney Hugh (O/1104)
IHS. In loving memory of Sidney Hugh NEWELL, who died at Rawalpindi 18 Nov 1902 in his 29th year. Thanks be to God which giveth us the victory through our Lord Jesus Christ. 1.COR.XV.57. NIYAZ ALI, RAWALPINDI. (82)(93)

NEWMAN, Alice Evanthea (VII/1387)
Alice Evanthea NEWMAN. Born 17 Jan 1884. Died 12 Dec 1954. Erected by her son. (93)

NEWTON, Vivian Aubrey (X/860)
Vivian Aubrey NEWTON. 30 Aug 1888. Died 6 Mar 1967. A friend to all. Beloved of all. A man to be remembered.
(93)

NICHOLAS (LL/231)
.... child of Gunner George and Kate NICHOLAS, who fell asleep on 13 May 1908. Aged 2 yrs 4 mths. Suffer little children to come unto me for of such is the kingdom of heaven.
(82)(93)(WM)

NICHOLS, William (see ROYAL HORSE ARTILLERY (1))

NICHOLSON (A/111)
... Infant son of George and Sarah NICHOLSON. Born 18 Feb. Died 4 May 1880. He shall gather the lambs with his arm, and carry them in his bosom. (93)(WM)

NICHOLSON, Charles George (III/489)
Sacred to the memory of a devoted and loving husband and father Charles George NICHOLSON. Inspector of Her Majesty's Customs, Burma, retired. Born 10 Nov 1888. Died 8 Dec 1944.
(82)(93)(WM)

NIXON, H A (W/882)
H A NIXON, beloved son of Joseph and Leonora NIXON, who died 23 May 1911. Aged 1 yr 7 mths 18 days. (82)(93)

NOAD, W (see ROYAL ARTILLERY (8))

NOBLE, Betty (W/917)
In ever loving memory of darling Betty. Daughter of Regimental Quartermaster Sergeant and Mrs NOBLE. 2nd Battalion The Sherwood Forresters. Born Kuldana 20 Jul 1923. Died Rawalpindi 19 Apr 1924. Another jewel added to his crown.
(82)(93)

NODDLE, G (see ROYAL ARTILLERY (6))

NOLAN, John Luke   (R/279)
In loving memory of John Luke NOLAN, Lieutenant Royal
Engineers, aged 27 yrs, who was killed in an avalanche on
Khillanmarg, Kashmir on 1 Mar 1936. Eternal rest give to him
O Lord and let perpetual light shine upon him.   (93)
     (see HINGSTON, Alfred Bose)

NORMAN, Eliza Ellen   (BB/22)
To the memory of Eliza Ellen, the beloved wife of Major F B
NORMAN, Bengal Staff Corps, who died at Rawalpindi 6 Jan 1870.
Aged 35 yrs 17 days. Therefore be ye also ready: for in such
an hour as ye think not the son of man cometh. Matthew
XXIV.42. NUND RAM, DELHI.   (82)(93)(PS)

NORRIS, George Charles   (LL/237)
In ever loving memory of George Charles NORRIS, son of Farrier
Quartermaster Sergeant and Mrs NORRIS, who died at Rawalpindi
14 May 1907. Aged 11 mths 28 days.   (93)(WM)

NORTH, A (see WEST RIDING REGIMENT (1))

NORTH, Charles   (L/1063)
IHS. Sacred to the memory of No 6563 Lance Corporal Charles
NORTH. E Company 1st Royal Munster Fusiliers. Died
Rawalpindi 14 Feb 1908.   (82)(93)

NVX (?NYX), Mary Ellen   (BB/29)
Sacred to the memory of Mary Ellen. The beloved daughter of
Bazaar Sergeant J NVX (?NYX) and Catherine his wife. Died 1
Dec 1864. Aged 10 mths. Of such is the kingdom of heaven.
Ere sin could blight or sorrow fade, death came with friendly
care, the opening bud to heaven conveyed, and bade it blossom
there. NUND RAM, DELHI.   (93)(WM)

Incomplete inscriptions from damaged and broken headstones

NO NAME
No 2295 Private John ......
10th Royal Hussars.... (82)

NO NAME   (J/440)
Our darling Biddy.   (93)(mb)

NO NAME   (M/1183)
"Thorough". Erected by his brother officers of the 5th
Fusiliers.   (93)

NO NAME   (JJ/341)
In loving memory of our darling Marie Enid. Aged 10 mths 14
days. O God thou hast taken back what but for a time was
given.   (82)(93)(WM)(mb)

NO NAME
Sacred to the memory of Frederick George William. The infant son of William and Georgina..... *(82)*

NO NAME *(HH/320)*
To the memory of Alfred .... O God thou hast taken back what but for a time was given, teach us to bow to Thy will on earth for our treasure in safe in heaven. *(93)(BS)(mb)*

NO NAME *(GG/210)*
..John ... HM's 70th ... Derynane near ...... the County of Kerry, Ireland .... Rawalpindi 15 Mar 1865. Aged 28 yrs. Everyone that saith unto me Lord .... enter into the Kingdom. *(93)(BS)*

NO NAME
Died 7 Jun 1868. The wife of Sergeant ..... of 6th Royal Regiment. *(82)*

NO NAME *(EE/81)*
Born at Murree 2 Jun 1868. Died at Rawalpindi 3 Sep 1868. *(93)*

NO NAME *(EE/90)*
Mona. 7 Nov 1869. *(82)(93)(WM)(mb)*

NO NAME *(DD/78)*
Neil. Born 13 Dec 1872. Died 10 Apr 1873. .... Richard ......ember 1870. *(93)*

NO NAME *(GG/212)*
Sacred to the memory of Isabella Grace who died at Jhelum 15 Dec 1872. Aged 6 weeks. Also Frances who died at Rawalpindi 21 Aug 1874. Aged 6 weeks 3 days. The beloved children of... *(93)(BS)*

NO NAME
Sacred to the memory of Henry. Died 11 Mar 1876. Aged 7 mths and Edith, died 1877..... *(82)*

NO NAME *(HH/321)*
... Queen's Regt ... departed this life 20 Nov 1877. Aged 30 yrs. *(93)(BS)*

NO NAME
...... Sergeant Instructor 1st Battalion 17th Regiment. Died 22 Apr 1879. Aged 34 yrs. *(82)*

NO NAME *(HH/330)*
In memory of Anne. The beloved wife of Sergeant..... Commissariat Department who died 4 Sep 1879. May she rest in peace. Erected by her sorrowing husband and fond children. *(82)(93)(BS)*

NO NAME *(C/97)*
IHS. In affectionate remembrance of our dear mother, who died 17 Aug 1880. Aged 53 yrs. Blessed are the dead that die in the Lord. EARLE, MEERUT. *(82)(93)(PS)(mb)*

NO NAME   *(C/99)*
Sacred to the memory of our dear mother. Died 19 Feb 1881.
                                          (82)(93)(PS)

NO NAME   *(A/128)*
Died 28 Jun 1884. Aged 10 mths. A flower too frail to bloom
on earth.   *(93)(BS)*

NO NAME   *(A/131)*
In loving memory of our little James who died 2 Apr 1885.
Aged 13 mths 11 days. Suffer little children to come unto me
and forbid them not for of such is the kingdom of heaven.
                                          (82)(93)(WM)

NO NAME   *(B/138)*
In memory of Florry. 5 Aug 1888. Not lost but gone before.
                                          (93)(PS)(mb)
     (see TROLLOP, Florence)

NO NAME   *(K/629)*
... Died Rawalpindi 8 May 1892. Aged 20 yrs.   *(93)(BS)*

NO NAME   *(K/626)*
.... who died at Rawalpindi 15 Sep 1892. Aged 30. *(93)(BS)*
     (Regiment is possibly 1st King's Royal Rifles)

NO NAME   *(K/627)*
George R....   3rd Dragoon Guards who died at Rawalpindi 23
Sep 1892. Aged 30.   *(93)(BS)*

NO NAME   *(K/609)*
In loving memory of Charlotte Alice. Beloved wife of Sergeant
..... who departed this life at Rawalpindi 2 Nov 1892.
                                          (82)(93)(BS)(mb)

NO NAME
Died Rawalpindi 26 Jul 1895. Aged 23 yrs.   *(82)*

NO NAME   *(N/1464)*
Aged 1 yr. Died 23 Dec 1895. Asleep in Jesus.   *(82)(93)*

NO NAME
Marjorie Cecil Rachel. Wife of ..... Born 31 Dec 1873. Died
29 Dec 1899.   *(82)*

NO NAME   *(P/1290)*
.... on 28 Dec 1903. Aged 23 yrs. Erected by the officers,
NCOs and men of the battery.   *(93)(PS)*

NO NAME   *(LL/245)*
H company. 1st .... who died at Rawalpindi 30 Jun 1904. Aged
25 yrs. Erected by H company as a token of respect. Gone but
not forgotten.   *(93)(WM)*

NO NAME   *(L/1065)*
... on 24 Jan 1906. Age 34 yrs. Requiescat in pace. Erected
by the officers, NCOs and men of No 6 MB RGA.   *(93)(BS)*

NO NAME   (AA/1/634)
.. No .. Carriage .. William Arthur ... Heavy Battery RGA ...
died at Rawalpindi 18 (28?) Oct 1906. Erected by the
officers, NCOs and men as a token of respect. *(93)(BS)*

NO NAME   (AA/1/260)
21 Jul 1907. Aged 25 yrs.   *(93)*
    (Regiment is possibly 10th Hussars)

NO NAME   (AA/1/262)
Died of enteric fever 16 Sep 1907. Aged 27.   *(82)(93)*
    (Regiment is possibly 10th Hussars)

NO NAME   (LL/229)
... who died on 9 Nov 1908. Aged 5 yrs 3 mths 11 days. We
miss her, Oh how sadly. Loving hearts alone can tell. We
have lost her. Heaven has found her. Jesus hath done all
things well.   *(93)(WM)*

NO NAME   (W/886)
Our darling son Regie. Son of ...1/5th Fusiliers. Died 12
Dec 1909.   *(93)*
    (see WOOLL, Madelaine Grace)

NO NAME   (O/1081)
... and died at Rawalpindi 1 Jun 1910. Aged 11 mths. *(93)*

NO NAME
Our dear little Alfie. Aged 5 yrs 6 mths who died 15 Feb
1912. Born 10 Aug 1907.   *(82)*

NO NAME   (W/931)
Died 4 Dec 1930. Suffer little children to come unto me. *(93)*

NO NAME
Unseen but loved. 19 Oct 1932. Baby Lee. *(82)*

NO NAME   (W/960)
Died 19 Jan 1933.   *(93)*

NO NAME   (V/997)
2nd Battalion Argyll and Sutherland Highlanders. Born 18 Jul
1915. Died 30 Apr 1935.   *(82)(93)*

NO NAME   (IV/565)
.... Born Dec 1890. Died 22 Nov 1935 at Rawalpindi. Now the
labourers task is o'er.   *(93)*

NO NAME   (V/523)
Died 15 Jan 1942. Safe in the arms of Jesus.   *(93)(WM)*

NO NAME   (V/538)
1/D.C.L. 1/IAOC. Died 16 Dec 1945. Aged 3 mths & 8 mths. *(93)*

NO NAME   (VI/463)
25 Sep 1946. Died 27 Sep 1946. The Lord gave and the Lord
hath taken away. Blessed be the name of the Lord.   *(93)(WM)*

O'CONNELL, D (see ROYAL ARTILLERY (6))

O'CONNOR, Annie   (K/606)
In loving memory of Annie. The dearly beloved wife of Captain G O'CONNOR, Queen's Bays, who died painlessly on 12 May 1893.
          (82)(93)

O'CONNOR, Joycie
In loving memory of our dear little Joycie. (Mother's joy) Beloved child of William and A O'CONNOR. Died........
          (82)(mb)

O'DONNELL, Catherine Jane   (JJ/355)
In loving memory of Catherine Jane, the beloved wife of Captain John O'DONNELL, King's Dragoon Guards, who died at Rawalpindi on 19 Mar 1888. Aged 39 yrs 10 mths. For I know that my redeemer liveth and in the last day I shall rise out of the earth. Requiescat in pace. Deeply regretted by her sorrowing husband and children.   (82)(93)(WM)

O'DONNELL, K (see 1ST KING'S DRAGOON GUARDS (1))

O'DONOGHUE, M Oliver   (R/286)
Sister M Oliver O'DONOGHUE. Died 23 Mar 1939. RIP.
          (82)(93)(WM)

O'DWYER, Michael   (KK/236)
Sacred to the memory of Michael O'DWYER, HM's 88th Regiment, born in the parish of Six Mile Bridge, County Clare, Ireland, who departed this life 21 Apr 1867. Aged 25 yrs. May he rest in peace. Amen.   (93)(BS)

O'HARA, Denzil Desmond   (W/889)
Our darling Denzil Desmond. The beloved son of Arthur and May O'HARA. Born 7 Aug 1913. Died 5 Jun 1914. Aged 10 mths.
          (93)

O'LAUGHLIN, Martin   (V/990)
In loving memory of Martin O'LAUGHLIN. Died Rawalpindi 14 Feb 1932. Born: 1872. Until the day breaks and the shadows flee away.   (82)(93)

O'LOUGHLIN, Michael William   (B/137)
Michael William O'LOUGHLIN. Born 12 Feb 1890. Died 10 Jun 1890. For of such is the kingdom of heaven. (93)(WM)

O'REILLY, Lawrence   (VII/1371)
Sr Lawrence O'REILLY. PBVM. Born Dunmore, Ireland 24 Jun 1891. Died Wah 5 Dec 1979.   (93)(WM)

O'SHEA, D (see 70TH REGIMENT (3))

O'SHEA, M Josephine   (VII/1348)
Reverend Mother M Josephine O'SHEA. Died 22 Oct 1944. RIP.
                                       (82)(93)(WM)

O'SULLIVAN, Ellen Margaret   (I/405)
May she rest in peace. In loving memory of Ellen Margaret
O'SULLIVAN who died Rawalpindi 28 Aug 1894. Deeply regretted.
                                       (82)(93)

O'SULLIVAN, O D (see ROYAL ARTILLERY (9))

O'SULLIVAN, Winifred   (VII/1378)
Mrs Winifred O'SULLIVAN. Died at Rawalpindi 31 May 1956.
                                       (93)(WM)

OAKES, Percy Herbert   (N/1443)
In fond and loving memory of Percy Herbert OAKES. Lieutenant,
King's Own Scottish Borderers. Beloved son of Lizzie Hare and
the late Major Augustus Richard OAKES, MSC. Born 7 Jan 1871.
Died 14 Mar 1894. Even so Father. Erected by his brother.
                                       (82)(93)

OAKES, Samuel (see 98TH REGIMENT (1))

OBEY, James Godfrey
To the memory of James Godfrey. Infant son of Sergeant J and
E OBEY. 2nd Battalion 60th Rifles. Born at Nowshera 5 Oct
1872. Died Rawalpindi 21 Dec 1874. Aged 2 yrs 2 mths. The
Lord gave, the Lord has taken away, blessed be the name of the
Lord. May he rest in peace.   (82)

ODELL, John (see ROYAL ARTILLERY (5))

ODELL, William Henry   (N/1462)
IHS. In memory of Major William Henry ODELL. 2nd Oxfordshire
Light Infantry. Born 6 May 1852. Died 8 Nov 1894. Erected by
the officers of his regiment.   (82)(93)

OFFILL, A? (see 60TH ROYAL RIFLES (1))

OGILVIE, Alex L S   (H/588)
Alex L S OGILVIE, BSC. Died Rawalpindi 1 Apr 1887.(82)(93)(WM)

OGILVIE, Minnett Emily Grisel   (M/1209)
In loving memory of Minnett Emily Grisel. Dearly loved
daughter of Captain E C OGILVIE, Royal Engineers, and Kathleen
his wife. Died 14 Apr 1904. Aged 18 mths.   (82)(93)

OGLE, Robert Valentine
To the memory of Private Robert Valentine OGLE, F Troop, 8th
King's Royal Irish Hussars, who died Rawalpindi 8 Feb 1881.
Aged 32 yrs.   (82)

OLDEN, C   (IV/582)
Sacred to the memory of No 5496453. Private C OLDEN. A Company
1st Battalion The Hampshire Regiment. Died at Rawalpindi 16
May 1936. Age 21 yrs. Erected by all ranks of his company.(93)

OLDER, Winefred Clara   (M/1211)
Our little darling Winefred Clara, infant daughter of SQMS
Albert and Emily OLDER, who died 6 Nov 1899. Aged 8 mths 15
days.   (82)(93)

OLIVER, Arthur Harrison   (M/1176)
In loving memory of Arthur Harrison OLIVER. Lieutenant 84th
Punjabis. Died Rawalpindi 8 Nov 1911. Aged 22 yrs.
                                         (82)(93)(mb)

Alice Owen GANNON

OLLENBACH, Susan Bertha   (X/824)
In loving memory of our dear mother Susan Bertha OLLENBACH of
Mandalay, Burma. Wife of the late Mr P S OLLENBACH of Patna.
Born 12 Jul 1889. Died 29 Aug 1946.   (82)(93)

OLLIVER, J (see 1ST KING'S DRAGOON GUARDS (1))

OLSON, Edwin Alvin
Edwin Alvin OLSON. Born 1 Mar 1885 in Swedeburg, Nebraska,
USA. Died 31 May 1921 Rawalpindi. ULC Mission, Rajahmundry.
                                         (82)

ORCHARD, G E   (see ROYAL ARTILLERY (6))
OSBORN, W   (see DONALDSON, Lionel)

OSBORNE, A S   (VII/1388)
A S OSBORNE. Died 6 May 1955.   (93)

OSBORNE, E   (see 1ST KING'S DRAGOON GUARDS (1))
OSBORNE, R A   (see 1ST KING'S DRAGOON GUARDS (1))
OTTER, A   (see ROYAL ARTILLERY (3))

OTTING, Mary Ann Elizabeth   (I/409)
In loving memory of Mary Ann Elizabeth OTTING, who died on 14 Sep 1897. Aged 51 yrs 4 mths. Deeply regretted by her sorrowing children. Thy will be done. (93)

OWEN, Ivy Florence   (M/1203)
In loving memory of Ivy Florence. Mother's pet. Beloved daughter of T and A OWEN. Born 7 Dec 1904. Died 6 May 1905. He has taken home our darling, placed our bud amongst his flowers, taken home the babe he lent us, to a better world than ours. God is love. (82)(93)

OWEN, Kathleen Wilmer   (M/1155)
In loving memory of Kathleen Wilmer. The beloved wife of T OWEN, Store Sergeant, Ordnance Department. Died 1 Jan 1902. Aged 28 yrs. Sleep on beloved. Underneath are the everlasting arms. (82)(93)

OWEN, Richard   (D/1113)
In loving memory of No 5719 Private Richard OWEN. C Squadron 21st Empress of India Lancers. Died 9 Jun 1913. Aged 35 yrs 4 mths. (82)(93)

OWINGS (see RICE, Robert)

PACE, Charles Percy   (X/764)
In loving memory of Charles Percy PACE. Beloved husband of Eileen Mary PACE. Born 25 Apr 1879. Died.... (82)(93)

PACE, Thomas   (G/418)
3rd Dragoon Guards. Sacred to the memory of Corporal Thomas PACE. Died Rawalpindi 17 Aug .... (82)(93)(BS)

PACKER, S (see ROYAL ARTILLERY (9))

PACY, Dorothy Irene   (VV/527)
In ever loving and cherished memory of our beloved baby and sister Dorothy Irene PACY who passed away on 11 Dec 1942. Aged 1 yr 8 mths. (93)

PAGE, Ansel Osmond   (VII/1336)
Ansel Osmond PAGE. N W Railway. Beloved husband of Maud. Born 11 Aug 1907. Died 29 Aug 1958. Erected by a sorrowing wife and children. (93)

PAINE, Diane Mary Hares
In precious memory of Diane Mary Hares PAINE. Died 17 Apr 1929. Aged 3 mths. (82)

PAINES, Fredrick William
Fredrick William. The beloved child of F and M PAINES. 2nd Battalion 8th The King's Regiment. Died 22 Dec 1878. Aged 1 yr. Suffer little children to come unto me. *(82)*

PAINTER, Charles *(P/1276)*
In memory of No 5607 Private Charles PAINTER, F Company 1st Wiltshire Regiment, who died 28 Sep 1903 at Rawalpindi. Aged 21 yrs 3 mths. Erected by his comrades. RIP. *(82)(93)(PS)*

PAIS, Ivy
In loving memory of Ivy PAIS. Dearly loved daughter of Mr and Mrs PAIS. *(82)*

PALMER, Renee *(III/487)*
Renee. Dearly beloved wife of Charles A PALMER and mother of Timothy and John. Died 5 Nov 1944. Aged 28. *(93)*

PANIZ, Giuseppe *(F/387)*
Giuseppe PANIZ. Nato e marto 2 Luglio 1970. I genitori e il fratellino. *(93)(WM)*

PARDOE, E (see GORDON HIGHLANDERS (4))
PARFITT, F (see ROYAL HORSE ARTILLERY (2))

PARKER, Fergus Erskine Wiremu *(VI/468)*
In loving memory of our darling baby Fergus Erskine Wiremu. Infant son of Mr and Mrs L Clement PARKER. Born 12 May 1940. Died 31 Dec 1940. *(82)(93)(WM)*

PARKES, S (see SOMERSET LIGHT INFANTRY (1))

PARKINSON, Emily *(F/394)*
In loving memory of our little Emily. The beloved daughter of Sergeant Major and Emily PARKINSON. 2nd King's Own Scottish Borderers. Died 27 Mar 1896. Aged 1 yr. *(82)(93)*

PARNELL, J E *(D/174)*
Sacred to the memory of J E PARNELL. Died 19 Nov 1880.
(93)(BS)

PARROTT, Norman Francis *(W/923)*
In sweet remembrance of Norman Francis. Beloved son of Lance Corporal and Mrs PARROTT. 1st King's Royal Rifles. Drowned in the bath 17 Nov 1925. Aged 1 yr 9 mths.
(82)(93)

PARRY, W *(Z/651)*
Sergeant W PARRY. 1st Battalion Lancashire Fusiliers. Died at Rawalpindi 2 Oct 1908. Aged 34 yrs. Gone but not forgotten. *(82)(93)*

PARSICK, Horace John *(M/1149)*
In loving memory of Horace John PARSICK. Pleader, High Court and Notary Public. Born 22 Sep 1846. Died 17 Jan 1903. Erected by his surviving son Charles Edmund PARSICK.
(82)(93)

PARSICK, Mary Evangeline
In loving memory of Mary Evangeline. Wife of Horace J H PARSICK. Born 11 May 1855. Died 29 Dec 1878.
(82)(mb)

PASBORG, Eric Peter   *(Y/707)*
Eric Peter PASBORG. 6 Apr 1981 - 8 Apr 1981.   *(93)(WM)*

PASSANT, Richard   *(CC/38)*
Sacred to the memory of Richard PASSANT. Band, HM's 2/8th The King's Regiment. Died Rawalpindi 8 Jun 1878. Aged 23 yrs. This tomb is erected by his brother bandsmen as a slight token of the affection they entertained for him. He is not dead but sleepeth.   *(82)(93)(PS)*

PASSY, Harry Everard   *(M/1173)*
Jesu Mercy. To the beloved memory of Harry Everard PASSY. Lieutenant Colonel Indian Army. Born 28 Aug 1854. Died 22 Dec 1904.   *(82)(93)*

PATERSON, J A   *(D/182)*
In memory of Lieutenant J A PATERSON, King's Dragoon Guards who died 10 Jun 1884. Aged 34 yrs.   *(82)(93)(PS)*

PATMORE, Francis (see GORDON HIGHLANDERS (1))

PATRICK, Thomas Eric
Thomas Eric PATRICK, who died 25 Sep 1897. Aged 55 yrs 4 mths 18 days.   *(82)*

PATTERSON, J A (see 1ST KING'S DRAGOON GUARDS (1))

PATTERSON, Neome Rose   *(X/770)*
Neome Rose. Wife of Joel Griffen PATTERSON. Died 24 Nov 1959. Aged 64 yrs. (poem)   *(93)*

PATTERSON, T (see 1ST KING'S DRAGOON GUARDS (1))

PAXTON, Harriet Mary   *(VII/1379)*
Mum. Harriet Mary PAXTON. Died 18 Jun 1953. Born 3 Aug 1870.
(93)(WM)

PAYNE, Diane Mary Nares   *(W/928)*
In precious memory of Diane Mary Nares PAYNE, who died 17 Apr 1929. Aged 3 mths.   *(93)*

PAYNE, Gerald Stuart   *(W/912)*
Our darling Boo Boo. Gerald Stuart. Son of Captain and Mrs C J PAYNE. Born 17 Aug 1921. Died 13 Feb 1922.   *(93)*

PAYNE, Henry James   *(X/796)*
IHS. Sacred to the memory of Henry James PAYNE, beloved husband of Caroline Maud PAYNE, who fell asleep 24 Dec 1938. May his spirit be with the peace of God which passeth all understanding.   *(93)*

PAYNE, I (see GORDON HIGHLANDERS (4))

PAYNE, Oscar Duke (VII/1404)
Oscar Duke PAYNE. Died 20 Apr 1966. Inserted by his wife.
(93)(WM)

PEARCE, Ellen Millicent (W/902)
RIP. Thy will be done. In loving memory of our dearest Pet Ellen Millicent, the baby child of Ellen and Harold PEARCE, who left our dear home 1 Jun 1920. Age 1 yr 4 mths. As in life we fondly loved her, we'll forget her not in death, but before God's holy altar, pray her soul may be at rest. A reaper came one morning, he came to gather flowers, and from amongst some lillies, that day he gathered ours. Erected by her sorrowful parents. (93)

PEARCE, H (see SOMERSET LIGHT INFANTRY (1))

PEARCE, Lillian Adelaide (B/149)
In loving memory of Lillian Adelaide. Dearly loved daughter of Alice and Robert PEARCE. Quartermaster Sergeant 2nd Royal Sussex Regiment. Born 25 Feb 1888. Died 8 Nov 1888.
(82)(93)(WM)

PEARL, V G (VII/1334)
With deepest affection of my darling son V G PEARL. Died 30 Jan 1941. He was the favourite, and the flower and the youngest of the four. So sweet, so calm, so kind, so meek, so softly worn, so sweetly weak, so tearless yet so tender kind, and grieved for those he left behind.
(82)(93)

PEAT, L L (S/305a)
RIP. Sacred to the memory of No 4966437 Private L L PEAT. A Company 2nd Battalion Sherwood Forresters. Died 1 Oct 1925. Aged 21 yrs. (82)(93)

PECK, Winifred
In ever loving memory of Winifred, the beloved daughter of Thomas and Margaret PECK, who died of cholera 18 Nov 1887. Aged 8 yrs 7 mths. (82)

PEIRCE (sic), Helen M B (X/849)
Helen M B PEIRCE (sic) of Cumberland, who gave nearly four years of loving service at the Station School and passed to her rest 8 Oct 1955. (93)

PEMBLE, K E (see ROYAL ARTILLERY (6))

PENFOLD, R (see ROYAL ARTILLERY (2))

PENNING (see De PENNING)

PENROSE, Amelia Priscilla and William Henry
Sacred to the memory of Amelia Priscilla PENROSE. Died 19 Nov 1928. Aged 76 yrs 9 mths. Also her husband William Henry PENROSE. Died 3 Oct 1931. Aged 80 yrs.
(82)

PENTICOST, P   (V/998)
In memory of No 3907504 Gunner P PENTICOST, 1st South Wales
Borderers, who was accidentally killed at Westridge on 14 Jan
1935. Erected by the officers, Warrant Officers, NCOs and men
of his regiment.   (82)(93)

PEPPER, George Albert Peene   (A/120)
Sacred to the memory of George Albert Peene, the beloved son
of George and Mary Ann PEPPER, who died on 29 Nov 1882. Aged
11 mths 8 days.   (82)(93)(PS)

PERCY, Keith Harold Oscar   (X/768)
Keith Harold Oscar PERCY. Headmaster, Lawrence College, Ghora
Gali. Died on 16 Mar 1960. Aged 78. RIP.
                                              (93)

PEREIRA, Lawrence Michael Justinian   (JJ/346)
Lawrence Michael Justinian. Infant child of Francis Caridade
and Anna Florinda PEREIRA. Born 8 Jan 1887. Died 15 Aug 1887.
Aged 7 mths 7 days. Sinite parvulos venire ad me quia ipsorum
est pegnum coelorum.   (82)(93)(PS)

PEREIRA, X   (HH/326)
Sacred to the memory of X PEREIRA. Born in Goa .....
                                              (93)(BS)

PERRETT, Alfred
In memory of Private Alfred PERRETT. 2nd Battalion C Company
Wiltshire Regiment. Died Rawalpindi 28 Aug 1884. Aged 22
yrs.   (82)

PETER, S B   (Y/684)
3/5th Gurkha Battalion. Rifleman S B PETER. 22 Jul 1917.
                                              (82)(93)

PETERS, Allan D Fraga   (VII/1383)
Allan D Fraga PETERS. 23 Jan 1950.   (93)

PETERS, Anna Mary   (R/278)
IHS. In undying and cherished memory of our precious mother
and devoted wife Anna Mary PETERS, who passed away peacefully
on 8 Feb 1936. Born 12 Dec 1872. Erected by her sorrowing
husband, children and grandchildren. Just a sad and fond
remembrance, loving hearts must ache the same, beside your
grave we'll often stand, with hearts that are crushed and
sore. But in the gloom dear these sweet words will come. Not
lost but gone before.   (82)(93)

PETERS, May   (VII/1364)
In loving memory of May PETERS, who passed away on 6 Jul
1947. Gone but not forgotten. Erected by her sister-in-law B
PETERS.   (93)

PETTITT, J (see ROYAL ARTILLERY (3))

PHARAOH, Herbert Henry   (Q/1311)
In loving memory of Herbert Henry PHARAOH, Corporal, 3rd
Battalion Rifle Brigade, who died from dysentery contracted on
the return march from the Tochi Valley on 2 Dec 1897. Aged 27
yrs. Interred at Rawalpindi. Thy will be done.   *(93)(PS)*

PHELAN, M (see ROYAL ARTILLERY (6))

PHILLIPS, E G   *(Y/685)*
Sacred to the memory of No 26071 Gunner E G PHILLIPS, A
Ammunition Column, Royal Horse Artillery, who departed this
life 29 Jul 1914 at Rawalpindi. Aged 33. Erected by the
officers, NCOs and men of Mountain Battery, Royal Horse
Artillery, and A Ammunition Column, Royal Horse Artillery.
                                        (82)(93)(WM)

PHILLIPS, Elizabeth   *(X/801)*
Sacred to the memory of Elizabeth. Dearly loved wife of Major
J B PHILLIPS. The Queen's Royal Regiment. Born 11 Jun 1908.
At rest 21 Oct 1941. Grant unto her O Lord eternal rest and
may perpetual light shine upon her. May she rest in peace.
Amen.   *(82)(93)*

PHILLIPS, Ellen   *(D/166)*
In loving memory of Ellen. Beloved wife of Alfred PHILLIPS.
Died 28 Mar 1882 in her 30th year. Into thine hand I commit
my spirit. Thou hast redeemed me O Lord God of truth.
                                        (82)(93)

PHILLIPS, H (see 1ST KING'S DRAGOON GUARDS (1))

PHILLIPS, Hope Asha May   *(X/765)*
Hope Asha May PHILLIPS. Died 20 Dec 1961. Inserted by her
children and grandchildren.   *(93)*

PHILLIPS, Minnie Louisa   *(D/159)*
In memory of Minnie Louisa. Daughter of V J and M J PHILLIPS.
Born 25 Jun 1885. Died 30 Nov 1885. Safe above.   *(82)(93)*

PHILLIPS, Wilfred   *(A/117)*
In memoriam. Wilfred. Son of Wilfred and Ellen PHILLIPS.
Died 18 Sep 1881. Aged 18 mths.   *(93)*

PIAIR, Blanche   *(S/304)*
In loving memory of our darling Blanche. Daughter of Mr and
Mrs F A PIAIR. Born 8 Sep 1913. Died 13 Aug 1925. RIP. In
early morn, when all was still, God gave his great command,
and silently you passed away, into a better land. God knows
how much we loved you, and counts the tears we shed, and
whispers hush she only sleeps, our loved one is not dead.
                                        (82)(93)

PICKUP, J   *(Y/687)*
Sacred to the memory of No. 23735 Acting Bombadier J PICKUP,
No 6 Mountain Battery Royal Garrison Artillery, who was
accidentally drowned at Rawalpindi 26 Oct 1913. Erected by
the officers, NCOs and men of his battery.   *(82)(93)(WM)*

PIERCE, Helen M B (see PEIRCE, Helen M B)

PIGOTT, Douglas   (L/1028)
In loving memory of Douglas PIGOTT. Born 8 Dec 1905.   Died 16
Apr 1906.   Safe in God's love will we meet.   (82)(93)

PIGOTT, Kenneth   (S/294)
In ever loving and undying memory of our darling Dad Kenneth
PIGOTT.   Born 4 Feb 1864.   Died 12 Jul 1918.   Aged 54 yrs 5
mths.   (82)(93)

PIKE, ?Ada   (A/108)
?Ada ... The beloved child of H and E PIKE. D/4.   R.A.   Died
21 Jun 1879. Aged 5 1/2 yrs.   (82)(93)(BS)

PIKE, E   (see ROYAL HORSE ARTILLERY (2))
PILCHER, S (see KING'S DRAGOON GUARDS (1))

PILL   (W/942)
... Dearly beloved daughter of Sergeant and Mrs PILL.   2nd
Battalion Gloucestershire Regiment.   (93)

PILLING, G Taylor   (X/760)
2nd Lieutenant G Taylor PILLING of Sheffield, England,   32nd
Ox and Bucks Light Infantry,   who died at Rawalpindi 23 Dec
1924. Aged 21 yrs.   (93)

PINK, A (see SOMERSET LIGHT INFANTRY (1))

PLUMMER, Alfred J   (Z/658)
Sacred to the memory of No 7352 Private Alfred J PLUMMER,   G
Company 1st Royal Sussex Regiment, who died Rawalpindi 24 Aug
1909. Aged 29 yrs.   Erected by his comrades of G company as a
token of respect.   (82)(93)(PS)

POCOCK, Frank William   (BB/12)
Sacred to the memory of Frank William POCOCK. Extra Assistant
Commissioner. Died Rawalpindi 8 Jan 1877. Aged 26 yrs.
                                          (82)(93)

PODMORE, H (see 1ST KING'S DRAGOON GUARDS (1))
POLLARD, A (see SOMERSET LIGHT INFANTRY (1))

POLLOCK, Anne
Baby Anne POLLOCK.   Daughter of Conductor and Mrs J POLLOCK.
Born 16 Jul 1945. Died 16 Jul 1945.   (82)

POLLOCK, Hugh
No 4442 Sergeant Bugler Hugh POLLOCK. 2nd Battalion Highland
Light Infantry. Died Rawalpindi 8 Aug 1897. Aged 32 yrs.(82)

PONTEFRACT, J (see WEST RIDING REGIMENT (1))

POPE, Earnest(sic) Wilfred   (VII/1337)
Loves tribute to the sacred and beautiful memory of my beloved
husband and our dear Daddy Earnest (sic) Wilfred POPE.   Died
18 Oct 1942. Aged 43 yrs.   (82)(93)

POPELY, Edward V R   *(W/947)*
Edward V R POPELY, beloved son of S. Srgt and Mrs E S POPELY,
IASC, who was called to heaven on 18 Apr 1925. Aged 9 mths 14
days. Only for a short time lent, was our baby dear,
our God took back the gift he sent and left us weeping here.
Safe in the arms of Jesus. Thy will be done. *(82)(93)*

POPLAR, Arthur (see ROYAL HORSE ARTILLERY (1))

PORTER, J H   *(V/985)*
In loving memory of No 3704951 Private J H PORTER. B Company
2nd Battalion The King's Own Royal Regiment. Died Rawalpindi
23 May 1929. Aged 27 yrs. .... by all ranks of the company.
                                  (82)(93)

POTTER, Olive Eliza   *(H/598)*
In loving remembrance of my dear wife Olive Eliza POTTER, who
died 28 Aug 1888. Aged 22 yrs 68 days. This stone is erected
by her sorrowing husband. Thy will be done. *(82)(93)(PS)*

POTTS, Thomas Fredrick   *(X/862)*
In loving memory of Major Thomas Fredrick POTTS. Royal Engineers. Born 15 May 1888. Died 10 Mar 1969. Till we meet
again. Erected by his sorrowing wife and family.
                                  (82)(93)

POWELL, Edith May
Edith May POWELL. Wife of Colonel John POWELL. Born 20 Jan
1872. Died 11 Feb 1943.   *(82)*

POWELL, G   *(IV/551)*
In memory of No 4031226 Private G POWELL. 1st Battalion
K.S.L.I. Died 4 Sep 1933. Erected by his comrades.
                                  (82)(93)

POWELL, James *(E/194)*
In loving memory of
James POWELL. Died
10 Feb 1887. Aged
74 yrs and 3 mths.
(82)(93)(WM)

POWELL, John
(see
ROYAL ARTILLERY (4))

POWELL, William
(see
ROYAL ARTILLERY (4))

<u>ROYAL ARTILLERY (4))</u>

PRATICE, James *(G/433)*
Sacred to the memory of No 127 Sergeant James PRATICE, 78th Highlanders (late 72nd Highlanders), who died at Rawalpindi 31 Dec 1888. Aged 36 yrs. The hour of my departure comes, I hear the voice that calls me home. At last O Lord let troubles cease, and let thy servant die in peace. *(82)(93)*

PRATT, Edward *(P/1282)*
Sacred to the memory of A^c Bombadier Edward PRATT, F Battery, Royal Horse Artillery, who died 7 Jul 1903. Aged 29 yrs. Erected by his comrades. *(93)(PS)*

PRATT, George
In affectionate remembrance of George PRATT. Schoolmaster. Died 2 Dec 1872. Aged 34 yrs. *(82)*

PREEDY, Caroline Anne *(Q/1322)*
IHS. RIP. In loving memory of Caroline Anne PREEDY, the beloved wife of Gunner F PREEDY, No 5 MB, R A, who died at Rawalpindi 21 Nov 1896. Aged 32 yrs. Good in heart in friendship sound, patient in suffering, beloved by all around. Her trials are o'er, her work forever done, a life of everlasting joy she has now begun. This stone was erected by her sorrowing husband. *(82)(93)(PS)*

PRICE, Amy Constance *(M/1217)*
Gentle Jesus meek and mild, look upon a little child, pity my simplicity, suffer me to come to thee. In memory of Amy Constance (little Tommy), beloved daughter of Sergeant Major and Mrs PRICE, Somerset Light Infantry, who died 9 Dec 1900. Aged 4 yrs and 7 mths. Go to prepare a place for you. *(93)*

PRICE, Charles Daniel
Charles Daniel PRICE. Died 9 Jan 1920. Aged 59 yrs. *(82)*

PRICE, Owen *(IV/520)*
In loving memory No 3955843 Private Owen PRICE. 2nd Battn The Welch Regt. Died Rawalpindi 29 Nov 1931. Aged 23 yrs. *(82)(93)*

PRICE, T (see ROYAL HORSE ARTILLERY (2))
PRIESTLEY, J (see WEST RIDING REGIMENT (1))

PRIESTLEY, Louisa Jane *(A/114)*
Sacred to the memory of Louisa Jane, the beloved daughter of Quartermaster Sergeant and Mrs PRIESTLEY, who departed this life 26 Feb 1881. Aged 5 yrs 2 mths. She sleeps in peace. *(93)*

PRING, E G *(Y/731)*
To the memory of No 2306825 L/Corporal E G PRING, Royal Corps of Signals, who died at Rawalpindi 8 Feb 1926. Aged 22 yrs. Erected by all ranks of No 1 (Line) Company, B Corps Signals and comrades of D Divisional Signals. *(93)*

PROBETS, William
Driver William PROBETS. F Company 1st Wiltshire Regiment. Died Rawalpindi 12 Feb 1905. Aged 28 yrs. Erected by his brother. *(82)*

HARLEY STREET CEMETERY

PROCTOR, Horace   (Y/686)
Rifleman Horace PROCTOR, A Company, 4th Battalion, King's Royal Rifle Corps, who was drowned at Baracow 16 Apr 1914. Aged 21 yrs. Erected by the officers and NCOs and men of his company.   (82)(93)

PULSFORD, W H (see ROYAL ARTILLERY (6))

PYE, Edward
Sacred to the memory of No 9804 Shoeing Smith Edward PYE. 57th Battery RFA. Died Rawalpindi 16 Dec 1904. Aged 26 yrs.
                                                    (82)

PYMENT (see ROYAL GARRISON ARTILLERY (2))

PYMONT, A   (O/1110)
Sacred to the memory of No 26243 Gunner A PYMONT. No 7 MB RGA who died at Rawalpindi 1 Jun 1908.   (82)(93)(PS)

QUAINTON, Margaret Anne   (VI/458)
In loving memory of Margaret Anne QUAINTON. Born 11 Jan 1964. Died 3 Jun 1966. (poem)   (93)

QUAMBER, A W   (X/817)
In loving memory of Mrs A W QUAMBER (Una SWIFT). Born 29 Jan
1890. Died 15 Jan 1942.   *(93)*

QUAMBER, Ernest   *(X/816)*
Rest in peace. In loving memory of Mr Ernest QUAMBER. Born 1
Apr 1923. Died 6 Jan 1969.   *(93)*

QUAMBER, Oscar Julian   *(X/789)*
In loving memory of Oscar Julian QUAMBER. Born 1 Jul 1913.
Died 23 Dec 1934.   *(93)*

QUICK, Derrick   *(T/366)*
In loving memory of our Derrick. The infant son of D H and
Mrs A N QUICK. Born 29 Mar 1928. Died 29 Mar 1928. Here lies
our darling little son who from our arms has flown,unto a
brighter world above, where sorrow ne'er is known.RIP.*(82)(93)*

QUICK, Margaret   *(M/1133)*
In loving memory of Margaret QUICK who died 19 Apr 1898. Aged
45 yrs 6 mths. Deeply regretted. By her sorrowing husband
and children.   *(82)(93)*

QUIGLEY, Elizabeth Ann   *(X/790)*
Peace perfect peace. Sacred to the memory of Elizabeth Ann
QUIGLEY. The dearly beloved wife of the late John QUIGLEY.
Died 25 May 1935. Aged 79 yrs 11 mths. We miss her and
mourn her in silence unseen and dwell in the memories of days
that have been. Unknown to the world, she stands by our side
and whispers these words "Death cannot divide". Eternal rest
give to her O Lord, and let perpetual light shine upon her.
May she rest in peace.   *(82)(93)(WM)*

QUIGLEY, John   *(X/742)*
Peace perfect peace. Sacred to the memory of John QUIGLEY,
the dearly beloved husband of Mrs Elizabeth QUIGLEY, who died
suddenly of heart failure at Rawalpindi on 12 Mar 1930. Aged
79 yrs. Forget no, nor never will, we loved him here, we love
him still, nor love him less, although he's gone, from us to
his eternal home. We miss him and mourn him in silence
unseen, and dwell in the memories of days that have been.
Unknown to the world he stands by our side, and whispers these
words, death cannot divide. In loving cherished memory of our
darling Daddy. Eternal rest give to him O Lord, and let
perpetual light shine upon him. May he rest in peace. Amen.
Erected by his sorrowing wife and children. *(82)(93)*

QUIN, Edward   *(D/165)*
Sacred to the memory of Private Edward QUIN, 8th Kings Royal
Irish Hussars, who was killed at Rawalpindi 17 Aug 1882. Aged
23 yrs.   *(93)(BS)*

QUINN, George   *(S/288)*
In memory of No. 4036 Sergeant George QUINN. 10th Royal
Hussars.   *(82)(93)*

QUINN, J   (see GORDON HIGHLANDERS (4))

QUINTON, Albert (see ROYAL HORSE ARTILLERY (1))

RABJOHNS, Dollie   (III/483)
In loving memory of Dollie. Dearly beloved wife of CSM W
RABJOHNS. 1/Glosters. Born 3 Mar 1899. Died 28 Jun 1942.
                                                 (93)

RADFORD, James
No 8992 Lance Corporal James RADFORD. C Company 1st Battalion
Royal Sussex Regiment. Died Rawalpindi 3 Aug 1914. Aged 25
yrs.   (82)

RALSTON, William J H   (IV/496)
In loving memory of Major William J H RALSTON, 2/7th Rajputs,
Indian Army, the dearly loved husband of Kitty RALSTON, who
fell asleep suddenly at Rawalpindi 14 Feb 1928. Aged 45 yrs.
                                          (82)(93)(WM)

RAMPLING, Clara Sophia   (Q/1313)
In loving memory of Clara Sophia, the beloved wife of Sergeant
RAMPLING, Royal Artillery, who died at Rawalpindi 19 Jan 1897.
                                              (82)(93)

RANDALL, W (see ROYAL HORSE ARTILLERY (3))

RANDALL, William   (N/1428)
Sacred to the memory of Bombadier William RANDALL. B Battery
Royal Horse Artillery. Died Rawalpindi 24 Jun 1895. Aged 24
yrs.   (82)(93)(BS)

RANSOM, J C (see ROYAL HORSE ARTILLERY (3))

RANSOM, John Charles   (K/632)
Sacred to the memory of Bombadier John Charles RANSOM, B
Battery Royal Horse Artillery, who was accidentally drowned in
the Sohan River Rawalpindi 24 May 1892. Aged 24 yrs.
                                          (82)(93)(BS)

RATCLIFFE, Isabelle   (IV/577)
Sacred to the memory of Isabelle. Wife of Sergeant R
RATCLIFFE, Royal Corps of Signals. Died Rawalpindi 29 Mar
1936. Erected by all ranks of A Corps Signals. (82)(93)

READ, Stanley John   (Y/719)
Sacred to the memory of No 1039385 Driver Stanley John READ,
126th Battery, Royal Field Artillery, who departed this life
on 4 Oct 1921. Aged 20 yrs.   (82)(93)

RECTOR, Gail Judith   (VI/471)
In loving memory of Gail Judith. Infant daughter of Trevor
and Marjorie RECTOR. Born 4 Dec 1939. Died 23 Dec 1940.
                                              (82)(93)

REED, Arthur   (Y/715)
In memory of No 5373306 Private Arthur REED. D Company 2nd
Battalion Oxfordshire and Bucks Light Infantry. Died at
Rawalpindi 5 Jul 1924.   (82)(93)

REEHIL, Augustine   (VII/1356)
Sister M Augustine REEHIL. Died 14 Jul 1960. RIP.   (93)(WM)

REES, Elsie Agnes   (V/999)
Rest in peace. In ever loving memory of our beloved mother
Elsie Agnes REES. Born 16 Dec 1876. Died 30 Dec 1934.
                                                (82)(93)

REEVE, Henary (sic)   (G/413)
Sacred to the memory of No 3162 Private Henary (sic) REEVE,
who died at Rawalpindi 5 Jun 1890. Aged 20 yrs 5 mths. E
Troop, 3rd Dragoon Guards.   (82)(93)(BS)

REGAN, James   (F/383)
Sacred to the memory of James REGAN. Erected by his wife.
Sweet Jesus Mercy. RIP.   (82)(93)

ROADSIGN OUTSIDE FLASHMAN'S HOTEL, RAWALPINDI

REID, Alex Ashley Edward (see ROYAL ARTILLERY (5))

REID, Arthur   (Z/663)
Private Arthur REID. 10th Royal Hussars ....   (93)

REID, Cissy Maud   *(M/1202)*
Our darling Cissy Maud. Daughter of Sergeant and Mrs REID. 12th Royal Lancers. Died 12 May 1905. Aged 2 yrs 8 mths. We loved her, O no tongue can tell, how much we loved her and how well. God loved her too and thought it best to take her home with him to rest.   *(82)(93)*

REID, William (see ROYAL HORSE ARTILLERY (1))

REILLY, Ellen   *(GG/226)*
Sacred to the memory of Ellen, the beloved wife of Sergeant Instructor in Musketry J REILLY, HM's 38th Regiment, who died at Rawalpindi 24 Apr 1871. Aged 33 yrs. *(82)(93)(BS)*

REILY, Mary Anthony   *(VII/1372)*
Sister Mary Anthony REILY. Presentation Sister. Born in Westmeath, Ireland 13 Aug 1891. Died Rawalpindi 15 Jun 1974.
                                           (93)(WM)

REMBLANCE, William   *(P/1270)*
Sacred to the memory of No 9831 Gunner William REMBLANCE, 57th Battery, RFA, who died at Rawalpindi 20 Aug 1902. Age 24 yrs 3 mths. Erected by the officers, NCOs and men of the Battery.   *(93)(PS)*

RENAULT, John (see ROYAL ARTILLERY (5))

RENNIE, William   *(O/1101)*
In memory of No 7357 Private William RENNIE, 2nd Gordon Highlanders, who died at Baracao on 12 Jul 1902. Aged 20 yrs. Gone but not forgotten. Erected by the officers, NCOs and men of F company.   *(93)*

RENNY, George (see ROYAL ARTILLERY (10))

RENNY, Harriett Charlotte   *(N/1457)*
In loving memory of Harriett Charlotte, dearly loved wife of Major George B RENNY, Indian Staff Corps, who died 27 Apr 1895. Born Feb 1850. Thy will be done. *(82)(93)*

REVENING, T H (see ROYAL ARTILLERY (6))

REYNOLDS, Frederick R   *(P/1251)*
Sacred to the memory of Frederick R REYNOLDS. 4th Royal Irish Dragoon Guards. Died 22 Feb 1901. Aged 26 yrs. Erected by comrades of D Squadron.   *(82)(93)*

RICE, Percy   *(IX/1010)*
In memory of Percy RICE, Apprentice IAOC, who was accidentally drowned at Chaklala 28 Sep 1939. Erected by his officers and comrades.   *(93)*

RICE, Robert   *(L/1031)*
Robert RICE. 2nd King's Royal Rifle Corps. Died 16 Nov 1901. A token of respect from Rifleman OWINGS, 4th King's Royal Rifle Corps, 1913.   *(82)(93)(PS)*

RICH, Henry Bayard   (E/185)
In loving memory of Henry Bayard RICH, Captain Royal Engineers, who died from the effect of an accident at polo 17 Nov 1884.   (82)(93)(WM)

RICHARDS, Charles   (Z/671)
In memory of No 1840 Private Charles RICHARDS. 10th Royal Hussars. Died Rawalpindi....   (82)(93)

RICHARDS, David Poley   (D/180)
In memory of David Poley RICHARDS. Died 24 Oct 1880. Aged 73 yrs.   (93)

RICHARDS, E   (IV/578)
In memory of No 3908086 Private E RICHARDS. 1st Battalion South Wales Borderers. Died Westridge 12 Apr 1936. Erected by the officers, warrant officers, NCOs and men of his Regiment.   (82)(93)

RICHARDS, Edward Groves   (X/744)
In affectionate remembrance of Edward Groves RICHARDS, Lieutenant, Indian Army Service Corps, who died at Rawalpindi 19 Mar 1931. Aged 33 yrs 8 mths. Erected by his brother officers. RIP.   (82)(93)(end)

RICHARDS, Francis Howe   (X/792)
In memory of Francis Howe RICHARDS, DSO. Commanding 5th Field Brigade, Royal Artillery. Accidentally killed by a falling boulder on Kohala Road. 20 Apr 1937. Aged 46. (82)(93)(WM)

RICHARDSON, F (see SOMERSET LIGHT INFANTRY (1))

RICKARDS, Mary   (N/1472)
In loving memory of Mary. Infant daughter of Cecilia and Edward RICKARDS. Died 25 Feb 1899.   (93)

RICKMAN, G J (see 1ST KING'S DRAGOON GUARDS (1))

RICKMAN, George James
In loving memory of George James. The beloved son of Frederick and Mary RICKMAN. King's Dragoon Guards. Died 19 Aug 1886. Aged 3 mths 15 days.   (82)

RICKMAN, May   (JJ/347)
In loving memory of little May, the beloved daughter of Frederick and Mary RICKMAN. King's Dragoon Guards. Died 22 Apr 1887. Aged 3 yrs 1 mth. But to us this dear one was but lent, we thought her surely given, but Jesus called her and she went to dwell with him in heaven. (82)(93)

RIDDELL, R S (see 70TH REGIMENT (1) and (5))

RIELLY, Mary   (AA/6)
Sacred to the memory of Mary, the beloved wife of Sergeant D RIELLY, HM's 70th Regiment, who departed this life on 13 Oct 1858. Aged 28 yrs. Also her infant son who died 8 Nov 1858. Aged 1 yr 3 mths.   /continued.........

REILLY, Mary (cont)
Mourn not for me my husband dear, we are not dead but sleeping here. We were not yours, but Christ's alone, He loved us best and took us home. J BURNS.   *(82)(93)(BS)*

RIFFEN, William   *(L/1050)*
Sacred to the memory of No 4418 Driver William RIFFEN, 57th Battery, Royal Field Artillery, who died at Rawalpindi on 15 May 1903. Aged 25 yrs 3 mths. Erected by the officers, NCOs and men of the battery.   *(93)*

RING, James   *(M/1135)*
Sacred to the memory of Lieutenant Colonel James RING, Royal Army Medical Corps, who died at Rawalpindi on 16 Oct 1898. Erected by his brother officers in token of their high esteem. Resurgam.   *(82)(93)(mb)*

RIORDAN, Michael (see ROYAL ARTILLERY (5))

RITCHIE, Henry   *(D/167)*
In loving memory of Henry RITCHIE. Born 5 Apr 1841. Died 19 Jul 1881. In the midst of life we are in death.
                                        (82)(93)(WM)

ROACH, Jack Herbert   *(M/1218)*
In loving memory of our dearly beloved son Jack Herbert ROACH. Born Nowshera 5 Feb 1901. Died Rawalpindi 4 Apr 1901.
                                        (82)(93)

ROBERTS, Frank   *(Q/1319)*
Frank ROBERTS, Rifle Brigade, who departed this life at Rawalpindi 11 Jul 1897. Aged 25 yrs. The Lord gave and the Lord hath taken away, blessed be the name of the Lord. More than conquerors through him that loved us.   *(82)(93)*

ROBERTS, John (see 98TH REGIMENT (1))
ROBERTS, T   (see ROYAL GARRISON ARTILLERY (4))

ROBERTSON, Elsie Isabel
Elsie Isabel. The darling child of John ROBERTSON, SMD, and Isabella, his wife. Born 25 Feb 1892. Died 22 Jun 1893. *(82)*

ROBEY, Henry Lewis (see ROYAL ARTILLERY (5))

ROBEY, Louis Harry   *(I/407)*
Pray for the repose of the soul of Louis Harry ROBEY of 5 Company, SDRA, who died Rawalpindi 5 May 1894.
                                        (82)(93)(BS)(mb)

ROBINSON, A E
In memory of Gunner A E ROBINSON, No 8 Mountain Battery, Royal Garrison Artillery. Died Rawalpindi 16 Apr 1908. NYAZ ALI & CO, RAWALPINDI.   *(82)*

ROBINSON, Charles Frederick   *(B/145)*
In loving memory of Charles Frederick. Infant son of Captain C T ROBINSON. Born 9 Dec 1889. Died 26 Nov 1890. *(82)(93)*

ROBINSON, Elizabeth Ann (VV/528)
In loving memory of darling Betty. Elizabeth Ann ROBINSON. Daughter of Captain and Mrs ROBINSON, IAOC. Born 28 Nov 1942. Died 6 Jul 1943. (93)

ROBINSON, Fanny Clara (X/745)
IHS. In thee have I trusted. Fanny Clara. Beloved wife of Henry Poston ROBINSON. Government Service, Retired. Born 28 Jul 1856. Died 12 Mar 1931. At rest with God. Erected by her family as a humble token of their deep love and reverence and of their lasting sorrow. (82)(93)

ROBINSON, Henry Poston (X/804)
In thee have I trusted. Sacred to the memory of Henry Poston ROBINSON. Government Service Retired. Born 24 Aug 1847. Died 25 Nov 1931. At rest with God. Erected by his family as a humble token of their deep love and reverence and of their lasting sorrow. (82)(93)

ROBINSON, John (P/1287)
Sacred to the memory of No 3839 Private John ROBINSON, H Company, 1st Battalion Wiltshire Regiment, who died Rawalpindi 11 Dec 1903. Aged 27 yrs 9 mths. Erected by H Company as a mark of esteem. Gone but not forgotten. (82)(93)

ROBINSON, T (see UNNAMED REGIMENT (1))

ROBINSON, T
Sacred to the memory of Private T ROBINSON, who died of cholera on the march from Mianmir to Rawalpindi 4 Nov 1887. Aged 24 and 1/2 yrs. Also Private J W JOHNSON who was drowned while bathing in the park at Rawalpindi 18 Mar 1888. Aged 21 yrs. (82)

ROBINSON, William (GG/214)
Sacred to the memory of Lance Corporal William ROBINSON. B Company 70th Regiment. Died at Rawalpindi 21 Dec 1871. Aged 24 yrs. This stone is erected by the officers, non commissioned officers and men of the company as a mark of respect to his memory. (82)(93)(BS)

ROBSON (O/1077)
IHS. In loving memory of the beloved infant daughter of G and M ROBSON. Died 23 Dec 1894 at Rawalpindi. (82)(93)

ROCKER, Teddy (W/952)
Sacred to the memory of Teddy. Beloved son of Corporal and Mrs ROCKER. 2nd Ox and Bucks Regiment. Born 9 Dec 19.. Died 27 Nov 19... (82)(93)

RODHAM, C H B (X/870)
Jesus is the resurrection and the life. He who believes in him shall never die. Brigadier (Retired) C H B RODHAM, SQA, CBE, DSO, MC. Born 1902. Died 16 Jun 1973. Served in the British Army for 28 yrs. Served in the Pakistan Army for 15 yrs. Director Pakistan Sports Board for 11 yrs. Erected by Mohd Ishtiaq and family. (93)

RODRIGUES, Frederick George   (VII/1366)
Frederick George RODRIGUES (Freddie). Born 17 Apr 1895. Died 27 Feb 1949. Erected by wife and children. *(93)(WM)*

ROGARS, J   (AA/1)
Sacred to the memory of the under mentioned men who died at Rawalpindi on the following dates: Private J ROGARS. Died 30 Aug 1874. Aged 22 yrs........... *(93)*

ROGERS, J H (see 1ST KING'S DRAGOON GUARDS (1))

ROGERS, John   (E/201)
Sacred to the memory of Private John ROGERS, who departed this life 8 Oct 1887. Aged 21 yrs. Follow peace with all men and holiness without which no man shall see the Lord. (HEB XII.14) Erected by the officers, NCOs and men of his troop. *(82)(93)*

ROGERS, Lillie and Kathleen   (L/1053)
In sacred and loving memory of Lillie, the beloved wife of Conductor J ROGERS, who departed this life 22 Nov 1904. Aged 28 yrs. And her little Kathleen, who fell asleep 26 Mar 1904. Aged 6 mths. Lord thy will be done. *(82)(93)*

ROGERS, Mary Anne   (JJ/357)
Sacred to the memory of Mary Anne, the dearly beloved wife of George Joseph ROGERS, Army Commisseriat Department, who departed this life on 5 Aug 1867. Aged 29 yrs. Deeply and sincerely regretted. She was a fond and devoted wife and mother, loving sister and a sincere friend. The Lord gave and the Lord hath taken away, blessed be the name of the Lord. Requiescat in pace. SUNTOKE AND SON, AGRA. *(82)(93)(WM)*

ROGERS, Maude Edith   (DD/59)
Sacred to the memory of Maude Edith. Beloved child of Captain and Mrs R G ROGERS. 20th Regiment, PI. Died 29 Nov 1866(?) .... Aged 4 mths 22 days. It is not the will of your Father which is in heaven that one of these little ones should perish. SOOKH LALL & CO, SCULPTORS. *(82)(93)(PS)*

ROGERS, William George   (VII/1340)
IHS. In loving memory of William George ROGERS. Born 11 Jul 1870. Died 16 Jul 1944. Rest in peace. Hold thou thy cross before my closing eyes, shine through the gloom and point me to the skies. Heaven's morning breaks and earths vain shadow flee in life, in death, O Lord, abide with me. *(82)(93)*

ROONEY, R   (Y/740)
Sacred to the memory of No 1054429 Signaller R ROONEY, 33rd Field Battery Royal Artillery, who died at Rawalpindi 23 Feb 1927. Aged 23 yrs 1 mth. Erected by the officers, NCOs and men of the battery. *(82)(93)*

ROPER, John Riddall Stokley
Captain John Riddall Stokley ROPER, RA. Died 9 Jan 1935. May he rest in peace. *(82)*

ROSS, George Edward   (O/1082)
In loving memory of George Edward ROSS. The beloved son of
James George and Mary ROSS. Born 2 Mar 1890. Died 20 Aug
1898. Deeply regretted by his sorrowing father. Suffer
little children to come unto me and forbid them not, for of
such is the kingdom of God. MARK 10.14.
                                             (82)(93)

ROSS, Joseph (see ROYAL GARRISON ARTILLERY (3))

ROSS, Mary   (J/446)
In loving memory of Mary ROSS. Beloved wife of James George
ROSS. Died 7 Jun 1891. Aged 29 yrs 1 mth. Not lost but gone
before to be with God which is very far better.
                                             (82)(93)(mb)

ROSS, Walter   (III/484)
In memory of our loved one Walter ROSS. Died 24 May 1942.
Aged 61 yrs.   (93)

ROTTON, Douglas Edward   (B/139)
In loving memory of Douglas Edward. Only child of Bertha and
Horace ROTTON. Died 10 May 1887. Aged 10 mths 27 days.
                                             (82)(93)

ROUTLEFF, George Cyril   (A/110)
In loving memory of George Cyril. The dear child of Conductor
and Mrs A J ROUTLEFF. Died 23 Dec 1879. Aged 1 mth 8 days.
                                             (82)(93)

ROUTLEFF, Winifred Daisy   (CC/37)
In loving memory of Winifred Daisy. The beloved child of Conductor W J ROUTLEFF. Born 19 Jun 1878. Died 13 Feb 1879.
                                             (82)(93)

ROVERY, F (see ROYAL FIELD ARTILLERY (1))

ROWAN, H   (BB/10)
Erected by the non commissioned officers and men of I Battery,
Royal Horse Artillery, A Brigade. Sacred to the memory of
Trumpeter C D WOODS. Died 15 Dec 1877. Aged 19 yrs. Also
Gunner H ROWAN. Died 26 Jul 1878. Aged 25 yrs.
                                             (82)(93)(BS)

ROWBURY, Elizabeth   (JJ/362)
IHS. In loving memory of our mother Elizabeth ROWBURY,
relict of the late J ROWBURY, who died at Murree on 20 Sep
1890. Aged 63 yrs 7 mths 14 days. Requiescat in pace.
                                             (82)(93)(WM)

ROWBURY, James   (E/202)
Sacred to the memory of James ROWBURY, who died 11 Nov 1887.
Aged 69 yrs 10 mths 17 days. I am the resurrection and the
life. He that believeth in me though he is dead shall live.
JOHN.XI.25.   (82)(93)(WM)

ROWELL, Annie Ellen (M/1206)
Annie Ellen ROWELL. Daughter of Frank and Annie Ellen ROWELL. 3 days old. Born 29 Apr 1904. Died 3 May 1904. Suffer little children to come unto me. (82)(93)

ROWLEY, Harry (Z/659)
In memory of No 5502 Private Harry ROWLEY. 10th Royal Hussars who died at Rawalpindi ...... (93)(WM)

ROY, Johnson William (X/853)
Johnson William ROY. 28 Aug 1899. Died 20 Apr 1964. Inserted by his sorrowing wife Kathleen and his children Kenneth, Theresa and Joseph. (93)

ROYAL, J (see YORKSHIRE REGIMENT (1))

ROYDS, Gerard Wilfred (X/854)
Gerard Wilfred ROYDS. Beloved husband of Sadie. Died as a result of an air crash 12 Dec 1964. Aged 61 yrs. (93)

ROYDS, Sarah (X/855)
Sarah ROYDS. Beloved wife of Gerrie. Died as a result of an air crash 12 Dec 1964. Aged 49 yrs. (93)

RUDD, Lily Clara (N/1478)
Our darling Lily Clara. Died 3 Apr 1898. Aged 7 mths 23 days. Daughter of Robert and Edith E RUDD. Colour Sergeant Queen's Royal West Surrey Regiment. Had he asked us, we should say, Lord we love her let her stay. In lonely grief we sigh, for our dear babe no longer nigh. (82)(93)(PS)

RUDDOCK, Fred (see 70TH REGIMENT (4))

RUIZ, Bernard (VIII/1419)
Bro. Bernard RUIZ. FMS. Born 20 Aug 1916. Rel Profession 8 Sep 1934. Died 25 Feb 1982. Fondly remembered by his family, Marist Brothers, his friends and his former pupils.
 (93)(WM)

RUNDALL, C D
Sacred to the memory of Lieutenant C D RUNDALL. XIX PNI. Died Rawalpindi 24 Jan 1870. Aged 24 yrs. (82)

RUSSELL, G (see 70TH REGIMENT (1))

RUSSELL, J (EE/80)
Sacred to the memory of Corporal J RUSSELL. HM's 70th Regiment. Died 1872. Aged 28. Erected by the officers, non commissioned officers and men of the above as a tribute of respect. (82)(93)(BS)

RUSSELL, P (see SOMERSET LIGHT INFANTRY (1))

RUTHERFORD, James Simmers (X/838)
Sacred to the memory of Major James Simmers RUTHERFORD. Royal Signals who was tragically killed in an accident at Jhelum on 3 Feb 1951. (93)

RUTHERFORD, Thomas S (N/1433)
Sacred to the memory of Corporal Thomas S RUTHERFORD, B Squadron, 4th Royal Irish Dragoon Guards, who died 24 Dec 1895. Aged 27 yrs. *(82)(93)(PS)*

RUTLEDGE, Olive Brenda
To the glory of God and in loving memory of Olive Brenda RUTLEDGE. Dearly beloved wife of Lieutenant L H RUTLEDGE. 1st/8th Gurkha Rifles. Born 19 Oct 1887. Died 13 May 1919.
(82)

RUTTER, A E (P/1245)
Acting Corporal G FRANKLIN. 3rd Battalion Rifle Brigade. Died Rawalpindi 17 Aug 1900. Aged 23 yrs 11 mths. Also of Acting Corporal A E RUTTER of the same Battalion, who died at Rawalpindi 28 Aug 1900. Aged 28 yrs. Erected by the Corporals of the 3rd Battalion Rifle Brigade as a mark of esteem.
(82)(93)

RYALL, Margaret Ada and Ruth Catherine (D/155)
Sacred to the memory of Margaret Ada. Beloved wife of Sergeant O R RYALL, Commissariat Department, who departed this life on 1 Dec 1883. Aged 29 yrs and 4 mths. Also of Ruth Catherine, their daughter, who departed this life 30 Nov 1883 aged 10 days. *(82)(93)(BS)*

RYAN, James (HH/328)
Sacred to the memory of Lieutenant James RYAN. Assistant Engineer, Military Works. Born in Limerick 7 Jul 1833. Died Rawalpindi 9 Jan 1883. Erected by his sorrowing widow and children. *(82)(93)*

RYAN, Thomas (L/1057)
Sacred to the memory of No 8405 Private Thomas RYAN, F Company 1/The Cannaught (sic) Rangers, who died of cholera at Rawalpindi on 12 May 1908. Aged 28 yrs and 1 mth. Erected by the officers, NCOs and men of his company.
(93)

RYAN, W C (P/1277)
Quartermaster Sergeant W C RYAN who departed this life 28 Jan 1903. Aged 38 yrs. Erected by his comrades of F Battery Royal Horse Artillery. Had he asked us, well we know, we should cry, O spare this blow. Yet with streaming tears should pray, Lord, we love him, let him stay.
(82)(93)

RYMILLS (M/1224)
... son of Fred and Nellie RYMILLS who died at Rawalpindi 9 Aug 1902. Aged 1 yr 6 days. Thy will be done.
(82)(93)

RYMILLS, Martha Ellen (P/1275)
In loving memory of Martha Ellen. Beloved wife of Corporal F G RYMILLS. Died 15 Nov 1903. Aged 24 yrs 6 mths. Erected by her husband. RIP. *(82)(93)*

SADLEIR, Josey   (M/1200)
In sweet memory of Josey. Son of Sergeant and Mrs SADLEIR. S
& T Corps. Born 6 Oct 1904. Died 21 May 1905.
                                        (82)(93)

SADLER, Bertie
In memory of our little treasure Bertie. Died 25 Apr 1885.
Aged 4 mths. The dearly loved child of Sergeant E A and Mrs E
SADLER. Royal Artillery.   (82)

SADLER, H   (IV/511)
No 6137022 Private H SADLER of HQ wing, 1st Battalion East
Surrey Regiment. Died Rawalpindi 4 Dec 1929. Aged 24 yrs.
Erected by all ranks of HQ wing.   (82)(93)

SALKELD   (W/970)
In memory of the infant son of Lieutenant Colonel and Mrs P E
SALKELD who died 28 May 1947. Aged 12 hours.
                                        (82)(93)

SALT, Frances Patricia   (W/911)
Frances Patricia. Daughter of Lieutenant and Mrs A C J SALT,
STC. Died 9 Feb 1921. Aged 16 days. Suffer little children
to come unto me.   (93)

SAMPSON, E   (D/164)
Sacred to the memory of Private E SAMPSON, 8th King's Royal
Irish Hussars, who died at Rawalpindi 25 Oct 1882.
                                        (82)(93)(BS)

SAMPSON, W   (N/1450)
In loving memory of Sergeant W SAMPSON, 1st Devon Regiment,
who died at Rawalpindi 6 Dec 1893. Aged 32 yrs. This stone is
erected as a token of esteem by his..... (82)(93)(PS)

SAMUEL, Joseph   (IV/544)
Sacred to the memory of No. 781165 (?) Driver Joseph SAMUEL.
4th Field (Coles Kop) Battery, Royal Artillery. Died
Rawalpindi 29 Nov 1932. Aged 22 yrs.   (82)(93)

SAMUELLS, Alexander Ingle   (C/96)
Sacred to the memory of Captain Alexander Ingle SAMUELLS,
Second In Command, 32 Punjab Pioneers, who died at Rawalpindi
7 Jul 1880. Aged 37 yrs.   (93)(mb)

SANDERS, A C   (Y/708)
Sacred to the memory of No 4963656 Boy A C SANDERS. HQ Wing.
2nd Battalion The Sherwood Forresters. Died 21 Nov 1923.
Aged 17 yrs 4 mths.   (82)(93)

SANDERSON, Constance Lucy Cecilia   (M/1208)
In loving memory of Constance Lucy Cecilia. Beloved daughter of Edward and Lucy SANDERSON. Died Rawalpindi 18 Apr 1904. Aged 7 mths 14 days. Had he asked us, well we know, we would cry, O spare this blow....   (82)(93)

SANDERSON, J   (Y/737)
In memory of No 18764 Private J SANDERSON. No 25 MT Company, Royal Army Service Corps. Died at Rawalpindi 16 Oct 1922. Erected by all ranks of the company.   (82)(93)

SANGSTER, Charlotte (see GORDON HIGHLANDERS (4))

SANKER, Elizabeth Rose
In loving memory of our darling baby Elizabeth Rose. The beloved daughter of Phillip and Elizabeth SANKER. Died 3 Nov 1897. Aged 3 mths.   (82)

SANKER, Katherine Frances
In loving memory of our darling baby Katherine Frances. The beloved daughter of Phillip and Elizabeth SANKER. Died 30 Nov 1897. Aged 3 1/2 mths.   (82)

SARATT, R
No 2312168(?) Signalman R SARATT, Royal Corps of Signals, who died Rawalpindi 18 Jul 1924. Aged 20 yrs. Erected by his comrades of No 2 Wireless Company, B Corps Signals from his loving Mum and Dad.   (82)

SARGENT, Henry   (G/417)
Sacred to the memory of Lance Corporal Henry SARGENT who died at Rawalpindi 1 Aug 1890. Aged 29. Erected by the NCOs and men of C Troop as a mark of respect.   (82)(93)(BS)

SARGON, John   (VI/459)
In loving memory of John SARGON. Born 9 Jan 1966. Died 23 Jan 1966. (poem)   (93)

SASS, Alfred   (C/106)
In proud memory of Alfred SASS. Construction Engineer. Jhelum Valley Railway. Born 27 Feb 1829 at Bloomsbury (England). Died 27 Jun 1879. To one we owe so much yet know so little. RIP. Erected by his grandsons Alfred, Joseph and Leonard.   (93)

SAVAGE, Arthur (see ROYAL HORSE ARTILLERY (1))

SAWERS, David   (O/1105)
In memory of Gunner David SAWERS, No 86 Company Royal Garrison Artillery, who died at Rawalpindi 4 Jan 1903. Aged 21 yrs 11 mths. Erected by the officers, NCOs and men of his Company as a token of their esteem and regard. NEYAZ ALI, SCULPTOR, RAWALPINDI.   (82)(93)

SAWYER, Elizabeth (see ROYAL HORSE ARTILLERY (1))

SAWYER, Elizabeth Rose   (F/392)
In loving memory of our darling baby Elizabeth Rose, the
beloved daughter of Philip and Elizabeth SAWYER, who died on
3 Nov 1897. Aged 3 mths. In a world of pain and care, Lord
thou wouldst no longer leave it, to thy meadows bright and
fair, lovingly thou dost receive it. Clothed in robes of
spotless white, now it dwells with thee in light. *(93)*

SAWYER, Katherine (see ROYAL HORSE ARTILLERY (1))

SAWYER, Kathleen Frances   (F/390)
In loving memory of our darling baby Kathleen Frances, the
beloved daughter of Philip and Elizabeth SAWYER, who died on
30 Nov 1897. Aged 3 mths. In a world of pain and care, Lord
thou wouldst no longer leave it, to thy meadows bright and
fair, lovingly thou dost receive it. Clothed in robes of
spotless white, now it dwells with thee in light. *(93)*

SAYNTOR, W S (see 60TH ROYAL RIFLES (1))

SCAMMELL, L E W
No 7887086 L E W SCAMMELL. 1st Light Tank Company, Royal Tank
Regiment. Died Rawalpindi 19 May 1939. Aged 23 yrs.
                                          (82)

SCHILT, Victor John   (Y/714)
Victor John SCHILT. Born London 25 Oct 1951. Died Chitral 28
Jul 1976.   *(93)(WM)*

SCOTT, Arthur Wellesley   (DD/70)
Sacred to the memory of Arthur Wellesley. Eldest son of John
and Mary SCOTT. Born 19 Jun 1853. Died 20 Jan 1871.
                                          (82)(93)(PS)

SCOTT, E   (AA/1/259)
No 5067 Private E SCOTT who died at Rawalpindi 17 Mar 1907.
Aged 26 yrs. 10th Royal Hussars.   *(82)(93)*

SCOTT, Henry Hare   (D/170)
Sacred to the memory of Henry Hare SCOTT, Ex Engineer, who
died at Rawalpindi 22 Dec 1880. Aged 45 yrs. Because I live
ye shall live also.   *(82)(93)(PS)*

SCOTT, Mary   (W/900)
In loving memory of Mary, the daughter of W H and E SCOTT, who
died 12 Apr 1915. Aged 6 mths 12 days. Of such is the
kingdom of God.   *(82)(93)*

SCOTT, Mary   (M/1167)
In loving memory of Mary SCOTT. Born 29 Dec 1836. Died 28 Dec
1906. Peace.   *(82)(93)(end)*

SEATON, Duncan McLaughlan   (M/1137)
In memoriam. Duncan McLaughlan SEATON. Fellow of the
Institute of Actuaries. Died at Rawalpindi 31 Oct 1899. No
cross, no crown.   *(82)(93)(end)*

SEATON, Harry   *(CC/34)*
In memory of Lieutenant Harry SEATON. 8th The King's
Regiment. Born at Leeds, Yorkshire 26 Sep 1857. Died ....
                                           (82)(93)(PS)

SEATON, Liston   *(D/163)*
Liston.   Infant son of T and S SEATON. Died Dec 1887. Aged
14 mths.   *(93)(BS)*

SECCO, Alberto   *(VI/457)*
Alberto SECCO.   12 May 1983.   Tarbela Anche da Lontano I tuoi
Genitori ti Ricorderanno sempre.   *(93)*

SEDDON, Roger John   *(VII/1390)*
Roger John SEDDON. Died 25 Oct 1961. Aged 36.   *(93)*

SELLERS, John   *(III/474)*
In memory of No 1059954 Sergeant John SELLERS.   63rd Field
Battery Royal Artillery. Died at Rawalpindi 9 Aug 1937.
Erected by officers, NCOs and men of the battery. *(93)*

SENIOR, H (see ROYAL FIELD ARTILLERY (1))

SERGENT, H   *(P/1244)*
In memory of Gunner H SERGENT, 24 Company, ED RGA, who died 13
Jul 1901. Aged 28 yrs. Erected by his comrades.
                                           (82)(93)(PS)

SERROT, J R   *(JJ/363)*
In memory of J R SERROT. Born in France 5 Jul 1843. Died 6
Jul 1891.   *(82)(93)(BS)*

SEXEY, J (see 1ST KING'S DRAGOON GUARDS (1))

SEXY, Joseph   *(H/591)*
1st King's Dragoon Guards.   Sacred to the memory of Private
Joseph SEXY. Died 7 Jun 1888. Aged 24 yrs. Truly my hope is
even ......   *(82)(93)(BS)*

SEYMOUR, Edward Victor Francis   *(IV/498)*
Sacred to the memory Edward Victor Francis SEYMOUR. Captain
9th Hodson's Horse. Born 5 Aug 1887. Died 16 Apr 1927.
                                           (93)(WM)

SEYMOUR, R W (see KING'S DRAGOON GUARDS (1))

SEYMOUR, Robert William   *(H/594)*
In memory of Robert William SEYMOUR. Schoolmaster 1st King's
Dragoon Guards. Died 1 Aug 1888. Aged 32 yrs 5 mths.
                                           (82)(93)(WM)(mb)

SHACKLETON, Frederick William   *(W/901)*
Frederick William.   Son of Frederick Walter and Ellen
SHACKLETON. Died 11 Jul 1918. Not gone from memory, not
gone from love, but gone to his father's home above.
                                           (82)(93)

SHALOM, Sabina					(VII/1327)
Mother Sabina SHALOM. Born 1896. Died 14 Aug 1972. *(93)(WM)*

SHAPIRO, William Cumins			(X/867)
William Cumins SHAPIRO. 5 Feb 1932. Died 28 Jul 1974 at Tarbela. Rest in peace. *(93)*

SHARDLOW, E (see ROYAL ARTILLERY (6))

SHARP, Francis William				(Z/639)
Sacred to the memory of No 1203 Sergeant Francis William SHARP, No 3 Mountain Battery, Royal Garrison Artillery, who died Rawalpindi 16 Jun 1908. Aged 37 yrs 4 mths. *(82)(93)*

SHARPE, Agnes					(IV/548)
Sacred to the memory of Agnes, the dearly beloved wife of Staff Sergeant T M SHARPE, IAOC, who died at Rawalpindi on 20 Jun 1932. Aged 37 yrs. Erected by her sorrowing husband. Life's sweetest memory, heaven's welcome guest, my dearest treasure, God loved her best. *(82)(93)(WM)*

SHAUNNESSY, John				(R/272)
In loving memory of No 3955657 Private John SHAUNNESSY. 2nd Battalion The Welch Regiment. Died at Rawalpindi 13 Dec 1932. Aged 25 yrs. *(82)(93)*

SHAW, E (see 1ST KING'S DRAGOON GUARDS (1))

SHAW, E^{dn}					(H/592)
Sacred to the memory of Private E^{dn} SHAW. Died 9 Jun 1888. Aged 22 yrs. 1st King's Dragoon Guards. For they ....
(82)(93)(BS)

SHAW, Kathleen Isobel				(W/953)
In sacred and loving memory of our precious little GooGoo. Kathleen Isobel. Dearly loved little daughter of Mr and Mrs A E SHAW. Died 5 Nov 1926. Aged 2 yrs 3 mths. A perfect little form, eyes of the tenderest blue, curls just kissed by the sun's last rays, and a heart that was straight all through. Jesus loves me this I know. *(82)(93)(mb)(end)*

SHAW, Thomas Charles				(X/806)
In loving memory of our dear father Thomas Charles SHAW. Died 28 Jun 1945. Aged 87 yrs. *(93)*

SHEAHAN, John					(GG/228)
In memory of Robert CLEMMETT and John SHEAHAN of B Company of HM's 36th Regiment, who departed this life at Rawalpindi on 6 Sep and 21 Nov 1870. Respectively 31 and 27 yrs. *(82)(93)(BS)*

SHELDON
Baby SHELDON. 6 Jan 1932.			*(82)*

SHENLEY, J					(Z/637)
J SHENLEY, The Royal Irish Regiment, who died at Rawalpindi on 6 Apr 1908. Aged 29 yrs. Erected by his comrades of his regiment.					*(93)(WM)*

SHEPHERD, Charles   *(C/104)*
Charles SHEPHERD. Pension Conductor. Born 2 Nov 1817. Died
5 Jul 1879.   *(82)(93)(BS)*

SHEPPERSON, Robert   *(H/605)*
Thy will be done. In loving memory of Robert SHEPPERSON.
Died 11 Oct 1888. Aged 21.   *(82)(93)*

SHERLOCK, T (see 1ST KING'S DRAGOON GUARDS (1))

SHERLOCK, T   *(JJ/354)*
D Troop Kings Dragoon Guards. Sacred to the memory of Private
T SHERLOCK. Died 17 May 1888. Aged 21 yrs. *(82)(93)*

SHIELDS, C   (see 5TH REGIMENT (1))
SHIELDS, E   (see 1ST KING'S DRAGOON GUARDS (1))
SHIELDS, John   (see KING'S OWN SCOTTISH BORDERERS (1))

SHIER, Sheila   *(VIII/1411)*
Sheila (nee GOSSE) Wife of Scott SHIER. Born 13 Aug 1925 in
Quetta. Died 7 Mar 1984 in Rawalpindi. *(93)(WM)*

SHRIMPLIN, William (see ROYAL ARTILLERY (6))]

SHRIVES, J   *(J/453)*
In loving memory of Colour Sergeant J SHRIVES, 1st
Bedfordshire Regiment, who died of enteric fever on 21 Jun
1891 on his 28th Birthday.   *(82)(93)(BS)*

SIBLEY, Thomas (see ROYAL HORSE ARTILLERY (1))
SIMMONDS, A   (see 1ST KING'S DRAGOON GUARDS (1))

SIMMONDS, Arthur   *(H/590)*
1st King's Dragoon Guards. Sacred to the memory of Private
Arthur SIMMONDS, who died 11 May 1888. Aged 24 yrs. This
stone was ......   *(82)(93)(BS)*

SIMPSON, A H (see ROYAL ARTILLERY (6))

SIMS, William   *(N/1438)*
IHS. Sacred to the memory of No 2402 Bandsman William SIMS,
2nd King's Own Scottish Borderers, who died during the Chitral
Campaign at Jambatai Kotal on 22 Jun 1895. Aged 22 yrs. No
2109 Lance Corporal Bandsman John BOLTON, 2nd King's Own
Scottish Borderers, who died at Rawalpindi 22 Feb 1896. Aged
23 yrs. Erected by their brother bandsmen as a token of
respect. Thy will be done.   *(82)(93)*

SINCLAIR, Cynthia May
In loving memory of our darling baby Cynthia May. Infant
daughter of Mr and Mrs W S SINCLAIR. Born 4 Jul 1930. Died 4
Dec 1930.   *(82)(end)*

SINDEN, T (see ROYAL ARTILLERY (9))

SINEL, M H (see ROYAL ARTILLERY (8))

SINEL, M H (Q/1304)
In memory of Corporal M H SINEL, No 5 Company, Western Division Royal Garrison Artillery, who died at this station on 10 Jun 1899, aged 27 yrs, whose death is much regretted by his comrades. (82)(93)

SKELLY, C J (IX/1011)

In memory of

No 5618733

Private C J SKELLY.

1st Battalion

The Devonshire

Regiment.

Died at Rawalpindi

9 Apr 1939.

(82)(93)

SKEWS, A (see RIFLE BRIGADE (2))

SKINNER, A (see 1ST KING'S DRAGOON GUARDS (1))

SKINNER, Albert Edward Bertie (H/597)
In loving memory of Albert Edward Bertie SKINNER of Winchelsea, who died of cholera at Rawalpindi 7 Aug(*) 1888. Aged 24 yrs. Requiescat in pace. (82)(93)(WM)
   (* = Headstone reads: Agust 7th 1888)

SKIPTON, G T Kennedy (see ROYAL ARTILLERY (6))

SLADEN, T (DD/51)
Sacred to the memory of Private T SLADEN, HM's 85th Regiment, who died at Rawalpindi on 3 May 1872. Aged 35 yrs 6 mths. This was erected by his Merghul wife as a token of his loss.
  (82)(93)(BS)

SLATTERY, J   (L/1061)
In loving memory of No 6205 Private J SLATTERY,   E Company
1st Battalion The Royal Irish, who died at Rawalpindi 26 Jun
1906. Aged 27 yrs. Erected by the officers, NCOs and men of
his company.   (82)(93)

SMAILS, Gertrude (see BARTLETT, Gertrude)

SMEE, F   (P/1248)
In memory of No 3867 Private F SMEE. B Company 3rd Rifle
Brigade. Died 10 Jul 1900. Erected by his comrades.   NIYAZ
ALI, RAWALPINDI.   (82)(93)(PS)

SMEE, Maurice   (JJ/349)
In loving memory of Maurice. Born 26 Jun 1886. Died 30 Jan
1887. Beloved son of Mr and Mrs SMEE, Military Works.
Blessed in the arms of Jesus.   (82)(93)(PS)

SMEE, Thomas and Alice Maud   (HH/340)
In loving memory of Thomas. Born 13 Apr 1884. Died of
measles 25 Mar 1886. Alice Maud. Born 13 Jul 1878. Died of
typhoid fever 29 Oct 1886. Beloved children of Mr and Mrs
SMEE, Military Works.   (82)(93)(PS)

SMELLIE, Ann Shirley   (X/751)
Ann Shirley. The beloved daughter of Corporal and Mrs L
SMELLIE, RAMC (Burma). Born 17 Aug 1943 ....   (82)(93)(WM)

SMITH   (W/887)
Lost awhile our treasured love, saved forever, safe above.
Dearly beloved son of Lance Corporal and Mrs SMITH, North
Stafford Regiment, who died at Rawalpindi 19 Nov 1914.   Aged
7 mths.   (93)

SMITH, Annie and Norman   (H/583)
In loving memory of Annie. The beloved wife, and Norman,
infant son of .... SMITH.......   (93)

SMITH, Derek A   (VII/1402)
Derek A SMITH. Died 23 Apr 1971. Aged 47 yrs. Mourned by
wife Rita and children.   (93)(WM)

SMITH, Edith O (see ROYAL FIELD ARTILLERY (2))

SMITH, F   (N/1424)
Sacred to the memory of Private F SMITH who died at Rawalpindi
28 Sep 1895. Aged 22 yrs. Erected by the officers, NCOs and
men of his Squadron as a mark of respect.   (93)(BS)

SMITH, Frank Morse   (X/751)
In most loving memory of Frank Morse SMITH. Aged 38 yrs. The
dear husband of Elsie M SMITH of Los Angeles, California, USA.
Killed in an automobile accident 1 Apr 1928.   (82)(93)

SMITH, G C
No 91241. G C SMITH. 69th Battery Royal Field Artillery.
Died Rawalpindi 31 Mar 1905. Aged 35 yrs. (82)

SMITH, Geoffrey					(M/1181)
Rest in peace. In loving memory of Lieutenant and Adjutant
Geoffrey SMITH, DSO, RFA. Died Rawalpindi 12 Nov 1910.
					(82)(93)(mb)

SMITH, George					(P/1292)
Sacred to the memory of Private George SMITH, 1st Wiltshire
Regiment, who departed this life at Rawalpindi 7 Jan 1904.
Deeply lamented by all. Erected by his comrades and fellow
temperance workers. O weary hearth, there is a home beyond
this world of toil and care, who would not fain be resting
there.					(82)(93)

SMITH, Henry William				(O/1128)
Henry William SMITH, Telegraph Master, Indian Telegraphs,
aged 42 yrs 1 mth, who was accidentally drowned 2 May 1909.
					(82)(93)

SMITH, J H					(Q/1298)
In memory of No 5169 Private J H SMITH. C Company 1st
Battalion The Queens (RWS) Regiment who died at Rawalpindi 22
Feb 1899. Aged 20 yrs 8 mths. Erected by the officers, NCOs
and men of his company.			(82)(93)(PS)

SMITH, Jeannie Davidson				(O/1114)
Sacred to the memory of Jeannie Davidson, beloved wife of
Sergeant A L SMITH, 1st Royal Munster Fusiliers, who died at
Rawalpindi 29 Jan 1908. Aged 27 yrs 6 mths. Asleep in Jesus.
					(82)(93)

SMITH, John
Sacred to the memory of Private John SMITH of 79th Cameron
Highlanders who departed this life on 3 Jul 186? in the 23rd
year of his age. This stone is erected by his disconsolate
widow who mourns the loss of an affectionate husband and a
tender father.					(82)

SMITH, John					(Y/695)
In loving memory of No 2070 Rifleman John SMITH. A Company
2nd Battalion Rifle Brigade. Died Rawalpindi 2 Feb 1913.
Aged 26 yrs 8 mths. This stone is erected by his sorrowing
comrades. I have loved thee with an everlasting love .... in
loving kindness have I drawn thee.		(82)(93)

SMITH, Margaret Douglas Sydney			(X/828)
In ever loving memory of Margaret Douglas Sydney SMITH. Wife
of Sydney SMITH, Esq. DIG, Punjab Police. Died 8 Jan 1948.
Aged 84 yrs. Those who bring sunshine into the lives of
others cannot keep it from themselves. J M BARRIE.
					(82)(93)

SMITH, Nalchtine
Our darling Nalchtine(?). Infant son of Quartermaster Sergeant SMITH and his wife Norah. 5th SDRA. Born 19 Aug 1894.
Died 3 Oct 1894.				(82)

SMITH, Norah   (I/396)
In loving memory of Norah, the beloved wife of Quartermaster
Sergeant M SMITH, who died at Rawalpindi on 21 Mar 1896.
                                          (82)(93)(WM)

SMITH, O   (Z/641)
Sacred to the memory of No 4968 Private O SMITH. D Squadron
9th Lancers. Died Rawalpindi 22 Jul 1904. Aged 25 yrs.
                                          (82)(93)(PS)

SMITH, Sydney   (X/763)
In loving memory of Sydney SMITH. Son of General C F SMITH,
ICS. Died 4 Apr 1924. Aged 74 yrs. In his life he was
without guilt.   (82)(93)

SMITH, T (see GORDON HIGHLANDERS (4))

SMITH, Thomas   (KK/265)
IHS. Sacred to the memory of Thomas SMITH, Drum Major HM's
81st Regiment, who died on 22 Jan 1861. Aged 35 yrs. Deeply
regretted by all who knew him. Leaving a disconsolate widow
and three children to deplore his loss. This tomb is erected
by the band and the drummers as a mark of esteem for which
they held him during his service of 22 years amongst them.
                                          (82)(93)

SMITH, W (see ROYAL ARTILLERY (6))
SMITH, W (see RIFLE BRIGADE (2))

SMITH, W
Yea though I walk through the valley of the shadow of death, I
fear no evil. Thou art with me. Major W SMITH. Royal Artillery. Died 27 Jan 1879. Aged 30 yrs 5 mths. *(82)*

SMITH, William (see 98TH REGIMENT (1))

SMITH, William   (EE/87)
Sacred to the memory of Private William SMITH, late of G
Company HM's 70th Regiment, who died at Rawalpindi on the 18
Mar 1872. Aged 36 yrs. This was erected by the officers, NC
officers and men of G Company and his widow as a mark of their
esteem and regret at his loss. Looking unto Jesus.
                                          (82)(93)(BS)

SMITHERS, William   (Y/717)
In loving memory of my darling husband William SMITHERS, who
departed this life 18 Oct, 1924.   (93)

SMITHURST, Ashley   (VV/525)
In loving memory of Ashley. Our beloved son. Born 29 Nov
1962. Died 13 Dec 1962. Geoffrey and Bridget SMITHURST.
                                          (93)(WM)

SMYTH, Aloysius   (VII/1370)
Sister Aloysius SMYTH, PBVM. Born Kilkenny, Ireland 30 Jul
1916. Died Sargodha 7 Jan 1979.   (93)(WM)

SMYTH, G   (see ROYAL HORSE ARTILLERY (2))
SMYTHE, Henry (see ROYAL HORSE ARTILLERY (1))

SOMERVILLE, Willie   (LL/232)
Willie.   Only child of Sergeant and the late Mrs SOMERVILLE.
1st Battalion Northumberland Fusiliers. Died at Rawalpindi 25
May 1908. Aged 13 mths. Thy will be done.   *(82)(93)(WM)*

SOUTHGATE, R H (see 1ST KING'S DRAGOON GUARDS (1))

SOWMAN, Charlotte Olive   (P/1253)
In loving memory of Charlotte Olive, the beloved wife of Sub
Conductor J SOWMAN,   who departed this life 6 Jan 1901.
Aged 21 yrs. She is not dead but sleepeth.   *(82)(93)*

SPEAR, Peggy Patricia   (T/378)
Peggy Patricia. Dearly beloved daughter of Lance Sergeant and
Mrs SPEAR. Royal Garrison Artillery. Lord in thy gracious
keeping, here we leave our darling sleeping.
                                     (82)(93)(WM)

SPEARMAN, John Noel   (W/885)
John Noel. Beloved son of Mr and Mrs A H SPEARMAN, The Home-
stead, Rawalpindi. Born Christmas Day 1909. Died 7 Jan 1910.
Mourn not for me my parents dear, I am not dead but sleeping
here, Christ came and took me to his care. E'er sin could
blight his angel here.   *(82)(93)*

SPENCER, E (see ROYAL GARRISON ARTILLERY (4))

SPENCER, Ethel   (BB/26)
Ethel SPENCER. Born 30 Jun 1876. Died 30 Mar 1877.
                                     (82)(93)

SPENCER, F
In memory of 7943 Private F SPENCER. D Company 2nd Royal
Irish Fusiliers. Died 7 Jul 1905. Erected by the officers,
NCOs and men of his company.   *(82)*

SPENCER, George (see 98TH REGIMENT (1))

SPENCER, Harry
In loving memory of our darling little Harry. Son of Alfred
and Jessie SPENCER. 1st Battalion West Yorkshire Regiment.
Died 20 Feb 1907. Aged 1 yr 7 mths.   *(82)*

SPENCER, Robert Donald   (X/826)
Robert Donald SPENCER. Indian Police Retired. Died 15 Mar
1947.   *(82)(93)*

SPENDER, Isabella   (O/1087)
In loving memory of Isabella SPENDER, beloved daughter of
Corporal and Mrs SPENDER, 38th Battery Royal Field Artillery,
who died 2 Mar 1914. Aged 4 mths. Safe in the arms of Jesus.
Safe on his gentle breast, there by his arm shaded, sweetly
her soul shall rest.   *(82)(93)*

SPICER, George (see ROYAL FIELD ARTILLERY (2))

SPICER, H (Q/1300)
Sacred to the memory of No 1795 Private H SPICER, C Company 3rd Battalion The Rifle Brigade, who died at Rawalpindi on 17 Mar 1899. Aged 25 yrs. Come unto me all ye that labour and are heavy laden and I will give you rest. NEYAZ ALI, RAWALPINDI. (82)(93)(PS)

SPOONER, Frank George Malcolm (X/875)
Frank George Malcolm SPOONER. Born 24 Mar 1948 Plymouth. Died 18 Mar 1972 accidentally at Sohawa. (93)(WM)

SPRATT, R L (Y/716)
No 2312169 Signalman R L SPRATT, RCS, who died at Rawalpindi on 18 Jul 1924. Aged 20 yrs. Erected by his comrades of No 2 Wireless Company, B Corps Signals. He's gone like a flower cut down in full bloom, from the sunshine of life to the shade of the tomb. But death cannot sever the chain of our love nor steal the fond hope, we shall meet him above. From his loving Mum and Dad. (93)(WM)

SPRENT, Ella May (N/1473)
Ella May, daughter of Sergeant and N SPRENT, 4th Dragoon Guards, who died 23 Jan 1899. Aged 1 yr 3 mths. (93)(PS)

SPRINGETT, Mary (S/310)
RIP. In loving memory of Mary. Dearly beloved wife of R Q SPRINGETT. Born 19 Aug 1902. Died 10 Jan 1931. Erected by her sorrowing husband. When the soft dews of kindly sleep, my wearied eyelids gently steep. Be my last thought how sweet to rest, forever on my Saviour's breast. AHMED BUX, SCULPTOR, RAWALPINDI. (82)(93)

SQUIER, Frank Trevetan (P/1266)
Bombadier Frank Trevetan SQUIER, 104 Company Royal Garrison Artillery, who died at Rawalpindi 3 Jul 1902. Aged 25 yrs. Erected by the officers, NCOs and men of 104 Company. Until the day dawns. If thou shouldst call me to resign what most I prize it ne'er was mine. I only yield thee what was thine. Thy will be done. (93)(PS)

ST JOHN, Oliver (X/756)
XIX Hyderabad Regiment. Sacred to the memory of Major Oliver ST JOHN, 1st Battalion 19th Hyderabad Regiment (Russells), who died at Rawalpindi 18 Dec 1925. Aged 44 yrs. Erected by his brother officers. (93)

STACEY, Ivor Mark (W/955)
Sacred to the memory of Ivor Mark. Son of Mr and Mrs A M STACEY, RAOC. Born 31 Jan 1928. Died 23 Nov 1928. Who plucked this flower? The Master, and the gardener held his peace. (82)(93)

STANDEN, C H (Z/670)
Sacred to the memory of Sergeant C H STANDEN, who departed this life 3 Jan 1912. Aged 32 yrs. (82)(93)

STAINES, F J   (S/308)
Sacred to the memory of No 4797615 Lance Bombadier F J
STAINES. 3rd Light Battery, Royal Artillery. Died Rawalpindi
25 Dec 1930. Aged 24 yrs.   (82)(93)

STAINTON, Vernon Bruce   (X/822)
In loving memory of Vernon Bruce STAINTON, OBE, Indian Civil
Service. Died 10 Apr 1946. Aged 42 yrs.   (82)(93)

STANIFORTH, Charles (see 98TH REGIMENT (1))

STANIFORTH, George (see 98TH REGIMENT (1))

STANLY, Ann Sophia   (L/1046)
IHS. Rest in peace. In loving memory of Ann Sophia STANLY,
beloved wife of Sergeant H C STANLY, 104 Company HB Royal
Garrison Artillery, who died on 19 Oct 1902. Aged 27 yrs.
Erected by her sorrowing husband. M HUSSAIN, SCULPTOR,
RAWALPINDI.   (82)(93)

STANTON, A F C   (S/297)
Sacred to the memory of No 7143017 Regimental Quartermaster
Sergeant A F C STANTON. 1st Battalion The Connaught Rangers.
Died 25 Sep 1921. Claude STANTON. Aged 37 yrs. Erected by
his loving wife and son.   (82)(93)

STAPLETON, Margaret   (M/1136)
In loving memory of Margaret, the beloved wife of Arthur
STAPLETON, who died Rawalpindi 19 Nov 1898. Aged 29 yrs 6
mths 17 days. Sleep my love sleep.   (82)(93)

STAPLEY, H   (J/438)
Sacred to the memory of Sergeant H STAPLEY, who died at
Rawalpindi 21 Jul 1891. Aged 39 yrs. Erected by his brother
NCOs as a mark of ......   (82)(93)(BS)

STARKE, Philip Henry Ravenscourt   (IV/518)
In memory of Signalman Philip Henry Ravenscourt STARKE. Died
Rawalpindi 19 Dec 1929. Erected by all ranks B Corps Signals.
                                       (82)(93)

STARR, John Edmund   (X/785)
In loving memory of our dear father John Edmund STARR. Died 2
Nov 1933. Aged 59 yrs 3 mths. Father in thy gracious
keeping, leave we now our loved one sleeping. Erected by his
sorrowing children.
                                       (82)(93)(end)

STAY, Frank (see ROYAL HORSE ARTILLERY (1))

STEAD, Thomas   (L/1049)
Sacred to the memory of No 15750 Driver Thomas STEAD. 57th
Battery Royal Field Artillery. Died Rawalpindi 13 May 1903.
Aged 32 yrs.   (82)(93)

STEELE, J (see 1ST KING'S DRAGOON GUARDS (1))

STEMP, Lewis James					(IV/543)
In memory of No 1072316 Driver Lewis James STEMP. 4th Field (Coles Kop) Battery Royal Artillery. Died Rawalpindi 29 Dec 1932. Aged 24 yrs 3 mths.		(82)(93)

STEPHENS, A					(X/876)
In memory of our beloved mother Mrs A STEPHENS. Died 5 Apr 1971.		(93)(WM)

STEVENS, A (see 1ST KING'S DRAGOON GUARDS (1))

STEVENS, Charles Mordaunt			(N/1458)
In loving memory of Captain Charles Mordaunt STEVENS, King's Own Yorkshire Infantry, who died at Rawalpindi 3 Nov 1895. Aged 38.		(82)(93)

STEVENS, E H (see ARMY SERVICE CORPS (1))

STEVENS, James Hay				(V/992)
In memory of No 2979384 Private James Hay STEVENS. A(S) Company.....		(82)(93)

STEVENS, Lena					(Y/700)
In loving memory of Lena (Sis), the dearly beloved wife of Colour Sergeant H STEVENS, 2nd Battalion Rifle Brigade, who departed this life 15 Feb 1913. We loved thee well, but Jesus loved thee best. Sleep on beloved. (82)(93)

STEVENS, Martha E				(DD/71)
In remembrance of Martha E STEVENS, the beloved daughter of Private Edmund STEVENS, 2/9th Regiment, who died at Rawalpindi 28 Apr 1876. Aged 4 mths.	(93)

STEVENS, W E					(V/1000)
In memory of No 739506 Staff Sergeant W E STEVENS, IASC. Erected by the officers, Warrant Officers and NCOs of the IASC (MT), Chaklala. Died 15 Nov 1933.	(82)(93)

STEVENSON, Alexander				(O/1127)
In loving memory of Alexander STEVENSON. Lieutenant Royal Munster Fusiliers who died 1 Nov 1909.	(82)(93)

STEWARD, William Arthur
No 34627 Carriage Smith William Arthur STEWARD. 91st Heavy Battery, Royal Garrison Artillery. Died Rawalpindi 28 Oct 1906.		(82)

STEWART					(V/978)
In memory of Gunner STEWART. No 12 Pack Battery, Royal Garrison Artillery. Died Rawalpindi 2 Nov 1923. Erected by all ranks of the Battery.	(82)(93)

STEWART, A					(O/1111)
38th Battery RFA. In memory of No 49949 Driver A STEWART, who died at Rawalpindi 31 Dec 1913.	(82)(93)(BS)

STEWART, Douglas Gordon (X/856)
Douglas Gordon STEWART. Died 12 Dec 1964. Aged 49. Husband of Anne and father of Douglas, Alan and Fiona. *(93)*

STEWART, Florence Matilda (BB/23)
Sacred to the memory of Florence Matilda. Daughter of J STEWART. Conductor and Sub Engineer, PWD. Died 28 Jan 1876. Aged 7 yrs 6 mths. Safe in the arms of Jesus. *(93)(PS)(mb)*

STEWART, Henrietta Adelaide (H/604)
Sacred to the memory of Henrietta Adelaide STEWART. Died 31 Oct 1888. Aged 51 yrs 8 mths. For me to live is Christ and to die to gain. *(82)(93)(PS)*

STEWART, Lucy Sarah
In memory of Lucy Sarah. Wife of Harry H A STEWART, Esq. Captain 9th Regiment. Here awaits the resurrection. Born 13 Jul 1849. Died 26 Jul 1875. *(82)*

STINSON, T (Z/634)
UBIQUE. Sacred to the memory of No 40392 Gunner T STINSON. No 5 AG, Royal Field Artillery. Died Rawalpindi 1 Jul 1907. This stone is erected by the officers, NCOs and men of the column as a token ..... *(82)(93)*

STIRLING, Morris (Q/1297)
Sacred to the memory of Private Morris STIRLING, 4th (Royal Irish) Dragoon Guards, who died at Rawalpindi 16 Jun 1898. Aged 28 yrs. Erected by the officers, NCOs and men of C Squadron. *(82)(93)*

STOCK, Tony (W/936)
In loving memory of Tony. Beloved son of CQMS and Mrs STOCK. 2nd Suffolk Regt. Born 30 Jun 1939. Died 30 Nov 1939. *(82)(93)*

STOCKER, William (see 98TH REGIMENT (1))

STODDARD, Agnes Gertrude (N/1423)
In loving memory of Agnes Gertrude STODDARD. Born 5 Feb 1864. Died 25 Apr 1895. Thy will be done. *(82)(93)(BS)*

STOKES, S (see ROYAL ARTILLERY (6))

STOLBERG, Eric Albert (VII/1345)
My father Eric Albert STOLBERG. 13 Feb 1959. Aged 78 yrs. Erected by Harold STOLBERG. *(93)*

STONE, George A S (J/450)
George A S STONE. Lieutenant Royal Engineers. Died of fever at Rawalpindi 28 Oct 1890. *(82)(93)*

STONE, Ivy Muriel (M/1180)
In loving memory of Ivy Muriel STONE, beloved wife of Frederick William STONE, who departed this life 4 Mar 1911. Aged 28 yrs 11 mths. *(82)(93)*

STOREY, R D (see SOMERSET LIGHT INFANTRY (1))

STOTT, J   (see 60TH ROYAL RIFLES (1))
STRAFFORD, J (see 36TH REGIMENT (1))

STRATFORD, F   (IV/508)
In memory of No 781860 Driver F STRATFORD. 14th Field Battery, Royal Artillery. Died Rawalpindi 4 Nov 1930. Aged 22.   (82)(93)

STRATFORD-COLLINS, John   (M/1172)
Sacred to the memory of Major General John STRATFORD-COLLINS, CB, of Wythall, Ross, Herefordshire, who died Rawalpindi of cholera whilst commanding the 2nd (Rawalpindi) Division on 27 Apr 1908. Aged 57. Erected as a token of esteem and respect by all ranks of 1st Battalion The Queen's Regiment, which he commanded from Sep 1896 to 1901. Pristinae Virtutis Memor.
                                      (82)(93)

STRATTON (see ROYAL FIELD ARTILLERY (2))

STRATTON, H A   (AA/1/258)
Sergeant H A STRATTON. 1st Battalion The Royal Irish, who died at Rawalpindi on 20 Nov 1906. Aged 34 yrs. Erected as a token of respect by the members of the Sergeants Mess, the NCOs and men of G Company. RIP.   (93)

STRETTELL, John Dashwood   (W/956)
24 Oct 1928. John Dashwood STRETTELL. (93)

STROUD, F W   (P/1291)
In loving memory of Private F W STROUD, 1st Battalion Wiltshire Regiment, who departed this life at Rawalpindi 5 Jan 1904. Aged 35 yrs 8 mths. This stone was erected by his comrades.   (82)(93)

STRUTTON, H A
Sacred to the memory of No 2934 Sergeant H A STRUTTON. G Company 1st Battalion The Royal Irish. Died Rawalpindi 20 Nov 1906. Aged 34 yrs.   (82)

STUDD, F   (Z/668)
In memory of No 5476 Private F STUDD, 10th Royal Hussars, who died Rawalpindi 19 Jul 1912. Aged 28 yrs. (82)(93)

STUDLLEY(?) (see ROYAL HORSE ARTILLERY (2))
STURGIS, T G (see 1ST KING'S DRAGOON GUARDS (1))

STURGIS, Thomas Guy   (G/430)
Thomas Guy STURGIS. Elder son of Samuel Harman STURGIS. Born 13 Jul 1867. Died of enteric fever 19 Jul 1889. (82)(93)(WM)

STURNEY (see ROYAL ARTILLERY (7))
STURT, W (see WEST RIDING REGIMENT (1))
STURTON (see ROYAL ARTILLERY (6))

STYLES, J E   (Y/691)
In loving memory of Sergeant J E STYLES. D Company 2nd Battalion North Stafford Regiment.   /continued........

STYLES, J E (cont)
Died Rawalpindi 13 Aug 1913. Aged 39 yrs. Erected by the officers, sergeants, NCOs and men of his company as a token of respect. Rest in peace. *(82)(93)*

STYLES, J
Sergeant J STYLES. 4th Dragoon Guards who died at Rawalpindi 29 Mar 1901. Aged 36 yrs. *(82)*
(In Yapton Church, Sussex there is an MI which gives his names at James Henry and the date of death 30 Mar 1901)

SULLEN, George Oswald *(HH/337)*
In sweet memory of George Oswald. Dearly loved child of Samuel and Rose SULLEN. 28 Apr 1881. O lovely bud, so young and fair, called forth by early doom ....*(82)(93)(WM)*

SULLIVAN, J (see 36TH REGIMENT (1))

SULLIVAN, John *(KK/264)*
Sacred to the memory of John SULLIVAN, who departed this life... *(93)(BS)*

SULLY, C (see 1ST KING'S DRAGOON GUARDS (1))

SULLY, Charles Wesley *(E/183)*
In loving memory of Private Charles Wesley SULLY. A Troop 1st Dragoon Guards. Died Rawalpindi 25 Jun 1884. Aged 26 yrs. And God shall wipe away all tears from their eyes and there shall be no more death, neither sorrow nor crying, neither shall there be any more pain for the former things are passed away. This stone was erected by the officers, NC officers and men of his troop as a token of esteem. *(82)(93)(BS)*

SUMMERS
Child of QS and Mary SUMMERS, 1st Royal Sussex Regiment, who died 11 Dec 1911. Aged 3 yrs. *(82)*

SUMNER, L *(IV/570)*
Sacred to the memory of No 5493495 Private L SUMNER. D Company The Hampshire Regiment .... *(93)*

SUTCLIFFE, George *(E/192)*
Sacred to the memory of Private George SUTCLIFFE. 1st West Riding Regiment. Died Rawalpindi 14 May 1886. Aged 39 yrs. This stone is erected by the NC officers and men of his company as a token of ..... *(82)(93)(BS)*

SUTTON, Arthur
No 1403995 Sergeant Arthur SUTTON. 1st Indian Divisional Signals. Died Rawalpindi 27 Apr 1927. Aged 39 yrs. *(82)*

SUTTON, Bridget, James Henry and William *(GG/218)*
Sacred to the memory of Bridget, James Henry and William. The beloved wife and children of Private William SUTTON. HM's 70th Regt. James Henry died 9 Dec 1870. Aged 1 yr 9 mths. William died 2 Jun 1872. Aged 4 mths. Bridget died 13 Aug 1872. Aged 24 yrs. Jesus, we came at thy command. *(82)(93)(BS)*

SUTTON, Harold
Harold. The beloved son of Alice Mary and George William
SUTTON. Schoolmaster 3rd Dragoon Guards. Died Rawalpindi 28
Apr 1892. Aged 4 mths. Thy way, not mine, O Lord.
(82)

SWAN, T H   *(M/1153)*
Our friend sleepeth.   Sacred to the memory of T H SWAN, who
died 7 Feb 1902. Aged 68 yrs.   *(82)(93)*

SWEALES, Elaine Sara   *(VI/470)*
In ever loving memory of Elaine Sara. Dearly loved daughter
of Staff Sergeant A and Mrs R SWEALES, RAMC. Died 8 Dec 1940.
We mourn for you in silence and oft recall your name. What
would we give to hold you in our arms and to see your lovely
smile.   *(82)(93)(WM)*

SWEENEY, Peter Lawrence   *(III/488)*
Peter Lawrence SWEENEY. Born 12 Aug 1953 in Bombay. Died 28
Aug 1982 in Islamabad.   *(93)(WM)*

SWIFT, Stanley   *(Z/652)*
In loving memory of Mr Stanley SWIFT. Born 25 Feb 1893. Died
1 Feb 1966.   *(93)(WM)*

SWIFT, Una (see QUAMBER, A W)

SWINDON, F   *(P/1259)*
Sacred to the memory of No 4440 Private F SWINDON, D Company
The Queen's, who died at Rawalpindi 4 Jan 1902. Aged 27 yrs.
Erected by D Company as a mark of respect. *(82)(93)*

SWON, William   *(Q/1317)*
Sacred to the memory of Private William SWON, who died at
Rawalpindi 8 Sep 1896. Aged 26 yrs.   *(82)(93)(BS)*

SYMONS, N (see 70TH REGIMENT (1))

TABRAM, John   *(Q/1308)*
In memory of No 3710 Private John TABRAM, 1st Battalion
Devonshire Regiment, who died at Rawalpindi 22 Feb 1898 from
the effects of wounds received at Karappa with the Tirah
Expeditionary Force. Aged 25 yrs. RIP. *(82)(93)*

TALBOT, Frederic Augustus   *(DD/45)*
To the memory of Frederic Augustus TALBOT, who departed this
life at Rawalpindi on 11 Sep 1863. Aged 35. In the midst of
life we are in death.   *(82)(93)(WM)*

(For illustration, see page 120)

TALBOTT, Henry   (E/196)
Sacred to the memory of Private Henry TALBOTT. B Company 2nd
Battalion Royal Sussex Regiment. Died 29 Aug 1887.   Aged 28
yrs. His end was peace. Erected by the officers, NCOs and
men of his company as token of esteem.   (82)(93)

TAPSALL, Robert Henry   (N/1456)
Sacred to the memory of Assistant Surgeon Robert Henry
TAPSALL. Died 26 Dec 1895. Erected by his brother medical
warrant officers.   (82)(93)(PS)(mb)

TATE, Harold   (VV/535)
In ever loving memory of Harold. Born 13 Oct 1948. Died 4 Aug
1949. Dearly beloved son of Captain and Mrs H A R TATE. (93)

TATHAM, J T
Sergeant Major J T TATHAM. Royal Artillery.   Died Rawalpindi
19 Nov 1878.   (82)(mb)

TAYLOR, Alexander Vernon
In loving memory of Alexander Vernon TAYLOR.   Died 15 Feb
1939. Aged 72 yrs.   (82)

TAYLOR, Elizabeth Mary and Alexander Vernon (V/1001)
In loving memory of Elizabeth Mary. The beloved wife of A V
TAYLOR, DSP. Died 2 Feb 1930.   In loving memory of Alexander
Vernon TAYLOR who died on 15 Feb 1939. Aged 72 yrs. (82)(93)

TAYLOR, G
2nd Lieutenant G TAYLOR, Pilling, Sheffield, England.   52nd
Ox and Bucks Light Infantry. Died Rawalpindi 23 Dec 1924.
Aged 21 yrs.   (82)

TAYLOR, George   (P/1294)
No 3480 Driver George TAYLOR. 57th Battery Royal Field Artillery. Died Rawalpindi 28 Dec 1903. Aged 23 yrs. Erected by
the officers, NCOs and men of the battery.   (82)(93)(PS)

TAYLOR, George William   (Y/712)
In memory of No 5373272 Corporal George William TAYLOR. D
Company 2nd Battalion Ox and Bucks Light Infantry. Died at
Rawalpindi 30 Jun 1924.   (93)

TAYLOR, Ivan G E   (V/977)
In loving memory of Ivan G E TAYLOR, who died on 16 Jan 1927.
Aged 47. Thy will be done, O God.   (82)(93)

TAYLOR, James (see 9TH REGIMENT (1))
TAYLOR, J C   (see ROYAL ARTILLERY (6))

TELLIS, Hilda   (VII/1407)
Hilda TELLIS.   11 Nov 1975. Aged 68. Erected by her husband
Stan TELLIS.   (93)

TELLIS, STAN H   (VIII/1414)
Stan H TELLIS.   Born 29 Oct 1904. Died 3 Nov 1981.   Erected
by W J TELLIS.   (93)(WM)

TELLIS, William Joseph   (VIII/1409)
William Joseph TELLIS. Born 1 Nov 1911. Died 18 Mar 1987. *(93)*

TENNER(?)   (A/119)
.... Robert and Ellen TENNER(?). 39th Regiment who died 2 Jan 1873. Aged 13 mths.   *(93)(BS)*

TERRY, David (see ROYAL GARRISON ARTILLERY (3))

THACKWELL, Matilda and Rees   (DD/55)
Here sleeps in Jesus Matilda, the beloved wife of Reverend R THACKWELL, who departed this life 17 Feb 1873. Aged 34 yrs. Also Rees. The infant son of the Reverend and Matilda THACKWELL, who died 20 Feb 1873. Aged 4 days. Them also that sleep in Jesus will God bring with him. *(82)(93)(PS)*

THIPTHORPE, Keith Duncan   (W/908)
In loving memory of Keith Duncan, the darling infant son of William Henry and Mary Olivia THIPTHORPE, who left us on 28 Mar 1919. Aged 6 mths. Safe in the arms of Jesus. *(93)*

THOMAS, Anna Francis (sic)   (L/1072)
Anna Francis (sic). Mother of Joseph E H THOMAS, who died on 13 Nov 1909. Aged 48 yrs.   *(93)(BS)*

THOMAS, B (see RIFLE BRIGADE (2))

THOMAS, Fredrick   (IV/563)
In loving memory of Fredrick THOMAS, beloved son of Staff Sergeant and Mrs A THOMAS, IASC, age 22 yrs 7 mths, who died at Rawalpindi 15 Nov 1934, who is deeply mourned by his Dad, Ma and sisters. Gone my son but not forgotten. RIP. *(82)(93)*

THOMAS, G (see RIFLE BRIGADE (2))
THOMAS, H (see 1ST KING'S DRAGOON GUARDS (1))

THOMAS, Harry   (E/191)
Sacred to the memory of Private Harry THOMAS, who departed this life 28 Apr 1886. Aged 21 yrs. D Troop, 1st King's Dragoon Guards.   *(82)(93)(BS)*

THOMAS, I L   (IV/549)
In memory of No 784223 Lance Bombadier I L THOMAS. 7th Field Battery Sandham's Company Royal Artillery. Died at Rawalpindi 14 Mar 1932. Aged 22 yrs.   *(82)(93)*

THOMAS, J   (IV/516)
In memory of No 784837 Driver J THOMAS. 14th Field Battery, Royal Artillery. Died at Rawalpindi 25 Oct 1931. Aged 24 yrs.   *(82)(93)*

THOMAS, Joseph   (DD/63)
In memory of Corporal Joseph THOMAS, 4th Queen's Own Hussars, who departed this life at Rawalpindi on the 8 Mar 1873. Aged 33 yrs. Farewell my wife and child dear, my death will cost you many a tear. Yet blest with hope we'll meet again, in heaven above farewell till then.   *(82)(93)(BS)*

THOMAS, Walter Joseph   (P/1261)
In loving memory of Private Walter Joseph THOMAS. D Company
2nd King's Royal Rifles. Died at Rawalpindi 9 Jun 1902. Aged
24 yrs 7 mths. This stone is erected as a mark of respect by
the WOs and Sergeants of the Brigade and the officers, NCOs
and men of D Company, 2nd Kings Royal Rifles.   (82)(93)

THOMPSON, David Boxwell Harding   (A/124)
David Boxwell Harding.   Beloved son of David and Bella
THOMPSON. Born 8 Oct 1882. Died 22 Dec 1882. (93)(BS)(mb)

THOMPSON, J   (IV/502)
Sacred to the memory of No 6449473 Gunner J THOMPSON, 33rd
Field Battery Royal Artillery, who died at Rawalpindi 19 Sep
1928. Aged 28 yrs. Erected by the officers, NCOs and men of
the Battery.   (82)(93)

THOMPSON, James (see GORDON HIGHLANDERS (5))
THOMPSON, James (see KING'S OWN SCOTTISH BORDERERS (2))

THOMPSON, Maggie   (O/1086)
In loving memory of Maggie. Dearly beloved daughter of
Sergeant and Mrs THOMPSON. 21st Empress of India Lancers.
Died at Rawalpindi 4 Dec 1912. Aged 3 yrs 4 mths. Deeply
mourned. Asleep in Jesus. One more in heaven.   (82)(93)

THOMSON, A (see ROYAL GARRISON ARTILLERY (4))

THORNDIKE, Francis Henry   (H/603)
In loving memory of Francis Henry THORNDIKE. Major 2nd Battalion Royal Sussex Regiment. Born 27 Nov 1852. Died 22 Nov
1888.   (82)(93)(WM)

THORNTON, M   (S/301)
Sacred to the memory of No 7144479 Private M THORNTON. 1st
Battalion The Connaught Rangers. Died 30 Mar 1922. RIP.
                                         (82)(93)

THORNTON, W (see GORDON HIGHLANDERS (3))

THROPP, A   (V/984)
In memory of No 7256921 Private A THROPP. Royal Army Medical
Corps. Died suddenly at Rawalpindi 24 Feb 1929. Erected by
his comrades.   (82)(93)

THRUSSELL, Herbert   (N/1427)
Sacred to the memory of Herbert THRUSSELL, B Company 3rd Battalion the Rifle Brigade, Prince Consort's Own, who died at
Rawalpindi 22 Jun 1895. Aged 24 yrs. This stone was
erected.....   (82)(93)(PS)

THRUSSELL, James   (W/965)
In cherished memory of little James. Dearly loved son of Mr
and Mrs T THRUSSELL. Born 29 Sep 1933. Died 30 Sep 1933. He
was lent but for a little while. Safe in the arms of Jesus.
                                         (82)(93)

THRUSSELL, John Oscar *(W/929)*
In cherished memory of John Oscar. Dearly loved son of Mr and Mrs T THRUSSELL, IAOC. Born 7 Jul 1931. Died 23 Sep 1931. The cup was bitter, the sting severe, to part with one we loved so dear, the trial is hard, we'll not complain, but trust in God to meet again. Safe in the arms of Jesus. *(93)*

TIMMS, F (see SOMERSET LIGHT INFANTRY (1))
TIMMS, J (see 1ST KING'S DRAGOON GUARDS (1))

TIMS, J M *(VII/1344)*
Mrs J M TIMS.
Born 22 Jul 1915.
Died 13 Jul 1976.
RIP. *(93)*

TIPPETTS, H
(see 1ST KING'S DRAGOON GUARDS (1))

TIPTON, J
Devonshire Regiment.
Private J TIPTON.
Died 5 Dec 1897.
Aged 22 yrs.
(82)

TITLEY, J
(see ROYAL ARTILLERY (6))

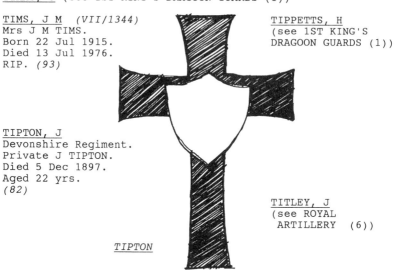

TIPTON

TODD, George *(E/190)*
In memory of Lance Corporal George TODD, Bandsman Henry MOORE and Charles G FROST, the 2nd Battalion The Royal Irish Regiment, who were killed in a railway accident on 15 Mar 1885. *(82)(93)(BS)*

TODD, Susie *(K/613)*
In loving memory of Susie. The loved wife of Sub Conductor T R TODD, Ordnance Department. Born 26 Dec 1872. Died at Rawalpindi 8 Jan 1893. Good was her heart and friendship sound, patient in pain and loved by all around. Her griefs are o'er, her pain for ever done. A life of everlasing joy she has now begun. Thy will be done. *(82)(93)(WM)*

TOMPKINS, Thomas *(K/623)*
Sacred to the memory of No ..488 Private Thomas TOMPKINS. ... King's Royal Rifles. Died 7 Aug 1892. Aged 22 yrs. This stone was erected by the officers, NCO and men of H Company. *(82)(93)(BS)*

TOMKINSON, Monica Ann *(VII/1400)*
Monica Ann. Daughter of Leslie and Monica TOMKINSON of Cheshire, England. Born 6 Feb 1934. Died 25 Jun 1967. *(93)*

TOOTH, A (see ROYAL GARRISON ARTILLERY (1))
TOOTH, A (see ROYAL GARRISON ARTILLERY (4))

TOPHAM, Hal   (M/1189)
In loving memory of Hal TOPHAM. The dearly loved husband of Jeani TOPHAM. Died 21 Aug 1908. Aged 48 yrs 6 mths. Blessed are the pure in heart for they shall see God.   (82)(93)(mb)

TOPPING, Ellen Laura
Ellen Laura. Daughter of Sergeant and Mrs TOPPING. 1st Battalion King's Royal Rifle Corps who died at Rawalpindi 1 Dec 1923. Aged 3 yrs 2 mths.   (82)

TOWERS, Elsie   (W/898)
The dearly loved daughter of Sergeant and Elsie TOWERS, who died 27 Jan 1920. Aged 1 yr 1 mth. Had he asked us, well we know, we should cry, O spare this blow. Yes with streaming tears should pray, Lord we love her, let her stay. Father in thy gracious keeping, leave we now our darling sleeping.
                                         (82)(93)

TOWEY, J (see ROYAL GARRISON ARTILLERY (1))

TOWNLEY, George   (M/1184)
In loving memory of George TOWNLEY. Died 16 Oct 1909 in his 53rd year. Even so Father for so it seemeth good in thy sight.   (82)(93)

TRAFFORD, Edward Le Marchant   (H/587)
Edward Le Marchant TRAFFORD, Major 5th Northumberland Fusiliers. Son of the late Major General T S TRAFFORD, who died Rawalpindi 9 Jan 1888. Aged 42 yrs.   (82)(93)(WM)(mb)

TRATTNER, Werner   (VIII/1422)
Werner TRATTNER. Lilienfeld 6 Feb 1959. Rawalpindi 28 Aug 1978. Verunglueckt auf seiner Maturareise. RIP. (93)

TRAVERS, Betty Catherine   (III/480)
In memory of Betty Catherine. Dearly loved wife of Captain W H C TRAVERS, Royal Engineers. Born 30 Apr 1912 and passed to rest 30 Apr 1939. A little while and ye shall not see me, and again a little while and ye shall see me because I go to the Father.   (82)(93)

TREADWELL, William   (L/1027)
In loving memory of our darling William. Son of John and Jane TREADWELL. Born 16 Jun 1900. Died 3 Nov 1903.   (82)(93)

TREBY, A   (see SOMERSET LIGHT INFANTRY (1))
TREHANE, W C (see SOMERSET LIGHT INFANTRY (1))

TREVELYAN, Frank
Bombadier Frank TREVELYAN. 104 Company Royal Garrison Artillery. Died Rawalpindi 3 Jul 1902. Aged 25 yrs. Erected by the officers, NCOs and men of 104 Company.   (82)

TROLLOP, Florence
Our darling Florence. Daughter of Sergeant and Mrs TROLLOP.
1st Wiltshire Regiment. *(82)(mb)*
    (see NO NAME (B/138))

TROTTER, Alexander James   (AA/4)
Here rest the beloved remains of Alexander James TROTTER.
Lieutenant Bengal Artillery. Second son of the late Archibald
TROTTER, Esq of Dreghorn, Scotland. He was drowned in crossing
the Jhelum 4 Oct 1856 in the 24th year of his age. This stone
is erected by his widowed mother and his sorrowing relations
in England. *(93)(WM)*

TROTTER, Edwin William   (M/1148)
In loving memory of Edwin William TROTTER. Born 11 Sep 1829.
Died 10 Apr 1903. Peace perfect peace. AHMUD BUX, RAWALPINDI.
(82)(93)(end)

TROTTER, Ellen   (IV/541)
Mother Ellen TROTTER. Born 1853. Died 1933. *(82)(93)*

TROTTER, Gilbert Ralph Abercromby John (M/1190)
Captain Gilbert Ralph Abercromby John TROTTER. 56th Punjab
Rifles, Frontier Force. 2nd son of Colonel TROTTER of
Colinton, Midlothian. Born 28 Jan 1880. Died 4 Jan 1913.
(82)(93)

TRUEMAN, Barbara   (W/888)
Barbara. The beloved only child of Sergeant and Mrs TRUEMAN.
2nd Battalion Rifle Brigade. Born 7 Jan. Died 21 Sep 1914.
Safe in the arms of Jesus. *(93)*

TUBB, W (see SOMERSET LIGHT INFANTRY (1))

TUGWELL, George   (Q/1324)
Sacred to the memory of No 913 Private George TUGWELL, G Company, 3rd Battalion Rifle Brigade, Prince Consort's Own,
who died at Rawalpindi 14 Dec 1896. Aged 23 yrs 11 mths.
Gone but not forgotten. Erected by his comrades. *(82)(93)(PS)*

TUNY, Belaso   (V/1014)
Mrs Belaso TUNY. Mother of Joseph. Died 25 Dec 1919. Aged
90 yrs. *(82)(93)*

TURBAN, Albert Maurice   (X/844)
Albert Maurice TURBAN. 1892 - 1965. *(93)*

TURBAN, Florentine Florence Amelia (X/843)
In ever loving memory of my beloved wife Florentine Florence
Amelia TURBAN. Died at Murree 16 Sep 1953. *(93)*

TURNBULL, John   (BB/14)
In memory of John TURNBULL. District Superintendent of
Police, Rawalpindi. Died 23 Aug 1876. Aged 37 yrs. The Lord
giveth his beloved sleep. This stone is placed by his brother
officers in token of esteem and regard. *(82)(93)*

TURNER, Albert E   (P/1272)
Sacred to the memory of No 5249 Private Albert E TURNER, D
Company 1st Battalion The Queen's, who died at Rawalpindi 24
Jan 1902. Aged 22 yrs.   Erected by D Company as a mark of
respect.   (82)(93)

TURNER, Amy Hilda   (B/143)
Amy Hilda TURNER. Aged 3 yrs 3 mths.   (82)(93)(mb)

TURNER, Emma Maria   (M/1158)
IHS. In loving memory of our dear mother Emma Maria TURNER,
who departed this life at Rawalpindi 9 Oct 1901. Aged 59 yrs.
Widow of the late S C TURNER. Loco Foreman SI Railway,
Trichinopoly. At rest.   A loving mother true and kind, she
was to us in heart and mind. She always strove to do her
best, and now she is for ever blest. We should not call her
back again, our loss is her eternal gain. Her sufferings on
the earth are o'er we mourn but still God's will be done.
AHMUD BUX, RAWALPINDI, UMBALA & PESHAWAR. (82)(93)(mb)(end)

TURNER, J W   (VII/1328)
J W TURNER. Died 19 Aug 1961.   (93)(WM)

TURNER, Sarah and Kate Issabell Traver   (DD/52)
Sacred to the memory of Sarah. The beloved wife and Kate
Issabell Traver, the beloved daughter of Bugler Alere (Sic)
TURNER. HM 23 P.N.I. Died at Rawalpindi 31 Aug ... (93)(BS)

TURNER, T (see ROYAL GARRISON ARTILLERY (2))

TURNER, T   (Z/648)
No 33183 Gunner T TURNER. No 7 Mountain Battery Royal Garrison Artillery, who died Rawalpindi on 30 May 1908.
                                          (82)(93)(PS)

TWYMAN, Johnny   (Z/645)
In loving memory of Johnny. Dearly loved child of John and
Rosa TWYMAN. Died 17 Nov 1907. Aged 7 mths. Until the day
break.   (82)(93)(WM)

TYLER, Arthur Edmund
My own darling husband Arthur Edmund TYLER. S & T Corps.
Born 11 Apr 1875. Died 17 Feb 1922.   (82)

TYRRELL, Trevor Hardinge   (O/1089)
In ever loving memory of Trevor Hardinge TYRRELL .... (93)

UNWIN, A W   (Y/729)
Sacred to the memory of No 4962842 Company Sergeant Major A W
UNWIN. LRC Company, 2nd Battalion, The Sherwood Foresters.
Died 12 Jul 1925. Aged 34 yrs.   (82)(93)

UTTING, Ann Elizabeth
In loving memory of Ann Elizabeth UTTING, who died 14 Sep 1897. Aged 51 yrs 4 mths. *(82)*

VALLER, Ernest (see ROYAL HORSE ARTILLERY (1))

VALLER, Ernest   *(P/1238)*
Sacred to the memory of Ernest VALLER, who died at Rawalpindi 8 May 1900. Aged 29 yrs. Erected by his comrades of K Battery Royal Horse Artillery. *(82)(93)*

VAN CUYLENBURG   *(W/927)*
In ever loving memory of our little darling Elsie Evelyn. Beloved and only child of Assistant Surgeon and Mrs V A VAN CUYLENBURG, IMD. Born 20 Aug 1925. Died 4 Oct 1931 at Murree. Aged 6 yrs 1 mth 14 days. *(82)(93)(mb)*

VANDEMERE, Frank (see ROYAL HORSE ARTILLERY (1))

VANEY, Peta   *(X/815)*
In ever loving memory of Peta VANEY. Beloved wife of Lieutenant Colonel L S VANEY, IAOC, who died at Rawalpindi 10 Nov 1942. *(82)(93)*

VANSTONE, Hazel   *(W/925)*
In loving memory of our darling Hazel, beloved child of F/S Sergeant and Mrs VANSTONE, who passed away 3 Apr 1932. Aged 7 mths. Jesus called a little child unto him.
(82)(93)

VAUGHAN   *(W/966)*
Beloved child of Sergeant and Mrs VAUGHAN. Royal Tank Corps. Born 15 Jan 1931. Died 28 Feb 1933. If thou shouldst call me to resign, what most I prize, it ne'er was mine, I only yield thee what is thine. Thy will be done.
(82)(93)

VESEY, W   *(LL/243)*
Sacred to the memory of No 3693 Corporal Rough Rider W VESEY, B Squadron 9th Queens Royal Lancers, who died at Rawalpindi 24 Apr 1904. Aged 28 yrs 11 mths. Erected as a token of esteem by his comrades. *(82)(93)(WM)*

VICKERS, A (see WEST RIDING REGIMENT (1))

VICKERY, C (see ROYAL HORSE ARTILLERY (3))

VICTORIA MEMORIAL

Until the Suez Crisis, this nine foot tall marble statue of Queen Victoria stood at the end of the Mall, near St Paul's Church. It had been commissioned in 1901, at the time of the Queen's death, by the Rawalpindi Queen Empress Memorial Fund, and was designed by J H Gardner of the Statuary & Granite Co of London. In the autumn of 1990 it was rescued by the British High Commission from a garden in Rawalpindi, and now has a new home overlooking the courtyard of the BHC in Islamabad, mounted on a new marble base, and flanked by 4 cypress trees. The execution of the engraving is very fine, and represents Queen Victoria at the time of her Coronation in 1838.

VIDA, Olive Jane   (R/285)
In ever loving and cherished memory of Olive Jane. The dearly
beloved and precious wife of Captain A St J VIDA, AF (I) ITD,
who died on 19 Sep 1938. Dearest, sweetest, best in all the
world to me, how can I live without thee, how forego, thy
sweet converse and love so dearly joined, to live in this
dreary world, saddened and forlorn. Rest in peace. She
toiled for me, she gave her precious life, to love and home,
a mother and a wife. Her golden heart had room for one and
all, but poured itself unstinted to each call. Cheerless
wife, O incomparable and precious mother, a queen among women.
The most cherished and priceless of my treasures, Olive
darling, hath been taken from me when I needed and longed for
you most. The sun hath forever set upon my horizon and the
transcendent rays that permeated my home forever extinguished.
                                            (82)(93)(mb)

VIDEION, Harold Charles   (DD/60)
Sacred to the memory of Harold Charles. Son of Louise and
Hiram VIDEION. Born Apr 1868. Died Mar 1869. Aged 11 mths.
                                            (82)(93)(BS)

VIGAR, Joseph   (Y/739)
In loving memory of No 6136220 Private Joseph VIGAR ......
                                            (82)(93)

VON GOLDSTEIN, Jessie McIntyre   (M/1177)
In loving memory of Jessie McIntyre, wife of George von
GOLDSTEIN, who died Rawalpindi 4 Oct 1911.*(82)(93)*

VON HENNING, Carl Ferdinand   (O/1124)
Carl Ferdinand Von HENNING who passed away at Rawalpindi on 28
Apr 1905. Aged 48 yrs. Deeply mourned by his wife and
children. The longest day has its evening, the hardest work
its end. The sharpest pain its contended and everlasting
rest.   *(93)*

VYSE, Charles Frederick   (N/1461)
Sacred to the memory of Major Charles Frederick VYSE, XXVII
Punjab Infantry, who departed this life at Rawalpindi 18 Nov
1894. Aged 44 yrs. This monument is erected by his brother
officers. Peace perfect peace. With loved ones far away, in
Jesus' keeping, we are safe and they.   *(82)(93)*

WADE, Elizabeth Jane   (IV/580)
Sacred to the memory of ....Elizabeth Jane ... of A WADE.
?Died Easter Morn 1937. .....Lissie darling thou hast left
me.......   *(93)*

WADE, Samuel C (BB/27)
In memory of Samuel C WADE, Hospital Steward, Her Majesty's 79th Cameron Highlanders, who died at Rawalpindi on 5 May 1864. Aged 33 yrs.
(93)

WADSWORTH, David Andrew (VI/461)
In loving memory of David Andrew, infant son of BSM and Mrs WADSWORTH, who was taken away from us 17 Aug 1949. Aged 7 mths 5 days.
(82)(93)(WM)

WAGHORNE, F (see ARMY SERVICE CORPS (1))

WAGSTAFF, L W (Y/709)
Sacred to the memory of No 4962586 Lance Sergeant L W WAGSTAFF. HQ Wing. 2nd Battalion The Sherwood Forresters. Died 24 Dec 1923. Aged 31 yrs 7 mths. *(82)(93)*

WAILES, Derrick Henry
Derrick Henry WAILES. Born 8 Oct 1920. Died 12 Apr 1921.
(82)

WAKEFIELD, Florence (X/798)
Peace. In loving memory of Florence WAKEFIELD. A sweet and beloved mother and wife of A B WAKEFIELD. Died 24 Feb 1940. Aged 55. Farewell in hope and love, in faith and peace and prayer, till he whose home is ours above unite us there.
(82)(93)

WAKEFIELD, George Edward Campbell & George Colin (X/810)
In beloved memory of George Edward Campbell WAKEFIELD, CIE, OBE. Born 16 Apr 1873. Died 9 Mar 1944 after many years service in British India and Indian States. Also to the blessed memory of his youngest son George Colin WAKEFIELD. 3rd/16th Punjab Regiment. Born 15 Sep 1914. Killed in action at Singapore 11 Feb 1942. Their lives beautiful memories, their absence a silent grief. *(82)(93)*

(There may be a further WAKEFIELD grave beside this but the stone was too heavy to turn over to read)

WALDREN, Herbert C (IV/503)
In memory of No 6079480 Lance Bombadier Herbert C WALDREN. 3rd Light Battery Royal Artillery. Died Rawalpindi 13 Nov 1928. Aged 24 yrs. *(82)(93)*

WALES, W J (LL/242)
Sacred to the memory of No 4981 Private W J WALES, B Squadron 9th Queen's Royal Lancers, who died at Rawalpindi 23 May 1904. Aged 21 yrs. Erected by the officers, NCOs and men of his Squadron. *(82)(93)*

WALKER, Alice Mary (M/1160)
Alice Mary. The beloved wife of Major A L WALKER, Royal Artillery. Died 31 Jan 1904. *(82)(93)*

WALKER, J (see WEST RIDING REGIMENT (1))

WALKER, Lily Irene   (IX/1009)
Resting. Sacred to the memory of Lily Irene. Beloved wife of
Captain H M L WALKR. IE. Born 30 Jun 1888. Died 1 Dec 1941.
                                          (82)(93)

WALKER, T   (O/1103)
Sacred to the memory of Gunner T WALKER, F Battery Royal
Horse Artillery, who died 6 Nov 1902. Aged 24 yrs. Erected
by his comrades.   (82)(93)(PS)

WALKINSHAW, John (see KING'S OWN SCOTTISH BORDERERS (1))

WALL, Frank   (see RIFLE BRIGADE (1))

WALLACE, Michael
In loving memory of Gunner Michael WALLACE, 5th Company Royal
Garrison Artillery, who died 16 Jun 1900. (82)

WALLER, Claude   (B/142)
In loving memory of Claude. Infant son of Captain J D WALLER,
Royal Artillery. Aged 2 mths 18 days. Safe in the arms of
Jesus.   (82)(93)

WALLHEAD (see ROYAL ARTILLERY (7))

WALSH, G (see 60TH ROYAL RIFLES (1))

WALSH, Mary   (L/1020)
In loving memory of little Mary. Child of E and P WALSH.
Died 21 Sep 1899. Dear Lord in thy keeping leave we here our
darling sleeping.   (93)

WALSH, P (see 70TH REGIMENT (1))

WALSH, William Henry   (UA/972)
William Henry. The beloved son of Corporal and Mrs WALSH.
Royal Signals. Born 26 Jul 1934. Died 1934. (82)(93)

WALTER, Cecil Ernest   (A/115)
In loving remembrance of Cecil Ernest. Son of Charles and
Annie WALTER. Born 29 Jan 1881. Died 7 May 1881. Safe in the
arms of Jesus.   (82)(93)(WM)

WALTON, John
In memory of No 950 Private John WALTON. 10th Royal Hussars.
Died Rawalpindi....   (82)

WAPLES, Derrick Henry   (W/921)
Our darling son Derrick Henry WAPLES. Born 8 Oct 1920. Died
12 Apr 1921. Suffer little children to come unto me and
forbid them not for of such is the kingdom of heaven.
                                          (93)

WARBURTON, Alfred George   (V/995)
In loving memory of Alfred George WARBURTON. Chelsea
Pensioner, Royal Artillery. Died 10 Oct 1946. Aged 88 yrs 6
mths.   /continued..........

WARBURTON, Alfred George (cont)

For I know whom I have believed and am persuaded that he is able to keep that which I have committed unto him against that day. 11 TIMOTHY 1.12. He is not dead, dear one of my affection, but gone unto that school where he no longer needs my poor protection and Christ himself doth rule. Erected by H O WARBUTON, Military Engineering Services. *(82)(93)(end)*

WARBURTON, Clara Agnes (V/975)
In ever loving and tender memory of Clara Agnes WARBURTON, the dearly beloved wife of Mr A G WARBURTON, who was called to her eternal rest on 2 Jan 1939. Aged 78 yrs 5 mths. Deeply regretted by her husband, children and grandchildren. Peace. Precious in the sight of the Lord is the death of his saints. PSALM 116.V.15. Erected by her sorrowing husband, children and grandchildren. *(82)(93)*

WARD, Harry Lyman (X/841)
Peace. Harry Lyman WARD. Born 29 May 1891 Bradford, Pennsylvania, USA. Died 16 Jan 1952 Dhulian Oil Field. *(93)*

WARD, Mary (DD/61)
...... Mary .... the beloved child of Major D WARD RE. *(93)*

WAREHAM, Frederick
Sacred to the memory of Private Frederick WAREHAM. H Company 1st Battalion Wiltshire Regiment. Died Rawalpindi 24 May 1905. Aged 24 yrs. *(82)*

WARNE, Nellie (LL/241)
Nellie, beloved daughter of Frank and Sophia WARNE, who died at Rawalpindi 9 Mar 1907. Aged 1 yr 11 mths. Her suffering is now o'er. Safe in the arms of Jesus. *(82)(93)(WM)*

WARNER, G F (IV/547)
Sacred to the memory of No 2316069 Corporal G F WARNER. Royal Corps of Signals. Died Rawalpindi 3 Sep 1932. Aged 28 yrs. Erected by all ranks of 1st Indian Divisional Signals. *(82)(93)*

WARNER, William (Q/1303)
In memory of No 4530 Private William WARNER, C Company 1st Battalion The Queen's Royal West Surrey Regiment, who died at Rawalpindi 7 Nov 1898. Aged 23 yrs. Erected by the officers, NCO and men of the company. *(82)(93)(PS)*

WARRE-CORNISH, Francis Thackeray (M/1157)
Captain Francis Thackeray WARRE-CORNISH, Adjutant 17th Bengal Lancers, who died at Rawalpindi 20 Oct 1901. Aged 30 yrs. Erected by his brother officers, British and native, who deeply mourn his loss. *(82)(93)(mb)*

WARREN, A E
In memory of No 5884 Corporal A E WARREN. C Squadron 1st King's Dragoon Guards. Died 16 Sep 1910. Aged 29. *(82)*

WARRY, Adeline, Sarah *(M/1233)*
In loving memory of Adeline Sarah. Dearly loved daughter of Sergteant T C and E WARRY. 2nd ... Rifles....
(82)(93)

WASHHAND, T (see 1ST KING'S DRAGOON GUARDS (1))

WATERPARK (see CAVENDISH, Henry)

WATERS, Owen
Sacred to the memory of No 67495 Bombadier Collar Maker Owen WATERS. 57th Battery Royal Field Artillery. Died Rawalpindi 31 May 1902. Aged 33 yrs 2 mths. *(82)*

WATKINS, A (see 1ST KING'S DRAGOON GUARDS (1))
WATKINS, W (see RIFLE BRIGADE (2))
WATKINS, W (see ROYAL ARTILLERY (3))

WATSON, Alan Holmes *(IV/516)*
In memory of Alan Holmes WATSON. Lieutenant Royal Artillery. Died 6 Aug 1931. Aged 32. *(82)(93)*

WATSON, Clifford Eustace *(LL/230)*
Our darling Clifford Eustace. The beloved son of AR Quartermaster Sergeant J H WATSON, AOC, and Flora his wife. Born 7 May 1907. Died 14 Nov 1908. Suffer little children to come unto me. God has taken home our darling, placed our bud amongst his flowers. Taken home the baby he lent us to a better world than ours. *(82)(93)(WM)*

WATSON, J (see 70TH REGIMENT (2))

WATSON, Nita *(X/830)*
In undying memory of Nita WATSON, wife of John WATSON, who died 19 Mar 1948. Aged 44. She devoted her life to those dear to her. *(93)*

WATSON, Wilfred *(M/1212)*
In loving memory of Little Wilfred. Little son of Fred and Ada WATSON. No 2 MB RA. Died Rawalpindi 12 Nov 1899. Aged 8 mths. Of such is the kingdom of heaven. *(82)(93)*

WATTS, John (see ROYAL GARRISON ARTILLERY (3))

WATTS, R (see GORDON HIGHLANDERS (3))

WAUGH, Robert *(V/996)*
Sacred to the memory of No 1038844 Sergeant Robert WAUGH. 73rd Field Battery, Royal Artillery. Died 5 Nov 1935. Aged 35 yrs. *(82)(93)*

WEARE, Elsie E
Elsie E WEARE. Aged 23 mths. 15 Jan 1879. *(82)(93)*

WEBB, Audrey   (W/932)
In loving memory of Audrey WEBB. Aged 1 yr 8 mths. Darling baby of Staff Sergeant and Mrs A WEBB, IAOC. Died 18 Feb 1934. I wonder, oh I wonder, where the little faces go that come and smile and stay awhile then pass like flakes of snow. There is no need to wonder, in that bright land so far, we shall find the little faces, with their guardian angels there.   *(82)(93)*

WEBB, W (see 36TH REGIMENT (1))

WEEDON, William   *(P/1243)*
Sacred to the memory of No 4611 Gunner William WEEDON, 57th Battery Royal Field Artillery, who died at Rawalpindi 5 Jul 1901. Aged 25 yrs. Erected by the officers, NCOs and men of the Battery.   *(82)(93)(PS)*

WELCHMAN, May Beatrice   *(III/491)*
In precious memory of May Beatrice, very dearly loved wife of Lieutenant P A WELCHMAN, IAOC, who passed away on 5 Apr 1946. Aged 47 yrs. Until we meet again.   *(93)(WM)*

WELDON, Charles   *(JJ/356)*
Northumberland Fusiliers. Sacred to the memory of Sergeant Michael GORDON, who died at Rawalpindi 15 Jan 1889. Aged 34 yrs. And Sergeant Charles WELDON, who died at Rawalpindi 15 Jan 1889.   *(82)(93)(BS)*

WELLER, H (see 1ST KING'S DRAGOON GUARDS (1))

WELLS, Bonny
Our Bonny. The beloved daughter of Colour Sergeant S and E WELLS. King's Own Scottish Borderers. Aged 1 yr 6 mths. *(82)*

WELLS, Jeannie   *(M/1231)*
Our darling pet Jeannie. The beloved daughter of W H and J E WELLS. Ordnance Department. Born 5 Nov 1901. Died 13 Apr 1902. Aged 5 mths 8 days.   *(82)(93)*

WELTON   *(W/895)*
Child of William Avis WELTON, Indian Ordnance Department, who died 5 Dec 1913. Aged 1 yr 6 mths 5 days.   *(82)(93)*

WEST, Jack Reginald   *(W/918)*
Jack Reginald. Son of Sergeant and Mrs J O WEST. Born 20 Jun 1920. Died 22 Nov 1921. Aged 1 yr 5 mths. Till we meet.
                                           (82)(93)

WESTON, John (see ROYAL FIELD ARTILLERY (2))
WESTWOOD, Ed (see ROYAL ARTILLERY (6))

WHALLEY, John   *(O/1088)*
In loving memory of John. Infant son of Colour Sergeant and Mrs WHALLEY. 2nd North Staffordshire Regiment. Died 22 Dec 1914. Aged 3 mths. Jesus called a little child. *(82)(93)*

WHEELER, C C (see ROYAL HORSE ARTILLERY (2))

WHEELER, John (see 98TH REGIMENT (1))

WHEELER, William and Thomas　　　　　*(M/1210)*
Safe in the arms of Jesus. In memory of William and Thomas. The beloved sons of Sergeant Thomas and Ellen WHEELER. 51st Royal Artillery. Aged 2 yrs 7 mths and 1 mth 4 days. Died 17 Sep 1899 and 7 Jan 1900.　　　　　*(82)(93)*

WHITE, Anne　　　　　*(JJ/353)*
Sacred to the memory of Mrs Anne WHITE, the beloved wife of Thomas WHITE, who departed this life 4 Feb 1888, aged 58 yrs, leaving her loving husband, grandson and friends to mourn her loss. This is erected by her bereaved and sorrowful husband and grandson. We loved her dear, Oh, no tongue can tell, how much, how fondly, and how well. God loved her too and thought it best to call her home to heaven to rest. My sins forgiven, my soul is free to God and Heaven now away I flee.
　　　　　(82)(93)(WM)

WHITE, E (see 60TH ROYAL RIFLES (1))

WHITE, E
No 4233 Private E WHITE. A Squadron 3rd King's Own Hussars. Died Rawalpindi 14 Mar 1907. Aged 25 yrs. IMTIAZALLY & CO, SIALKOT.　　　　　*(82)*

WHITE, J A (see ROYAL HORSE ARTILLERY (2))

WHITE, Richard　　　　　*(GG/208)*
Sacred to the memory of Private Richard WHITE, HM's 38th Regiment, who departed this life at Rawalpindi on 30 Aug 1867. Aged 32 yrs. This was erected by the 88th Connaught Rangers.　　　　　*(82)(93)(BS)*

WHITE, Thomas Kyran William　　　　　*(VI/469)*
In memory of Thomas Kyran William. Infant son of Major and Mrs T K WHITE. Died 20 Nov 1940.　　　　　*(82)(93)*

WHITE, William　　　　　*(VII/1401)*
Rev William WHITE, MHM. Born 30 Jan 1885 England. Ordained 1917 Mill Hill. Died 1 Feb 1967 Rawalpindi.　*(93)*

WHITING, John (see RIFLE BRIGADE (1))

WHITTACKER, Mary Queenie　　　　　*(L/1030)*
Mary Queenie WHITTACKER, CTD, who departed this life 28 Jul 1901. Aged 36 yrs and 9 mths.　　*(93)*

WHITTAKER, William　　　　　*(CC/40)*
Master Sergeant William WHITTAKER, 1st Battalion 6th Royal Regiment, who departed this life on 15 Nov 1868. Aged 39 yrs. This was erected by his three brothers who deeply lament his loss.　　　　　*(82)(93)(BS)*

WICKS, A R　　　　　*(N/1444)*
Sacred to the memory of Sergeant A R WICKS, 4th Dragoon Guards, who died at Rawalpindi 14 May 1896. *(82)(93)(BS)*

WICKS, Frederick William   (Q/1307)
In loving memory of Corporal Frederick William WICKS, 4th
(Royal Irish) Dragoon Guards, who died at Rawalpindi 13 May
1898. Aged 22 yrs 8 mths. Deeply regretted by all ranks.
Jesus saith: Thy brothers shall rise again. This stone was
erected by a sorrowing comrade. I have loved thee with an
everlasting love.   (82)(93)

WICKS, Joseph (see 9TH REGIMENT (1))

WIGHTMAN, Walter   (N/1446)
Sacred to the memory of Walter WIGHTMAN, youngest son of
Arthur WIGHTMAN of Blackwall, who died 28 May 1896. Aged 28.
                                            (82)(93)(PS)

WIGMORE, Claude Wesley and Evelyn Linda   (O/1076)
Claude Wesley. Died 22 Feb 1904. Aged 3 1/2 mths. Also
Evelyn Linda who died at Cherat 13 Jul 1902. Aged 5 days.
Beloved children of H and E WIGMORE, Ordnance Department.
                                            (82)(93)

WIGNALL, Percy   (M/1214)
The Lord giveth and the Lord hath taken away. Our little
Percy. The beloved son of Colour Sergeant and Annie WIGNALL.
3rd Battalion Rifle Brigade. Died 11 Dec 1899. Aged 1 yr.
                                            (82)(93)

WILD, Clara   (BB/13)
Sacred to the memory of Clara. The dearly beloved wife of
Lieutenant Colonel E J WILD, Bengal Infantry. Died 9 Oct
1876. Rock of ages cleft for me, let me hide myself in thee,
Holy, holy, holy Lord, God Almighty, early in the morning our
song shall rise to thee.   (82)(93)(PS/WM)
        (This headstone is known as The Growing Stone)
                    (see following page)

WILD, W (see ROYAL HORSE ARTILLERY (3))

WILD, Walter   (N/1431)
Sacred to the memory of Gunner Walter WILD. B Battery Royal
Horse Artillery. Died Rawalpindi 13 Jul 1895. Aged 20 yrs.
Erected by the officers, NCOs and men of B Battery.
                                            (82)(93)(BS)

WILDING, Horace   (III/477)
Per Adua ad Astra. No 519040 LAC Horace WILDING. No 39
Bomber Squadron RAF. In remembrance of Horace, dearly loved
son of A and E WILDING, who was fatally injured at Rawalpindi
while serving with the RAF on 23 Jun 1938. Aged 26 yrs.
                                            (82)(93)

WILKIE, Mary and Bob   (N/1447)
In memory of Mary. The beloved wife of Battery Quartermaster
Sergeant WILKIE. No 2 Ammunition Column, Royal Field Artillery. Died 9 Nov 1916. Aged 36 yrs 9 mths. Also of Little
Bob who preceeded his mother on 12 Oct 1915. Aged 22 days.
                                            (82)(93)(WM)

CLARA WILD

The Growing Stone

Since at least the 1920's, there has been talk about a headstone in Rawalpindi which "grows". There is some confusion as to whether the original "Growing Stone" was even in the Harley Street cemetery, but a poor photocopy of a photo taken in 1929 appears to confirm that it belongs to Clara Wild. The stem of her headstone doesn't survive, and the circular top now lies flat on the top of the "rock". The recent picture (below) shows the marks where the rock has reputedly grown. A newspaper article in 1982 claimed the Growing Stone to be that of "a soldier who led a bad life". The Author would appreciate any further information readers might have.

WILKINSON, George   (EE/92)
Sacred to the memory of Color (sic) Sergeant George WILKINSON.
70th Regiment who died at Rawalpindi on the 5 Jan 1874. Aged
27 yrs.   (82)(93)(BS)

WILKINSON, Joan   (UA/974)
In loving memory of our beloved daughter Joan WILKINSON. Died
11 Mar 1938. Suffer little children to come unto me.
                                            (82)(93)

WILL, John Ogilvie   (IV/554)
In loving memory of 2nd Lieutenant John Ogilvie WILL, ULIA,
attached to 2nd Battalion Welch Regiment. Died Rawalpindi 18
Apr 1934. Aged 20 yrs 1 mth.   (82)(93)

WILLASEY-WILSEY, Harry (see WILSEY, Harry Willasey)

WILLBOND, Cicilia Mary (May)   (L/1036)
In loving memory of Cicilia Mary (May). Beloved daughter of
Sergeant and Bridget WILLBOND. Royal Irish Regiment. Born 18
Mar 1907. Died 19 Mar 1908. RIP.   (82)(93)

WILLCOX, William   (N/1440)
Bays. Sacred to the memory of Private William WILLCOX, who
died at Rawalpindi of enteric fever 14 Dec 1893. Erected by
the officers, NCOs and men of C Squadron as a mark of respect.
                                            (93)(BS)

WILLIAM   (HH/331)
.... child of Mr and Mrs F P WILLIAM ..... The Kingdom of
God....   (93)(BS)

WILLIAM, Agnes Mary   (VII/1394)
Agnes Mary. Wife of Peter WILLIAM. Died 6 Aug 1970.   (93)

WILLIAMS   (see ROYAL HORSE ARTILLERY (2))
WILLIAMS, C   (see 70TH REGIMENT (1))
WILLIAMS, Edward   (see ROYAL HORSE ARTILLERY (3))

WILLIAMS, F   (IV/513)
No 1081938 Lance Bombadier F WILLIAMS. 33rd Field Battery
Royal Artillery. Died Rawalpindi 13 Jul 1929. Aged 24 yrs 9
mths. Erected by the officers, NCOs and men of his battery.
                                            (82)(93)

WILLIAMS, Gladys Ada Mary   (M/1170)
Jesu save. Gladys Ada Mary WILLIAMS. The dearly loved wife
of the Reverend J E H WILLIAMS. Priest Chaplain of Westridge,
Rawalpindi. Born 17 Oct 1887. Fell asleep in Jesus 30 Dec
1907.   (82)(93)

WILLIAMS, Gladys Mary and John Geoffrey   (M/1234)
Gladys Mary. Beloved and only child of Reverend J E H and
Gladys WILLIAMS. Born 22 Dec 1907. Died 31 Mar 1908. Also
John Geoffrey (Kippy). Aged 3 yrs. The beloved son of Rever-
end J E H and Brenda WILLIAMS. Died 11 Jul 1919.
                                            (82)(93)

WILLIAMS, J C　　　　　　　　　　　　　　　(S/318)
In loving memory of J C WILLIAMS who died 7 Feb 1928. Eternal rest give unto him O Lord. RIP.　　　(82)(93)(WM)

WILLIAMS, John　　　　　　　　　　　　　　(G/414)
Sacred to the memory of John WILLIAMS. "Native Christian". Born 6 Feb 1851. Fell asleep 15 Jun 1890. I believe in the communion of saints, the forgiveness of sins, the resurrection of the body, and the life everlasting. (+ short Urdu text)
　　　　　　　　　　　　　　　　　　　　　　(82)(93)(BS)

WILLIAMS, Kathleen　　　　　　　　　　　　(R/270)
IHS. In loving memory of my beloved daughter Kathleen WILLIAMS. Born 1 Sep 1915. Died 13 Mar 1932. Gone from us my beloved daughter to the world where there is no sorrow and pain. Thinking not of her poor mother, whom she left to mourn in vain.　　　　　　　　　　　　　　　(82)(93)(WM)

WILLIAMS, Violet Campbell　　　　　　　　(O/1083)
IHS. Violet Campbell WILLIAMS. Aged 13 mths. Died 5 Nov 1899. At Rest. NEYAZ ALI, SCULPTOR, RAWALPINDI. (82)(93)

WILLIAMS, W (see ROYAL ARTILLERY (3))

WILLIAMS, William　　　　　　　　　　　　(G/424)
Sacred to the memory of Band Sergeant William WILLIAMS, 2nd Battalion Seaforth Highlanders, who died at Rawalpindi 12 Feb 1890. Aged 28 yrs 5 mths. Behold how good and how pleasant it is for brethren to dwell together in unity. PSALM CXXXIII.
　　　　　　　　　　　　　　　　　　　　　　(82)(93)

WILLIAMSON, T (see 1ST KING'S DRAGOON GUARDS (1))

WILLIS, Emmiline Rose
Our little darling Emmiline Rose. Daughter of Sergeant and Mrs WILLIS. 10th Royal Hussars. Died 15 Apr 1908. Aged 6 mths 3 weeks.　　　　　　　　　　　　(82)(mb)

WILLIS, Marie Lousia (sic)　　　　　　　(LL/236)
Our darling little Marie Lousia (sic). Daughter of Sergeant and Mrs WILLIS, 10th Hussars, who departed this life.......
　　　　　　　　　　　　　　　　　　　　　　(93)(WM)

WILLIS, Mollie　　　　　　　　　　　　　　(L/1042)
My darling wife Mollie who died at Rawalpindi 9 May 1904. Aged 29 yrs. Erected by Sergeant J WILLIS. 2nd Royal Irish Fusiliers.　　　　　　　　　　　　　　(82)(93)

WILSEY, Harry Willasey and Edward Henry (X/813)
In ever loving memory of my beloved husband Harry Willasey WILSEY, Major S & T Corps, who died at Rawalpindi 17 Mar 1943. Aged 54 yrs. Also in proud and loving memory of our very dear son Edward Henry WILSEY (Ned) Lieutenant 93rd Burma Regiment, who fell at Kut-El-Amara Jan 1917. Aged 23 yrs. Goodbye our treasured darlings, your bright souls far away, in Jesus' precious keeping, we are safe and they.
　　　　　　　　　　　　　　　　　　　　　　(82)(93)

WILSON, Dorothy *(A/121)*
In memory of Dorothy. Aged 15 mths. Youngest child of Colonel WILSON. Died 1 Nov 1888. It is well with the child for in heaven their angel .... Always behold the face of ... which is in heaven. *(93)(BS)*

WILSON, Dorothy Maud
Dorothy Maud WILSON. Daughter of G H and M V WILSON, King's Royal Rifles. Died Rawalpindi 20 Mar 1904. Aged 2 yrs 11 mths. *(82)*

WILSON, Eleanor Frances *(X/805)*
In affectionate memory of Eleanor Frances. Dearly loved wife of W WILSON. Died 6 Oct 1945. Aged 73 yrs. A loving wife and devoted mother. *(82)(93)*

WILSON, Hugh *(III/494)*
In loving memory of Hugh WILSON who died at Rawalpindi 30 Mar 1952. Aged 57. RIP. *(93)*

WILSON, Ida Gladys and Gwendoline Mary *(M/1232)*
Ida Gladys. Beloved daughter of G H and M V WILSON. King's Royal Rifles. Born Rawalpindi 31 Mar 1902. Died 30 May 1902. Also Gwendoline Mary. Born South Africa 29 Sep 1898. Died Calcutta 29 Apr 1899. Aged 7 mths. If thou shouldst call me to resign what most I prize it ne'er was mine. I only yield thee what is thine. *(82)(93)*

WILSON, James *(G/416)*
3rd Dragoon Guards. Sacred to the memory of Private James WILSON, who died at Rawalpindi 18 Jun 1890. Aged 30. Erected by the NCOs and men of C Troop as a mark of respect. *(82)(93)(BS)*

WILSON, James *(P/1264)*
Sacred to the memory of Gunner James WILSON. F Battery Royal Horse Artillery, who died 28 Jun 1902. Aged 23 yrs. Erected by his comrades. AHMUD BUX, RAWALPINDI. *(82)(93)(PS)*

WILSON, John *(DD/46)*
Sacred to the memory of Assistant Surgeon John WILSON. 13th Regiment Bengal Cavalry. Born 9 Apr 1834. Died 27 Mar 1862. Aged 28 yrs. *(82)(93)(PS)*

WILSON-ALLEN, Lillian Florence
In loving memory of our pet Lillian Florence. The darling daughter of Sergeant John and May WILSON-ALLEN. 10th Hussars. Died on 9 Nov 1908. Aged 5 yrs 3 mths 11 days. *(82)*

WINCHELSEA, Albert Edward Bertie Skinner
In loving memory of Albert Edward Bertie Skinner WINCHELSEA. Died of cholera at Rawalpindi 7 Aug 1888. Aged 24 yrs. *(82)*

WINGFIELD, S H *(IV/573)*
In memory of Farrier Corporal S H WINGFIELD, 13th/18th Royal Hussars (QMD), who died at Rawalpindi 29 Jan 1937. Aged 35 yrs. Erected by his comrades. *(93)*

WINN, C C (see RIFLE BRIGADE (2))

WINSER, W (see RIFLE BRIGADE (2))

WINSLOE, Alfred Raynaud (X/775)
Alfred Raynaud WINSLOE. Colonel. Royal Engineers. Born 25 Oct 1868. Died 16 Jan 1932. Requiescat in pace.
(82)(93)(PS)

WINTER, E C T (see ROYAL ARTILLERY (6))

WINTER, Louisa Fredrika (X/755)
To the memory of my beloved mother Louisa Fredrika WINTER. Widow of Thomas WINTER. Born 24 Jul 1856. Died 22 Jan 1927. Aged 70 yrs 6 mths. After life's fitful fever, she sleeps well. Underneath are the everlasting arms. Rest in peace.
(82)(93)

WINTER, Thomas (X/774)
In loving memory of Thomas WINTER. Born in Dublin 11 Jan 1853. Died 13 Jul 1918. Aged 65 1/2 yrs. *(82)(93)(mb)*

WISENTHAL, A (Q/1316)
In loving memory of A WISENTHAL. Born in Austria in the year 1859. Died in Rawalpindi 25 Aug 1896. Aged 37 yrs.
(82)(93)(PS)

WITNEY, G (see 1ST KING'S DRAGOON GUARDS (1))

WOOD, Elanor C (S/312)
Sacred to the memory of my beloved mother Elanor C WOOD, who died on 22 May 1929. Aged 83. RIP. *(93)*

WOOD, Elizabeth Jane
Sacred to the memory of Elizabeth Jane. Wife of George Henry WOOD of Peshawar and Murree. Died 17 Nov 1882. Aged 43 yrs.
(82)

WOOD, Mary J (X/809)
In loving memory of our sister Mary J WOOD, who passed away 9 Jun 1944. Born 10 Jan 1871. *(82)(93)*

WOOD, Myra Anna Home (Y/681)
Myra Anna Home. Wife of J J WOOD. Deputy Superintendent Telegraphs. Died Rawalpindi 22 Aug 1918. Aged 36 yrs. Deeply mourned by her sorrowing husband and children. O Lord into thy hands we commend her spirit. Rest in peace.
(82)(93)(WM)

WOOD, Willie (L/1066)
My dearly loved son Willie WOOD, who died 30 Nov 1906 at Rawalpindi. Aged 25 yrs. Lord I hear thy voice and quit the world for you. Lord teach me to give back to thee the treasure thou didst lend to me. Eternal rest give unto him O Lord and let perpetual light shine upon me. Rest in peace my darling. *(82)(93)*

WOODHOUSE, Campbell H and Rosanna Louisa *(H/589)*
Sacred to the memory of Campbell H WOODHOUSE, Esquire. Captain 2nd Royal Sussex Regiment. Son of Henry R WOODHOUSE, Esq, of Wyndham Place, Bryanston Square, London and of Rosanna Louisa, his wife, who died from effects of an accident at Rawalpindi 4 Mar 1886. Aged 27 yrs. This monument is erected in affectionate remembrance by his brother officers.
(82)(93)(WM)

WOODS, C D *(BB/10)*
Erected by the noncommissioned officers and men of I Battery, Royal Horse Artillery, A Brigade. Sacred to the memory of Trumpeter C D WOODS. Died 15 Dec 1877. Aged 19 yrs. Also Gunner H ROWAN. Died 26 Jul 1878. Aged 25 yrs.
(82)(93)(BS)

WOODWARD, Jos *(DD/66)*
Sacred to the memory of Private Jos WOODWARD of F or Captain L C BROWNRIGG'S Company, 2nd Battalion, 60th Royal Rifles, who departed this life 16 Feb 1875. Aged 37 yrs. This tablet was erected by the officers, noncommissioned officers and men of the above company as a mark of their esteem. *(82)(93)*

WOOLL, Madeline Grace *(W/880)*
Madeline Grace. Beloved daughter of Sergeant Major George WOOLL and Grace his wife. 1/5th Fusiliers. Died 19 Feb 1911. Aged 1 yr 5 mths. God has taken home our darling .... picked our bud .... taken back the babe he lent us, to a better world than ours. *(82)(93)*

(see NO NAME - W/886)

WOOTON, F (see ROYAL ARTILLERY (3))

WORTH, Joan Antionette *(T/375)*
Joan Antionette WORTH. The daughter of Corporal and Mrs WORTH. Royal Signals. Died Rawalpindi 14 Nov 1930. Aged 1 yr 10 mths. Lord teach me to confide with thee the treasure thou didst trust with me. *(82)(93)(WM)*

WRIGHT   (see ROYAL FIELD ARTILLERY (1))
WRIGHT, Ada (see ROYAL ARTILLERY (6))

WRIGHT, Ann *(EE/88)*
Sacred to the memory of Ann WRIGHT. The beloved wife of John WRIGHT. Private HM's 36th Regiment. Died 27 Feb 1872. Aged 31 yrs. E.H. 36TH REGT. *(82)(93)(BS)*

(for illustration, see following page)

WRIGHT, F (see ROYAL HORSE ARTILLERY (2))

WRIGHT, G *(EE/195)*
Sergeant C COLEMAN. Died Rawalpindi 8 Jan 1888. Also G WRIGHT, who died at Rawalpindi on 16 Nov 1887. This stone is erected by their brother sergeants. *(82)(93)(BS)*

WRIGHT, Ann

WRIGHT, J (see ROYAL HORSE ARTILLERY (2))

WRIGHT, James Johnstone   (V/981)
In loving memory of James Johnstone WRIGHT. Senior Chaplain Church of Scotland. Died Rawalpindi 12 Apr 1928. Aged 55 yrs.   (82)(93)

WRIGHT, John   (V/986)
In loving memory of my dearly beloved husband John WRIGHT. Called to rest 20 Mar 1934. Safely anchored in Christ the rock of ages.   (82)(93)

WRIGHT, R (see SOMERSET LIGHT INFANTRY (1))

WRIGHT, Thomas   (GG/217)
Sacred to the memory of Thomas WRIGHT. Band. 6th Royal Regiment who died on 21 Sep 1869. Aged 16 yrs 9 mths. Erected by his parents. Jesus saw this young stranger clothed in innocence and love and to save him from all danger, took him to himself above.   (82)(93)(BS)

WYNNE, Alice Matilda   (GG/206)
In memory of Alice Matilda WYNNE. Born 16 Mar and died 8 Aug 1873.   (82)(93)(BS)

YARNOLD, W (see 70TH REGIMENT (2))

YATES, Morris (X/837)
In memory of Morris YATES, DSO, OBE. Brigadier, Royal Artillery. Born 15 Sep 1900. Died 23 Jan 1951 while serving as a volunteer in the Royal Pakistan Army. *(93)*

YOUNG, Kate
Our darling Kate. The dearly loved child of William and Louisa YOUNG. Aged 5 yrs 1 mth 3 days. Born 12 Apr 1888. Died 15 May 1893. *(82)*

YOUNG, Phyllis Irene (W/948)
Phyllis Irene. Beloved daughter of Sergeant and Mrs YOUNG. 1st King's Royal Rifle Corps. Died 7 Apr 1925. Aged 8 mths. Suffer little children to come unto me. *(82)(93)*

YOUREY, W (see ROYAL ARTILLERY (3))

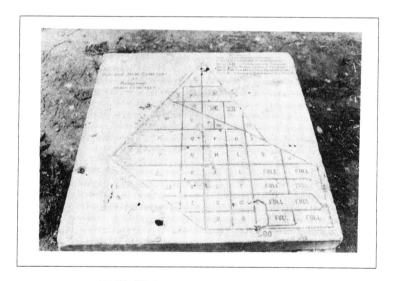

PLAN OF HARLEY STREET CEMETERY

(CC/43)

This marble plaque hangs on the wall of the cemetery lychgate. The burial places of the different denominations are detailed, and the plan forms the basis of the maps (see page 212).
(82)(93)(W)(WM)

HARLEY STREET REGIMENTAL INSCRIPTIONS

ARMY SERVICE CORPS (1)   (Y/679)
Sacred to the memory of the officers, NCOs and men of the 28th
MAC who have died while serving on the North West Frontier:

Captain A A GEDDES	ASC		
	Died Rawalpindi		5 Jul 1916
M2/166637	Lce Corporal W A CRAGG ASC		
	Died Rawalpindi		2 Feb 1917
M2/076674	MSS W R FERNS ASC		
	Died at Dera Ismail Khan		29 Jul 1917
DM2/129563	Private J M BAINBRIDGE ASC		
	Died at Rawalpindi		26 May 1918
M2/166392	Private F WAGHORNE ASC		
	Died Rawalpindi		7 Jul 1916
M2/175204	Private J FINDLATER ASC		
	Died Rawalpindi		14 Jul 1916
M2/166440	Private E H STEVENS ASC		
	Died at Rawalpindi		18 Jul 1916
M2/166384	Private F BRIDGLAND ASC		
	Died at Rawalpindi		29 Aug 1916

(82)(93)(WM)

GORDON HIGHLANDERS (1)

No 4465	Private James ERRINGTON	Died Jambata Kota
	16 Jun 1895	
No 4435	Private Harold JOHNSON	Died Jambata Kota
	19 Jul 1895	
No 3692	Private Francis PATMORE	Died Rawalpindi
	29 Nov 1895	

    Sleep thy last. Sleep from care and sorrow,
    Rest where no one weep till the eternal morrow,
    Though dark waters roll o'er the silent river,
    Thy fainting soul Jesus can deliver.
                                  (82)(93)

GORDON HIGHLANDERS (2)   (N/1425)
The NCOs and men of G Company 1st Gordon Highlanders who died
during the Chitral Campaign:

No 2014	Sergeant A KENT	Died Jambatai
No 3194	Lance Corporal W HYLAND	Died Jambatai
No 4360	Private W ANDREWS	Died Barchanrai
No 3681	Private J BAILEY	Died Rawalpindi
No 3834	Private J CARSWELL	Died Cherat
No 1638	Private G COWBOROUGH	Died Malakand
No 2016	Private T DONALDSON	Died Jambatai
No 4288	Private F HUGHES	Died Jambatai
No 4066	Private P KENNEDY	Died Jambatai

(82)(93)(PS)

GORDON HIGHLANDERS (3)　　　　　　　(Q/1309)
Sacred to the memory of:
No 2914　　Private C CONNON
　　　　　Died enteric fever at Sabathu　　　Jul 1893
No 3749　　Private James HENDERSON
　　　　　Died enteric fever at Umballa　　　Jan 1894
No 4555　　Private A FRANCES
　　　　　Killed at the storming of the Malakand　Apr 1895
No 4445　　Private W THORNTON
　　　　　Died enteric fever at Rawalpindi　　Oct 1895
No 5276　　Private J HENDERSON
　　　　　Died enteric fever at Kohat　　　　Dec 1897
No 3862　　Private R WATTS
　　　　　Died enteric fever at Rawalpindi　　Jan 1898
They did their duty. Erected by the officers, NCOs and men of C Company, 1st Battalion, Gordon Highlanders. AHMUD BUX.
(82)(93)

GORDON HIGHLANDERS (4)　　　　　　　(N/1435)
F Company 1st Gordon Highlanders. Sacred to the memory of
No 4689　　Private E PARDOE
　　　　　Killed storming the Malakand Pass　3 Apr 1895
No 4376　　Private I PAYNE
　　　　　Died Rawalpindi　　　　　　　　9 Dec 1895
No 4619　　Private E BAKER
　　　　　Died Gharial　　　　　　　　　24 May 1895
　　　　　Armourer Sergeant A J CRUTCHLEY
　　　　　Died Gharial　　　　　　　　　30 May 1896
No 2893　　Sergeant F MARTIN
　　　　　Died Madras　　　　　　　　　6 Jul 1897
No 1208　　Corporal J BELL
　　　　　Killed storming the Dargai Heights　20 Oct 1897
No 4299　　Private J QUINN
　　　　　Killed storming the Dargai Heights　20 Oct 1897
No 3868　　Private A CIVIL　　　　　　Died of wounds
　　　　　received storming Dargai Heights　21 Oct 1897
No 3411　　Private J DAVIE　　　　　Died of wounds
　　　　　received storming Dargai Heights　22 Oct 1897
No 3773　　Private T SMITH
　　　　　Died Tirah　　　　　　　　　21 Nov 1897
No 5297　　Private J LOFTHOUSE
　　　　　Died Gharial　　　　　　　　　29 May 1898
　　　　　Child Charlotte SANGSTER　　　2 Jun 1898
Erected by the officers, NCOs and men of F Company. Asleep in Jesus. Blessed sleep from which none ever wake to weep.
(82)(93)

GORDON HIGHLANDERS (5)　　　　　　　(D/1093)
Sacred to the memory of
Sergeant James THOMPSON who died at Rawalpindi
　　　　　　　　　　　28 Dec 1894　　　Aged 32 yrs
Sergeant Alex KENT who died at Landi Kotal
　　　　　　　　　　　14 Jun 1895　　　Aged 28 yrs
Sergeant John HUNTER who died at Cherat
　　　　　　　　　　　4 Jan 1896　　　Aged 28 yrs
RIP. Erected by the Sergeants 1st Gordon Highlanders.　*(93)*

1ST KING'S DRAGOON GUARDS (1)   (G/421)
Sacred to the memory of the undermentioned NCOs, men, women
and children of the 1st Kings Dragoon Guards:

1064	Private R BAMBRICK	11 Jan 1884	26 yrs 11 mths
	Lieutenant J A PATTERSON	11 Jun 1884	35 yrs
1747	Private C SULLY	25 Jun 1884	32 yrs 11 mths
2374	Private R W COLLYER	22 Sep 1884	24 yrs
2424	Private T COOMBES	22 Oct 1884	21 yrs 10 mths
762	Private H PODMORE	30 Oct 1884	37 yrs 4 mths
1296	Private W HOULDSWORTH	22 Nov 1884	29 yrs
2470	Private W LAMMAS	21 Feb 1885	20 yrs
2403	Private G JACKSON	3 Jul 1885	21 yrs
2630	Private J KILCULLEN	5 Jul 1885	22 yrs
2449	Private D HEHIR	7 Jul 1885	23 yrs
2279	Staff Sergeant J BELL	5 Aug 1885	35 yrs
2261	Private W McCUTCHEON	16 Mar 1886	31 yrs
2255	Private E MINCHER	23 Mar 1886	28 yrs 1 mth
2777	Private H THOMAS	30 Apr 1886	26 yrs
2524	Private C BATCHELOR	17 Oct 1886	21 yrs
2167	Private E CALLINGHAM	12 Nov 1886	29 yrs
1461	Private A STEVENS	26 Nov 1886	30 yrs 5 mths
2475	Private R BUTLER	9 Jan 1887	23 yrs
1765	Corporal H BOGGISS	17 Jan 1887	29 yrs
3122	Corporal T WILLIAMSON	31 Jul 1887	29 yrs
1357	FQMS A HANCOCK	28 Mar 1887	34 yrs 5 mths
3007	Private C KEOUGH	15 Apr 1887	22 yrs 7 mths
2901	Private J HICKMAN	13 Sep 1887	22 yrs
2786	Private H WELLER	20 Sep 1887	25 yrs 11 mths
2581	Private J H ROGERS	9 Oct 1887	21 yrs
2598	Private H ASHBY	21 Nov 1887	29 yrs 7 mths
995	Corporal J LUNNY	10 Dec 1887	37 yrs 2 mths
775	Private T WASHHAND	14 Dec 1887	38 yrs 8 mths
2392	Trumpeter W HILLMAN	24 Jan 1888	19 yrs 5 mths
1200	Private J TIMMS	24 Feb 1888	23 yrs 7 mths
2336	Private R H SOUTHGATE	19 Mar 1888	22 yrs
3071	Private R FINDLAY	8 May 1888	21 yrs
3083	Private A SIMMONDS	13 May 1888	24 yrs 3 mths
3075	Private T SHERLOCK	19 May 1888	21 yrs 1 mth
2526	Private J SEXEY	7 Jun 1888	24 yrs 9 mths
3143	Private E SHAW	9 Jun 1888	22 yrs
Schoolmaster R W SEYMOUR		1 Aug 1888	32 yrs 5 mths
1919	Sergeant J STEELE	6 Aug 1888	33 yrs
3113	Private H PHILLIPS	6 Aug 1888	23 yrs
3026	Private J EDMONDS	6 Aug 1888	21 yrs
2920	Private N NAISBETT	6 Aug 1888	22 yrs
2443	Private H TIPPETTS	6 Aug 1888	24 yrs
2857	Lance Corporal A SKINNER	7 Aug 1888	24 yrs
2967	Private W GRIMES	7 Aug 1888	21 yrs
2706	Private T PATTERSON	7 Aug 1888	21 yrs
2562	Private R McFARLANE	9 Aug 1888	26 yrs
2863	Lance Corporal W CAMPION	10 Aug 1888	23 yrs
3252	Corporal J OLLIVER	10 Aug 1888	29 yrs
2577	Private I DAVIS	12 Aug 1888	25 yrs
3107	Private A WATKINS	12 Jul 1888	20 yrs 3 mths
2353	Lance Corporal S PILCHER	14 Aug 1988	25 yrs 9 mths
2221	Private J MOORE	15 Aug 1888	29 yrs 7 mths
			/continued....

1ST KING'S DRAGOON GUARDS (cont)

2469	Private G WITNEY	16 Aug 1888	24 yrs 10 mths
2583	Private T KANE	20 Aug 1888	23 yrs 11 mths
2512	Private A R MASON	20 Aug 1888	30 yrs 3 mths
2903	Private R BOATWRIGHT	1 Sep 1888	22 yrs 4 mths
2528	Private H BARNES	19 Dec 1888	24 yrs 6 mths
3002	Pte C F CHRISTOPHERSON	27 Jan 1889	24 yrs 2 mths
2917	Private E SHIELDS	5 Apr 1889	22 yrs
3120	Private C MORRIS	18 Apr 1889	22 yrs
2981	Private R LEWCOCK	11 May 1889	20 yrs 11 mths
3050	Private T HARRISON	27 May 1889	
2635	Private F GOLLAGHY	8 Jun 1889	
3252	Lce Corporal T G STURGIS	19 Jul 1889	
2858	Lance Corporal G BLAKE	2 Sep 1889	

Women

Mrs C GWILLIAM	28 Nov 1885	28 yrs
Mrs A JOHNSON	2 Feb 1886	32 yrs
Mrs K O'DONNELL	Feb 1888	
Mrs A A LOWING	6 Aug 1888	26 yrs
Mrs E OSBORNE	12 Aug 1888	31 yrs
Mrs T McKNIGHT	15 Sep 1888	32 yrs

Children

Child R A OSBORNE	9 Apr 1884	4 mths
M G McKNIGHT	28 Jun 1884	10 mths
E H EDWARDS	18 May 1885	5 yrs 1 mth
A COLLINS	20 Aug 1885	3 mths
A JONES	28 Apr 1886	6 mths
R H LAWRENCE	28 Apr 1886	6 mths
G J RICKMAN	20 Aug 1886	2 mths
D COLLINS	12 Oct 1888	3 mths
H BARGER	Apr 1888	4 mths
W R DONN	22 Nov 1888	5 mths
E McGILL	13 Dec 1888	5 mths

(82)(93)

KING'S OWN SCOTTISH BORDERERS (1)   *(I/400)*
Sacred to the memory of

Private John KELLY	Died	9 Jun 1896	Aged 27 yrs
Corporal John WALKINSHAW	Died	2 Nov 1895	Aged 26 yrs
Corporal Alfred HAWKINS	Died	27 Nov 1894	Aged 20 yrs
Private William MORTON	Died	5 May 1894	Aged 24 yrs
Private John SHIELDS	Died	20 Feb 1897	Aged 27 yrs

This stone was erected by the officers, NCOs and men of E Company King's Own Scottish Borderers as a mark of respect. AHMUD BUX, SCULPTOR, RAWALPINDI AND UMBALA.   *(82)(93)*

KING'S OWN SCOTTISH BORDERERS (2)

  William LAWRIE   Colour Sergeant A Company 2nd Battalion
    King's Own Scottish Borderers.
    Died Rawalpindi 18 Aug 1897. Aged 33.
  Sergeant Alex KENT who died at Jambat Kotal 14 Jun 1895.
    Aged 28 yrs.
  Sergeant John HUNTER who died at Cherat 4 Jan 1896.
    Aged 28 yrs.
  Sergeant James THOMPSON who died at Rawalpindi
    28 Dec 1894. Aged 32 yrs.   *(82)*

RIFLE BRIGADE (1)   (N/1426)

In memory of Lance Corporal Thomas DICKENSON, 3rd Battalion Rifle Brigade (PCO). Died 15 Jun 1895. Aged 21 yrs.

Also to those below who died during the Tochi Valley Expedition 1897-1898:

Lance Corporal	Alfred FAULKNER	17 Aug 1897
	Died Sherani	Aged 21
Lance Corporal	Frank WALL	19 Aug 1897
	Died Sherani	Aged 21
Lance Corporal	John WHITING	29 Aug 1897
	Died Sherani	Aged 25
Lance Corporal	Albert DOREY	31 Aug 1897
	Died Sherani	Aged 22
Corporal Henry	HOLLAND	8 Sep 1897
	Died Sherani	Aged 25
Acting Corporal	William MITCHELL	7 Sep 1897
	Died Atta-Khel	Aged 21
Acting Corporal	Samuel MOUNSEY	22 Oct 1897
	Died Bannu	Aged 27
Acting Corporal	Benjamin BARLOW	1 Nov 1897
	Died Kohat	Aged 33

Erected by the Corporals of the Battalion as a mark of esteem and respect. FEYAZ ALI, AMBALA.   *(82)(93)*

RIFLE BRIGADE (2)
Sacred to the memory of

Major The Honourable C C WINN	Died Ambala
2nd Lieutenant KANE	Died Miranshah
Acting Corporal E DOREY	Died Sherani
Private W WATKINS	Died Sherani
Acting Corporal W MILLS	Died.....
Private W WINSER	Died Sherani
Private E DOUTHWAITE	Died Sherani
Private GUTTERIDGE	Died Datta Khel
Private W BROWN	Died Datta Khel
Private F LEWINS	Died Datta Khel
Private A SKEWS	Died Datta Khel
Private F LAWRENCE	Died Miranshah
Private H GARLTON	Died Bannu
Private LUNN	Died Bannu
Private B THOMAS	Died Gumbat
Private W DAWES	Died Umballa
Private W SMITH	Died Umballa
Private G THOMAS	Died Umballa
Private A GONNESBY	Died Jullunder
Private J HATHERILL	Died Solon
Private J DICKENS	Died Kuldana
Private W HURST	Died Murree

F Company, 3rd Battalion, Rifle Brigade. *(82)*

ROYAL ARTILLERY (1)   (BB/11)
In memory of :
John EVANS   Gunner 15/9th Battery.
                        Died at Rawalpindi 15 Nov 1877. Aged 33.
Also
William COOK.   Gunner. 15/9th Battery.
     Accidentally killed at Rawalpindi 15 Jan 1877. Aged 31.
John LAWRENCE.   Gunner. 15/9th Battery.
                        Died Khaira Gali 3 Aug 1877.   Aged 26.
James DOHERTY   Gunner. 15/9th Battery.
                        Died at Umballa 1 Jan 1876.   Aged 28.
                                (82)(93)(BS)

ROYAL ARTILLERY (2)   (C/103)
Sacred to the memory of the following men of D Battery 4th Brigade Royal Artillery, who died while the Battery was quartered at Rawalpindi:
Gunner A BONHAM   17 Nov 1878
Farrier Sergeant R PENFOLD   7 Dec 1878
Trooper D HAMILTON   16 Aug 1879
Sergeant J McCONNELL   15 Dec 1879
Gunner J EARLE   17 Sep 1879
Gunner H HITCHCOCK   27 Oct 1879
Driver W ALLAN   4 Dec 1879
Gunner R LILLEY   8 Dec 1879
Gunner J BOOTH   17 May 1880
Gunner J JEPSON   14 Jun 1880
Gunner A LEARMOUTH   14 Jan 1881
Gunner W McGRATH   27 Aug 1881
                                (82)(93)

ROYAL ARTILLERY (3)   (G/429)
This monument was erected by the officers, NCOs and men of No 15 (Late 7/1) Eastern Division, Royal Artillery, as a mark of respect to their departed comrades.
Bombadier W HANNANT   Bombadier W WATKINS
Gunner C FANCE   Gunner J McGREGOR
Gunner F WOOTON   Gunner J GIBBS
Gunner A OTTER   Gunner J PETTITT
Gunner J BROWN   Gunner W WILLIAMS
Gunner J DUGGAN   Gunner J BRIMSON
Gunner W YOUREY   Bombadier J LUMSDAIN

Also of Catherine the beloved wife of Sergeant E APPLEYARD.
They rest from their labours.   (82)(93)(BS)

ROYAL ARTILLERY (4)   (G/420)
Sacred to the memory of the noncommissioned officers and men of 60th Field Battery, Royal Artillery, who departed this life during the stay of the Battery in this station from 19 Feb 1891 to 18 Jan 1894.
Gunner Frederick NEIL   29 Mar 1891 at Jhansi
Gunner John POWELL   11 Jul 1891
Driver John MOFFAT   31 Jul 1891
Bombadier James CARTLEDGE   6 Sep 1891
                                        /continued..........

- 199 -

ROYAL ARTILLERY (4) (cont)
Driver William BROWN   15 Oct 1891
Driver William POWELL   12 Jan 1892
Gunner Edward MOTT   16 Jan 1892
Bombadier Patrick DOLAN   26 Mar 1892
Gunner Charles HODDER   29 Sep 1892
Bombadier James HARRISON   7 May 1892
Bombadier Clifford ANDREWS   23 Jun 1892
Gunner John LATIMER   11 Jun 1893.
This memorial is erected by the officers, NCOs and men of the
60th Field Battery, Royal Artillery, as a mark of esteem.
FAIYAZ ALLY & SONS, SCULPTOR, UMBALLA AND RAWALPINDI.
                                          (82)(93)(PS)
     (See page 137 for illustration)

ROYAL ARTILLERY (5)   (I/395)
Sacred to the memory of the undermentioned NCO and gunners of
5 Company, SD Royal Artillery. Erected by the officers, NCOs
and men of the Company:
Gunner John RENAULT   Gunner Richard LEONARD
Gunner Michael RIORDAN   Gunner Richard HALLIGAN
Gunner George CHILCOTT   Gunner John HEALY
Gunner Dan MAGEE   Gunner Jeramiah FEHILY
Gunner Henry Lewis ROBEY   Gunner Patrick McCOURT
Corporal Alex Ashley Edward REID
Gunner T McCAUSLAND   Gunner John ODELL
Gunner Thomas KENNEDY   Gunner Henry COX
Gunner Hurst COWEN   Gunner Patrick DOWDALL
Gunner F C KELLY   Bombadier John HOSFORD
                                          (82)(93)(BS)

ROYAL ARTILLERY (6)   (M/1235)
10th Field Battery Royal Artillery. In memory of the officers, NCOs and men who died in India from 1884 to 1898:
1884
Driver M BOLLEY   at Kirkee
1885
Lieutenant A H SIMPSON   at Kirkee
Gunner W BARRETT   at Kirkee
1886
Gunner T CONSTABLE   at Karachi
1887
Gunner W SMITH   at Karachi
Sergeant W H PULSFORD   at Karachi
1888
Driver M HANNON   at Karachi
1889
Gunner G NODDLE   at Karachi
Corporal F MONKS   at Karachi
Driver J HANNEN   at Karachi
Gunner D O'CONNELL   at Karachi
1891
Gunner T MATHESON   at Dalhousie
Bombadier Collar Maker William HERBERT   at Multan
Bombadier George KYLE   at Multan
                                       /continued........

ROYAL ARTILLERY (6) 1891   (cont)

Driver Ed WESTWOOD   at Multan
Driver William SHRIMPLIN   at Multan
1893
Major G T Kennedy SKIPTON   at Multan
Gunner James DAWSON   at Dalhousie
Gunner H R FINCKE   at Meean Meer
1893   Women
Mrs STURTON   at Multan
Mrs MILLER   at Multan
1892   Children
Ada WRIGHT   at Multan
1895
Gunner W EGGERS
Corporal T H REVENING
1896
Gunner M PHELAN
Driver J C TAYLOR
Gunner J TITLEY
1897
Gunner J MONKTON
Trumpeter G E ORCHARD
Gunner L ANDERTON
Gunner E C T WINTER
Driver D DOBSON   Women
Driver A LOMAX   K E PEMBLE   1896
Gunner C FIELDER   S STOKES   1897
1898   Children
Driver J JOHNSON   G GOWTON   Male 1894
Gunner E SHARDLOW   G H W JUPP   Male 1897
Driver W J LANCE   E V ADAMSON   Male 1897
Driver A ALLSEBROOK   J A GUEST   Male 1898
                                                    (82)(93)(PS)

ROYAL ARTILLERY (7)   (Q/1315)
Sacred to the memory of the noncommissioned officers and men of No 7(?) Mountain Battery Royal Artillery who died between the years 1895 and 1898. Erected by the officers, NCOs and men as a mark of esteem and respect.

Khyra Gali
Bombadier HADDON   9 Jun 1896   Aged 30
Chitral Relief Force
Gunner STURNEY   16 Sep 1895   Aged 25
Malakand Field Force
Gunner BLISSETT   1 Aug 1897   Aged 26
Bombadier DAVIES   27 Dec 1897   Aged 26
Tpr MALLON   28 Sep 1897   Aged 25
Gunner JOHNSON   12 Nov 1897   Aged 26
Rawalpindi
Qtr Master Sergeant COLLISTER 20 Feb 1897   Aged 36
Corporal WALLHEAD   22 Jan 1897   Aged 30
Bombadier MANUEL   30 May 1898   Aged 30
NYAZ ALI, SCULPTOR, SUDDAR BAZAAR, RAWALPINDI.
                                           (82)(93)

- 201 -

ROYAL ARTILLERY (8)　　　　　　　　　(Q/1312)
In memory of

Corporal M H SINEL　　　　　　Gunner W HALL
Gunner W NOAD　　　　　　　　Gunner J BOSLEY

All of No 5 Company, Western Division, Royal Artillery who died at this station 1895 - 1899. Erected by their comrades. AHMUD BUX & SONS, SCULPTOR, UMBALLA AND RAWALPINDI.
　　　　　　　　　　　　　　　　　　　(82)(93)(PS)

ROYAL ARTILLERY (9)　　　　　　　　(Q/1321)
Sacred to the memory of

Corporal T SINDEN　　　　　Died Rawalpindi
　　　　　　　　　　　　14 Nov 1896　　Aged 23 yrs 9 mths
Gunner D O'SULLIVAN　　　　Died Rawalpindi
　　　　　　　　　　　　 9 Oct 1896　　Aged 25 yrs 5 mths
Sergeant S PACKER　　　　　Died Rawalpindi
　　　　　　　　　　　　14 Jun 1898　　Aged 28 yrs
Gunner G A S MODGET　　　　Died Rawalpindi
　　　　　　　　　　　　15 Jul 1898　　Aged 24 yrs 6 mths
also
No 11666　Gunner John HAWKINS　Died Rawalpindi 1 May 1899
No 93110　Gunner John DAVIES　Died Rawalpindi 27 Dec 1899

No 5 MB, Royal Artillery. AHMUD BUX & SON, SCULPTOR, RAWALPINDI AND UMBALLA.　　　　　*(82)(93)*

ROYAL ARTILLERY (10)　　　　　　(DD/56)
The undermentioned noncommissioned officers and men of D Battery 16th Brigade RA, who have died since the arrival of the Battery at Rawalpindi:

Gunner George RENNY　　　　　　22 Jul 1872
Driver John BATES　　　　　　　 3 Sep 1872
Wheeler Sergeant R E JARRETT　 31 Mar 1873
Driver James HILLYER　　　　　 ?6 May 1873
Gunner Patrick MATTHEWS　　　　18 May 1873

Erected by the officers, noncommissioned officers and men of the Battery as a mark of esteem and respect 24 Sep 1873.
　　　　　　　　　　　　　　　　　　　(82)(93)(BS)

ROYAL FIELD ARTILLERY (1)　　　　　(I/404)
Sacred to the memory of the warrant officers, NCOs and men of No 2 Column Royal Field Artillery, who died Rawalpindi during the war 1914-1918:
At Rawalpindi
No 1197　　BSM F ROVERY　　　　24 May 1917
No 9759　　Gunner A LEWINGTON　15 Jul 1918
No 214380　Gunner H SENIOR　　 13 Jul 1918
No 781498　Gunner WRIGHT　　　 1 Nov 1918
No 45379 　Gunner LOUDEN　　　 14 Jun 1918 at Simla.
　　　　　　　　　　　　　　　　　　　(82)(93)(PS)

ROYAL FIELD ARTILLERY (2)   (Z/660)

67th Battery Royal Field Artillery. In memory of men, women and children of 67th Battery, Royal Field Artillery who died during the stay of the battery at Rawalpindi:

Men
```
16953      John ACTON           Died 12 Oct 1907
5778       James COOK           Died  9 May 1908
45541      George SPICER        Died  9 May 1908
33227      George COOK          Died 23 May 1908
14079      Richard FLINDAL      Died  3 Jul 1908
99755      John WESTON          Died 27 Jul 1908
32282      Samuel JOHNSON       Died 27 Oct 1909
20375      Patrick COUGHLAN     Died  5 Apr 1910
```
Children
```
           Robert GAWKRODGER    Died 31 Jul 1908
           Phylis E HOME        Died 18 Nov 1908
           Edith O SMITH        Died 12 Apr 1909
```
Women
```
           Mrs COLLINS          Died 31 Aug 1908
           Mrs STRATTON         Died 27 Sep 1909
```
                                          (82)(93)(WM)

ROYAL GARRISON ARTILLERY (1)   (LL/244)
To the memory of the NCOs and men who died on field service Aden Hinterland 1903-1904. The strife is o'er, the battle done.
```
RGA 49     Bombadier T CHESTER    Died Dthalla
           1 Jun 1903             Aged 27
RGA 1151   Bombadier G HANKERS    Died Dil-hajira
           11 Nov 1903            Aged 25
RA 96499   Gunner F GALE          Died Aden
           21 Mar 1904            Aged 29
RGA 25990  Gunner F BISHOP        Died Rawalpindi
           25 Jun 1904            Aged 28
RA 92137   Bombadier A TOOTH      No 2 MB RGA (attached)
           Died Alsalula          26 Feb 1903  Aged 28
RA 88184   Corporal J TOWEY       Died Dthalla
           16 May 1903            Aged 30
```

Erected by the officers, NCOs and men of No 6 MB, RGA.
                                          (82)(93)(PS)

ROYAL GARRISON ARTILLERY (2)   (Z/678)
Erected by officers, non commissioned officers and men of 7th Mountain Battery, Royal Garrison Artillery in memory of their comrades who died during the time the battery served at Rawalpindi and in the Murree Hills 1907 - 1911:

```
33183      Gunner T TURNER      Died 30 May 1908
26243      Gunner A PYMENT      Died  1 Jun 1908
21297      Gunner A BROOKS      Died  5 Jun 1908
23964      Gunner L BOURKE      Died 25 Dec 1907
```
                                          (82)(93)(WM)

ROYAL GARRISON ARTILLERY (3)   (P/1255)
Sacred to the memory of the undermentioned NC officers and men of No 1 Mountain Battery, Royal Garrison Artillery:

RA/18072	Gunner John WATTS	who died at Simla 26 Jun 1895	Aged 41 yrs
RA/72365	Gunner Alfred JAMES	who died Camp Rajpur 30 Dec 1895	Aged 27 yrs
RA/75380	Bombadier Thomas ASHBY	who died at Malakand Kotal 6 Aug 1897	Aged 27 yrs
RA/99120	Bombadier Joseph ROSS	who died at Nowshera 14 Aug 1897	Aged 24 yrs
RA/88064	Gunner David TERRY	who died at Nowshera 25 Jun 1898	Aged 25 yrs
RA/70152	Gunner Henry JOHNSON	who died Khyra-Gali 1 Oct 1898	Aged 32 yrs
RA/3191	Gunner John L(?D)OUDWELL	who died at Landikotal 7 Aug 1899	Aged 25 yrs
RA/2294	Bombadier John CORRIGAN	who died at Peshawar 29 Dec 1899	Aged 28 yrs

Erected by the officers, NCOs and men of No 1 MB, RGA as a token of respect.   *(82)(93)(PS)*

ROYAL GARRISON ARTILLERY (4)   (P/1236)
This stone is erected by the officers and men of No 2 Mounted Battery Royal Garrison Artillery to the memory of their comrades who died between 1898 and 1904:
Sergeant A THOMSON
Sergeant J BENJAMIN
Sergeant T ROBERTS
Sergeant Farrier E DAY
Corporal W E HOPPER
Bombadier A TOOTH
Bombadier S MARSHALL
Gunner H B ELSON
Gunner E SPENCER
Gunner S BALDWIN
Gunner G CLARKE

(82)(93)

ROYAL HORSE ARTILLERY (1) - SEE FOLLOWING PAGE

ROYAL HORSE ARTILLERY (1)   (HH/327)

Sacred to the memory of the NCOs and men of K Battery, Royal Horse Artillery who died during the years 1897-1902. Erected by the officers, NCOs and men of the Battery as a mark of their respect and esteem. NEYAZ ALI, SCULPTOR, RAWALPINDI.

At Sialkot
Gunner Herbert BARBER   Died 7 Sep 1903   Aged 28
Driver Alfred DARBY   Died 9 Sep 1903   Aged 26
At Rawalpindi
Gunner Rowland BOWELL   Died 14 Jul 1897   Aged 22
Gunner Alfred COOPER   Died 5 Jul 1898   Aged 34
Driver Frank VANDEMERE   Died 30 Dec 1898   Aged 25
Driver Arthur POPLAR   Died 5 Jun 1899   Aged 22
Gunner Henry SMYTHE   Died 13 Feb 1899   Aged 29
Driver Ernest VALLER   Died 8 May 1900   Aged 29
Elizabeth. Daughter of Sergeant P SAWYER.
                              Died 4 Nov 1897. Aged 4 mths
Katherine. Daughter of Sergeant P SAWYER.
                              Died 29 Nov 1897. Aged 5 mths
William. Son of Corporal W COOKE.
                              Died 4 Apr 1898. Aged 3 mths
Acting Bombadier Frederick MEYERS
                              Died 13 Sep 1903.   Aged 26
Jessie FITT   Died 7 Sep 1903.   Aged 27
Cecil FITT   Died 7 Sep 1903.   Aged 6
At Cliffden
Barbara. Wife of Gunner BARNES Died 27 Aug 1898   Aged 27
At Lower Topa
Driver Charles HICKMAN   Died 2 Jun 1899   Aged 21
Driver Robert NEALE   Died 3 Jun 1902   Aged 28
Gunner Robert CLIFFORD   Died 26 Aug 1902   Aged 24
At Jamrud
Driver Alfred LUDKIN   Died 30 Oct 1897   Aged 22
Staff Sergeant Thomas SIBLEY Died 1 Nov 1897   Aged 28
At Peshawar
Driver Albert QUINTON   Died 8 Sep 1897   Aged 25
Driver Frank STAY   Died 3 Nov 1897   Aged 25
Bombadier William NICHOLS   Died 7 Nov 1897   Aged 26
Gunner Denis HAYES   Died 4 Nov 1897   Aged 23
Trooper Arthur SAVAGE   Died 30 Dec 1897   Aged 26
Driver Richard McLEOD   Died 5 Jan 1898   Aged 21
Driver Arthur DOWNS   Died 6 Mar 1898   Aged 20
Gunner William REID   Died 9 Sep 1903   Aged 28
Driver William MOORE   Died 12 Sep 1903   Aged 34
Driver William HAGYARD   Died 18 Oct 1903   Aged 24
                                  (82)(93)(PS)

(see previous page for illustration)

ROYAL HORSE ARTILLERY (2)   (J/443)
In memory of soldiers, women and children T Battery, Royal Horse Artillery (late MB RHA), who died Rawalpindi from Nov 1887 to 19 Oct 1891:

Lieutenant G R COOKES   Corporal W I ALLEN
Bombadier M COOPER   Bombadier J MORGAN
Bombadier A E FOWLER   Trumpeter A MOORE
Gunner G BENNETT   Gunner R BIRCHELL
Gunner F CHILVERS   Gunner M CONNOR
Gunner T PRICE   Gunner W HOOKER
Driver C HURRELL   Driver C JACKSON
Driver A LANE   Driver G MOON
Driver E PIKE   Driver J WRIGHT
Driver C C WHEELER   Driver G SMYTH
Gunner J BROWN   Gunner J A WHITE
Driver ... WILLIAMS   Gunner T P FLANAGAN
Gunner P FLYNN   Gunner W MARCH
Gunner A MARSTON   Gunner W MANLEY
Gunner F PARFITT   Gunner F WRIGHT
Driver H CARVER   Driver J CUMMING
Driver J HOWARD

Women and Children
...   Daughter of Sergeant W G STUDLLEY (?)
...   Son of Driver G BATES
C ELLIS   Wife of Sergeant Farrier ELLIS
S ELLIS   Son of Sergeant Farrier ELLIS
A L KERRY   Son of Sergeant Major KERRY
G J MacDONALD   Daughter of Sergeant Farrier MacDONALD

This monument is erected by the officers, NCOs and men of T Battery, Royal Horse Artillery on 19 Oct 1891.
                                                (82)(93)(BS)

ROYAL HORSE ARTILLERY (3)   *(M/1143)*
B Battery, Royal Horse Artillery.
In memoriam. Dec 1891 to Nov 1896.
Major G W CAMPBELL
Lieutenant E H DAVIS
Corporal G GOULD
Bombadier Collar Maker GREENE
Acting Bombadier J C RANSOM
Acting Bombadier W RANDALL
Gunner J MANNION
Gunner H KNOWLES
Gunner D CURTIS
Gunner C VICKERY
Gunner W WILD
Driver W FOSTER
Driver E E HAYES
Annie HARMER
Bertha NASH
Edward WILLIAMS
Ruley ASPIN
AHMUD BUX,
RAWALPINDI AND UMBALA.

(82)(93)(PS)

SOMERSET LIGHT INFANTRY (1) (CC/42W)
In loving memory of the NCOs and men of the 1st F.S.Gn.Bn. Somerset Light Infantry who died during 1917 - 1919:

34592	A/Colour S. M.S PARKES		34568	Pte W TUBB
34811	Sergeant E FRYER		275431	Pte H LUCKETT
34626	Lance Corporal P DAVY		37846	Pte T MERRY
34406	Lance Corporal F TIMMS		39824	Pte M G MUNDAY
34474	Pte W BACK		39686	Pte H PEARCE
241004	Pte J BARNARD		34552	Pte A PINK
275265	Pte H BRINKLER		39809	Pte A POLLARD
33655	Pte A CLARIDGE		275114	Pte F RICHARDSON
2319	Pte F COX		34772	Pte P RUSSELL
275424	Pte P O GAME		39672	Pte R D STOREY
240677	Pte L H HARDING		37852	Pte A TREBY
34655	Bugler J HAWTIN		742457	Pte W C TREHANE
51551	Pte W LLOYD		39674	Pte R WRIGHT

Erected by the officers, NCOs and men of the Battalion.
AHMUD BUX, SCULPTOR. (82)(93)(WM)

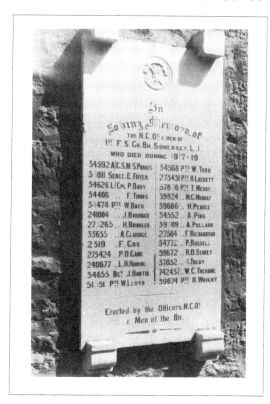

UNNAMED REGIMENT (1)   (H/584)

Sacred to the memory of
Private T ROBINSON who died of cholera on the march from Mian Mir to Rawalpindi   4 Nov 1887.   Aged 24 1/2 yrs.
Also Private J W JOHNSON, who was drowned while bathing in the park in Rawalpindi   18 Mar 1888.   Aged 21 yrs.
Private W GILBERT killed in Black Mountain Expedition
                         2 Nov 1888   Aged 22
Private G BLAIR. Died Rawalpindi 5 Feb 1888.   Aged 22 yrs.
Sergeant GORDEN. Died Rawalpindi 9 Feb 1888(9?) Aged 40 yrs.
Rest in peace.   Erected by the officers, NCOs and men .....
                                          (82)(93)(BS)

WEST RIDING REGIMENT (1)   (E/186)
Sacred to the memory of the undermentioned men of F Company, 1st Battalion West Riding Regiment who have died in this country since 1 Jan 1880:
At Lucknow: Private J LUBY
            Private W BEEBY
            Private C GRAHAM
            Private W STURT
            Private W DRISCOLL
            Corporal J GROVER
            Private D DAY
            Private M DUFFY
            G BRIGGS   at Nowshera
            Private T ADAMS   at Rawalpindi
            Private J PRIESTLEY   at Rawalpindi
            Private A NORTH
            Private J HEELING
            Private J WALKER
J PONTEFRACT and A VICKERS.   This monument was erected by the officers, NC officers and men of the company as a token of remembrance.   (82)(93)(PS)

YORKSHIRE REGIMENT (1)   (Y/680)
To the memory of:
No 21668   Private D NEWBY
No 39918   Private J ROYAL
No 21831   Private A J MAHON
No 22244   Private T BRADY

who died Rawalpindi 1917-1918. Erected by all ranks 1st GN Battalion (Alexandra, Princess of Wales's Own) Yorkshire Regiment.   (82)(93)

5TH REGIMENT (1)
In memory of the undermentioned men of the 1st/5th Regiment who died at Rawalpindi:
Private M HYNES   28 Jan 1880
Private J BIRKS   12 Jan 1880
Private J HERRING   25 Dec 1879
Private C SHIELDS   28 Feb 1880
This stone was erected by the NC officers and men of the detachment as a mark of esteem.   (82)

9TH REGIMENT (1)   (BB/20)
The undermentioned men of F Company 2/9th Regiment, who have died since the arrival of the Battalion at Rawalpindi:

Private Samuel HOWARD	19 Apr 1875	Aged 20 6/12 yrs
Private John MARTIN	11 Jul 1875	Aged 22 7/12 yrs
Private Michael KEEFE	11 Feb 1876	Aged 36 7/12 yrs
Private Frederick MEALE	18 Aug 1876	Aged 21 2/12 yrs
Private James TAYLOR	18 Aug 1876	Aged 21 1/12 yrs
Private Francis McCANN	4 Sep 1876	Aged 39 11/12 yrs
Private Frederick JONES	1 Jan 1877	Aged 27 yrs
Private William DAVIS	5 Apr 1877	Aged 28 3/12 yrs
Colour Sergeant Joseph WICKS	25 Jul 1877	Aged 35 11/12 yrs

(82)(93)(BS)

36TH REGIMENT (1)   (DD/65)
Sacred to the memory of Drum Major J SULLIVAN, Colour Sergeant W WEBB and Sergeant J STRAFFORD. HM's 36th Regiment who died at Rawalpindi 24 Dec 1868, 17 Sep 1870 and 14 Feb 1872 respectively. Aged 31, 28 and 28 years. This stone is erected by their brother sergeants as a tribute of their love and esteem.
(82)(93)(BS)

60TH ROYAL RIFLES (1)   (BB/24)
Undermentioned noncommissioned officers and men of E Company 2nd Battalion 60th Royal Rifles, who have died since the arrival of the battalion in India in 1867:

Private J STOTT	Jan 1868
Private W COLE	May 1868
Private J GIBSON	Jan 1869
Lance Corporal H COX	Apr 1869
Sergeant W BOLTON	May 1869
Private J DONOVAN	May 1871
Private M McDONALD	Dec 1871
Private W S SAYNTOR	Jun 1873
Private C FARMER	Nov 1873
Private E WHITE	Jan 1874
Sergeant .. OFFILL	Sep 1874
Private J DICKS	Oct 1874
Private G WALSH	Nov 1875

Erected by the noncommissioned officers. *(82)(93)(BS)*

70TH REGIMENT (1)   (EE/91)
The undermentioned men of A Company 70th Regiment who have died since the arrival of the Corps at Rawalpindi.

Private G RUSSELL	Died 26 Dec 1871	Aged 21
Private C WILLIAMS	Died 2 Apr 1872	Aged 36
Private N SYMONS	Died 17 June 1872	Aged 24
Private P WALSH	Died 11 Dec 1873	Aged 32
Private D CALDER	Died 14 Feb 1874	Aged 29
Private William ELLIS	Died 2 Sep 1874	Aged 24

Erected by Lieutenant R S RIDDELL, Commanding, and NC officers and men of the company as a tribute of respect.
(82)(93)(BS)

70TH REGIMENT (2)   (BB/25)
In affectionate remembrance of the undermentioned men of G Company HM's 70th Regiment, who died as stated below:
Private P DORAN   Accidentally killed   28 Dec 1871
Private T MATTHEWS   Died at Lawrencepure   23 Jan 1873
Private W HALL   Died at Murree   21 May 1873
Lance Corporal W YARNOLD   Died at Rawalpindi   15 May 1873
Private J WATSON   Died at Rawalpindi   4 Oct 1874
This stone was erected by the officers, NCO and men of C Company as a token of respect and esteem. *(82)(93)(BS)*

70TH REGIMENT (3)   (DD/57)
Sacred to the memory of the undermentioned men of E Company 70th Regiment:
Private William MORLEY   Died 13 Jan 1872   Aged 21 yrs
Private D O'SHEA   Died 7 Sep 1872   Aged 22 yrs
Private J JENKINSON   Died 15 Oct 1875   Aged 23 yrs
This stone is erected by the officers, NC officers and men of the Regiment as a mark of esteem.   *(82)(93)(BS)*

70TH REGIMENT (4)   (DD/50)
Sacred to the memory of the undermentioned men, who died at Rawalpindi on the following dates:
Private George DEAN   Died 23 May 1872   Aged 25 yrs
Private William FRANCIS   Died 27 May 1872   Aged 21 yrs
Private Fred RUDDOCK   Died 28 May 1872   Aged 20 yrs
Private Thomas BAND   Died 7 Jun 1872   Aged 21 yrs
This is erected by the officers, NC officers and men of D Company HM's 70th Regiment as a mark of esteem and regard for their loss.   *(82)(93)(BS)*

70TH REGIMENT (5)   (GG/225)
In memory of the undermentioned men of A Company 70th Regiment who have died since the arrival of the Corps at Rawalpindi:
Private H HEHIR   Died 18 Jan 1872   Aged 20
Private J LAPPIN   Died 6 Apr 1873   Aged 36
Private P DOHERTY   Died 28 Sep 1874   Aged 37
Erected by Lieutenant R S RIDDELL (Commanding) and NC officers and men of the company as a tribute of respect.
                                          (82)(93)(BS)

98TH REGIMENT (1)   (AA/7W)
The undermentioned men of No 9 Company HM's 98th Regiment, who died while serving in the Punjab:
Samuel OAKES   24 Aug 1858
John ROBERTS   17 Jul 1860
William SMITH   15 Jun 1860
Thomas CAMPBELL   16 Oct 1861
William STOCKER   30 Oct 1861
William MASON   17 May 1862
John WHEELER   29 Sep 1862
George SPENCER   22 Oct 1862
Also Charles STANIFORTH, who died 2 Nov 1862 leaving a dear wife and child to mourn his loss. Also George, son of the above, who died Karachi on the 13 Mar 1860. Prepare to meet thy God. This monument is erected by their comrades.
                                              (82)(93)

HARLEY STREET CEMETERY MAPS

An old map has been traced and used as the basis for surveying the cemetery. As the routes of the majority of the original footpaths still survive, the blocks marked on this map were still identifiable, and have therefore been used for mapping the cemetery. The many modern well-used paths have not been added, except for where they are so well established that a new block (with new lettering) has been created to make it easier to search for particular graves.

Each inscription in the list has an italic letter/number at the top, which indicates which block, followed by a plot number. It should be noted that these plot <u>numbers</u> (as opposed to the letters which do come from the original maps) are entirely drafted by the Author and bear no relation to any that might appear in Burial Registers or other old documents.

The first map (page 212) covers the whole cemetery, with the subsequent pages being divided into:

Page 213	Map	AA	1 – 8	Page 220	Map	VI	457 – 472
	Map	BB	9 – 29		Map	III	473 – 495
	Map	CC	30 – 43		Map	IV	496 – 522
Page 214	Map	DD	44 – 78				540 – 582
	Map	EE	79 – 93	Page 221	Map	VV	523 – 539
	Map	C	94 – 106		Map	H	583 – 605
Page 215	Map	A	107 – 131		Map	K	606 – 632
	Map	B	132 – 149		Map	Z	634 – 678
	Map	D	150 – 180	Page 222	Map	Y	679 – 741
Page 216	Map	E	181 – 203		Map	X	742 – 879
	Map	FF	195, 204	Page 223	Map	W	880 – 971
	Map	GG	205 – 228		Map	U	972 – 974
	Map	LL	229 – 245		Map	UU	1015 – 1019
Page 217	Map	AA1	246 – 262	Page 224	Map	IX	1009 – 1013
			633				
	Map	KK	263 – 265		Map	V	975 – 1008
	Map	R	266 – 287				1014
	Map	S	288 – 319		Map	L	1020 – 1072
Page 218	Map	HH	320 – 340	Page 225	Map	O	1073 – 1129
	Map	JJ	341 – 363		Map	M	1130 – 1235
	Map	T	364 – 378		Map	P	1236 – 1296
	Map	F	379 – 394	Page 226	Map	Q	1297 – 1324
Page 219	Map	I	395 – 412		Map	VII	1325 – 1407
	Map	G	413 – 436	Page 227	Map	VIII	1408 – 1422
	Map	J	437 – 456		Map	N	1423 – 1479

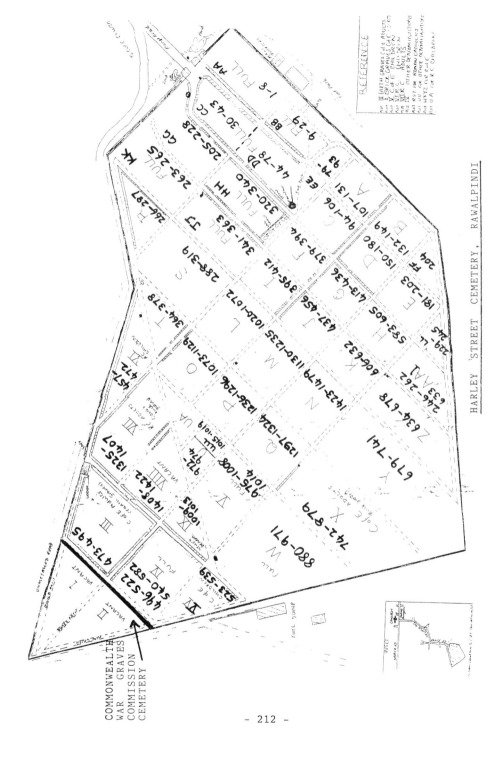

HARLEY STREET CEMETERY, RAWALPINDI

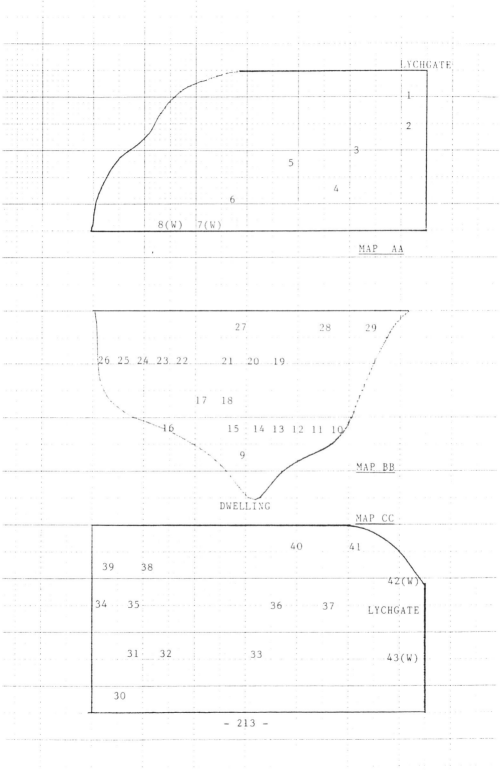

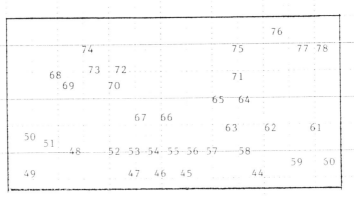

MAP DD

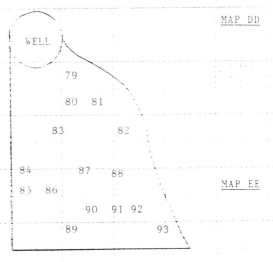

MAP EE

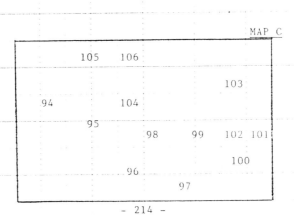

MAP C

```
                108              107
112 110 109
     111
113 114 115  116    117    118 119
                              120     MAP A
           126              121
       127     125 124
128
    129                      122
       130  131                 123
```

```
                      139
149 146 144 142 140    138

148 147 145 143 141
                      137           MAP B
                         136
                   135
    132          133    134
```

```
   180 179 178     177
                              175
       170 171 172   173 176 174
          169 168
                   167    153    150   MAP D
          164  165  166
       158 157 156 155 154   152 151

          163 162   161 160 159
```

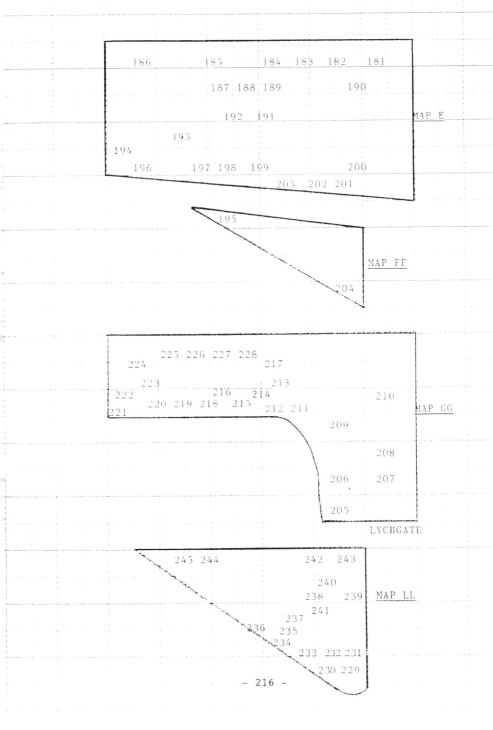

- 216 -

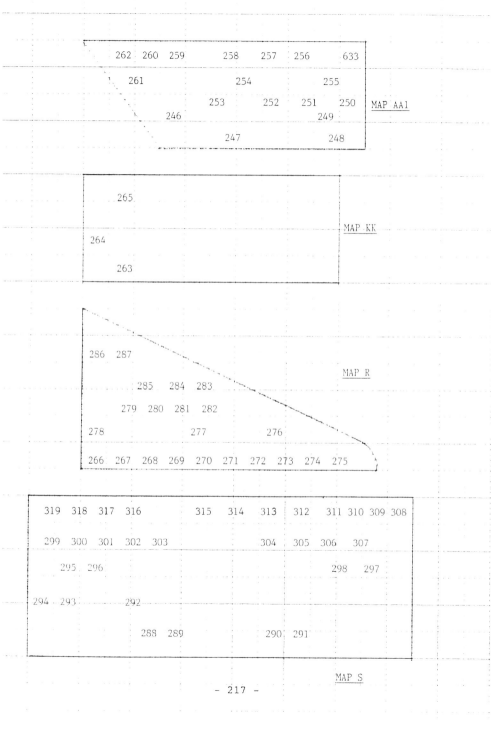

```
                339 340                          334
            338     336 335       337                   333
                            331        332                      MAP HH
                                           320
                    328                         329
                                                   321
      327   326   325                324  323 322 320
```

```
                    361
            363 362    360 358 357 355 354
                                356       353
                        359                 352          MAP JJ
                    343
            341        344      345
                                    346  348
                342                   347 349 350 351
```

```
                377
              376
              375
                374
                  373   372
                          371                MAP T
                      366   370
              364 365         368
            378         367       369
```

```
                                    394 393
                        389      390         391 392
                            385
                388           384  382 381 380            MAP F
                        386         383         379
                    387
```

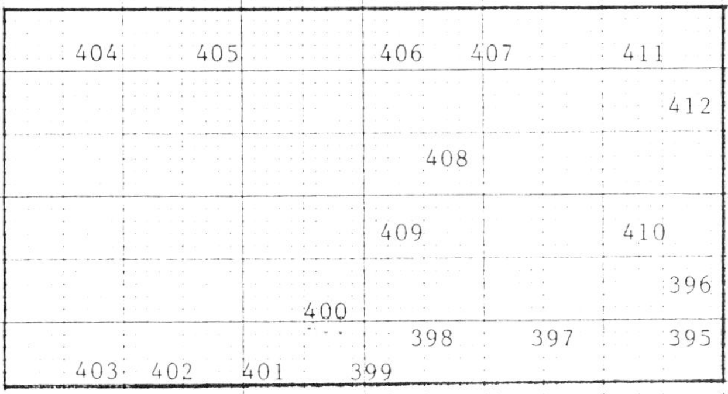

```
    404    405       406  407    411
                                  412
                     408
                     409       410
                                  396
                400
                     398  397    395
       403 402  401  399
                              MAP I
```

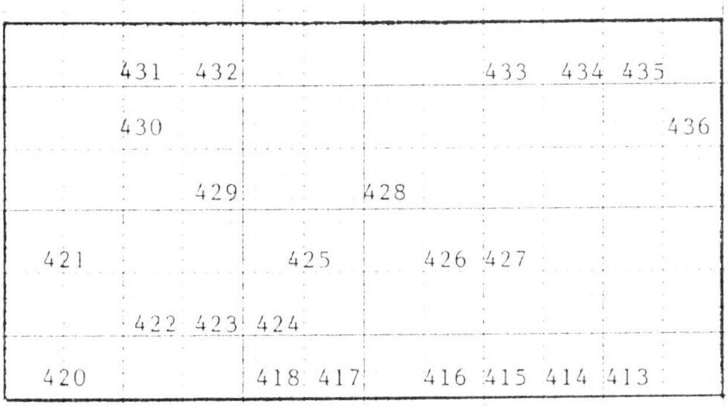

```
       431 432        433 434 435
       430                      436
          429    428
  421        425    426 427
       422 423 424
  420        418 417  416 415 414 413
                              MAP G
```

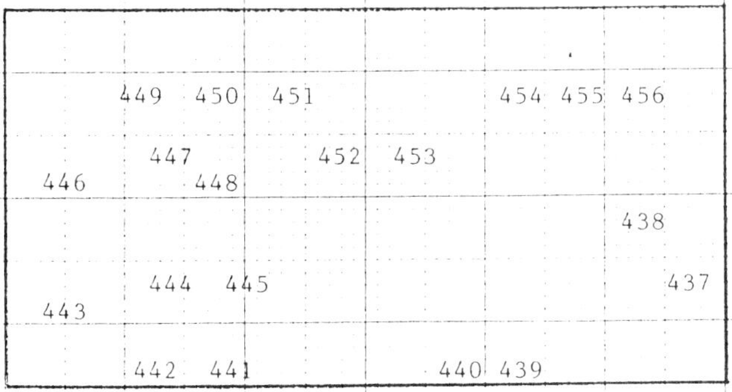

```
       449 450 451      454 455 456
          447      452 453
  446        448
                                438
          444 445
  443                           437
          442 441       440 439
                              MAP J
```

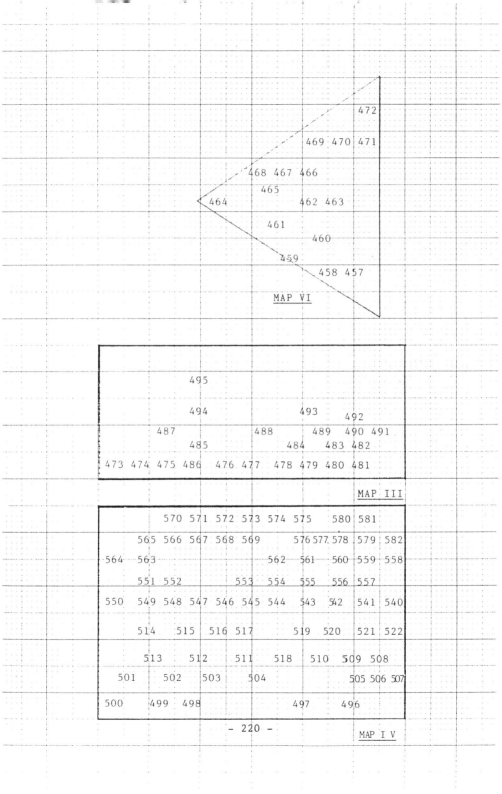

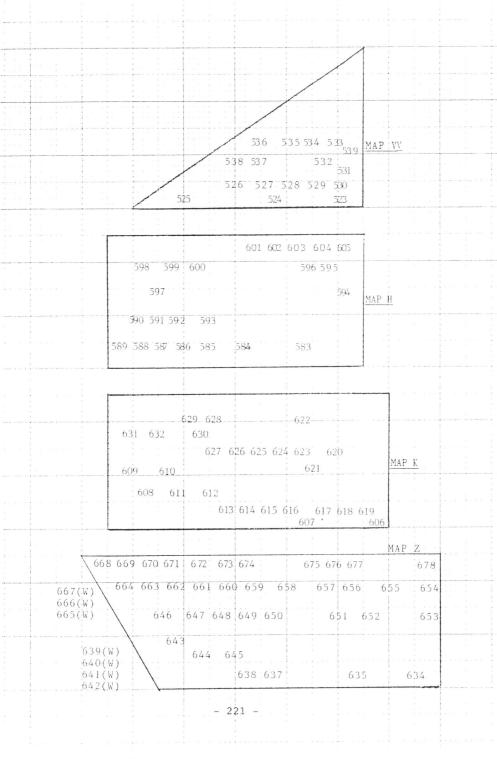

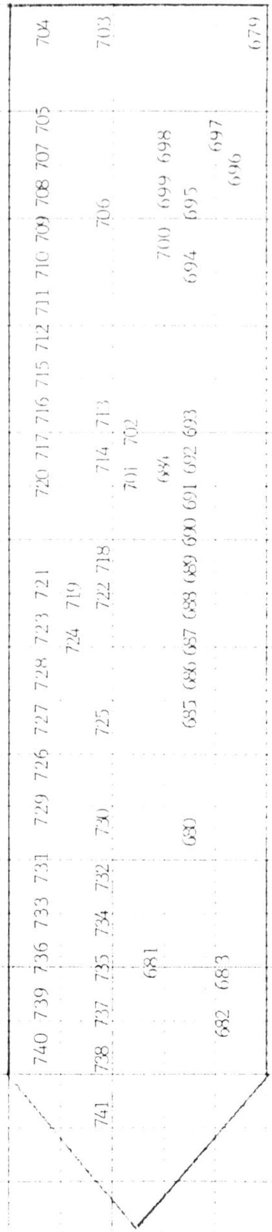

MAP Y

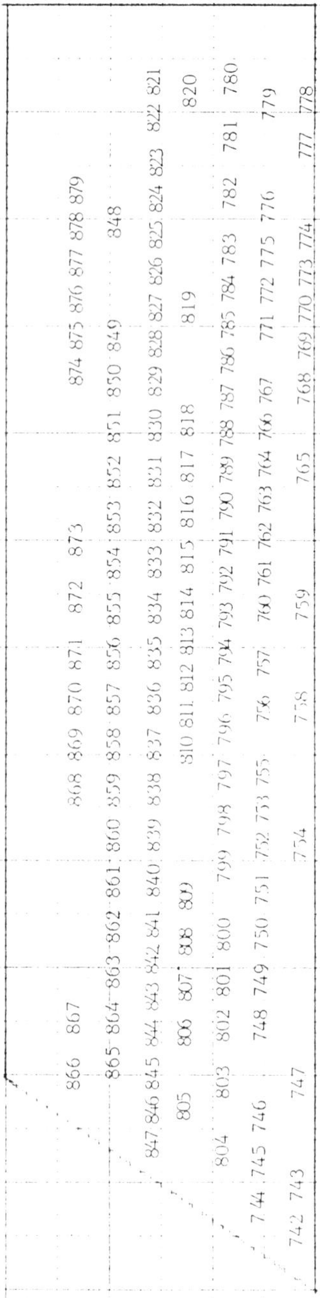

MAP X

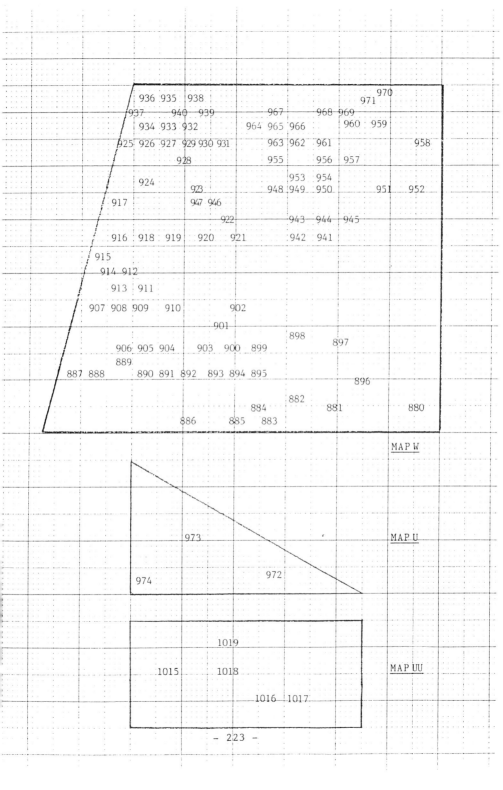

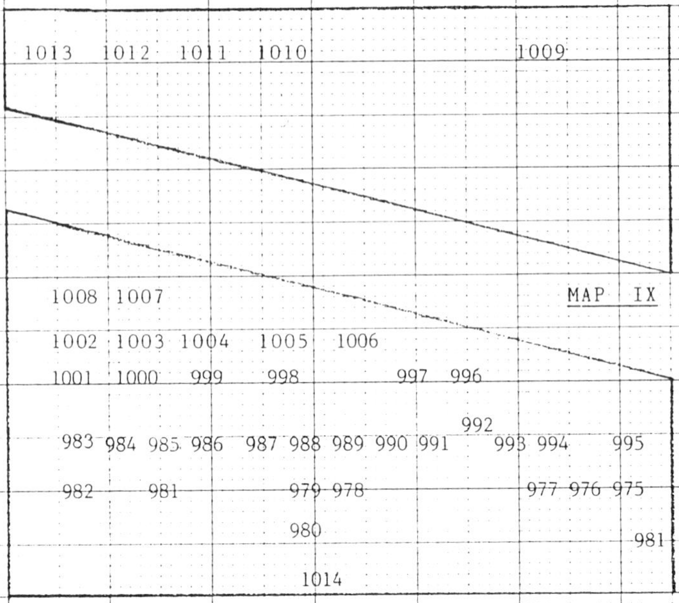

```
1013   1012  1011  1010                1009
```

```
1008  1007                                          MAP IX
1002  1003  1004  1005  1006
1001  1000   999   998         997   996
                                  992
     983 984 985 986 987 988 989 990 991   993 994    995
     982    981        979 978              977 976 975
                        980
                                                      981
                       1014
```
MAP V

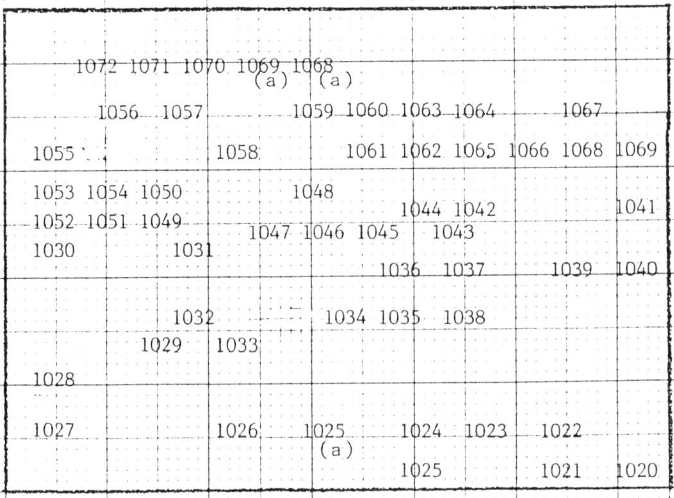

```
        1072 1071 1070 1069 1068
                      (a)  (a)
           1056  1057         1059 1060 1063 1064        1067
1055             1058           1061 1062 1065 1066 1068 1069
1053 1054 1050        1048
1052 1051 1049                     1044 1042              1041
                 1047 1046 1045   1043
1030      1031
                                    1036  1037   1039 1040
             1032          1034 1035 1038
        1029      1033
1028
1027           1026    1025     1024  1023    1022
                        (a)
                                1025          1021  1020
```
MAP L

```
                                    1129
                  1111 1112 1113 1115 1116 1119 1120 1121 1122 1123 1128 1127
          1109 1110        1114       1117 1118              1124 1125 1126
          1108 1107 1106   1105  1104 1103   1102 1101 1100 1099 1098 1097
   1089 1090                                              1096 1095      1094
                           1091           1092                 1093
    1088 1087 1086 1085    1081 1080   1079              1076
                     1084 1083   1082        1078 1077   1075 1074 1073
```

MAP O

```
  1235                       1227        1225              1224
                            1230
    1234 1233 1232      1231 1229 1228    1226  1223 1222  1221
    1220 1219 1218 1217       1216 1215 1214         1213 1212 1211 1210

        1199 1200 1201 1202 1203            1204 1205  1206    1207 1208 1209

         1198 1197 1196      1195        1194 1193   1192    1191 1190

     1174 1175 1176 1177 1178   1179 1180 1181  1182 1183 1184 1185 1186 1187  1188 1189
                                            1164
     1173      1172 1171 1170   1169 1168  1167   1166 1165 1163 1162    1161 1160

  1144 1145 1146 1147  1148  1149 1150 1151  1152 1153 1154 1155 1156 1157 1158   1159
  1142 1141 1140 1139        1138 1137      1136 1135 1134 1133 1132 1131  1130
1143
```

MAP M

```
   1296           1295 1294 1293 1292 1291 1290 1289 1288         1287
 1273  1274 1275       1276              1278 1282 1281 1284 1285 1286

                       1277              1279 1280              1283
                                                        1262
 1270 1269 1268 1267 1266 1265 1264 1263    1261 1260

              1271  1272                      1259 1258 1257   1256
                    1241 1242        1243 1244 1246 1247 1251 1252 1253
                  1239     1240           1245      1248 1249 1250
                                                                 1255
  1236 1237 1238                                                 1254
```

— 225 —

MAP P

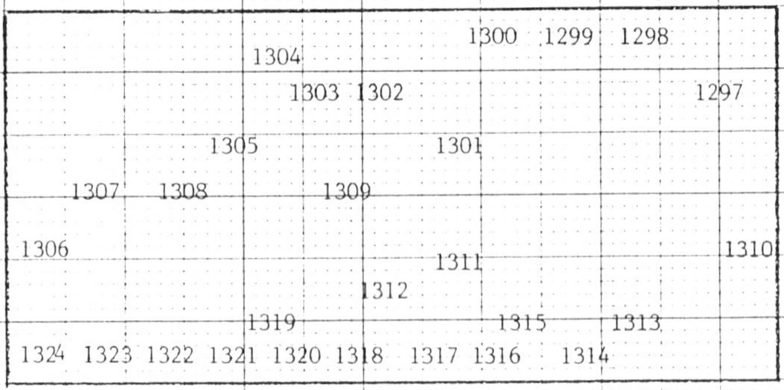
1300 1299 1298
1304
1303 1302
1297
1305
1301
1307 1308
1309
1306
1310
1311
1312
1319
1315
1313
1324 1323 1322 1321 1320 1318 1317 1316 1314

MAP Q

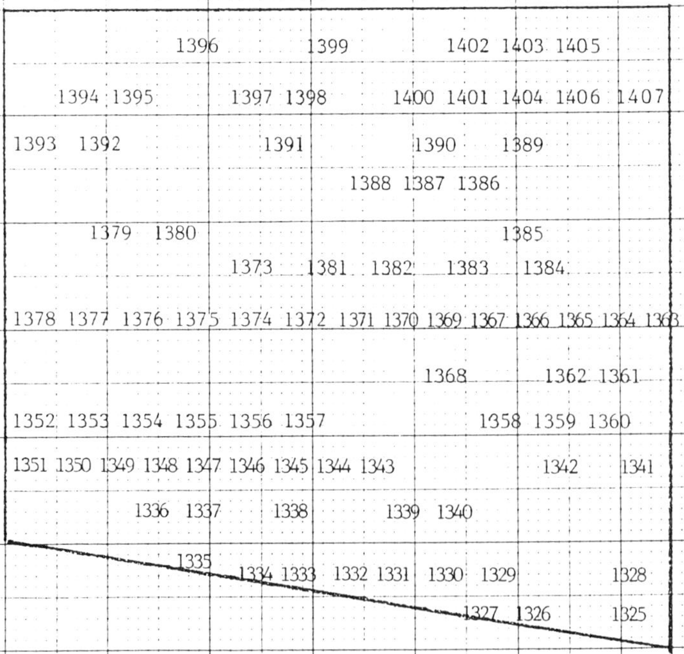
1396 1399 1402 1403 1405
1394 1395 1397 1398 1400 1401 1404 1406 1407
1393 1392 1391 1390 1389
1388 1387 1386
1379 1380 1385
1373 1381 1382 1383 1384
1378 1377 1376 1375 1374 1372 1371 1370 1369 1367 1366 1365 1364 1363
1368 1362 1361
1352 1353 1354 1355 1356 1357 1358 1359 1360
1351 1350 1349 1348 1347 1346 1345 1344 1343 1342 1341
1336 1337 1338 1339 1340
1335
1334 1333 1332 1331 1330 1329 1328
1327 1326 1325

MAP VII

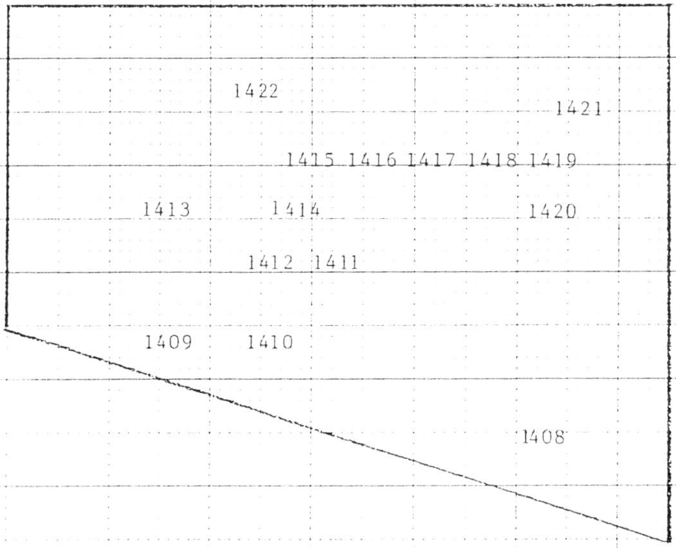

```
                1422
                                    1421
                        1415 1416 1417 1418 1419
        1413        1414                1420
                    1412 1411

            1409    1410

                            1408
```

MAP VIII

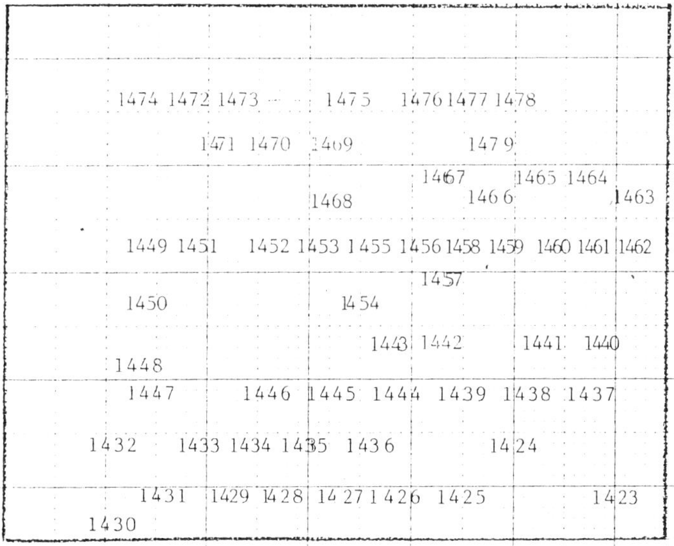

```
    1474 1472 1473    1475   1476 1477 1478
            1471 1470 1469        1479
                                1467    1465 1464
                        1468        1466            1463
    1449 1451    1452 1453 1455 1456 1458 1459 1460 1461 1462
                            1457
    1450            1454
                        1443 1442    1441 1440
    1448
        1447    1446 1445 1444 1439 1438 1437
    1432    1433 1434 1435 1436        1424
        1431 1429 1428 1427 1426 1425        1423
    1430
```

MAP N

PART II

ADDITIONAL INSCRIPTIONS

The inscriptions which follow are from the Rawalpindi cemeteries and churches other than the Harley Street cemetery:

```
Murree Road Cemetery    Old Cemetery            Parsee Cemetery
Westridge Cemetery      Christchurch            St Andrew's Church
St Joseph's Cathedral   St Mary's Church        St Paul's Church
Sacred Heart Church     Nicholl Memorial Church
```

Refer to Page 5 for a key to the abbreviations.

A plotted map of Westridge cemetery follows at page 282.

THE CHAPEL IN WESTRIDGE CEMETERY

ABBOTT, John (see ROYAL ARTILLERY (2))

ADAMS, Joseph   WESTRIDGE *(P2)*
In affectionate memory of Joseph ADAMS. Loco foreman, N W Railway Shed, who departed this life at Rawalpindi Railway Hospital 30 Jul 1904. Aged 59 yrs and 4 days. Deeply regretted by his sorrowing wife. Gone but not forgotten. All ye who come my grave to see, prepare yourselves to follow me, think of the time and don't delay, for youth and age will soon pass away. Life is uncertain, death is sure, sin is the wound and Christ is the cure. Oh, death, where is thy sting; Oh, grave, where is thy victory, but thanks be to God which giveth us the victory through our Lord Jesus Christ.   *(82)(93)*

ALEXANDER, G   (see GORDON HIGHLANDERS)
ALEXANDER, J   (see 3RD (PRINCE OF WALES'S) DRAGOON GUARDS)
ALLEN, W   (see 9th LANCERS)
ALLISON, A J   (see RIFLE BRIGADE)
ANSCOMBE, G A H   (see 36TH SIKHS)

ANTHONY, Joseph Stanislaus   WESTRIDGE *(F4)*
In loving memory of Joseph Stanislaus ANTHONY. Guard NW Railway, Rawalpindi. Beloved son of Gilbert and Christina ANTHONY, who departed this life on 5 May 1907. Aged 25 yrs 3 mths 5 days. Gone but never will be forgotten. (poem) *(82)(93)*

ARATHOON, Martha   WESTRIDGE *(W3)*
Simply to thy cross I cling. In ever loving and affectionate memory of Martha ARATHOON. Beloved wife of L ARATHOON. Born 16 Jun 1875. Died 25 Nov 1924. 40 yrs 5 mths 6 days. In our hearts your memory lingers, sweet and tender, fond and true. There is not a day, dear wife and mother, that we do not think of you. In life's delight in deaths dismay, in cloud and sunshine, night and day. Here and hereafter I am thine. A loving wife and affectionate devoted mother. Erected by her sorrowing husband and children.   *(82)(93)(end)*

ATKINSON, W W (see ROYAL GARRISON ARTILLERY (2))

AVIS, G   (see RIFLE BRIGADE)

AVIS, J C   (see GORDON HIGHLANDERS)

BACON, M (see 9TH LANCERS)

BAILEY, Grace   WESTRIDGE *(D2)*
In loving memory of Grace. The wife of J W BAILEY. N W Railway who died 13 Dec 1892. Aged 32 yrs. Universally regretted. The Lord shall be unto thee an everlasting light. Thy God, thy glory.   *(82)(93)*

BAKER, C   (see 9TH LANCERS)
BAKER, W   (see BEDFORDSHIRE REGIMENT)
BANKS, A   (see 9TH LANCERS)
BARCOCK, H   (see RIFLE BRIGADE)

BARKER, Robert John   WESTRIDGE *(M4)*
Our precious baby Robert John BARKER. Born 8 Jun 1925. Died 13 Apr 1926. Aged 10 mths 5 days. Thy will be done. RIP.
                                                (82)(93)

BARLOW, B   (see RIFLE BRIGADE)
BARR, J   (see GORDON HIGHLANDERS)
BARRON, A S N   (see ROYAL ARMY SERVICE CORPS)
BARSTOW, E L J   (see 36TH SIKHS)
BARTHOLOMEW, W   (see BEDFORDSHIRE REGIMENT)
BARTLETT, W T   (see ROYAL HORSE ARTILLERY (1))

BARTON, Ralph Edward   CHRISTCHURCH
In ever loving memory of Ralph Edward BARTON, Lieutenant, 8th Mountain Battery, Royal Artillery, third son of Colonel B L BARTON, ADC of Portsalon, County Donegal, Ireland, who died 3 Nov 1906. Aged 24 yrs. "And he was not, for God took him." Genesis. V.24. NEYAZ ALI & CO.   *(82)(93)(brass)*

BARTON, W   (see RIFLE BRIGADE)
BATES, J   (see BEDFORDSHIRE REGIMENT)
BATESON, G   (see RIFLE BRIGADE)
BAXTER, F   (see GORDON HIGHLANDERS)

BAXTER, Valentine Oscar Ridley   CHRISTCHURCH
In loving memory of "Boodlums" Valentine Oscar Ridley BAXTER. Born 3 May 1911. Died 20 Nov 1947. Erected by his ever loving wife, daughters, mother and sisters. *(82)(93)(WM)*

BAXTER, Valentine Oscar Ridley   WESTRIDGE
Valentine Oscar Ridley BAXTER. 36 yrs. Ever loving and devoted wife till eternity Kathleen. Daughters Gloria, Jacqueline, Valerie, Mums and sisters. *(82)*

BAYES, John   WESTRIDGE *(N2)*
Sacred to the memory of John BAYES, Locomotive Department, N W Ry, who died 28 Aug 1904. Resting. Erected by his brother officers and friends as a mark of esteem.   *(82)(93)*

BECKTON, J (see GORDON HIGHLANDERS)
BENN, G A (see BEDFORDSHIRE REGIMENT)

BENTON, Sarah Ann   OLD CEMETERY
Sacred to the memory of Sarah Ann, daughter of Colour Sergeant
Joseph and Marta BENTON, HM's 22nd Regiment, who departed
this life 14 Nov 1853. 11 yrs 11 mths. *(82)(93)(BS)*

BETTS, T (see BEDFORDSHIRE REGIMENT)

BEVERIDGE, Douglas   WESTRIDGE *(G3)*
In loving memory of our dear little Douglas. The beloved
child of Fred and Maud BEVERIDGE. Born 13 Oct 1907. Fell
asleep 18th April 1908. Age 6 mths 5 days. An angel took our
flower away, why should we then repine? If Jesus on his bosom
wears, a flower that once was mine. *(82)(93)*

BEVERIDGE, Maud Elsa   WESTRIDGE *(U2)*
Maud Elsa. Beloved wife of J F W BEVERIDGE. Born 4 Nov 1888.
Died 6 Jan 1915. Aged 26 yrs 2 mths 2 days. And oft shall we
weep adieu, you our loved one, good and true........
                         (82)(93)

BIGNELL, H G   CHRISTCHURCH
Sacred to the memory of Lieutenant H G BIGNELL, XXXVI Sikhs,
who died at Rawalpindi on 29 Apr 1907. This tablet is erected
by his brother officers.   *(82)(93)(brass)*

BILBY, R   (see ROYAL ARTILLERY (1))
BIRCHALL   (see ROYAL HORSE ARTILLERY (2))
BLACKBURN   (see 3RD (PRINCE OF WALES'S) DRAGOON GUARDS)

BLAIR, Arthur K   CHRISTCHURCH
Sacred to the memory of Captain Arthur K BLAIR, 36th Sikhs,
who died of cholera while on famine duty at Myani Satara 29
Jul 1900. This tablet is erected by his brother officers.
NEYAZ ALI, SCULPTOR AND ENGRAVER, RAWALPINDI. *(82)(93)(brass)*

BLAND, A C   (see ROYAL ARTILLERY (1))
BLISSET, J H (see RIFLE BRIGADE)
BODDY, H G   (see 4TH DRAGOON GUARDS (1))
BOND, C H   (see BEDFORDSHIRE REGIMENT)
BOOTH   (see 3RD (PRINCE OF WALES'S) DRAGOON GUARDS)
BOSKETT, H C (see 4th DRAGOON GUARDS (1))
BOSS, L   (see ROOKE, Agnes Emily)
BOURKE, W   (see ROYAL ARTILLERY (2))

BOURNE, Thomas   WESTRIDGE *(S2)*
In loving memory of Thomas BOURNE, who died at Rawalpindi on
the 19 Sep 1906. Aged 48 yrs. Erected by his brother masons.
We loved him, oh, no tongue can tell, how much we loved him
and how well. God loved him too, and thought it best to take
him home with him to rest.   *(82)(93)*

BOYCE, A (see ROYAL GARRISON ARTILLERY (1))

BOYD, R (see GORDON HIGHLANDERS)

BRENNAN, Catherine Gertrude   WESTRIDGE *(P3)*
In loving memory of Catherine Gertrude BRENNAN, beloved wife of Patrick Sandford BRENNAN, born 11 Aug 1889, who left for her eternal home on the 3 May 1935. A loving wife and affectionate mother. All the world is dark without you, Kitty darling, memory turns each thought to pain, home is vacant, life is weary, till in heaven we meet again. Jesus mercy, mercy mild. Erected by her sorrowing and heart broken husband and daughter.   *(82)(93)(end)*

BRIGGS, H   (see RIFLE BRIGADE)
BRIGGS, J   (see 9TH LANCERS)
BRINDLEY, J (see RIFLE BRIGADE)

BRISCO-OWEN, Clarence Morland   WESTRIDGE *(D3)*
In loving memory of Captain Clarence Morland BRISCO-OWEN, MC, who died 12 Sep 1919.   *(82)(93)*

BROOKE, A M (see KING'S OWN SCOTTISH BORDERERS)
BROOKE, F   (see BEDFORDSHIRE REGIMENT)

BROOKS, George Henry Knight   WESTRIDGE *(C1)*
In loving memory of George Henry Knight BROOKS, the dearly loved husband of Hannah Knight BROOKS, who departed this life on the 25 Feb 1922. Aged 75 yrs 4 mths and 18 days. A loving husband, and father so true and kind, a beautiful memory left behind. Heavenly father in thy gracious keeping leave we now thy servant sleeping. Peace perfect peace. *(93)*

BROOKS, Hannah Knight   WESTRIDGE *(R)*
In loving memory of Hannah Knight BROOKS, the dearly loved wife of the late George Henry Knight BROOKS, who departed this life on the 3 Oct 1923. Aged 65 yrs 3 mths 23 days. A loving wife and mother so true and kind, a beautiful memory left behind. Heavenly father in thy gracious keeping leave we now thy servant sleeping. Peace perfect peace. *(82)(93)(end)*

BROWN, A   (see GORDON HIGHLANDERS)
BROWN, A   (see 3RD (PRINCE OF WALES'S) DRAGOON GUARDS)
BROWN, E   (see BEDFORDSHIRE REGIMENT)
BROWN, H T   (see RIFLE BRIGADE)
BROWN, J   (see 9TH LANCERS)
BROWN, W J   (see RIFLE BRIGADE)

BROWNE, Ivy Grace   ST ANDREW'S CHURCH
To the glory of God. In loving memory of Ivy Grace. Dearly beloved daughter of Ezekiel and Edith BROWNE. Born 12 Jul 1902. Died 18 Jan 1923. I know whom I have believed and I am persuaded that He is able to guard that which I have committed unto Him against that day. II. Tim.1.12. *(93)(WM)*

BROWNLEE, T (see GORDON HIGHLANDERS)
BRYANT, A W (see RIFLE BRIGADE)
BRYSON, J   (see GORDON HIGHLANDERS)
BUCKLEY   (see 3RD (PRINCE OF WALES'S) DRAGOON GUARDS)
BUCKLEY, C   (see ROYAL ARTILLERY (2))
BUIST, J   (see GORDON HIGHLANDERS)

BUNBURY, G H ST P (see 36TH SIKHS)
BURKE, M J   (see ROYAL HORSE ARTILLERY (1))

BURNETT, Isabella Ann   WESTRIDGE *(K2)*
In loving memory of Isabella Ann, dearly beloved wife of D M
BURNETT, Government Telegraph Department, who died at Khushab
on the 19 Dec 1900. Aged 29 yrs 9 mths 19 days. Thy will be
done. We shall sleep but not forever, in the lone and silent
grave. Blessed be the Lord that taketh, blessed be the Lord
that gave. In the bright eternal city, death can never never
come.   In his own good time he'll call us from our rest to
home sweet home.   *(82)(93)*

BURRIDGE, T (see RIFLE BRIGADE)

BURROWES, L A   WESTRIDGE *(V1)*
In loving memory of our dear father L A BURROWES. Born
26-12-1861. Died 25-5-1924. Beautiful memory left behind of
our darling Dad........   *(82)(93)*

BURTENSHAW, H (see 4TH DRAGOON GUARDS)
BURTON, E V   (see 4TH DRAGOON GUARDS)
BUSBY, F   (see BEDFORDSHIRE REGIMENT)
BUSSEY, W   (see 4TH DRAGOON GUARDS)
BUTCHER, A R   (see 4TH DRAGOON GUARDS)

BUXTON, May   WESTRIDGE *(U1)*
In loving memory of May, the beloved daughter of W H BUXTON,
who died 20 May 1899.   Aged 15 yrs and 3 mths. Sadly missed,
in silence mourned. NEYAZ ALI, SCULPTOR, RAWALPINDI.
                                           (82)(93)

BUXTON, Rose Olive   WESTRIDGE *(S1)*
In loving memory of Rose Olive, beloved daughter of W H
BUXTON, who departed this life 24 Sep 1894.   Aged 2 yrs 24
days. Suffer little children to come unto me for of such is
the kingdom of heaven. FAIYAZ ALI & SONS, SCULPS, UMBALLA &
RAWALPINDI.   *(82)(93)*

CAIN, T (see BEDFORDSHIRE REGIMENT)

CALEY, H F   CHRISTCHURCH
In memory of Major General H F CALEY, formerly 64th Regiment
BNI, who after an honorable (sic) career of 59 years in India
died on the 21 Dec 1866 at Rawul Pindee of which station he
was Brigadier. Aged 74 yrs. This tablet is erected by
several of his friends and brother officers as a mark of
esteem and regard. MARTIN, SCULPTOR.   *(82)(93)(WM)*
     (for illustration, see Page 28)

CAMPBELL, W   (see GORDON HIGHLANDERS)
CANNON, C   (see RIFLE BRIGADE)

CARLTON, H C (see RIFLE BRIGADE)
CARPENTER, W (see RIFLE BRIGADE)
CASS, R (see BEDFORDSHIRE REGIMENT)
CAVENDISH, H (see RIFLE BRIGADE)

CELAND, Mavis Clare   WESTRIDGE *(X3)*
In fondest memory of our precious baby Mavis Clare CELAND. Called to rest 20 Oct 1920. Aged 15 yrs. Sweet flower farewell, too fair for earth, brief space to us thy charms were given. He who bestowed thee knew thy worth, and took thee our treasure to Christ in heaven. Call it not death, a few short day o'er, we shall meet thee in heaven to part no more. *(82)(93)*

CELAND, Terence Edward   WESTRIDGE *(O3)*
In cherished memory of our fondly loved laddie Terence Edward. Dear son of Mr and Mrs C J CELAND. Called to rest 1 Jan 1929. Aged 26 yrs. Only withdrawn from us a little space, gone home before, learning in paradise God's resting place, to love him more. Not sad but beautiful, his memory so dear, so bright, twill guide us through earth's darkness into God's light. Gone from our sight, but e'er near to our hearts. *(82)(93)*

CHANNELL, W V (see RIFLE BRIGADE)

CHAPMAN, Henry Howard   CHRISTCHURCH
Sacred to the memory of Henry Howard CHAPMAN, Lieutenant and Adjutant HM's 101st Regiment Royal Bengal Fusiliers and formerly of the 6th Bengal European Infantry, who fell in action at the Umbeyla Pass 18 Nov 1863. Aetat 25 yrs. He lost his life whilst in the gallant discharge of his duty and in a noble and unselfish endeavor (sic) to render help to a wounded brother officer. Friends and brother soldiers have erected this humble monument to his memory. RAMSUHOY, SCULPTOR, DELHI.   *(82)(93)(WM)*

CHEESEMAN, J (see ROYAL ARTILLERY (1))
CHILVERS   (see ROYAL HORSE ARTILLERY (2))

CHRISTY, Edwin   CHRISTCHURCH
King's Royal Irish Hussars. In memory of Edwin CHRISTY, 2nd Lieutenant VIIIth King's R I Hussars, who was accidently killed at Rawalpindi 13 Dec 1880. Aged 25 yrs. This tablet is erected by his brother officers. *(82)(93)(WM)*

CLARK, Ernest Picton   WESTRIDGE *(Z2)*
Our darling little Tiny Ernest Picton. Dearly loved son of Adam and Charlotte P CLARK. Born 13 Jul 1910. Fell asleep in Jesus 1 Sep 1913. Aged 3 yrs 11 mths and 18 days. Safe in the arms of Jesus. He has left us, Oh, for ever, he is resting now in peace, and our hearts cries will not cease. How we loved him, how we want him, how we call for him in vain. He has entered space supernal, free from sorrow, free from pain. Tiny darling, how we miss you, Oh that you were with us now, sweetest darling little angel, loved by everyone of us. God loved you too, he thought it best to take you home with him to rest.   *(82)(93)*

CLARK, F   (see 4TH DRAGOON GUARDS (1))
CLARK, W G   (see 4TH DRAGOON GUARDS (1))

CLARK, William James Hubert Picton   WESTRIDGE *(F3)*
William James Hubert Picton. Youngest son of John and Justina Picton CLARK. Born 15 Aug 1904. Fell asleep in Jesus 4 Apr 1908. Safe in the arms of Jesus. A flower to us was lent, a gift from God.......   *(93)*

CLARKE, Irene Constance   WESTRIDGE *(S)*
In loving memory of Irene Constance CLARKE (nee COLLINS). The dearly loved daughter of Patrick and Lillian COLLINS who left us for her heavenly home on 24 Sep 1928. Aged 27 yrs. Erected by her heartbroken parents. How we loved her no tongue can tell, how much we loved her and how well. God loved her too, he thought it best, to take her home with him to rest. Lord in thy gracious keeping, here we leave our darling sleeping. Thy will be done.   *(82)(93)(end)*

CLARKE, J A (see GORDON HIGHLANDERS)

CLAYTON, George Edward Cyril   WESTRIDGE *(Z)*
In loving memory of our darling son George Edward Cyril CLAYTON. Born 3 Oct 1919. Died 15 Oct 1924. We saw him fading like a flower, we could not make him stay, we nursed him with our tenderest care till God called him away. An angel took our flower away, but we will not repine, for Jesus in his bosom wears a flower that once was ours. *(82)(93)(end)*

CLAYTON, Harry Swinton   CHRISTCHURCH
In loving memory of Harry Swinton CLAYTON. Punjab Police. Born 27 Oct 1883. Died 26 Dec 1904. He giveth his beloved sleep. This tablet is erected by his parents as a token of undying affection.   *(82)(93)(brass)*

CLEAVER, E   (see RIFLE BRIGADE)
CLEMENTS, G F (see 4TH DRAGOON GUARDS (1))
CLEMSON, E   (see 4TH DRAGOON GUARDS (1))
CLOUGH, Frances Gertrude (see LAMB, Frances Gertrude)
COLE, W U   (see 3RD (PRINCE OF WALES'S) DRAGOON GUARDS)

COLEMAN, Elizabeth   WESTRIDGE *(Q4)*
In affectionate remembrance of Elizabeth, the dearly beloved wife of Fredrick J T COLEMAN, who departed this life at Westridge, Rawalpindi, India 1 Feb 1903. Aged 30 yrs 1 day. Rest in the Lord. "In the midst of life we are in death. Soon shall I join the ransomed far beyond the sky. Christ is my salvation, why should I fear to die? Soon my eyes shall behold him seated upon the bright throne. Then, oh then shall I see thee, beautiful beautiful home." Sung by her before death. NEYAZ ALI & SON, RAWALPINDI.   *(82)(93)*

COLEMAN, Fredrick J T   WESTRIDGE *(P4)*
Fredrick J T COLEMAN, who died at Rawalpindi on the 6 Aug 1922. Aged 53 yrs. Erected by his sorrowing widow. Gone but not forgotten.   *(82)(93)*

COLLINS, Audrey Mavis   WESTRIDGE *(K1)*
Our precious baby Audrey Mavis, who was called to heaven on
the 19 Jun 1933. Aged 4 1/2 months. Beloved daughter of Edna
and Denzil COLLINS. God has taken home our darling, placed
our bud amongst his flowers, taken back the babe he lent us to
a better world than ours.   *(82)(93)(end)*

COLLINS, Irene Constance (see CLARKE, Irene Constance)

COLLINS, John Stratford   CHRISTCHURCH
Sacred to the memory of Major General John Stratford COLLINS,
CB, of Wythall, who died at Rawalpindi on the 27 Apr 1908
while commanding the 2nd Rawalpindi Division. Erected by
those who served under him.   *(82)(93)(brass)*

BRITISH CAVALRY BARRACKS, RAWALPINDI

COLLINS, Mabel Annie   WESTRIDGE *(M)*
In loving memory of Mabel Annie, the dearly loved daughter of
Patrick and Lillian COLLINS, who left us for her heavenly home
on 10 Oct 1931. Aged 17 yrs. Had he asked us well we know,
we should cry, O spare this blow. Yes, with streaming tears
should pray, Lord we love her, let her stay. Gone from us,
but not forgotten, never shall thy memory fade. Sweetest
thoughts shall ever linger, round the spot where you are laid.
Thy will be done. Erected by her heartbroken parents.
                                       (82)(93)(end)

CONNELL, D (see ROYAL ARTILLERY (1))
CONNOR, J   (see RIFLE BRIGADE)

CONWAY, Bryan Adair   WESTRIDGE *(I3)*
In loving memory of Bryan Adair CONWAY. Born 4 Apr 1907.
Passed away 25 Nov 1908.   *(82)(93)*

COOK, G   (see BEDFORDSHIRE REGIMENT)
COOK, G   (see 9TH LANCERS)
COOK, H   (see ROYAL GARRISON ARTILLERY (1))
COOKES   (see ROYAL HORSE ARTILLERY (2))

COOPER, J	(see RIFLE BRIGADE)
COOPER, S	(see BEDFORDSHIRE REGIMENT)
COSTELLO, H T	(see BEDFORDSHIRE REGIMENT)
COULTER, T	(see BEDFORDSHIRE REGIMENT)
COUZENS, B A	(see 4TH DRAGOON GUARDS (1))
COWPER	(see ROYAL HORSE ARTILLERY (2))
COX, E I F	(see RIFLE BRIGADE)
COX, G	(see RIFLE BRIGADE)
COX, W A	(see RIFLE BRIGADE)
CRAYFORD, G	(see BEDFORDSHIRE REGIMENT)

CREAGH, Rachel and CREAGH, C P Brazier   CHRISTCHURCH
To the glory of God and in memory of Rachel. Wife of C P Brazier CREAGH. Captain in 9th Bengal Lancers. Born 31 Dec 1873. Died at Rawalpindi 29 Dec 1899. Also in memory of C P Brazier CREAGH. Her husband. Born Sep 4 1864. Died of wounds received at Leevw Kop, South Africa 27 Apr 1900. Thy grace is sufficient for me.   *(82)(93)(brass)*

CROSBIE, Charles   (see 4th DRAGOON GUARDS (2))

CRUNDEN, Eileen Stella   WESTRIDGE *(X2)*
Eileen Stella CRUNDEN, who died at Rawalpindi on 25 Oct 1909. Born 6 Mar 1891. Come unto me all ye that labour and are heavy laden and I will give you rest.   *(82)(93)*

CULLUM, H	(see ROYAL HORSE ARTILLERY (1))
CULVER, J	(see BEDFORDSHIRE REGIMENT)
CUNNINGHAM, C S	(see 36TH SIKHS)

CUNNINGHAM, Walter James Radcliffe   WESTRIDGE *(L2)*
In loving memory of Walter James Radcliffe CUNNINGHAM, who departed this life at Rawalpindi on 20 Aug 1906. Age 43 yrs 5 mths. Gone but not forgotten. Deeply regretted by his sorrowing wife and children. Forget him, no, we never will, we loved him here, we love him still, nor love him less although he's gone from us to his eternal home. Rest on dear husband thy labours o'er, thy willing hand will toil no more. In life thou wert loved and esteemed, in death thou are mourned and lamented.   *(82)(93)*

CUTTS (see 3RD (PRINCE OF WALES'S) DRAGOON GUARDS)

D'AGUILAR, C S   CHRISTCHURCH
Sacred to the memory of Captain C S D'AQUILAR, 84th Punjabis, who died at Rawalpindi on the 21 Mar 1912. This tablet is erected by his brother officers. P ORR & SONS, ART METAL WORKERS, MADRAS AND RANGOON.   *(82)(93)(brass)*

DE SOUZA, Michael   WESTRIDGE
In loving memory of Michael De SOUZA. Died 24 Sep 1926. Aged 53 yrs.   *(82)(end)*

DALE, S O (see RIFLE BRIGADE)

DARCY, M (see 4TH DRAGOON GUARDS (1))

DARLING, Isabel   WESTRIDGE *(A3)*
In loving memory of Isabel DARLING, dearly beloved wife of Thomas DARLING, who departed this life 7 Mar 1912. Aged 56 yrs. Deeply loved in life, deeply mourned in death. We loved her, oh, no tongue can tell, how much we loved her, and how well. God loved her too, he thought it best to take her home with him to rest.   *(82)(93)*

(Headstone is an angel, now with it's head missing)

DAVIS, Kenneth Lionel Hay   WESTRIDGE *(R2)*
Kenneth Lionel Hay DAVIS, who fell asleep in Christ on 26 Nov 1907. Aged 27 yrs 4 mths. Erected by his sorrowing mother, sisters and brother. (Illegible poem) *(82)(93)*

DAVIS, W   (see UNNAMED REGIMENT)
DAWE, W   (see RIFLE BRIGADE)
DAWES, P S   (see 4TH DRAGOON GUARDS (1))

DAY, Edward A F H   CHRISTCHURCH
To the memory of Lieutenant Edward A F H DAY, Royal Artillery, who died of typhoid fever at Kyra Gully 10 Jun 1884. This tablet is erected by some of his brother officers. COX & BUCKLEY, LONDON.   *(82)(93)(brass)*

DAY, H W   (see RIFLE BRIGADE)
DEADMAN, G E   (see BEDFORDSHIRE REGIMENT)
DEAN, S H   (see 4TH DRAGOON GUARDS (1))
DEFLY, T   (see RIFLE BRIGADE)
DERING, E W W   (see KING'S OWN SCOTTISH BORDERERS)
DEVINE, J   (see RIFLE BRIGADE)
DEWICK, A   (see RIFLE BRIGADE)
DILLON, H J   (see BEDFORDSHIRE REGIMENT)
DIMOND, F S   (see 3RD (PRINCE OF WALES'S) DRAGOON GUARDS)

DIRKBY, William   OLD CEMETERY
William. The beloved son of Colour Sergeant Hodgson and Jessy DIRKBY. HM's 22nd Regiment. Departed this life 8 Jun 1852. Aged 10 mths 19 days.   *(82)*

DODD, J   (see UNNAMED REGIMENT)
DOREY, A   (see RIFLE BRIGADE)
DOUBLEDAY, J   (see RIFLE BRIGADE)
DOUTHWAITE, E   (see RIFLE BRIGADE)
DOWNHAM, R   (see RIFLE BRIGADE)
DOWNING, J   (see ROYAL GARRISON ARTILLERY (1))
DOWNING, R   (see ROYAL FIELD ARTILLERY)

DOYNE, P K   CHRISTCHURCH
In memory of Lieutenant Colonel P K DOYNE, lately commanding 4th Dragoon Guards, who died at Simla 17 Jun 1900. Erected by his former brother officers.   *(82)(93)(brass)*

EAGLEN, E   (see QUEEN'S REGIMENT)
EBDON, H   (see QUEEN'S REGIMENT)
ECCLESTONE, A   (see SEAFORTH HIGHLANDERS)
EDWARDS, S E   (see 3RD (PRINCE OF WALES'S) DRAGOON GUARDS)

EDWARDS, Samuel Ernest   CHRISTCHURCH
In memory of Samuel Ernest EDWARDS, 2nd Lieutenant, 3rd Dragoon Guards, who died at Kasauli of typhoid fever on 15 Nov 1891. Aged 23 yrs. This tablet is erected by his brother officers. COX & BUCKLEY, LONDON.   *(82)(93)(brass)*

ELLIOTT, Charles Allen   CHRISTCHURCH
To the glory of God and in memory of Lieutenant Colonel Charles Allen ELLIOTT, CMG, DSO, Royal Engineers, who died at Rawalpindi 15 Aug 1919. Aged 48 yrs and 5 mths. Plot X3062.
                                          (82)(93)(brass)

ELLIS, J T (see RIFLE BRIGADE)

ELLIS, Kathleen   OLD CEMETERY
Kathleen, the dearly beloved wife of Colour Sergeant John ELLIS, HM's 22nd Regiment, who departed this life 12 Jul 1852. Aged 25 yrs 5 mths.   *(82)*

ELLISON, Florence   WESTRIDGE *(H2)*
Florence, the beloved wife of Charles H ELLISON, who died at Westridge 29 Jan 1898. Aged 22 yrs 7 mths.   *(82)(93)*

WESTRIDGE, RAWALPINDI

ELPHICK (see 3RD (PRINCE OF WALES'S) DRAGOON GUARDS)

EVANS, Pearl Helena Beatrice   WESTRIDGE *(N)*
In loving and undying memory of my darling daughter Pearl Helena Beatrice EVANS. Age 14 yrs 1 mths 25 days. Died 21 Feb 1932. Beside your grave we often stand, with hearts both crushed and sad. Our lips cannot speak how we loved you, nor words express what we wish to say. Only you know how we miss and want you, as we battle through life's rough way. Erected by her broken hearted mummy, brother and sister.   *(82)(93)*

EVANS, W (see ROYAL ARTILLERY (1))

EVEREST   (see 3RD (PRINCE OF WALES'S) DRAGOON GUARDS)

FAIRWEATHER, Lillian   WESTRIDGE *(O1)*
Lillian FAIRWEATHER. Beloved wife of Walter Edward FAIRWEATHER. Born 8 Mar 1858. Died 20 Nov 1918. Dear is the spot where our loved one is laid, dear is the memory that never can fade. Sweet is the hope that again we shall meet, all kneeling together at Jesus' feet. Days of sorrow now are mine, sorrow will I often tread and often I shed a silent tear for my loved one now gone to rest.   *(93)*

FARMER, J A   (see SHERWOOD FORESTERS)
FARRELL, B U (see ROYAL ARMY SERVICE CORPS)
FAULKNER, A   (see RIFLE BRIGADE)
FENNELL, W   (see 4TH DRAGOON GUARDS (1))

FERNANDEZ, Mary Magdalen   WESTRIDGE *(Q3)*
In ever loving and affectionate memory of Mary Magdalen FERNANDEZ. Beloved wife of J FERNANDEZ. Born in 1887. Died 23 Mar 1931. Aged 44 yrs. A loving wife and affectionate mother. Erected by her sorrowing husband and children. (Poem)   *(82)(93)*

FIELD, G (see RIFLE BRIGADE)

FITZ-MAURICE-DEANE-MORGAN,
Hamilton Robert Tilson Grogan   CHRISTCHURCH

In affectionate memory of Lieutenant The Hon Hamilton Robert Tilson Grogan FITZ-MAURICE-DEANE-MORGAN of the Royal Irish Regiment, eldest son of the 4th Baron MUSKERRY, who died at Murree on 30 Jul 1907. This tablet is erected by his widow and brother officers.   *(82)(93)(brass)*

FLANAGAN, F (see 4TH DRAGOON GUARDS (1))

FLEMING, George John   WESTRIDGE *(T3)*
George John. Dearly beloved husband of Eva Amelia FLEMING.
Born 21 Aug 1870.   Died 30 Sep 1923.   Aged 53 yrs 1 mth 9
days.   Erected by his sorrowing wife, six children and sister.
My God my Father whilst I stray, far from my home in life's
rough way.   Oh teach from heart to say, Thy will be done.
                                        (82)(93)

FLETCHER, A J   (see RIFLE BRIGADE)
FLETCHER, H   (see RIFLE BRIGADE)
FLOOD, H W   (see 4TH DRAGOON GUARDS (1))
FORBES   (see 3RD (PRINCE OF WALES'S) DRAGOON GUARDS)
FORBES-SEMPILL, D (see SEAFORTH HIGHLANDERS)
FORD, H R K   (see BEDFORDSHIRE REGIMENT)
FORDYCE, R   (see SEAFORTH HIGHLANDERS)

FOVET, Edna May   MURREE ROAD
Edna May FOVET. Missionary under WUMS. Born 7 Aug 1924.
Died 12 Aug 1958.   *(87)*

FOX, F H   (see 4TH DRAGOON GUARDS (1))
FRANCIS, G   (see RIFLE BRIGADE)
FRANKLIN, A   (see 4TH DRAGOON GUARDS (1))
FRANKLIN, J   (see 4TH DRAGOON GUARDS (1))

FRATEL, Mabel Jane   WESTRIDGE *(L4)*
In ever loving memory of our darling mother and grandmother
Mabel Jane FRATEL, who passed on to Jesus on 31 Jan 1943.
Buried in Maruyana.   *(82)(93)*

FREEMAN, F   (see 4TH DRAGOON GUARDS (1))
FREER, G   (see BEDFORDSHIRE REGIMENT)
FRENCHAM, F   (see 4TH DRAGOON GUARDS (1))

FRERE, Richard G   CHRISTCHURCH
Sacred to the memory of Lieutenant Richard G FRERE. HM's 13th
Light Infantry who died 17 Nov 1842. Aged 25 yrs. *(82)(93)(BS)*

CHURCH OF THE SACRED HEART, WESTRIDGE

GAGLIARDI, Louis P   SACRED HEART CHURCH
In perpetual memory of Captain Louis P GAGLIARDI.
Accidentally drowned at Amara 5 Sep 1917. Erected by his
relatives. Sweet Jesus Mercy.   *(94)*

   (This dedication is on the Font)

GALLAGHER, John Moran   WESTRIDGE *(Z1)*
In dear memory of John Moran GALLAGHER. Died at Attock 30 Dec
1882. Aged 50 yrs. Let my sorrow cease to flow; God has
recalled his own; Let my heart in every woe still say, Thy
will be done. In the midst of life we are in death. *(82)(93)*

GARDNER, Fredrick James   WESTRIDGE *(D4)*
Fred. In loving memory of Fredrick James GARDNER, who
departed this life on the 10 Feb 1913. Aged 47 yrs. Erected
by his sorrowing widow and three children. If thou shouldst
call me to resign what most I prize, it ne'er was mine. I
only yield thee what was thine. Thy will be done. *(82)(93)*

GARLAND, J (see QUEEN'S REGIMENT)

GARLIC, Alice Jane   WESTRIDGE *(D1)*
Our darling mother, Alice Jane GARLIC, who left us for her
eternal home on the 11 Mar 1921 at Rawalpindi. Aged 55 yrs 6
mths. All the world seems dark without you, memory turns each
thought to pain, time is vacant, life is weary, till in
heaven we meet again.   *(82)(93)*

GARRATT, W (see BEDFORDSHIRE REGIMENT)

GAULT, Andrew   WESTRIDGE *(C2)*
In loving memory of our dear brother Andrew GAULT, who
departed this life 29 Jun 1892 at Rawalpindi, India. Aged 37
yrs. It is past! He is gone and the spirit has fled. We
number him now with those who are dead. The last sigh is
breathed, the last prayer is given. He is gone from this home
to a better in heaven.   *(82)(93)*

GEACH, G B   (see 4th DRAGOON GUARDS (2))
GEDDES, A A   (see ROYAL ARMY SERVICE CORPS)
GEORGE, W   (see ROYAL ARTILLERY (1))
GILL, G   (see SHERWOOD FORESTERS)
GILMARTIN, J   (see 4TH DRAGOON GUARDS (1))
GLEDHILL, J   (see RIFLE BRIGADE)
GLEESON, F   (see ROYAL ARTILLERY (2))
GLYNN, R   (see ROYAL ARTILLERY (2))
GODDARD, E G   (see BEDFORDSHIRE REGIMENT)

GORDON, David and TURING, Arthur   CHRISTCHURCH
Sacred to the memory of Captain David GORDON. 36th Sikhs who died in the Kuram (sic) Valley 5 Jul 1897, and Lieutenant Arthur TURING. 36th Sikhs. Killed in action at the Shin Kamar Pass, Tirah 29 Jan 1898. This tablet is erected by their brother officers.   P ORR AND SONS, ART METAL WORKERS, MADRAS.
(82)(93)(brass)

GORDON, J	(see 4TH DRAGOON GUARDS (1))
GORDON, L	(see KING'S OWN SCOTTISH BORDERERS)
GORMAN, J	(see GORDON HIGHLANDERS)
GOSNEY, A	(see RIFLE BRIGADE)
GOULDING, A	(see 9TH LANCERS)
GRAY, J	(see 36TH SIKHS)
GREEN, G	(see BEDFORDSHIRE REGIMENT)
GREEN, G	(see 3RD (PRINCE OF WALES'S) DRAGOON GUARDS)

GREEN, Harry   WESTRIDGE *(V)*
A devoted husband and father, Harry GREEN, who departed this life on 18 Jan 1927. Aged 86 yrs. But oh, beyond this shadowland, where all is bright and fair, I know full well these dear old hands will palms of victory bear. Where crystal streams through endless years flow over golden sands and where the old grow young again I'll clasp my Harry's hands. RIP.   *(82)(93)(end)*

GRIFFIN, F	(see 4TH DRAGOON GUARDS (1))
GRIFFITHS, F	(see 9TH LANCERS)
GRIFFITHS, H	(see 4TH DRAGOON GUARDS (1))
GRIFFITHS, J W	(see ROYAL GARRISON ARTILLERY (2))
GROUNDSELL, Henry	(see TROUNDSELL, Henry)
GUDGIN, A	(see BEDFORDSHIRE REGIMENT)
GUNNING, O G	(see 36TH SIKHS)
GUNTER, J	(see ROYAL HORSE ARTILLERY (1))
GUTTRIDGE, F	(see RIFLE BRIGADE)
GUY, C	(see 9TH LANCERS)

HAGGER, A F	(see 4TH DRAGOON GUARDS (1))
HALLETT, S	(see 4TH DRAGOON GUARDS (1))
HAMILTON, J A	(see ROYAL ARMY SERVICE CORPS)
HAMILTON, W	(see GORDON HIGHLANDERS)
HANCOX, G E	(see RIFLE BRIGADE)
HARCOURT, L G M	(see ROYAL ARMY SERVICE CORPS)
HARDING, G A	(see RIFLE BRIGADE)

HARDING, Theodore Hubert John   WESTRIDGE *(Q)*
In loving memory of Theodore Hubert John (Bertie), the dearly loved son of Mr and Mrs T P HARDING, who departed this life on the 12 Dec 1930. Aged 15 yrs 5 mths and 15 days. Dear is the spot where our loved one is laid. Dear is the memory that never can fade. Sweet is the hope that again we shall meet all kneeling together at Jesus' feet.   *(93)*

HARDING, Theodore Parker　　　　　　　　WESTRIDGE　*(K)*
In loving memory of Theodore Parker HARDING, the dearly beloved husband of Lilian May HARDING, who departed this life on the 20 Jun 1933. Born 28 Jun 1882. Father while our eyes are weeping, o'er these spoils that death has won. We would at this solemn meeting calmly say "Thy will be done". Though today we're filled with mourning, mercy still is on thy throne, with thy smiles of love returning we can sing "Thy will be done". *(82)(93)*

HARGREAVES, G (see RIFLE BRIGADE)

HARRINGTON, Patrick Joseph　　　　　　　WESTRIDGE
Patrick Joseph HARRINGTON. Died Rawalpindi 13 Sep 1898. Aged 39 yrs 9 mths. *(82)*

HARRIS, G (see ROYAL ARTILLERY (2))

HARRIS, William　　　　　　　　　　　　　CHRISTCHURCH
To the glory of God and in affectionate memory of Lieutenant William HARRIS. 21st Regiment PNI. Suddenly called to his rest at Rawalpindi the 28 Nov 1876. Aged 27 yrs. The lectern was presented by his brother officers. *(82)(93)(brass)*

HART　　　　(see ROYAL HORSE ARTILLERY (1))
HART, R　　(see RIFLE BRIGADE)
HART, W　　(see 9TH LANCERS)

HARTT, Emily　　　　　　　　　　　　　　WESTRIDGE *(Y1)*
Sacred to the memory of Emily. The beloved wife of W E HARTT. Traffic Superintendent, PNSR. Died 28 Mar 1885.
(82)(93)

HARVEY, A　(see BEDFORDSHIRE REGIMENT)
HARVEY, W　(see BEDFORDSHIRE REGIMENT)
HATCH, W　　(see ROYAL HORSE ARTILLERY (1))

HAUGHTON, John　　　　　　　　　　　　　CHRISTCHURCH
In loving memory of John HAUGHTON, Lieutenant Colonel 36 Sikhs, who was killed on active service at Shin Kamar in Tirah on the 29th day of Jan 1898. God is Love. "Dulce et Decorum est pro Patria mori." *(82)(93)(brass)*

HAWES, G W　(see ROYAL HORSE ARTILLERY (1))
HAWKER, W　　(see GORDON HIGHLANDERS)
HAWKES, P　　(see RIFLE BRIGADE)
HAWS, J　　　(see BEDFORDSHIRE REGIMENT)
HAYNES, T　　(see BEDFORDSHIRE REGIMENT)

HEAD, Dickie　　　　　　　　　　　　　　WESTRIDGE *(V2)*
In loving memory of Dickie. Age 9 yrs 7 mths. Beloved child of Mrs HEAD, who died on 26 Oct 1918 after a long and painful illness borne patiently and bravely. *(82)(93)*

HEALY, Frances   WESTRIDGE *(C)*
In loving memory of our darling mother Frances Mary HEALY,
who died on the 20 Jul 1935. Aged 74 yrs. Thy voice is now
silent, thy heart is now cold, where thy smile and thy welcome
oft met us of old. We miss thee and mourn thee in silence
unseen and dwell in the memory of joys that have been.
                                              (82)(93)

HEANES, R   (see 9TH LANCERS)
HEDLEL   (see WILSON, Amabel)
HENRY, A W   (see 4TH DRAGOON GUARDS (1))
HERBERT, C   (see QUEEN'S REGIMENT)
HERRIDGE, W   (see 4TH DRAGOON GUARDS (1))

HETTINGA, Nicholas   ST JOSEPH'S CATHEDRAL
Nicholas HETTINGA. Bishop of Rawalpindi. 1947-1973. Born 8
Jul 1908. Died 26 Dec 1973.   *(94)*

HEWINGS, J   (see 4TH DRAGOON GUARDS (1))
HEWITT, A   (see BEDFORDSHIRE REGIMENT)
HEWITT, J W   (see BEDFORDSHIRE REGIMENT)
HIGGET, A   (see ROYAL HORSE ARTILLERY (1))

HIGHFIELD, Hilda Margaret Charlotte   WESTRIDGE *(G4)*
Hilda Margaret Charlotte. The beloved wife of Charles
HIGHFIELD. Born 28 Feb 1886. Died 30 Jan 1904. Blessed are
the dead which die in the Lord. RIP. *(82)(93)*

HILL, Alfred Osborne   WESTRIDGE *(S3)*
In loving memory of my beloved husband Alfred Osborne HILL,
who died on the 22 Mar 1929. Aged 46 years 10 mths 9 days.
                                       (93)

        (On same stone as McGOWAN, Patrick)

HILL, W   (see RIFLE BRIGADE)
HILLIER, J   (see BEDFORDSHIRE REGIMENT)
HODGKINS, T H   (see RIFLE BRIGADE)
HODKINSON, P   (see ROYAL HORSE ARTILLERY (1))
HOLLAND, H   (see RIFLE BRIGADE)

HOLMES   WESTRIDGE *(C4)*
Infant child of Assistant Surgeon and Mrs J A HOLMES. Born 1
Mar 1910. Died 3 May 1911. Safe in the arms of Jesus. AHMUD
BUX, SCULPTOR, RAWALPINDI.   *(82)(93)*

HOPCROFT   (see 3RD (PRINCE OF WALES'S) DRAGOON GUARDS)
HORGAN, D   (see ROYAL ARTILLERY (1))
HORNE, A   (see BEDFORDSHIRE REGIMENT)
HORSCHELL, F   (see GORDON HIGHLANDERS)
HORSENELL, L   (see 9TH LANCERS)
HUNT, W   (see RIFLE BRIGADE)

HURRELL, Alfred David   WESTRIDGE *(F1)*
IHS. In loving memory of my darling hubby Alfred David
HURRELL. Died on the 29 Mar 1921. Aged 52 yrs 7 mths and 17
days. I loved him in life he is dear to me still, but in grief
must bow to God's holy will. My sorrow is great, my loss
hard to bear, but angels, dear hubby, will tend you with
care. My home is all darkness from that fatal day when God in
his mercy called you away. Now the labourer's task is ended.
Peace perfect peace.   *(93)*

HUTCHISON, George   CHRISTCHURCH
Sacred to the memory of George HUTCHISON, Colonel of HM 80th
Regiment and Brigadier of the Sind Saugur District, who died
at Rawul Pindee on the 3rd of May 1859. Aged 63 yrs. He
served his country for the period of 46 years and during his
long and honorable (sic) career held many important staff
appointments and commands. His health was sacrificed by
exposure to the climate whilst engaged in the command of his
regiment at the beginning of the late war and Brigadier
HUTCHISON may be numbered amongst the many who have fallen in
consequence of the mutiny. He was a zealous and true soldier
and possessed a benevolent and amiable disposition to an
eminent degree. A good man obtaineth favour of the Lord.
Proverbs, XII.2. J BURNS.   *(82)(93)(WM)*

IBBITT, T (see BEDFORDSHIRE REGIMENT)
INGRIG, J (see GORDON HIGHLANDERS)
IRELAND   (see 36TH SIKHS)
IZZARD, A (see BEDFORDSHIRE REGIMENT)

JACKSON, J (see BEDFORDSHIRE REGIMENT)

JAMES, Arthur Wallesley (see KERR, Daniel)

JEFFERIES, A   (see ROYAL GARRISON ARTILLERY (1))
JEFFREYS, T   (see ROYAL HORSE ARTILLERY (1))
JOHNS, W   (see 9TH LANCERS)
JOHNSON, A   (see BEDFORDSHIRE REGIMENT)
JOHNSON, J   (see ROYAL ARTILLERY (1))
JOHNSTON, G F   (see 4TH DRAGOON GUARDS (1))
JONES, A   (see RIFLE BRIGADE)
JONES, C   (see RIFLE BRIGADE)
JONES, G   (see 3RD (PRINCE OF WALES'S) DRAGOON GUARDS)
JONES, H   (see RIFLE BRIGADE)
JONES, T F N   (see 4th DRAGOON GUARDS (2))

KANE, J F H   (see RIFLE BRIGADE)
KEELER, C   (see BEDFORDSHIRE REGIMENT)
KEELEY, A G   (see RIFLE BRIGADE)
KEEN, A   (see GORDON HIGHLANDERS)
KEEN, F   (see BEDFORDSHIRE REGIMENT)
KEENAN, G   (see GORDON HIGHLANDERS)

KELLY, ... St John   OLD CEMETERY
Sacred to the memory of ......St John KELLY, HM 22nd Regt, who departed this life on 12 Jul 1852. Aetat 25 yrs and 5 mths. Thy mercy Lord to me extend, on thy protection I depend.   *(93)(BS)*

KELSEY, John   OLD CEMETERY
Sacred to the memory of John KELSEY, Private, No 3 Company, HM's 87th Royal Irish Fusiliers, who died 22 Oct 1854. Aged 26 yrs.   *(82)(93)*

KERNAHAN, W   (see GORDON HIGHLANDERS)

KERR, Daniel and JAMES, Arthur W   WESTRIDGE *(T2)*
Our dear father Daniel KERR. Died 17 May 1906. Aged 70 years.
Underneath
Arthur Wallesley JAMES. Born 18 Jun 1881. Died 18 Sep 1906.
                             (93)

KERRISON, E   (see BEDFORDSHIRE REGIMENT)
KING   (see BEDFORDSHIRE REGIMENT)
KING, A V   (see 4TH DRAGOON GUARDS (1))
KING, W   (see 3RD (PRINCE OF WALES'S) DRAGOON GUARDS)
KNIGHT, H   (see RIFLE BRIGADE)

KNIGHT, Rose   WESTRIDGE *(T)*
In loving memory of my darling wife Rose, who passed away to eternal rest on 20 Apr 1925. Aged 38 yrs 6 mths 18 days. RIP. Erected by her sorrowing husband W C KNIGHT.   *(82)(93)*

L'ESTEVE   WESTRIDGE *(J4)*
In loving memory of our darling little boy. The dearly loved child of Oswald and Lilly L'ESTEVE. Born 28 Mar 1909. Died 7 Apr 1914. Aged 5 yrs 10 days. Only a little angel gone to its heavenly rest, only a little lamb safe on our Saviour's brest. (sic)   *(82)(93)*

LAING, Elizabeth Mabel (see SMITH, Elizabeth Mabel)

LAMB, Frances Gertrude   WESTRIDGE *(G2)*
Sacred to the memory of Frances Gertrude. The dearly loved wife of Arthur James LAMB and loving daughter of Mrs Frances CLOUGH. Died 9 Aug 1899. Aged 37 years and 6 mths. The cup was bitter, the sting severe to part with one we loved so dear. The trial is hard, we'll not complain but trust in Christ to meet again. NEYAZ ALI, SCULPTOR, RAWALPINDI. *(93)*

LANE   (see ROYAL HORSE ARTILLERY (2))

LANE, Brian Hill   CHRISTCHURCH
To the memory of Captain Brian Hill LANE. Army Veterinary Corps, who died Meerut 7 Nov 1911 from the result of an accident. Erected by his brother officers. SAFFIN & CO, REGENT STREET, LONDON.   *(82)(93)(brass)*

LANGFIELD, C   (see 4TH DRAGOON GUARDS (1))
LAVENDER, G   (see 9TH LANCERS)
LAVERS, E   (see 9TH LANCERS)
LAVERY, S   (see 4TH DRAGOON GUARDS (1))
LAWRENCE, F G   (see RIFLE BRIGADE)
LAWRENCE, G W   (see SHERWOOD FORESTERS)

LAWRENCE, George   WESTRIDGE *(S4)*
In affectionate memory of George LAWRENCE, the beloved husband of Elizabeth LAWRENCE, who died Rawalpindi 25 Jul 1888. Aged 34 yrs and 8 mths. I heard the voice of Jesus say: Come unto me and rest, lay down thou weary one, lay down, thy head upon my breast. I came to Jesus as I was, weary and worn and sad. I found in him a resting place and he has made me glad. Forever with the Lord.   *(82)(93)*

LAWSON, Margaret   WESTRIDGE *(R4)*
In loving memory of Margaret, the beloved wife of James LAWSON, who died at Westridge 25 Jun 1891. Aged 41 yrs.
                                          (82)(93)

LEE, D   (see QUEEN'S REGIMENT)
LEFTELY, J   (see 4TH DRAGOON GUARDS (1))
LENEY, W G   (see 4TH DRAGOON GUARDS (1))
LEVER, H R   (see ROYAL ARMY SERVICE CORPS)
LEWINS, E G   (see RIFLE BRIGADE)
LEWIS, W   (see 4TH DRAGOON GUARDS (1))
LEYDEN, J   (see 4TH DRAGOON GUARDS (1))

LIMA, Alice D   WESTRIDGE *(N4)*
In ever loving memory of my darling mother Alice D LIMA. Died on he 24 Jun 1939. Aged 68 years. Gone is the face we loved so dear, silent the voice we loved to hear. So far away from sight and speech but not too far for our thoughts to reach. A loving soul, so gentle and kind, a beautiful memory left behind. Erected by her sorrowing daughter, son-in-law and grand children. RIP.   *(82)(93)(end)*

LISLE, H   (see 4TH DRAGOON GUARDS (1))
LLOYD, C T   (see ROYAL ARMY SERVICE CORPS)
LOCKE, L A   (see 4TH DRAGOON GUARDS (1))

LOCKE, P   (see 4TH DRAGOON GUARDS (1))
LOCKYER, E   (see 4TH DRAGOON GUARDS (1))
LONIE, H   (see GORDON HIGHLANDERS)
LOUND, C M   (see SHERWOOD FORESTERS)
LOVELOCK, W R   (see RIFLE BRIGADE)

LOVETT, Douglas   WESTRIDGE
Douglas LOVETT. Born 12 Nov 1929. Died 7 May 1930. Aged 5 mths 25 days. We saw him fading like a flower. We could not make him stay. We nursed him with our tenderest care, till God called him away. But we will not repine, for Jesus in his bosom wears the flower that once was ours. DHYAN SINGH & SONS, LAHORE.   *(82)(93)*

LOWE, J   (see RIFLE BRIGADE)
LUNN, A   (see RIFLE BRIGADE)
LYNCH, S   (see ROYAL GARRISON ARTILLERY (1))

McANLEY (?McAULEY), D   MURREE ROAD
In sad and loving memory of Mrs D McANLEY (?McAULEY). Born 14 Dec 1887. Died 10 May 1966. Erected by her husband, sister, son and daughter-in-law and grandchildren. *(87)*

McANLEY, Robert   MURREE ROAD
Sacred to the memory of Robert McANLEY. Born 9 Oct 1879. Died 2 May 1881. Suffer little children to come unto me.*(87)*

McCONNELL, H   (see ROYAL GARRISON ARTILLERY (2))
MacDONALD, A   (see 9TH LANCERS)
McDONALD, J   (see GORDON HIGHLANDERS)
McELROY, B   (see GORDON HIGHLANDERS)
McENTIRE, J   (see UNNAMED REGIMENT)
MacFADYEN, I C   (see SEAFORTH HIGHLANDERS)
McFARLAND, R   (see 4TH DRAGOON GUARDS (1))
McGINN, T   (see BEDFORDSHIRE REGIMENT)

McGOWAN, Patrick   WESTRIDGE *(S3)*
My darling son Patrick McGOWAN. Died 12 Jun 1927. Aged 17 yrs 3 mths 17 days. You are gone dear son, but not forgotten, never shall your memory fade. Sad and loving thoughts shall linger round the spot where you are laid. RIP. *(82)(93)(end)*
    (on same stone as HILL, Alfred Osborne)

McGUIRE   (see 3RD (PRINCE OF WALES'S) DRAGOON GUARDS)
McINTYRE, J   (see 4TH DRAGOON GUARDS (1))

McKENZIE, Arthur William Frederick   WESTRIDGE *(T1)*
In loving memory of Arthur William Frederick, beloved son of Alexander and Alice McKENZIE, who died at Westridge, Rawalpindi, India on the 10 Jul 1892. Age 13 days.

                              /continued........

McKENZIE, Arthur William Frederick (cont)
A mortal bud of mortal birth to thee brief life was given. The flower that was too fair for earth called hence to bloom in heaven. NEYAZ ALI, SCULPTOR, RAWALPINDI. *(82)(93)*

WESTRIDGE, RAWALPINDI

MacKENZIE, A E   (see SEAFORTH HIGHLANDERS)

McKEOANE, John   OLD CEMETERY
Sacred to the memory of John McKEOANE. HM's 87th Royal Irish Fusiliers. Late of Tullamore, Kings County, Ireland. Departed this life 20 Jun 1855 at the age of 21 yrs after a short illness of 3 days. He was highly esteemed by his comrades while a soldier and at his death deeply lamented. This monument was erected by his countrymen as a token of their esteem and respect. May he rest in peace.   *(82)(93)*

MacLACHLAN, L C   CHRISTCHURCH
In memory of L C MacLACHLAN, Lieutenant and Adjutant 1st Battalion Kings Royal Rifles, who died at Rawalpindi 10 Mar 1895. This tablet was erected by the teams competing in the Rawalpindi polo tournament 1895.   *(82)(93)(WM)*

MacLACHLAN, N C	(see SEAFORTH HIGHLANDERS)
McLEAN, W	(see GORDON HIGHLANDERS)
McLEOD, J	(see GORDON HIGHLANDERS)
McMANN	(see 3RD (PRINCE OF WALES'S) DRAGOON GUARDS)
McNICOL, E	(see 9TH LANCERS)
McPHERSON	(see 3RD (PRINCE OF WALES'S) DRAGOON GUARDS)
McWILLIAM, T A	(see 4TH DRAGOON GUARDS (1))
MAJOR, S	(see ROYAL HORSE ARTILLERY (1))

MALL, Martha B   MURREE ROAD
Miss Martha B MALL. Born 14 Jan 1897. Died 23 Mar 1940. *(87)*

MANETTI, J   (see ROYAL HORSE ARTILLERY (1))
MANLEY   (see ROYAL HORSE ARTILLERY (2))
MARSHALL, G C   (see BEDFORDSHIRE REGIMENT)

MARSHALL, Robert Arthur   WESTRIDGE *(Q2)*
In loving memory of Robert Arthur. Son of the late E A MARSHALL. District Superintendent of Police. Died on 23 Jul 1909. Aged 39 yrs 4 mths. Gone from us but not forgotten. Never shall his memory fade. Sweetest thoughts shall ever linger round the spot where he is laid. Rest in peace, free from pain. Erected by his sorrowing sister Freda. *(82)(93)*

MARTIN, A D (see 36TH SIKHS)
MASLIN, W H (see RIFLE BRIGADE)

MASSEY, Ronald Anthony   MURREE ROAD
Ronald Anthony MASSEY. Son of Mr and Mrs J A MASSEY. Born 4 Nov 1958. Died 27 Oct 1974. We are confident, I say, and willing rather to be absent from the body and to be present with the Lord.   *(87)(WM)*

MASSY, J G A   CHRISTCHURCH
In affectionate memory of Captain J G A MASSY, The Royal Irish Regiment, of Kingswell, County Tipperary, who died at Srinagar on the 25th day of July 1908. Erected by his brother officers.   *(82)(93)(brass)*

MASTER, Ellen Harriet Martha   WESTRIDGE *(P)*
Sacred to the memory of our darling mother Ellen Harriet Martha, beloved wife of the late Gilbert Augustus MASTER, N W Railway, who left us for her heavenly home on 10 Mar 1930. Aged 60 yrs 3 mths 1 day. An affectionate wife and an untiringly devoted mother. Erected by her sorrowing children. We loved her well, no tongue can tell. How dearly how fondly and how well. Christ loved her too and thought it best to take her to his heavenly rest. Again we hope to meet in heaven where no farewell tears are shed. *(82)(93)(end)*

MASTER, Gilbert Augustus   WESTRIDGE *(Y2)*
Gilbert Augustus MASTER, who departed this life on 22 Nov 1910. Aged 38 years and 5 mths. Deeply regretted by his sorrowing wife and children. We miss him, oh how sadly, none but aching hearts can tell, the grief is sore, the loss severe to part with him we love so dear. We loved him yes, no tongue can tell how dearly, how fondly and how well. Christ loved him too and thought it best, to take him to his heavenly rest. Again we hope to meet in heaven where no farewell tears are shed.   *(82)(93)*

MATTHEW, A (see GORDON HIGHLANDERS)

MATTHEW, Harry   WESTRIDGE *(H)*
Sacred to the memory of Harry MATTHEW. Born 9 Dec 1888. Died 21 Feb 1935. Rest in peace.   *(82)(93)*

MATTHEWS   (see 3RD (PRINCE OF WALES'S) DRAGOON GUARDS)
MAVERS, R   (see GORDON HIGHLANDERS)
MELVIN, M   (see RIFLE BRIGADE)

MENDES   WESTRIDGE *(K4)*
The dearly beloved daughter of W J and S C MENDES. Born 2 Jun 1895. Died 3 Nov 1898 at Rawalpindi. Aged 3 yrs 4 mths.
(82)(93)

MENDHAM, C D   (see 4TH DRAGOON GUARDS (1))
MERCHANT, H M   (see ROYAL FIELD ARTILLERY)
MERRIMAN, G   (see 9TH LANCERS)
MERSH, J A   (see ROYAL HORSE ARTILLERY (1))
METCALFE, W   (see GORDON HIGHLANDERS)

MIDGLEY, Isabilla Toy   WESTRIDGE *(I2)*
Sacred to the memory of our loving and affectionate mother Isabilla (sic) Toy MIDGLEY, who departed this life on the 10 of Nov 1899. Aged 53 yrs.   *(82)(93)*

MILLER, Alan Stewart   CHRISTCHURCH
In memory of Alan Stewart MILLER. Lieutenant Royal Artillery (No 8 Mountain Battery) Born at Richmond, Yorkshire 4 Mar 1869. Died at Cherat 9 Aug 1895 from sickness contracted in the Chitral campaign of that year. Erected by his mother. May he rest in peace.   *(82)(93)(brass)*

MILLS, H G   (see RIFLE BRIGADE)
MILWARD-JONES, R A   (see 4th DRAGOON GUARDS (2))
MITCHELL   (see RIFLE BRIGADE)
MITCHELL, A   (see ROYAL HORSE ARTILLERY (1))
MITCHELL, J H   (see 36TH SIKHS)
MITCHELL, W J   (see RIFLE BRIGADE)
MOODY, C   (see 9TH LANCERS)
MOODY, D   (see GORDON HIGHLANDERS)
MOON   (see ROYAL HORSE ARTILLERY (2))
MOORE   (see ROYAL HORSE ARTILLERY (2))
MOORE, G   (see 4TH DRAGOON GUARDS (1))
MOORE, P A   (see RIFLE BRIGADE)

MOORSOM, Charles J   CHRISTCHURCH
In memory of Major General Charles J MOORSOM, late XXX Regiment, who commanded the Rawalpindi Division 1895-1899 and who died at Pretoria, South Africa 1908. BARTON SON AND CO, BANGALORE.   *(82)(93)(brass)*

MORLEY, E   (see 4TH DRAGOON GUARDS (1))
MORRISON, M   (see SEAFORTH HIGHLANDERS)

MOSS, Emily   WESTRIDGE *(E3)*
In loving memory of Emily MOSS. Died 2 Feb 1941. Aged 27 yrs. You were all alone my darling, when God gave you his great command. Without a farewell you passed away into a better land. God knows how much I miss you and he counts the tears I shed and whispers "Hush" she only sleeps, your darling is not dead.   *(82)(93)*

MOUNCEY, S (see RIFLE BRIGADE)

MULLENEX, Edwin Flatman   WESTRIDGE *(R1)*
In loving memory of Edwin Flatman MULLENEX. Born 16 Aug 1883.
Died 26 Sep 1883. Safe in the arms of Jesus.   *(82)(93)*

MULLENEX, Ernest Flatman   WESTRIDGE *(Q1)*
In loving memory of Ernest Flatman MULLENEX. Born 20 Sep 1884. Died 20 Dec 1884. Of such is the kingdom of God.
                                  (82)(93)

MULLENEX, Louisa Matilda   WESTRIDGE *(G)*
In loving memory of Louisa Matilda MULLENEX, who died at Rawalpindi on 29 Nov 1936. Aged 82 yrs 6 mths. Rest in peace.   *(82)(3)(end)*

MULLETT, L (see RIFLE BRIGADE)
MUNN   (see 3RD (PRINCE OF WALES'S) DRAGOON GUARDS)
MUNT, T R (see BEDFORDSHIRE REGIMENT)

MURRAY, A R   CHRISTCHURCH
Sacred to the memory of Lieutenant A R MURRAY, BSc who, after distinguishing himself in the Afghan War of 1878-79, survived only to die of cholera at Trete on the 18 Jul 1879. Aged 24 yrs. This stone is erected in affectionate remembrance of him by his brother officers of HM's 9th Regiment and 13th Bengal Lancers, in both of which regiments he had served. KUNNIAH LALL & SONS, SCULPTOR, DELHI.   *(82)(93)(WM)*

MURRAY, James   CHRISTCHURCH
In loving memory of Sergeant James MURRAY. Born 13 Jul 1842. Died 4 Sep 1897. During 18 years Church Clerk at Rawalpindi. AHMUD BUKSH, SCULPTOR, RAWALPINDI.   *(82)(93)(WM)*

MYERS, H (see ROYAL GARRISON ARTILLERY (1))

NEVAY, A (see GORDON HIGHLANDERS)

NEWELL, Elizabeth Catherine   WESTRIDGE *(B)*
In loving memory of our dear mother Elizabeth Catherine NEWELL, who died at Rawalpindi on 17 Jan 1940. Aged 77 yrs 3 mths. Until the day breaks and the shadows flee away. Hold thou thy cross before my closing eyes. Shine through the gloom and point me to the skies. Heaven's morning breaks, and earths vain shadows flee, in life, in death, O Lord, abide with me.   *(82)(93)*

NIXON, Grace Leonora   WESTRIDGE *(B1)*
Our only precious daughter Grace Leonora. Born on the 27 Mar 1917. Died on the 6 Aug 1922.

/continued........

NIXON, Grace Leonora (cont)
Gone from our midst, oh, how we miss you, loving you dearly your memory we keep. Never while life lasts will we forget you dear. To our hearts is the place where you sleep. Infant we believe we shall meet you again all kneeling together at Jesus' feet. Erected by her loving parents Joseph and Leonora NIXON. *(93)*

NOBLE, E E   (see SHERWOOD FORESTERS)
NORMAN, C   (see ROYAL GARRISON ARTILLERY (2))
NORMAN, F   (see 9TH LANCERS)
NORTH, W   (see BEDFORDSHIRE REGIMENT)
NORTON, H   (see BEDFORDSHIRE REGIMENT)

Incomplete inscriptions from damaged and broken headstones

NO NAME   WESTRIDGE
Died 3 Sep 1932. Born 8 Apr 1882.
(82)

NO NAME   WESTRIDGE *(N1)*
......who died at Westridge, Rawalpindi on 16 Sep 1919. Aged 42 yrs. She sleeps in peace, how sweet that rest, why then repine or shed a tear. The friend who orders all things best has moved her from the lower sphere. *(82)(93)*

NO NAME   WESTRIDGE *(O4)*
In loving memory of our little darling Denis Hugh....   *(93)*

NO NAME   WESTRIDGE *(B4)*
In loving memory of our little "angel" Louise Amelia. Rest in peace.   *(82)(93)*

NO NAME   WESTRIDGE *(E)*
Aged 63 yrs. Deeply mourned by her sorrowing husband and daughter. RIP.   *(93)*

NO NAME   WESTRIDGE *(G1)*
Erected by his brother officers, men and those who loved him. *(93)*

NO NAME   WESTRIDGE *(J1)*
He shall feed his flock like a shepherd, he shall gather the lamb with his arm, and carry them in his bosom. Suffer the little children to come unto me and forbid them not for of such is the kingdom of God. Erected by his sorrowing Mummy and Daddy.   *(93)(end)*

NO NAME   WESTRIDGE *(O)*
Erected by her sorrowing husband. Life's sweetest memory, heavens welcome guest. My dearest treasure, God loved her best. Always so true, unselfish and kind, few in this world her equal we'll find. A beautiful life that came to an end, she died as she lived, everyone's friend. *(93)(end)*

NO NAME   WESTRIDGE (Y)
Day by day a voice said cometh, enter thine eternal home,
asking not if we could spare his dear soul it summoned there.
Had he asked us, well we know, we should cry O spare this
blow. Saviour in thy gracious keeping, leave we now our loved
one sleeping till the resurrection morn. *(93)*

NO NAME   WESTRIDGE (I)
Rest in peace.   *(93)*

NO NAME   WESTRIDGE (P1)
.....on the 5 Nov 1918. Age 30 yrs. Thy will be done.
                                               (93)(WM)

NO NAME   WESTRIDGE (W1)
Not gone from mem'ry, not gone from love, but gone to her
Father's home above. Thy will be done. *(93)*

NO NAME   WESTRIDGE (B2)
Good was her heart and in friendship sound, patient in pain
and loved by all around. Her pains are o'er, her suffering
now is done, a life of everlasting joys now begun. We cannot,
Lord, thy purpose see, but all is well that's done by thee.
                                               (93)

NO NAME   WESTRIDGE (O2)
Age 53 yrs. Resting. Erected by his brother workmen as a
mark of esteem.   *(93)*

NO NAME   WESTRIDGE (J3)
Tender shepherd thou has stilled now thy little lamb's brief
weeping. Oh how peaceful, pale and mild, in it's narrow bed
'tis sleeping. And no sign of anguish sore, heaves that
little bosom more.   *(93)*

NO NAME   WESTRIDGE (Z3)
... who died at Rawalpindi on 15 May 1927. Aged 60 yrs 1 mth
and 1 week. (poem)   *(93)*

MARGALLA BARRACKS, RAWALPINDI

NO NAME   WESTRIDGE *(F)*
.......parents.   In our hearts your memory lingers, sweet and
tender, fond, true.   There is not a day, dear son and brother,
that we do not think of you.   *(93)*

NO NAME   ST ANDREW'S CHURCH
AMDG. In loving memory of my husband Henry. MCXIXXIII. *(93)*

O'HARA, J (see BEDFORDSHIRE REGIMENT)

O'SULLIVAN   WESTRIDGE *(A4)*
Wife of George O'SULLIVAN, who died at Rawalpindi 28 Oct 1918.
Aged 55 yrs. Thy will be done.   RIP. AHMUD BUX, SCULPTOR,
RAWALPINDI.   *(82)(93)*

O'SULLIVAN, Norah   WESTRIDGE
Sacred to the memory of Norah O'SULLIVAN.   Born Oct and died
.....   *(82)*

OAKES, P H (see KING'S OWN SCOTTISH BORDERERS)

OLIVER, Arthur Harrison   CHRISTCHURCH
Sacred to the memory of Lieutenant Arthur Harrison OLIVER,
84th Punjabis, who died at Rawalpindi on the 8 Nov 1911. This
tablet is erected by his brother officers.   P ORR & SONS, ART
METAL WORKERS, MADRAS AND RANGOON.   *(82)(93)(brass)*

ORMISTON, P (see GORDON HIGHLANDERS)

OWEN, Clarence Morland Brisco (see BRISCO-OWEN, Clarence M)

PADDAY, W H (see 36TH SIKHS)

PADGHAM, D G (see BEDFORDSHIRE REGIMENT)

PAGE, T   (see 3RD (PRINCE OF WALES'S) DRAGOON GUARDS)

PAINTER, Mollie Laura Arnaud   CHRISTCHURCH
Sacred to the memory of Mollie Laura Arnaud PAINTER.   Sister,
Queen Alexandra's Imperial Military Nursing Service.   Died
Trimulgherry 5 Jul 1941.   *(82)(93)(WM)*

*TWO VIEWS OF CHRISTCHURCH, RAWALPINDI
(SEE ALSO PAGE 281)*

PALMER, Gerald John   WESTRIDGE *(R3)*
In loving memory of Gerald John. The dearly loved child of Zena and Mervyn PALMAN. Born 16 Sep 1928. Died 14 Jul 1930.
(82)(93)(end)

PALMER, G J (see 4TH DRAGOON GUARDS (1))
PARKER, A   (see 4TH DRAGOON GUARDS (1))

PARSI CEMETERY PLAQUE
This cemetery, together with the buildings, well and compound wall, was erected to perpetuate the memory of the late Set Jehangirji Framji Jussawalla and Set Jamasji Hormasji Bogha, both of Rawalpindi, Parsi merchants, by their respective grandsons Set Dorabji Cowasji Jussawalla and Set Nasarwanji Jehangirji Bogha. Shanshai Month Tir 1267 Yezdezardi, January 1898.

PASSMORE, Keith   WESTRIDGE *(M1)*
In loving memory of Keith. Darling son of BQMS and Mabel PASSMORE. Died 17 Oct 1923. Aged 7 mths. This lovely bud so young and fair, called hence from early doom, just came to show how fair a flower in paradise will bloom.   *(82)(93)*

PASSY, Harry Everard   CHRISTCHURCH
Sacred to the memory of Lieutenant Colonel Harry Everard PASSY, Controller of Military Accounts, who died at Rawalpindi on the 22 Dec 1904. This tablet is erected by his brother officers. P ORR & SONS, ART METAL WORKERS, MADRAS, RANGOON & COLOMBO.   *(82)(93)(brass)*

PAYNE, E T   (see 4TH DRAGOON GUARDS (1))

PEARSON, Catherine Mary   WESTRIDGE *(J)*
Sacred to the memory of Catherine Mary PEARSON. Born 30 Jan 1859. Died 22 Dec 1933. Aged 74 yrs 11 mths 23 days. Father in thy gracious keeping, leave we now thy servant sleeping.
                                                  (82)(93)

PEAT, L L   (see SHERWOOD FORESTERS)
PELL   (see 3RD (PRINCE OF WALES'S) DRAGOON GUARDS)
PENN, J   (see BEDFORDSHIRE REGIMENT)
PENTLOW, S   (see 9TH LANCERS)

PERCY, Keith Harold Oscar   CHRISTCHURCH
In memory of Keith Harold Oscar PERCY. Headmaster, Lawrence College, Ghora Gali. Died on 15 Mar 1960. Age 78. *(82)(93)(WM)*

PERRY, H   (see BEDFORDSHIRE REGIMENT)
PETTY, E   (see RIFLE BRIGADE)
PHAROAH, H H   (see RIFLE BRIGADE)
PHILLIPS, A   (see GORDON HIGHLANDERS)
PIERCE, J   (see 9TH LANCERS)

PINNICER, Broome   WESTRIDGE *(D)*
In sacred and affectionate memory of my beloved husband Broome PINNICER, who fell asleep on the 21 Aug 1935. Aged 63 yrs 9 mths 19 days. We miss and mourn you in silence unseen. Unknown to the world you are still by our side, whispering my loved ones death cannot divide.   *(82)(93)*

PIRRIE, W F   (see 4TH DRAGOON GUARDS (1))
PITHER, A H   (see BEDFORDSHIRE REGIMENT)
POGAN, H   (see UNNAMED REGIMENT)
POLLOCK, J   (see 9TH LANCERS)

PONSONBY, Cecil Arnout   MURREE ROAD
In loving memory of Cecil Arnout PONSONBY. Born 30 Dec 1907.
Died 3 Oct 1914.   *(87)(WM)*

PONSONBY, Peter   MURREE ROAD
In loving memory of my beloved husband Peter PONSONBY. Born
20 Dec 1863. Died 12 Mar 1967.   *(87)*

POLYBLANK, Joseph Albert   WESTRIDGE *(F2)*
In loving memory of Joseph Albert. The beloved husband of
Caroline POLYBLANK who departed this life 3 Jan 1894. Aged 50
yrs. Light after darkness, gain after loss, strength after
weakness, crown after cross, sweet after bitter, hope after
fears, home after wandering, praise after tears, near after
distant, gleam after gloom, love after loneliness, life after
tomb. After long agony rapture of bliss, right was the
pathway leading to this.   *(82)(93)*

POTTER, S   (see UNNAMED REGIMENT)

POWELL, J   (see BEDFORDSHIRE REGIMENT)

POWELL, John   ST PAULS CHURCH
Sacred to the memory of Lieutenant Colonel John POWELL, CIE,
OBE, who died at Murree on 13 Jul 1938. Aged 82 yrs 6 mths. I
pray thee then write me as one of those who loved his fellow
men. "Heaven's light your guide."   *(82)(93)(brass)*

PRITCHARD, H (see RIFLE BRIGADE)

QUINLIN, M (see 4TH DRAGOON GUARDS (1))

RAE, R   (see 9TH LANCERS)

RAIKES, F S W   (see RIFLE BRIGADE)

RAPER, Lilian   WESTRIDGE *(E2)*
In loving memory of Lilian. Beloved wife of John C D RAPER, N
W Ry. Died 17 Aug. Age 27 years. Blessed are the pure in
heart for they shall see God.   *(93)*

REDMAN, J (see BEDFORDSHIRE REGIMENT)

REED, G   (see 3RD (PRINCE OF WALES'S) DRAGOON GUARDS)

REED, Margaret   WESTRIDGE *(X1)*
In loving memory of Margaret. The dearly beloved wife of William REED, Pensioner. Born 24 Aug 1836. Died 4 Sep 1886. Weep not for me my children dear, for I am not dead, but sleeping here. I am not yours, but Christ's alone He loved me best and took me home. This tablet is erected by her sorrowful daughter Elizabeth. KUNNIAN LAL & SONS, SCULPTOR, DELHI.
(82)(93)

REES, W   (see 4TH DRAGOON GUARDS (1))
REEVE   (see 3RD (PRINCE OF WALES'S) DRAGOON GUARDS)

REID, Thomas William   WESTRIDGE *(M2)*
Thomas William REID, N W Ry, who was accidentally killed whilst out shooting on 30 Mar 1906. Aged 29 years. Gone but not forgotten. Erected by his sorrowing brothers and sisters.
(93)

REYNOLDS, F R (see 4TH DRAGOON GUARDS (1))

RICH, Charles Lionel Mainwaring   CHRISTCHURCH
To the glory of God and in loving memory of Major Charles Lionel Mainwaring RICH. Deputy Judge Advocate General and late "Queen's Own" Corps of Guides, who died at Rawalpindi 10 Feb 1903. Aged 41 yrs. For I know whom I have believed and am persuaded that he is able to keep that which I have committed unto him against that day. II Timothy 1. Erected by his sorrowing widow.   *(82)(93)(brass)*

RICHARDS, E C (see RIFLE BRIGADE)
RICHARDSON   (see 3RD (PRINCE OF WALES'S) DRAGOON GUARDS)
RIDGE, J   (see 9TH LANCERS)
RIDGERS   (see 3RD (PRINCE OF WALES'S) DRAGOON GUARDS)

RILEY, Hope Ethel Reda   WESTRIDGE
In loving memory of Hope Ethel Reda. Beloved wife of H A RILEY. Died 21 Sep 1934.   *(82)*

ROBERTS, Dallis A   NICOLL MEMORIAL CH
Sacred to the memory of Rev Dallis A ROBERTS. Born 13 Dec 1942. Died 27 Dec 1988. Building of Independence and Church and Pastor for 18 years.   *(94)*

ROBERTS, David P   NICOLL MEMORIAL CH
Sacred to the memory of Revd David P ROBERTS. Born 19 May 1895. Died 28 Jan 1971. Builder of this church and Pastor for 50 years. Well done thou good and faithful servant. Enter thou into the joy of thy Lord. Math.25.21.   *(94)*

ROBERTS, W (see 4TH DRAGOON GUARDS (1))

ROBERTSON, Alexander   WESTRIDGE *(J2)*
In sacred memory of Alexander ROBERTSON, who died of apoplexy 20 Jul 1900. Aged 49 yrs 2 mths 27 days. God rest his soul in peace. NEYAZ ALI, SCULPTOR, RAWALPINDI. *(82)(93)*

ROBERTSON, P (see GORDON HIGHLANDERS)

ROBERTSON, W   (see GORDON HIGHLANDERS)
ROBINSON, C   (see ROYAL GARRISON ARTILLERY (1)

RODGERS, Winston, Desmond and Terence   ST JOSEPH'S CATHEDRAL
Pray for the donors Winston, Desmond and Terence RODGERS.
                                          (93)(WM)
       (This inscription is on the font)

ROGERS, H   (see BEDFORDSHIRE REGIMENT)
ROLPH, F   (see RIFLE BRIGADE)

ROOKE, Agnes Emily   ST ANDREW'S CHURCH
To the glory of God. In loving memory of Agnes Emily ROOKE.
During forty years missionary in India who worshipped in this
church   MCMVII-MCMXXIII.   Rejoice in hope. ROM.XII.12.
Presented by Dr Miss L BOSS. Rawalpindi 30 Nov 1935.   (94)

ROSE, W   (see BEDFORDSHIRE REGIMENT)

ROSSENRODE, Gertrude R   WESTRIDGE (I1)
In loving memory of Gertrude R ROSSENRODE. Born 26 Mar 1882.
Died 22 Oct 1918. Aged 36 yrs and 7 mths. Oh look with pity
on the scene of sadness and of dread and let thine angel
stand between the living and the dead. (82)(93)

RUFFETT, A   (see QUEEN'S REGIMENT)
RUTHERFORD, T S (see 4TH DRAGOON GUARDS (1))

SABER, Liliam   WESTRIDGE
In loving memory of Lilian. Beloved wife of John C D SABER.
N W Railway. Died 17 Aug .... Aged 27 yrs.   (82)

SADDLER, W   (see BEDFORDSHIRE REGIMENT)

SADLER, Eliza   WESTRIDGE (E1)
In loving and affectionate memory of my darling mother Eliza
SADLER who departed this life on 26 Mar 1921. Aged 83 yrs 9
mths 3 days. God granted one more angel to grace his
heavenly throne and so he took my darling mother and bade me
not to mourn. I tried so hard to keep her for she will be to me
dear, but Jesus said it could not be, He wanted her in
Heaven. Erected by her sorrowing daughter.
                                          (82)(93)

SAMUEL, Emanuel George   MURREE ROAD
In loving memory of Emanuel George. Beloved son of M R and B
SAMUEL who fell asleep 9 Nov 1914. Aged 4 1/2 mths. Suffer
little children to come unto me.   (87)

SANDERS, A C   (see SHERWOOD FORESTERS)
SANDERS, E   (see 4TH DRAGOON GUARDS (1))

SANDFORD, Catherine Gertrude Brennan   WESTRIDGE
In loving memory of Catherine Gertrude Brennan. Beloved wife of Patrick SANDFORD. Born 11 Aug 1889. Died 8 May 1935.
(82)

SANDIFORTH, C   (see ROYAL HORSE ARTILLERY (1))
SARGEANT   (see 3RD (PRINCE OF WALES'S) DRAGOON GUARDS)
SARTAIN, E   (see RIFLE BRIGADE)
SAVILLE, H   (see 4TH DRAGOON GUARDS (1))
SAVIN, J   (see ROYAL HORSE ARTILLERY (1))
SCOTT, E   (see BEDFORDSHIRE REGIMENT)
SCRIVENER, R A   (see 4TH DRAGOON GUARDS (1))
SCULLY, E   (see 4TH DRAGOON GUARDS (1))
SEMPLE, R   (see 4TH DRAGOON GUARDS (1))
SHAMBROOK, I M   (see BEDFORDSHIRE REGIMENT)
SHAMBROOK, J   (see BEDFORDSHIRE REGIMENT)
SHAMBROOK, J M   (see BEDFORDSHIRE REGIMENT)

SHARPE, Charles Thomas William Harry   WESTRIDGE *(L)*
Rest in peace. In loving memory of Charles Thomas William Harry SHARPE, the beloved son of Mrs Rose SHARPE, who died on the 31 Dec 1930. Aged 30 yrs 3 mths. Days and moments quickly flying blend the living with the dead. Soon will you and I be lying each within our narrow bed. *(82)(93)*

SHEEHAN, D   (see ROYAL FIELD ARTILLERY)
SHORTER, G   (see BEDFORDSHIRE REGIMENT)
SHRIVES, J   (see BEDFORDSHIRE REGIMENT)
SHRIVES, P   (see BEDFORDSHIRE REGIMENT)
SIBBALD, A   (see GORDON HIGHLANDERS)
SIMMONDS, G   (see RIFLE BRIGADE)
SIMMONS, W   (see RIFLE BRIGADE)
SIMPSON, J   (see GORDON HIGHLANDERS)
SKEWS, A   (see RIFLE BRIGADE)
SLADE, J   (see RIFLE BRIGADE)
SLATER, G   (see RIFLE BRIGADE)

SMITH, Agnes Sarah   CHRISTCHURCH
Sacred to the memory of Agnes Sarah, the beloved wife of Captain John SMITH, 51st Regiment, NI, who departed this life on the 11 Dec 1855. Aged 22 yrs. To depart and to be with Christ which is far better. Phil.1.C.23 verse. *(82)(93)(BS)*

SMITH, Agnes Sarah   OLD CEMETERY
Sacred to the memory of Agnes Sarah, the beloved wife of Captain J SMITH, 51st NI, who departed this life 11 Dec 1855. Aged 22 yrs. *(82)(93)(BS)*

SMITH, A J (see RIFLE BRIGADE)

SMITH, Alice   WESTRIDGE *(W2)*
In loving memory of Alice SMITH, the beloved wife of J W SMITH, Mutiny veteran, who departed this life on the 16 Apr 1915. Aged 49 yrs. Erected by her husband and children.
(82)(93)

SMITH, E (see BEDFORDSHIRE REGIMENT)

SMITH, Elizabeth Mabel   WESTRIDGE *(E4)*
In ever loving memory of Elizabeth Mabel (Tottie).   Dear wife
of Thomas SMITH and daughter of J G LAING. Called to rest   26
Dec 1907. Aged 28 yrs 1 mth 27 days.   Though death divides
your memory clings.   Farewell darling, rest in peace. Fond
memories of you ne'er will cease and oft shall we weep adieu.
For you, our loved one, good and true God grant us his grace
that we may prepare to meet you in heaven there's no parting
here.   *(82)(93)*

SMITH, F C   (see RIFLE BRIGADE)
SMITH, H R   (see 4TH DRAGOON GUARDS (1))
SMITH, J   (see SEAFORTH HIGHLANDERS)
SMITH, J   (see 3RD (PRINCE OF WALES'S) DRAGOON GUARDS)

SMITH, Lionel Henry Malir   WESTRIDGE *(L3)*
In loving memory of Lionel Henry Malir SMITH. Born 13 Nov
1887. Died at Rawalpindi on 22 Dec 1940. Aged 53 yrs 1 month
9 days. RIP.   *(82)(93)*

SMITH, Persis Priscilla   MURREE ROAD
In ever loving memory of Persis Priscilla. Wife of the late
Captain P P SMITH. Born 12 Nov 1905. Died 25 Jun 1970.
Erected by her daughter Enid NAJMUDDIN. *(82)(WM)*

SMITH, V   (see ROYAL HORSE ARTILLERY (1))
SMITH, W H   (see GORDON HIGHLANDERS)
SMITH, W J   (see RIFLE BRIGADE)

SPARKES, Winnie   WESTRIDGE *(B3)*
In loving memory of our darling little Winnie, dearly beloved
child of C W and A F SPARKES, who died at Rawal Pindi on the 1
Nov 1918 at the age of 11 years and 7 mths.   *(93)*

SPARKS, R   (see 4TH DRAGOON GUARDS (1))
SPITZER, R A   (see 4TH DRAGOON GUARDS (1))

SPLANE, Robert   WESTRIDGE *(U)*
In loving memory of our noble daddy Bertie, Robert SPLANE,
who gave his life to save anothers on the 16 Jul 1925. Fold
Daddy in thy arms, O Jesus, and let him henceforth be a
messenger of love between our aching hearts and thee. *(82)(93)*

SQUIER, F T (see ROYAL GARRISON ARTILLERY (2))

STAINTON, Vernon Bruce   CHRISTCHURCH
In loving memory of Vernon Bruce STAINTON, OBE. Indian Civil
Service. Born 31 Mar 1904. Died 10 Apr 1946. Deputy Commis-
sioner of Rawalpindi 1 Nov 1941 to 10 Apr 1946.*(82)(93)(brass)*

STAPELEY (see 3RD (PRINCE OF WALES'S) DRAGOON GUARDS)

STEPHENS, Ellen Isabel   WESTRIDGE
In beloved memory of our dear mother Ellen Isabel STEPHENS,
who died 30 Jan 1925. Aged 62 yrs.   *(82)(end)*

STERLING, M   (see 4TH DRAGOON GUARDS (1))

STEVENS, R   (see ROYAL HORSE ARTILLERY (1))
STEWART, A   (see 9TH LANCERS)

STEWART, Isabelle Darrow   MURREE ROAD
Sacred to the memory of Isabelle Darrow STEWART. 1888-1953.
The beloved wife of R R STEWART, DD. D.Sc. Principal Gordon
College. Blessed are they who die in the Lord. *(87)*

STOKES, S   (see BEDFORDSHIRE REGIMENT)
STONE, A   (see BEDFORDSHIRE REGIMENT)
STONE, A   (see 9TH LANCERS)
STRATTON, A   (see BEDFORDSHIRE REGIMENT)
STRAW, R   (see UNNAMED REGIMENT)
STRIVENS, B   (see ROYAL HORSE ARTILLERY (1))
STURMER, J A   (see 4TH DRAGOON GUARDS (1))
STYLES, J H   (see 4TH DRAGOON GUARDS (1))
SULLIVAN, T   (see BEDFORDSHIRE REGIMENT)
SULLIVAN, W   (see RIFLE BRIGADE)
SUTTON, E J   (see 4TH DRAGOON GUARDS (1))
SWAN, W   (see 4TH DRAGOON GUARDS (1))

TALBOT, A (see GORDON HIGHLANDERS)

TAPPIN, Queenie   WESTRIDGE *(C3)*
Queenie. Beloved wife of J C TAPPIN. Born 5 Mar 1878. Died
27 Dec 1911. How we loved her, no tongue can tell. How much
we loved her and how well. God loved her too and thought it
best to take our darling to her heavenly rest. *(82)(93)*

TARR, W S   (see ROYAL HORSE ARTILLERY (1))
TAYLOR, A T   (see 4TH DRAGOON GUARDS (1))
TAYLOR, W   (see 4TH DRAGOON GUARDS (1))
TAYLOR, W L   (see RIFLE BRIGADE)

TEAL, Arnold John   CHRISTCHURCH
In everlasting and loving memory of Dr. Arnold John TEAL, MBB
SDPH (London University), who died at Rawalpindi 27 Feb 1949.
Aged 47 yrs. A true Christian and a friend to all in need.
Ich din. At the going down of the sun and in the morning, we
will remember him. Erected by his wife and children.
                                        (82)(93)

TEAL, Arnold John   WESTRIDGE
In loving memory of Arnold John TEAL. Dearly loved husband of
Nes and father of Eleanor and John. Born 6 Oct 1901. Died 27
Feb 1949.   *(82)*

TEAL, Ernest Henry   ST MARY'S CHURCH
Sacred to the memory of Ernest Henry TEAL, who died at Murree
31 Oct 1920. Aged 14 yrs 9 mths. Erected by his sorrowing
parents. Rest in peace.   *(82)(WM)*

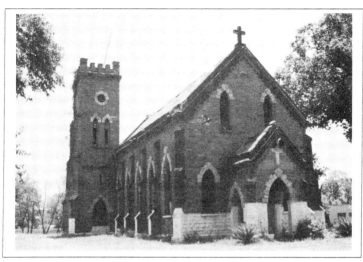

ST MARY'S CHURCH, WESTRIDGE

TEAL, Ernest Henry   WESTRIDGE *(H1)*
In ever loving memory of Ernest Henry TEAL, third son of Mr
and Mrs O J TEAL, who died in Murree as the result of a gun
accident. Born 21 Jan 1906. Died 31 Oct 1920. Rest in peace.
(82)(93)(end)

TEAL, Oswald John   CHRISTCHURCH
In ever loving and affectionate memory of Oswald John TEAL,
who died at Rawalpindi on 1 Dec 1945. Aged 78 yrs. He
worshipped in this church from 1904. A loving husband and
devoted father. Rest in peace.   *(82)(93)(WM)*

TEAL, Oswald John   WESTRIDGE
In loving and affectionate memory of Oswald John TEAL. Born
11 Dec 1867. Died 1 Dec 1945. A good Christian, husband, father and friend.   *(82)*

TEEDON, W   (see BEDFORDSHIRE REGIMENT)
TERRY, A   (see BEDFORDSHIRE REGIMENT)

THATCHER, Torin   CHRISTCHURCH
Sacred to the memory of Major General Torin THATCHER of the
Indian Army, who died at Murree on the 6 Oct 1903 in the 77th
year of his age. This tablet is placed here by friends of the
late General as a token of their respect and esteem.
(82)(93)(brass)

THOMAS, B   (see RIFLE BRIGADE)
THOMPSON, A   (see BEDFORDSHIRE REGIMENT)

```
THOMPSON, W J    (see RIFLE BRIGADE)
THOMSON, J W     (see 3RD (PRINCE OF WALES'S) DRAGOON GUARDS)
THOMSON, T       (see QUEEN'S REGIMENT)
TIDY, A G        (see RIFLE BRIGADE)
TILLER, G        (see ROYAL FIELD ARTILLERY)
TOMALIN, T       (see RIFLE BRIGADE)
TONKIN, R        (see RIFLE BRIGADE)
TOWEY, J J       (see 4TH DRAGOON GUARDS (1))
TRANTER          (see 3RD (PRINCE OF WALES'S) DRAGOON GUARDS)
```

TROTTER, Alexander James   CHRISTCHURCH
Sacred to the memory of 2nd Lieutenant Alexander James TROTTER of the Bengal Artillery. Drowned while crossing the River Jhelum near Katai on the 4 Oct 1856. Aetat 23. Requiescat in pace. LLEWELYN & CO, SCULPTORS, CALCUTTA.   *(82)(93)(BS)*

TROUNDSELL (?), Henry   WESTRIDGE *(H4)*
Henry TROUNDSELL (?GROUNDSELL), Guard N W Railway, who died at West Ridge 2 Nov 1905. Aged 35 years. Deeply lamented by his sorrowing wife.   *(82)(93)*

TUBINO, P (SEE 4TH DRAGOON GUARDS (1))

TURING, Arthur   CHRISTCHURCH
Sacred to the memory of Captain David GORDON, 36th Sikhs, who died in the Kuram (sic) Valley 5 Jul 1897, and Lieutenant Arthur TURING. 36th Sikhs. Killed in action at the Shin Kamar Pass, Tirah 29 Jan 1898. This tablet is erected by their brother officers. P ORR AND SONS, ART METAL WORKERS, MADRAS.
                                                (82)(93)(brass)

TURNER, Archibald James   WESTRIDGE *(H3)*
Our darling son. Archibald James. The dearly loved child of Rose and James TURNER. Died 9 Jul 1908. Aged 1 yr 4 mths. He has gone but not forgotten, never shall his memory fade. Sweetest thoughts shall ever linger around the tomb where Archie's laid. Thy will be done.   *(82)(93)*

```
TURNER, E  (see BEDFORDSHIRE REGIMENT)
TURNER, L  (see 9TH LANCERS)
TYLER, A   (see RIFLE BRIGADE)
```

UDAL, E R   CHRISTCHURCH
Sacred to the memory of Lieutenant E R UDAL, XXXVI Sikhs, who died at Bangalore on 3 Jun 1905. This tablet is erected by his brother officers.   *(82)(93)(brass)*

UNWIN, A W (see SHERWOOD FORESTERS)

VALENTINE, J (see GORDON HIGHLANDERS)
VARDON, C   (see ROYAL ARTILLERY (1))

VAUGHAN, Katherine   WESTRIDGE *(I4)*
In memory of Katherine VAUGHAN, dearly beloved mother of Peter VAUGHAN, who departed this life at Rawalpindi on 4 Mar 1901. Aged 60 yrs. Erected by her only sorrowing son. Lord I know it was thy will for me a mother's love to bear and so Lord Jesus be it still I consign her to thy care.   *(82)(93)*

VIEGAS, Annie   WESTRIDGE *(M3)*
In loving memory of (Mrs) Annie VIEGAS. Dearly loved mother and grandmother. Called to rest 5 Jan 1938. Erected by her sorrowing son, daughter-in-law, and grandchildren. (poem)
                                            (82)(93)

VIEGAS, Herbert William   WESTRIDGE *(K3)*
In ever loving memory of my beloved husband and devoted father Herbert William VIEGAS. Born 1 Apr 1898. Died 29 Apr 1941. Erected by his sorrowing wife and children. RIP. (poem)
                                            (82)(93)

VIEGAS, Thomas Manual   WESTRIDGE *(N3)*
In loving memory of Thomas Manual VIEGAS. Tommy. Late N W Railway. Dearly loved husband, father and grandfather. Called to rest 11 Oct 1936. Erected by his wife, children and grandchildren. RIP. (poem)   *(82)(93)*

VOEUX, S Des (see 36TH SIKHS)

WACKETT, T   (see BEDFORDSHIRE REGIMENT)
WAGSTAFFE, L W   (see SHERWOOD FORESTERS)
WALDEN, G   (see RIFLE BRIGADE)
WALKER, G H   (see 4TH DRAGOON GUARDS (1))
WALKER, W   (see BEDFORDSHIRE REGIMENT)
WALL, F P   (see RIFLE BRIGADE)
WALL, J   (see BEDFORDSHIRE REGIMENT)

WALLACE, Ethel   WESTRIDGE *(U3)*
Our dearly beloved mother Ethel WALLACE who departed this life on the 4 Jan 1924. Aged 64 yrs 7 mths. A loving mother true and kind, she was to us in heart and mind, she always strove to do her best, and now she is forever blest. We would not call her back again, our loss is her eternal gain. Her sufferings on this earth are o'er. We mourn, but still God's will be done.   *(82)(93)*

WALLACE, William   WESTRIDGE *(Y3)*
In loving memory of William WALLACE who died 6 Sep 1919. Aged
67 yrs 6 mths.   There is a link death cannot sever, love and
remembrance last forever. RIP.   *(82)(93)*

COFFIN CARRIER IN WESTRIDGE CEMETERY

WALSH, H   (see RIFLE BRIGADE)
WALSH, J T   (see 3RD (PRINCE OF WALES'S) DRAGOON GUARDS)
WALSH, T   (see 4TH DRAGOON GUARDS (1))
WALTON, J   (see 4TH DRAGOON GUARDS (1))
WARBURTON, J   (see UNNAMED REGIMENT)
WARD, A   (see 4TH DRAGOON GUARDS (1))
WARD, C   (see 9TH LANCERS)
WARD, R   (see ROYAL ARTILLERY (1))
WARREN, F   (see RIFLE BRIGADE)
WARREN, W   (see BEDFORDSHIRE REGIMENT)
WATERS, F C   (see 4TH DRAGOON GUARDS (1))
WATKINS, H   (see RIFLE BRIGADE)
WATSON, A   (see 9TH LANCERS)
WATTS, G   (see BEDFORDSHIRE REGIMENT)
WEBSTER, W J   (see 4TH DRAGOON GUARDS (1))
WEEKS, H V   (see 4TH DRAGOON GUARDS (1))
WEEKS, J T   (see RIFLE BRIGADE)
WELLS   (see 3RD (PRINCE OF WALES'S) DRAGOON GUARDS)
WELSH, M   (see GORDON HIGHLANDERS)
WEST, A H M   (see 36TH SIKHS)
WEST, G   (see BEDFORDSHIRE REGIMENT)
WESTERMAN, J   (see 4TH DRAGOON GUARDS (1))
WESTON, W   (see BEDFORDSHIRE REGIMENT)

WHEELER, Ellen Jane   OLD CEMETERY
Ellen Jane, the daughter of Colour Sergeant William and
Margaret WHEELER, HM's 87th Royal Irish Fusiliers, who died 2
Aug 1854. Aged 2 yrs 8 mths.   *(82)(93)*

WHEELER, T H   (see ROYAL FIELD ARTILLERY)
WHEELER, W T G   (see ROYAL FIELD ARTILLERY)
WHITE, J   (see BEDFORDSHIRE REGIMENT)
WHITE, J   (see GORDON HIGHLANDERS)
WHITE, J   (see SEAFORTH HIGHLANDERS)
WHITING, J   (see RIFLE BRIGADE)
WHITTY, B   (see RIFLE BRIGADE)

WICKHAM, Emilia   ST ANDREW'S CHURCH
AMDG. In piam memoriam. Emilia WICKHAM. Dedicat Emilia
Forrest. MCMXI.   *(94)*

WICKS, A   (see 4TH DRAGOON GUARDS (1))
WICKS, A R   (see 4TH DRAGOON GUARDS (1))
WIGHTMAN, W   (see 4TH DRAGOON GUARDS (1))
WILKINS, C   (see 9TH LANCERS)
WILKINS, W   (see RIFLE BRIGADE)
WILLIAMS, E   (see 3RD (PRINCE OF WALES'S) DRAGOON GUARDS)
WILLIAMS, J H   (see RIFLE BRIGADE)

WILLIAMS, Robert David   WESTRIDGE *(A1)*
In loving memory of our precious baby son Robert David
WILLIAMS. Born 6 Aug 1925 and left us for his eternal rest 16
Mar 1926. Aged 7 mths 10 days.   *(82)(93)*

WILLIAMS, T (see RIFLE BRIGADE)

WILSON   WESTRIDGE
...Caroline and Samuel WILSON. Born 28 Feb 1894. Died 6 Dec
1906.   *(82)*

WILSON, Amabel (sic) Pauline   WESTRIDGE *(A)*
Peace. In ever loving memory of my darling mother Amabel (sic)
Pauline WILSON. Born 23 Nov 1861. Died 28 Jan 1940. We'll
mourn for her in silence, no eye shall see us weep. But ever
in our aching hearts, her memory we will keep. Erected by
her sorrowing daughter Mrs HEDLEL, son-in-law and
grandchildren.   *(82)(93)*

WILSON, J (see 3RD (PRINCE OF WALES'S) DRAGOON GUARDS)
WILSON, S (see GORDON HIGHLANDERS)

WILSON, Samuel   WESTRIDGE *(A2)*
Thy will be done. In loving memory of Samuel WILSON, who was
killed while at Jahangera Road on 21 Dec *1913*. Aged 41 yrs 3
mths.   *(82)(93)*

WINDLEY, Roberti Joseph   ST JOSEPH'S CATHEDRAL
Orate proanima reverendissimi Dni Roberti Joseph WINKLEY
1916-1930. AB anno 1916 ad annum 1930 de Kafristan et Kashmir.
(Died 2 Nov 1930. Aged 70)   *(94)*

WINGRAVE, H   (see BEDFORDSHIRE REGIMENT)
WINN, R   (see 9TH LANCERS)
WINSOR, W   (see RIFLE BRIGADE)
WINTERBOTTOM, E   (see 9TH LANCERS)
WINTERHALDER   (see 3RD (PRINCE OF WALES'S) DRAGOON GUARDS)
WINTERSON, J   (see 4TH DRAGOON GUARDS (1))
WOODS, W   (see 3RD (PRINCE OF WALES'S) DRAGOON GUARDS)

WRAGGE, Edward Theophilus   WESTRIDGE *(X)*
In loving memory of Edward Theophilus WRAGGE, Hon Assistant Engineer, N W Railway, who died at Rawalpindi on 30 Aug 1928. Aged 51 yrs 5 mths 26 days. A true and loving husband and affectionate father and a sympathetic friend, his life was an inspiration to many and his memory endures imperishably enshrined in the hearts of his family circle and of all those who enjoyed his friendship.   *(82)(93)*

WRAY, A   (see BEDFORDSHIRE REGIMENT)
WRIGHT, C J   (see RIFLE BRIGADE)

WRIGHT, James Johnstone   ST PAULS CHURCH
In loving memory of James Johnstone WRIGHT. Senior Chaplain, Church of Scotland who died at Rawalpindi on 12th April 1928. Aged 55 yrs. Until the day breaks and the shadows flee away.
                                       (82)(93)(brass)

WROTTESLEY, William   (see 4th DRAGOON GUARDS (2))

WYATT, F O   CHRISTCHURCH
Sacred to the memory of the late Lieutenant Colonel F O WYATT, MVO, RGA, Commanding No 2 British Mountain Artillery Brigade, who died at Rawalpindi on 16 Dec 1919. This tablet is erected as a tribute of respect by the officers, noncommissioned officers and men of No 1 Mountain Battery, RGA and of the brigade of which he commanded.   *(82)(93)(brass)*

YOUNG, Duke Randolph   WESTRIDGE *(W)*
Loves best gift is remembrance. In ever loving and fond memory of my dear husband Duke Randolph YOUNG. Indian State Railways. Called to his eternal rest 10 Jun 1928. Aged 45 yrs. An affectionate husband and loving father. My toils on earth are over and my body here lies still, but back to God my soul I give, resigned to his sweet will. Safe in the "better land" I'll beg the dear "friend of mankind", to bless my wife and children whom with grief I leave behind. Jesus mercy.   *(82)(93)*

YOUNG, E (see BEDFORDSHIRE REGIMENT)

YOUNG, P (see ROYAL ARTILLERY (2))

REGIMENTS

BEDFORDSHIRE REGIMENT   CHRISTCHURCH
To the glory of God and in memory of the undernamed officers, NC officers, men, women and children of the 1st Bn Bedfordshire Regiment, who died while the regiment was stationed in the Rawalpindi District from Jan 1891 - Jan 1894.

At Rawalpindi
2nd Lieutenant H R K FORD
NC officers and men

Colour Sergeant J SHRIVES	Private A IZZARD
Sergeant H T COSTELLO	Private G A BENN
Lance Corporal R CASS	Private F BROOKE
Private J BATES	Private G GREEN
Private J WALL	Private J W HEWITT
Private W SADDLER	Private A TERRY
Private W NORTH	Private H PERRY
Private J REDMAN	Private E G GODDARD
Private A STONE	Private T WACKETT
Private F BUSBY	Private G SHORTER
Private H WINGRAVE	Private A STRATTON
Private J HAWS	Private S COOPER
Private J WHITE	Private W WESTON
Private A THOMPSON	
Private J HILLIER	Women
Private H J DILLON	Isabella Maud SHAMBROOK
Private W HARVEY	
Private W TEEDON	Children
Private W ROSE	Edward SCOTT
Private S STOKES	Jane PENN
Private T CAIN	Jane SHAMBROOK
Private J POWELL	Jessie May SHAMBROOK
Private D G PADGHAM	Percy SHRIVES
Private G WATTS	Ernest SMITH
Private T COULTER	Edith TURNER
Private A HORNE	Janet O'HARA
	Theresa Rose MUNT
	Annie JOHNSON
At Murree	
Private H ROGERS	Private A H PITHER
Private W BAKER	Private G COOK
At Kuldana	
Private G WEST	Private A HEWITT
Private F KEEN	Private G CRAYFORD
Private T IBBITT	Private T HAYNES
J JACKSON	
Children	
Esther BROWN	George FREER
At Campbellpore	
Private E YOUNG	
On Isazai Field Force 1892	
Sergeant G C MARSHALL	Private E KERRISON
Lance Corporal T SULLIVAN	Private A GUDGIN
Drummer T BETTS	Private W WALKER
Private A WRAY	Private H NORTON
Private W BARTHOLOMEW	Private G E DEADMAN
Private J CULVER	Private W GARRATT

BEDFORDSHIRE REGIMENT (cont)
En route to and from England
Mrs KING   Sergeant Major T McGINN
Corporal C KEELER   Private C H BOND
Private A HARVEY   Private W WARREN
This memorial is erected by the officers, NC officers and men
of the regiment.   *(82)(93)(brass)*

CONNAUGHT RANGERS   ST JOSEPH'S CATHEDRAL
1st Battalion The Connaught Rangers. 1922. Pray for the
donors.   *(93)(WM)*
     (This inscription is on one of two little fonts)

GORDON HIGHLANDERS   ST PAULS CHURCH
In memory of the following Warrant Officer, NCOs and men of
the 1st FS Garrison Battalion, Gordon Highlanders who died
while the battalion was on service in India 1917-1919.
CSM MOODY D   Private BROWN A
Sergeant KEEN A   Private BROWNLEE T
Lance Sergeant   CLARKE J A   Private BRYSON J
Lance Corporal HAMILTON W   Private BUIST J
Lance Corporal HAWKER W   Private CAMPBELL W
Lance Corporal MAVERS R   Private GORMAN J
Lance Corporal McLEOD J   Private HAMILTON W
Lance Corporal ROBERTSON P   Private HORSCHELL F
Private ALEXANDER G   Private INGRIG J
Private AVIS J C   Private KEENAN G
Private BARR J   Private KERNAHAN W
Private BAXTER F   Private LONIE H
Private BECKTON J   Private McDONALD J
Private BOYD R   Private McELROY B
                                      Private McLEAN W
Private MATTHEW A   Private SIMPSON J
Private METCALFE W   Private SMITH W H
Private NEVAY A   Private TALBOT A
Private ORMISTON P   Private VALENTINE J
Private PHILLIPS A   Private WELSH M
Private ROBERTSON W   Private WHITE J
Private SIBBALD A   Private WILSON S

Erected by the officers, warrant and noncommissioned officers
and men of the battalion. BARTON SON & CO, BANGALORE.
                                      (82)(93)(brass)

KING'S OWN SCOTTISH BORDERERS   CHRISTCHURCH
Sacred to the memory of the following officers of the 2nd Battalion King's Own Scottish Borderers.

2nd Lieutenant P H OAKES   14 Mar 1894
Lieutenant Colonel E W W DERING   2 Dec 1894
2nd Lieutenant A M BROOKE   30 May 1895
Major L GORDON   5 Feb 1896
This tablet is erected by their brother officers.
                                      (82)(93)(brass)

- 272 -

QUEEN'S REGIMENT   CHRISTCHURCH
Sacred to the memory of the following men of A Company 1st
Battalion The Queen's Regiment who died during the stay of the
regiment at Rawalpindi 1898 to 1902.
Private H EBDON   Private D LEE
Private A RUFFETT   Private J GARLAND
Private E EAGLEN   Private C HERBERT
Private T THOMSON
Erected by their comrades of "A" Company. AHMUD BUX & CO,
RAWALPINDI.   (82)(93)(brass)

RIFLE BRIGADE   CHRISTCHURCH
Rifle Brigade (3rd Battalion). Dedicated by their comrades to
the memory of
Major Frank Stewart Whittington RAIKES
2nd Lieutenant The Hon Henry CAVENDISH
2nd Lieutenant John Fielding Hill KANE

Sergeant A TYLER	Rifleman J COOPER
Sergeant G A HARDING	Rifleman MITCHELL
Corporal H HOLLAND	Rifleman F ROLPH
Acting Corporal A FAULKNER	Rifleman J SLADE
Acting Corporal F P WALL	Rifleman J H WILLIAMS
Acting Corporal J WHITING	Rifleman H FLETCHER
Acting Corporal W J MITCHELL	Rifleman G BATESON
Acting Corporal A DOREY	Rifleman T BURRIDGE
Acting Corporal S MOUNCEY	Rifleman F WARREN
Acting Corporal H H PHAROAH	Rifleman F GUTTRIDGE
Bugler G SIMMONDS	Rifleman P A MOORE
Rifleman G FRANCIS	Rifleman A J ALLISON
Rifleman H WATKINS	Rifleman H BRIGGS
Rifleman P HAWKES	Rifleman H WALSH
Rifleman J CONNOR	Rifleman W L TAYLOR
Rifleman E DOUTHWAITE	Rifleman W SULLIVAN
Rifleman J GLEDHILL	Rifleman W A COX
Rifleman J T ELLIS	Rifleman E I F COX
Rifleman H KNIGHT	Rifleman W H MASLIN
Rifleman C JONES	Rifleman H C CARLTON
Rifleman E SARTAIN	Rifleman T H HODGKINS
Rifleman H PRITCHARD	Rifleman B THOMAS
Rifleman J LOWE	Rifleman B BARLOW
Rifleman W WINSOR	Rifleman H G MILLS
Rifleman W BARTON	Rifleman H BARCOCK
Rifleman R DOWNHAM	Rifleman W J THOMPSON
Rifleman A JONES	Rifleman J H BLISSET
Rifleman T WILLIAMS	Rifleman W HILL
Rifleman E CLEAVER	Rifleman W HUNT
Rifleman A J SMITH	Rifleman G HARGREAVES
Rifleman G WALDEN	Rifleman W R LOVELOCK
Rifleman E PETTY	Rifleman J T WEEKS
Rifleman R TONKIN	Rifleman L MULLETT
Rifleman G SLATER	Rifleman A LUNN
Rifleman B WHITTY	Rifleman W V CHANNELL
Rifleman W J BROWN	Rifleman J DEVINE
Rifleman F G LAWRENCE	Rifleman G COX

/continued..........

RIFLE BRIGADE (cont)

Rifleman A J FLETCHER
Rifleman A JONES
Rifleman H T BROWN
Rifleman T DEFLY
Rifleman A DEWICK
Rifleman E G LEWINS
Rifleman A W BRYANT
Rifleman H JONES
Rifleman J BRINDLEY
Rifleman G E HANCOX
Rifleman C J WRIGHT
Rifleman A SKEWS
Rifleman E C RICHARDS
Rifleman R HART
Rifleman G FIELD
Rifleman S O DALE

Rifleman W J SMITH
Rifleman M MELVIN
Rifleman A G KEELEY
Rifleman C CANNON
Rifleman G AVIS
Rifleman A G TIDY
Rifleman T TOMALIN
Rifleman W WILKINS
Rifleman A GOSNEY
Rifleman W SIMMONS
Rifleman F C SMITH
Rifleman H W DAY
Rifleman W CARPENTER
Rifleman W HILL
Rifleman W DAWE
Rifleman J DOUBLEDAY

who died in the Tochi Valley, North West Frontier between July and December 1897.
(82)(93)(brass)

ROYAL ARMY SERVICE CORPS   CHRISTCHURCH
To the memory of officers of the Royal Army Service Corps who died while serving in India. Erected by brother officers of the Corps in India.

Captain Charles Trevor LLOYD
        Died at Murree   2 Jul 1906
Captain Lionel George Montagu HARCOURT
        Died at Quetta   4 Feb 1909
Captain Arthur Alexander GEDDES
        Died at Rawalpindi   5 Jul 1916
Lieutenant Colonel Harrie Reginald LEVER, OBE
        Died at Dera Ismail Khan 17 Nov 1920
Lieutenant Brian Usher FARRELL
        Died at Manzai   27 Jun 1921
Major John Alfred HAMILTON, DSO
        Died at Dera Ismail Khan 19 Jul 1921
Lieutenant Arthur Sidney Noel BARRON
        Died at Manzai   29 Jul 1922
(82)(93)(brass)

ROYAL ARTILLERY (1)   CHRISTCHURCH
In memory of the NC officers and men of No 9 Mountain Battery RA, who died during the period of 1884-94 whilst serving in the Rawalpindi District

Sergeant D CONNELL
Gunner J JOHNSON
Gunner R WARD
Gunner C VARDON
Gunner W EVANS

A/Bombadier W GEORGE
Gunner A C BLAND
Gunner R BILBY
Gunner J CHEESEMAN
Gunner D HORGAN

(82)(93)(brass)

ROYAL ARTILLERY (2)   CHRISTCHURCH
In memory of the following Noncommissioned Officers and men of No 1 (Mountain) Battery, 1st Brigade, Eastern Division Royal Artillery who died on service in Burma 1886-8.
- No 30329 Gunner William BOURKE
- No 29465 Gunner Robert GLYNN
- No 20437 Bombadier George HARRIS
- No 48926 Gunner John ABBOTT
- No 31920 Gunner Patrick YOUNG
- No 32344 Gunner Cornelius BUCKLEY
- No 50606 Gunner Francis GLEESON

Erected as a token of respect by the officers, noncommissioned officers and men of the battery. P ORR & SONS, MANUFACTURERS, MADRAS.   *(82)(93)(brass)*

ROYAL FIELD ARTILLERY   CHRISTCHURCH
Sacred to the memory of the following noncommissioned officer, men and children 51st Battery Royal Field Artillery who died at Rawalpindi 1899 - 1900:

Driver R DOWNING	16 Aug 99
SS Farrier G TILLER	1 Sep 99
Child W T G WHEELER	17 Sep 99
Child T H WHEELER	7 Jan 00
Child H M MERCHANT	27 May 00
Gunner D SHEEHAN	7 Jul 00

(82)(93)(WM)

A MILITARY BAND PLAYING OUTSIDE THE CLUB, RAWALPINDI

ROYAL GARRISON ARTILLERY (1)   CHRISTCHURCH
Sacred to the memory of the following NC officers and gunners of 74 Company of Royal Garrison Artillery, who died at Rawalpindi during the period 1906-1913.
Park Sergeant J DOWNING   Sergeant H COOK
Gunner A BOYCE   Gunner A JEFFERIES
Gunner S LYNCH   Gunner H MYERS
Gunner C ROBINSON
This tablet is erected in affectionate remembrance by their comrades who served with them in the Company. *(82)(93)(brass)*

ROYAL GARRISON ARTILLERY (2)   CHRISTCHURCH
Sacred to the memory of the NCOs and men of 104 Company, Heavy Battery, RGA, who died at Rawalpindi from Nov 1901 to December 1905.
          No 54945 Corporal J W GRIFFITHS
          No 21552 Bombadier F T SQUIER
          No 50365 Gunner W W ATKINSON
          No 25147 Gunner C NORMAN
          No 29582 Gunner H McCONNELL
Erected by the officers, NCOs and men of the battery.
                                 (82)(93)(brass)

ROYAL HORSE ARTILLERY (1)   CHRISTCHURCH
In memory of the NCO's and men of "J" Battery, Royal Horse Artillery who died during the Battery's term of service in India 1902-1907:
At Meerut
Gunner W HATCH   A/Bombadier R STEVENS
Gunner A HIGGET   Driver W T BARTLETT
Gunner W S TARR   Gunner J GUNTER
            Gunner J MIDDLEMAS
At Rawalpindi
Driver G W HAWES   SS T JEFFREYS
Gunner J SAVIN   Battery Sergeant Major S MAJOR
Gunner P HODKINSON   Bombadier J A MERSH
Corporal H CULLUM   A/Bombadier V SMITH
Driver J MANETTI   Driver A MITCHELL
Gunner C SANDIFORTH   A/Bombadier B STRIVENS
Battery Sergeant Major M J BURKE   also Mrs HART
This memorial is erected by the officers, noncommissioned officers and men of the battery. *(82)(93)(brass)*

ROYAL HORSE ARTILLERY (2)   CHRISTCHURCH
To the glory of God and in memory of
Lieutenant COOKES   Bombadier COWPER
Trumpeter MOORE   Gunner BIRCHALL
Gunner MANLEY   Driver MOON
Gunner CHILVERS   Driver LANE
of "N" Battery, "B" Brigade, Royal Horse Artillery, who died Rawalpindi during the year 1888. Thy will be done. This tablet is erected as a mark of respect by the officers, non-commissioned officers and men of the Battery. COX AND BUCKLEY, LONDON.   *(82)(93)(brass)*

SEAFORTH HIGHLANDERS   ST PAULS CHURCH
Names of the officers, NCOs and men in memory of whom the
above window was erected by the regiment:
    Major the Hon Douglas FORBES-SEMPILL, DSO
    Major Neil Campbell MacLACHLAN
    2nd Lieutenant Ian Campbell MacFADYEN (attached)
    Sergeant Alexander Evan MacKENZIE
    Private Robert FORDYCE
    Private John WHITE
    Private Albert ECCLESTONE
    Private John SMITH
    Private Murdo MORRISON
J WHIPPELL & CO LTD, EXETER AND LONDON   *(82)(93)*

Stained Glass Window Above
To the glory of God and in memory of the officers and men of
the 1st Battalion Seaforth Highlanders who were killed in action or died of wounds or disease in the Bazar Valley and
Mohmand Expeditions, North West Frontier 1908.
                                    (82)(93)

SHERWOOD FORESTERS   CHRISTCHURCH
Sacred to the memory of those warrant officers, noncommissioned officers, men and children of the 2nd Battalion, The
Sherwood Foresters, who died at Rawalpindi during the years
1923 to 1925.
    Boy A C SANDERS
    L/Sergeant L W WAGSTAFFE
    Private J A FARMER
    Private G W LAWRENCE
    CSM A W UNWIN
    Private L L PEAT
    George GILL (son of Private G GILL)
    Emily Elizabeth NOBLE (daughter of RQMS W J NOBLE)
    Cynthia Mary LOUND (daughter of Colour Sergeant E LOUND)
                                    (82)(93)(brass)

UNNAMED REGIMENT   OLD CEMETERY
To the memory of:
John McENTIRE   Died 27 Jul 1852   Aged 32
William DAVIS   Died 4 Sep 1852   Aged 32
Joseph WARBURTON   Died 25 Dec 1852   Aged 28
Hugh POGAN   Died 4 Jan 1853   Aged 29
Stephen POTTER   Died 9 Jan 1853   Aged 28
Richard STRAW   Died 24 Mar 1853   Aged 25
John DODD who was drowned whilst bathing 29 May 1853 Aged 25
                                    (82)

UNNAMED REGIMENT   OLD CEMETERY
...ove Comp...
1855.... Jul 18...   Jul 185...   Aug 185...   Sep 185...
                                    (93)(BS)

3RD (PRINCE OF WALES'S) DRAGOON GUARDS   CHRISTCHURCH
In memory of the following officers and noncommissioned officers and men of the 3rd (Prince of Wales's) Dragoon Guards, who died at Rawalpindi 1890-1892.

Major W U COLE
Sergeant STAPELEY
Sergeant Farrier HOPCROFT
Lance Corporal SARGEANT
Lance Corporal T PAGE
Lance Corporal ELPHICK
Lance Corporal TRANTER
Lance Corporal G GREEN
Lance Corporal McPHERSON
Trumpeter BUCKLEY
2nd Lieutenant S E EDWARDS
Private J ALEXANDER
Private RIDGERS
Private J T WALSH
Private McGUIRE
Private J W THOMSON
Private BLACKBURN
Private G JONES
Private J SMITH

Major F S DIMOND
Private REEVE
Private FORBES
Private J WILSON
Private MATTHEWS
Private RICHARDSON
Private WINTERHALDER
Private PELL
Private WELLS
Private BOOTH
Private E WILLIAMS
Private W WOODS
Private McMANN
Private MUNN
Private A BROWN
Private W KING
Private G REED
Private CUTTS
Private EVEREST

Erected by officers, nco and men of the regiment.   HART, SON, PEARD AND CO, LTD, LONDON.   (82)(93)(brass)

4TH DRAGOON GUARDS (1)   CHRISTCHURCH
4th Dragoon Guards. Dedicated by their comrades to the memory of the following NCOs and men of the 4th Dragoon Guards who died or were killed in action during their service in the Punjab from 4 Oct 1894 to 21 Jan 1903.

SSM G MOORE
SQMS F CLARK
Sergeant A W HENRY
Sergeant W HERRIDGE
Sergeant J LEYDEN
Sergeant H LISLE
Sergeant C D MENDHAM
Sergeant J H STYLES
Sergeant A T TAYLOR
Sergeant G H WALKER
Sergeant A R WICKS
L/Sergeant R A SCRIVENER
Corporal C LANGFIELD
Corporal S LAVERY
Corporal J WALTON
Corporal J WESTERMAN
Corporal A WICKS
Corporal SS A F HAGGER
L/Corporal J J TOWEY
L/Corporal H GRIFFITHS
L/Corporal L A LOCKE
L/Corporal T S RUTHERFORD
L/Corporal E J SUTTON

Private F FREEMAN
Private F FRENCHAM
Private F GRIFFIN
Private J GORDON
Private J GILMARTIN
Private J HEWINGS
Private S HALLETT
Private G F JOHNSTON
Private A V KING
Private J LEFTELY
Private W G LENEY
Private W LEWIS
Private P LOCKE
Private E LOCKYER
Private R McFARLAND
Private J McINTYRE
Private T A McWILLIAM
Private E MORLEY
Private G J PALMER
Private A PARKER
Private E T PAYNE
Private W F PIRRIE
Private M QUINLIN
/continued..........

4TH DRAGOON GUARDS (1) (cont)

L/Corporal R SEMPLE
Private H G BODDY
Private H C BOSKETT
Private H BURTENSHAW
Private E V BURTON
Private W BUSSEY
Private A R BUTCHER
Private W G CLARK
Private G F CLEMENTS
Private E CLEMSON
Private B A COUZENS
Private M DARCY
Private P S DAWES
Private S H DEAN
Private W FENNELL
Private F FLANAGAN
Private H W FLOOD
Private F H FOX
Private A FRANKLIN
Private J FRANKLIN
Private J WINTERSON

Private W REES
Private F R REYNOLDS
Private W ROBERTS
Private E SANDERS
Private H SAVILLE
Private E SCULLY
Private H R SMITH
Private R SPARKS
Private R A SPITZER
Private M STERLING
Private J A STURMER
Private W SWAN
Private W TAYLOR
Private P TUBINO
Private T WALSH
Private A WARD
Private F C WATERS
Private W J WEBSTER
Private H V WEEKS
Private W WIGHTMAN
(82)(93)(brass)

4th DRAGOON GUARDS (2)   CHRISTCHURCH
Sacred to the memory of
Rintoul Archer MILWARD-JONES, Lieutenant, 4th Dragoon Guards,
     who died at Murree October 5th 1897. Aged 31.
Thomas Frederick Newcome JONES, Captain, 4th Dragoon Guards.
     Shot on patrol near Jumrood October 10th 1897. Aged 31.
Charles CROSBIE, Lieutenant, 4th Dragoon Guards, who departed
     this life at Rawalpindi from an accident at polo January
     12th 1898. Aged 23.
Erected by their brother officers. Also of
Gabriel Burrell GEACH, Captain, 4th Dragoon Guards,
     who died at Murree 1st July 1899. Aged 37.
Hon William WROTTESLEY, Captain, 4th Dragoon Guards,
     who died at sea 1st Oct. 1899. Aged 36.
                               (82)(93)(brass)

CAMBRIDGE BARRACKS, RAWALPINDI

9TH LANCERS   CHRISTCHURCH
To the glory of God and in memory of our comrades, who fell in South Africa 1899-1902. This tablet is erected by the officers, NCOs and men of "C" Squadron, 9th Lancers.
2nd Lieutenant J POLLOCK
2nd Lieutenant The Honourable A MacDONALD

Sergeant W HART	Private C BAKER
Corporal C GUY	Private G COOK
Corporal C WILKINS	Private F GRIFFITHS
L/Corporal R HEANES	Private A GOULDING
Lance Corporal W JOHNS	Private L HORSENELL
Private W ALLEN	Private G LAVENDER
Private J BRIGGS	Private E LAVERS
Private A BANKS	Private E McNICOL
Private M BACON	Private G MERRIMAN
Private J BROWN	Private C MOODY
Private E WINTERBOTTOM	Private F NORMAN
Private J PIERCE	Private S PENTLOW
Private R RAE	Private J RIDGE
Private A STONE	Private A STEWART
Private L TURNER	Private R WINN
Private C WARD	Private A WATSON

P ORR, ART METAL WORKERS, MADRAS, RANGOON AND COLOMBO.
(82)(93)(brass)

9TH REGIMENT   CHRISTCHURCH
To the glory of God and in memory of 50 noncommissioned officers and privates, 6 women and 24 children belonging to the Corps who have died since leaving England in Oct 1874. The reredos is erected by the officers, noncommissioned officers and privates of HM's 2nd Battalion, 9th Regiment. 5 Nov 1877.
(82)(93)(brass)

A VIEW OF THE OLD CEMETERY

22ND REGIMENT   OLD CEMETERY
....members of the 22nd Regiment who died at Rawalpindi 1852 to 1853. *(names have all gone now)* *(82)*

36TH SIKHS   CHRISTCHURCH

Sacred to the memory of the undermentioned officers of 36th Sikhs who fell in action or died of wounds or disease contracted on active service during the war 1914-19.

Pekin
Major D de C IRELAND   7 Jan 1915
Neuve Chapelle
Captain W H PADDAY   21 Dec 1914
Beit-Aiessa
Captain J GRAY   12 Apr 1916
Captain A D MARTIN   17 Apr 1916
Kut-el-Amara
Lieutenant G A H ANSCOMBE   1 Feb 1917
Lieutenant E L J BARSTOW   1 Feb 1917
Lieutenant G H St P BUNBURY   1 Feb 1917
Lieutenant C S CUNNINGHAM   1 Feb 1917
Captain S Des VOEUX   1 Feb 1917
Lieutenant J H MITCHELL   1 Feb 1917
Cape Town
Brigadier General O G GUNNING, CMG,DSO   14 Nov 1917
Amara
Lieutenant A H M WEST   7 Jan 1918

ARMY & NAVY CS, LTD, BOMBAY.   (82)(93)(brass)

CHRISTCHURCH, RAWALPINDI (SEE ALSO PAGE 257)

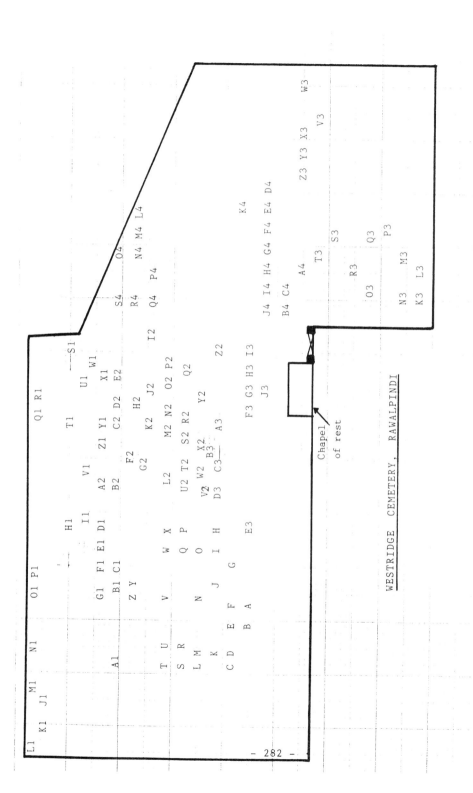

Appendix A

R E G I M E N T S

The following names have been extracted from the Inscriptions in all cemeteries included in this book. They are listed under the regimental names as they used to be known. The names on the Regimental plaques listed at the end of both sections of inscriptions have not been repeated. Other organisations such as the Railways, Masons etc are listed, and the various Indian Army regiments (eg. 19th Bengal Lancers, 3rd Punjab Cavalry) are collected together under the heading "Indian Army".

ARGYLL AND SUTHERLAND HIGHLANDERS : Downey. Morrison. No Name.

ARMY REMOUNT REGIMENT : Ablett. Jobson. Lipsham.

ARMY VETERINARY CORPS : Lane.

BEDFORDSHIRE REGIMENT : Ford. Johnson. Shrives.

BORDER REGT : Cootes. Hales. Holt. Lancaster. McLoughlin.

CARBINIERS : Hall.

COMMERCIAL : Mackenzie.

COMMISSARIAT DEPARTMENT : Loane. Rogers. Ryall.

CONNAUGHT RANGERS : Bland. Donoghue. Glen. Maffett. Ryan. Stanton. Thornton.

CUSTOMS : Nicholson.

DEVONSHIRE REGIMENT : Buxton. Casey. Crawford. Sampson. Skelly. Tabram. Tipton.

EAST SURREY REGT : Burwood. Cullimore. Harris. Hussey. Sadley.

ECCLESIASTIC/MISSIONARY : Antoninus. Armstrong. Beatty. Brown. Byrne. Coatsworth. de Ruyter. de Vreede. Downs. Finley. Fovet. Gillick. Gordon. Hill. Johnson. Kilcoyne. Kiernan. Luif. McCormick. MacDermot. McKelvie. McGuiness. Macken. Mallett. Michael. Milman. Mittleberger. Murray. O'Donoghue. O'Reilly. O'Shea. Olson. Reily. Reehil. Roberts. Rooke. Ruiz. Smyth. Thackwell. White. Williams. Williams. Wright.

EDUCATION : Housden. Percy. Pratt. Stewart.

GLOUCESTERSHIRE REGT : Banks. Gorwood. Hann. Pill. Rabjohns.

GORDON HIGHLANDERS : Bailey. Davidson. Duncan. Harris. Hurst. McRobb. Rennie.

HAMPSHIRE REGIMENT : Cook. Low. Olden. Sumner.

HIGHLAND LIGHT INFANTRY : Pollock.

INDIAN ARMY : Ames. Archibald. Baker. Battye. Bayly. Beaty. Bignell. Blair. Bond. Boutcher. Butler. Caley. Carnegy. Carr. Chapman. Chatterton. Creagh. D'Aquilar. De Cruz. Dickinson. Ewart. Gilmore. Goodwin. Gordon. Gwatkin. Harris. Haughton. Hill. Leeds. Lindsell. McCay. Macleod. Money. Monro. Morant. Murray. Norman. Oliver. Passy. Peter. Ralston. Renny. Rich. Rogers. Rundall. Rutledge. Samuells. Seymour. Smith. St John. Trotter. Turing. Turner. Udal. Vyse. Wakefield. Walker. Warre-Cornish. Wild. Wilson.

INDIAN ARMY CORPS OF CLERKS : Bake.

INDIAN ARMY NURSING SERVICE : Cann.

INDIAN ARMY ORDNANCE CORPS : Bristow. Carroll. Connolly. Croce. Hinge. Holmes. Rice. Robinson. Sharpe. Thrussell. Vaney. Watson. Webb. Welshman.

INDIAN CIVIL SERVICE : Darling. Mainprice. Pocock. Stainton.

INDIAN FINANCE DEPARTMENT : Farrell.

INDIAN MEDICAL SERVICE : Corry.

KING'S DRAGOON GUARDS : Jones. O'Donnell. Paterson. Rickman. Seymour. Shaw. Sherlock. Simmonds. Thomas. Warren.

KING'S OWN ROYAL REGIMENT : Godfrey. Porter.

KING'S OWN SCOTTISH BORDERERS : Bolton. Dering. Foy. Goodall. Gordon. Kirkwood. Lawrie. MacFarlane. McGown. Murphy. Oakes. Parkinson. Sims. Wells.

KING'S OWN YORKSHIRE (LIGHT?) INFANTRY : Stevens.

KING'S ROYAL IRISH FUSILIERS : Hunter. Lacy. McKeon. McKerney. McNabo. Sampson. Spencer.

KING'S ROYAL RIFLE CORPS : Bell. Bowles. Broome. Connicale. Eckert. Franklin. Franks. Hetherington. Homer. MacLachlan. Morris. Parrott. Proctor. Rice. Rough. Thomas. Tompkins. Topping. Wilson. Young.

KING'S SHROPSHIRE LIGHT INFANTRY : Brien. Carter. Coombes. Harvey. Lee. Murphy. Powell.

LANCASHIRE FUSILIERS : Bainbridge. Parry.

LEICESTERSHIRE REGIMENT : Langford.

MASON : Bourne. Ennis.

MEDICAL : Bowder. Finley. Finnerty. Ghosh. Gill. Godwin. Grose. Hart. Holmes. Jephson. Johnson. Jones. L'Fleur. Livingstone. MacKenzie. McMurray. Morris. Painter. Ring. Smellie. Sweales. Tapsall. Thropp. Van Cuylenburg.

MILITARY ACCOUNTS DEPT : Aikin. Davies. Hastings. Mark.

MILITARY ENGINEERING SERVICE : Hammond. Warbuton.

MILITARY WORKS SERVICE : Crunden. McDonough. MacGregor. Mitchell. Ryan. Smee.

NORFOLK REGIMENT : Cooper.

NORTH STAFFORDSHIRE REGIMENT : Farmer. Ingram. Lloyde. Styles. Whalley.

NORTHUMBERLAND FUSILIERS : Gordon. Lendon. Somerville. Trafford.

ORDNANCE DEPARTMENT : Bateman. Clements. Collis. Coplestone. Handley. Haswell. Lalor. Misson. Murphy. Owen. Todd. Wells. Welton. Wigmore.

OXFORDSHIRE AND BUCKINGHAMSHIRE LIGHT INFANTRY : Chambers. Coyne. Odell. Pilling. Reed. Rocker. Taylor.

POLICE : Blake. Clayton. Donaldson. Goldney. Marshall. Smith. Spencer. Turnbull.

POSTAL SERVICE : Bout.

PUBLIC WORKS DEPARTMENT : Albert. Barker. Beckett. Delaney. Jackson. Stewart.

QUEEN'S BAYS : Charles. O'Connor. Willcox.

QUEEN'S RWS REGIMENT : Corley. Cox. Crawley. Crees. Jenner. Lacey. Langton. Mallam. Manditt. Maskell. Rudd. Smith. Stratford-Collis. Swindon. Turner. Warner.

QUEEN'S ROYAL LANCERS : Horner.

QUEEN'S ROYAL REGIMENT : Phillips.

RAILWAYS : Adams. Anthony. Bailey. Bayes. Hartt. MacFarlane. Master. Page. Raper. Reid. Sass. Troundsell. Turner. Wragge. Young.

RIFLE BRIGADE : Allen. Barnard. Cavendish. Glayton. Cooper. Franklin. Frankline. Freeman. Gelder. Govier. Greenshields. Hand. Hill. McMahon. Pharaoh. Roberts. Rutter. Smee. Smith. Spicer. Stevens. Thrussell. Tugwell. Trueman. Wignall.

ROYAL AIR FORCE : Cooke. Kossakowski. Wilding.

ROYAL ARMY ORDNANCE CORPS : Blackman. Cornford. Davis.
Millard. Sanderson. Stacey.

ROYAL ARMY SERVICE CORPS : Birtwistle. Horner. Howard. Lloyd.

ROYAL ARTILLERY : Atkin. Barton. Bent. Bestford. Bruce.
Burbidge. Cardy. Carroll. Carter. Cater. Cook.
Coplestone. Cuddy. Davie. Davis. Day. Doherty. Donaldson.
Evans. Fleming. Fuller. Gallagher. Gardner. Gardy. Gray.
Hamilton. Hay. Hewitt. Hunt. Jackson. Kelly. Kilby.
Lawrence. Leyden. McCauley. MacDonald. McGregor. Mailyer.
Mariden. Matthews. Miller. Moore. Mortimer. Nelson.
Pike. Preedy. Rampling. Richards. Robey. Rooney. Roper.
Sadler. Samuel. Sellers. Smith. Staines. Stemp.
Stratford. Tatham. Thomas. Thompson. Waldren. Walker.
Waller. Warbuton. Watson. Waugh. Wheeler. Williams.

ROYAL CORPS OF SIGNALS : Bye. Caltress. Camp. Cann. Cole.
Draper. Ellis. Leeder. Pring. Ratcliffe. Rutherford.
Saratt. Spratt. Starke. Sutton. Walsh. Warner. Worth.

ROYAL ENGINEERS : Barton. Chester. Delaney. Elliott.
Hingston. Hodgson. Johnson. Kirby. Limond. Medley.
Morant. Nolan. Ogilvie. Potts. Rich. Stone. Travers.
Walker. Ward. Winsloe.

ROYAL FIELD ARTILLERY : Bagley. Baker. Benham. Bentley.
Browne. Earp. Fowler. Gittings. Gre... Griffen. Heath.
James. Jones. Lucas. Lynch. McCarthy. Merchant. Miller.
Pye. Read. Remblance. Riffen. Smith. Spender. Stead.
Stewart. Stinson. Taylor. Waters. Weedon. Wilkie.

ROYAL GARRISON ARTILLERY : Allen. Batchelor. Bourke.
Brooks. Burnidge. Byrne. Cadman. Clarke. Cleary. Clemo.
Davies. Feeley. Furr. Glasby. Green. Griffiths. Haugh.
Henderson. Hersey. Large. McConnell. Pickup. Pymont.
Robinson. Sawers. Sergent. Sharpe. Sinel. Spear. Squier.
Stanly. Steward. Stewart. Trevelyan. Turner. Wallace.
Wyatt.

ROYAL HORSE ARTILLERY : Anscomb. Aspin. Bowyer. Brogan.
Brooks. Brownbill. Burt. Cookes. Cupit. Curtis. Dobson.
Gardiner. Green. Hayes. Hodges. Hunter. Johnston.
Leicester. Loonam. McCaw. Maxwell. Nash. Phillips. Pratt.
Randall. Ransom. Rowan. Ryan. Valler. Walker. Wild.
Wilson. Woods.

ROYAL INDIAN ARMY SERVICE CORPS : Calder. Carter. Cheeseman.
Davison. Dunford. Griffin. Holdway. Lumsden. Richards.
Stevens. Thomas.

ROYAL IRISH DRAGOON GUARDS : Gordon. Jarmain. Rutherford.
Stirling.

ROYAL IRISH FUSILIERS : Caves. Daley. Donoghue. Fagan.
Kelsey. McKeoane. Wheeler. Willis.

ROYAL IRISH REGIMENT : Atherley. Bernard. Culleton. Fitz-Maurice-Deane-Morgan. Foley. Frost. Henley. Keating. Lawrence. Malone. Massy. Montgomery. Moore. Murphy. Shenley. Slattery. Stratton. Strutton. Todd. Willbond.

ROYAL MUNSTER FUSILIERS : Collins. McCourt. North. Smith. Stevenson.

ROYAL SCOTS FUSILIERS : Coyle. Craufurd. McCormack.

ROYAL SUSSEX REGIMENT : Alberry. Bailey. Birdwood. Bowers. Burke. Butler. Care. Carter. Craeer. Davis. Egan. Eldridge. Funnell. Green. Hearndon. Holden. Lamb. Pearce. Plummer. Radford. Talbott. Summers. Thorndike.

ROYAL TANK CORPS : Barton. Scammell. Vaughan.

ROYAL ULSTER RIFLES : Armstrong.

S & T CORPS : Bradley. Cadogan. Cobb. Graham. Sadler. Tyler. Wilsey.

SAPPERS AND MINERS : Dew.

SEAFORTH HIGHLANDERS : Campbell. Dixon. Douglass. Fraser. Gemmell. Halkett. Howarth. Williams.

SHERWOOD FORRESTERS : Farmer. Lawrence. Lound. Nobles. Peat. Sanders. Unwin. Wagstaffe.

SOMERSET LIGHT INFANTRY : Chaddock. Curry. Guppy. Price.

SOUTH WALES BORDERERS : Bromley. Ford. Hiley. Howells. Hughes. Penticost. Richards.

SUFFOLK REGIMENT : Lucas. Stock.

SUTHERLAND HIGHLANDERS : Thomas.

TELEGRAPH DEPT : Allen. Burnett. D'Cunha. Dodd. La Frenais. Smith. Wood.

WAR GRAVE : Cadogan. De Cruz.

WELCH REGT : Burn. Evans. Ogilvie. Price. Shaunnessy. Will.

WEST RIDING REGIMENT : Sutcliffe.

WEST YORKSHIRE REGIMENT : Spencer.

WILTSHIRE REGT : Ashley. Baily. Burt. Charlton. Gerring. Gray. Martin. Miles. Musselwhite. Painter. Perrett. Probets. Robinson. Smith. Stroud. Trollop. Wareham.

WORCESTERSHIRE REGIMENT : Dean. Jones.

1ST DRAGOON GUARDS : Colyer. Sully.

2ND DRAGOON GUARDS (QUEEN'S BAYS) : Allard. Gardiner. Luff.

3RD DRAGOON GUARDS : Brown. Edwards. Everest. Forbes. Maguire. Moore. Munn. No Name. Pace. Reeve. Sutton. Wilson.

3RD KING'S OWN HUSSARS : James. White.

4TH DRAGOON GUARDS : Allman. Bell. Brown. Chapman. Clarke. Crosbie. Doyne. Hook. Humphries. Johnston. Maughan. Mendham. Sprent. Styles. Wicks.

4TH QUEEN'S OWN HUSSARS : Boulter. Thomas.

4TH ROYAL IRISH DRAGOON GUARDS : Franklin. Reynolds. Wicks.

5TH FUSILIERS : Wooll.

6TH ROYAL REGT : Farrington. Mayr. No Name. Whittaker. Wright.

8TH KING'S ROYAL IRISH HUSSARS : Bolton. Christy. Clarke. Edden. Halliday. Mountford. Ogle. Quin.

8TH THE KING'S REGT : Connell. Enright. Paines. Passant. Seaton

9TH QUEEN'S ROYAL LANCERS : Avis. Bates. Cahoon. Charlesworth. Crosby. French. Hawkins. Hersey. Hird. Hoyes. Hulme. Hursey. Lewis. Luther. McCrea. Malone. Smith. Vesey. Wales.

9TH REGIMENT : Boughton. Chansey. Foley. Guazzaroni. Murray. Stevens. Stewart.

10TH ROYAL HUSSARS : Batten. Clothier. Collinson. Cunningham. Edwards. Glazier. Gray. Green. Hartley. Jones. King. Morgan. Neale. Quinn. Reid. Richards. Rowley. Scott. Studd. Walton. Willis. Wilson-Allen.

12TH ROYAL LANCERS : Reid.

13TH LIGHT INFANTRY : Frere.

14TH/20TH HUSSARS : Milroy.

17TH REGIMENT : Close. Fallon.

19TH REGIMENT Christopher. G........

21ST EMPRESS OF INDIA LANCERS : Blease. Harris. Holland. Owen. Thompson.

22ND REGIMENT : Benton. Dirkby. Ellis. Kelly.

30TH REGIMENT : Moorsom.

36TH REGT : Bevitt. Bryant. Clemmett. Sheahan. Keane. Wright.

38TH REGIMENT : Hynes. Nelson. Reilly. White.

60TH ROYAL RIFLES : Hill. Hyde. Obey. Woodward.

70TH REGT : Bleakley. Camp. Clark. Cleary. Connor. Delaney. Duffey. Forbes. Guthrie. Hughes. Jupp.... Leary. No Name. Rielly. Robinson. Russell. Smith. Sutton. Wilkinson.

78TH HIGHLANDERS : Pratice.

79TH CAMERON HIGHLANDERS : Baxter. Fraser. Smith. Wade.

80TH REGIMENT : Hutchison.

81ST REGIMENT : Anderson (? 31st Regt). Murphy. Smith.

85TH REGIMENT : Sladen.

88TH REGIMENT : O'Dwyer

****

Appendix B

CHAPLAINS OF CHRISTCHURCH, RAWALPINDI

Within the Christchurch hangs a board listing the Chaplains who have served at Christ Church:

Rev J M SHAW	1850
Rev R B MALTLY	1858
Rev J K STUART	1858
Rev N N PHELPS	1862
Rev A N IRVIN	1865
Rev M S LAING	1870
Rev W C BROMHEAD	1876
Rev W F ARMSTRONG	1877
Rev W M LETHBRIDGE	1887
Rev A W SPENS	1888
Rev J MOULSON	1893
Rev W B HANDFORD	1896
Rev H J SPENCE-GRAY	1899
Rev C STEWART	1901
Rev H A HARBERT (sic)	1905
Rev A J WHEELER	1907
Rev J BROOKES	1910
Rev W W CASTLE	1911
Rev A B F COLE	1916
Rev J E H WILLIAMS	1919
Rev R S B PROBY	1920
Rev H V ENGLAND	1923
Rev N E MARSHALL	1926
Rev J G LISTER	1929
Rev N E MARSHALL	1934
Rev G W JONES	1938
Rev F J FISH	1945

Appendix C

MISSING AND ADDITIONAL HEADSTONES

1982

The first of the two lists which follow gives the names of the headstones which were recorded in 1982, but were not located during the follow-up survey in 1993. As a map was not made during the initial 1982 survey, it has not been possible to assess whether all these missing headstones come from the same area of the cemetery. However, many of them are the older ones, and FARRINGTON, for example, was known to have been amongst the older graves on the left as you enter the cemetery through the lychgate.

Algar, Allen, Anderson, Apted, Babbett, Baily, Banks, Batten, Baxter, Beatty, Bent, Binge, Blackwell, Boileau, Boughton, Boulter, Broadway, Broome, Brown, Brownlee, Bruton, Burnidge, Buxton, Camp, Campbell, Chansey, Clarke, Clayton, Clements, Coates, Colyer, Cook, Costello, Crees, Crompton, Cullimore, Curley, Curry, de ...., D'Cunha, Daniel, Dobson, Doherty, Dunford, Egan, Evans, Farrington, Force, Freeman, Furr, G...., Galloway, Gardiner, Gelder, Glazier, Gray, Green, Griffen, Haswell, Haugh, Hay, Henley, Hersey, Hoare, Holden, Holland, Hynes, Irving, Jackson, Johnson, Johnstone, Jones, Joyce, Keough, Lacy, Lawrence, Lee, Lobo, Luff, MacBean, McCarthy, MacKay, Malone, Marshall, Martin, Mascarenha, Mayr, Montgomery, Morgan, Morley, Munn, Naylerrin, No Name, O'Connor, Obey, Ogle, Olson, Paine, Paines, Pais, Parsick, Patrick, Peck, Penrose, Perrett, Pollock, Powell, Pratt, Price, Probets, Pye, Radford, Rickman, Robertson, Robinson, Roper, Rundall, Rutledge, Sadler, Sanker, Saratt, Scammell, Sheldon, Sinclair, Smith, Spencer, Steward, Stewart, Strutton, Styles, Summers, Sutton, Tatham, Taylor, Tipton, Topping, Trevelyan, Trollop, Tyler, Utting, Wailes, Wallace, Walton, Wareham, Warren, Waters, Wells, White, Willis, Wilson, Wilson-Allen, Winchelsea, Wood, Young.

1993

The following headstones were recorded for the first time in 1993. During this latter survey, every stone that it was possible to turn over or clean was turned over or cleaned. The number is also increased by the inclusion of inscriptions which date from post-1947: these were omitted from the 1982 survey.

Alwyn, Andrews, Apps, Aspin, Bailie, Baker, Banach, Baptist, Barclay, Barker, Barnes, Barrett, Barritt, Batchelor, Bates, Beckett, Benjamin, Beville, Binge, Bishop, Bolton, Bookey, Borthwick, Bowman, Boydell, Boyle, Bradley, Briggs, Bright, Brisco, Britain, Brogan, Bruce, Brydone, Buchanan, Burdett, Burton, Burne, Bye, Care, Carroll, Chambers, Charles, Chester, Claish, Clarke, Coatsworth, Coldicott, Coldwell, Conway, Cooper, Cotter, Crawford, Crosse, Cunningham, De Costa, de Mars, D'Souza, D'Vaz, De Vreede, David, Davin, Davis, Dean,
/cont.............

Dearlove, Delm...., Disney, Donaldson, Donoghue, Drummond, Dun, Edden, Ellis, England, Ensor, Farnon, Farrell, Fencott, Fendall, Ferrier, Finner, Firth, Fitzpatrick, Flanagan, Flower, Forbes, Fordyce, Fox, Francis, Funnell, Gabriel, Gardener, Ghosh, Gill, Gillick, Gilliot(?), Gittings, Giuseppina, Glover, Gomes, Goodwin, Goss, Gre.., Grose, Guest, Gunson, Guppy, Gwatkin, Haglund, Hailstone, Hammond, Hansen, Harris, Harrison, Hart, Hawkins, Heard, Hellaby, Hennessy, Henry, Hering, Heymerdingner, Hill, Hingston, Hodgkins(?), Holmes, Hoss, Housto.., Howarth, Howie, Hoyes, Hurrell, Hursey, Isabella, Jackson, Jacobs, James, Johnson, Johnston,

SOLDIERS HOME, RAWALPINDI

Johnstone, Jones, Josiah, Jupp, Jupp..., Kedda, Kelly, Kennedy, Kenney, Kiernan, Kilcoyne, King, Klein, Koch, Kossakowski, Kunhardt, La..., Lamb, Ledlie, Leeder, Lewis, Lintott, Little, Loane, Lovett, Lucas, Lucien, Luif, Lush, Lynch, McCain, McCormich, McDermott, McDonald, McDonough, MacFarlane, McGuiness, McMann, Macken, Mainprice, Mallett, Manuals, Marks, Martin, Master, Matthews, Mealing, Meek, Mendham, Michael, Millard, Miller, Mitchell, Mittelberger, Money, Morrison, Muffett, Mumford, Munro, Murray, Myers, Nash, Neesam, Newbury, Newman, Newton, Nicholson, No Name, Nolan, Norris, Nvy(?Nyx), O'Dwyer, O'Hara, O'Loughlin, O'Reilly, O'Sullivan, Olden, Osborne, Otting, Pacy, Page, Palmer, Paniz, Parnell, Pasborg, Patterson, Payne, Paxton, Pearce, Peirce, Percy, Pereira, Peters, Pharaoh, Phillips, Pill, Pilling, Pratt, Price, Pring, Quamber, Quainton, Quin, Rabjohns, Reehil, Reid, Reily, Remblance, Rennie, Rice, Richards, Rickards, Riffen, Robinson, Rodham, Rodrigues, Rogars, Ross, Rowley, Roy, Royds, Ruiz, Rutherford, Ryan, Salt, Samuells, Sargon, Sass, Sawyer, Schilt, Seaton, Secco, Seddon, Sellers, Seymour, Shalom, Shapiro, Shaw, Shenley, Shier, Smith, Smithers, Smithurst, Smyth, Spooner, Spratt, Sprent, Squier, St John, Stephens, Stevens, Stewart, Stolberg, Stratton, Strettell, Sullivan, Sumner, Sweeney, Swift, Tate, Taylor, Tellis, Tenner(?), Thipthorpe, Thomas, Thompson, Thrussell, Tims, Tomkinson, Trattner, Trotter, Trueman, Turban, Turner, Von Henning, Wade, Walsh, Waples, Ward, Watson, Welchman, White, Whittacker, Willcox, William, Willis, Wilson, Wingfield, Wood, Yates.

SOURCES

GAZETTEER OF THE RAWALPINDI DISTRICT 1893-94
Punjab Government. (Lahore 1895)

MONTY'S GRANDFATHER : A LIFE'S SERVICE FOR THE RAJ
Brian MONTGOMERY   (Blandford Press,1984)
ISBN 0 7137 1401 8

PAKISTAN : PLACES OF INTEREST
Professor Masud-ul-Hasan. (Ferozsons Ltd, Lahore)

SOLDIERS OF THE RAJ
Compiled by William de RHÉ-PHILIPE and Miles IRVING, 1912
(Reprinted by the London Stamp Exchange Ltd, 1989)
ISBN 0-948130-77-6

SUPPLEMENTARY LIST OF INSCRIPTIONS ON TOMBS OR MONUMENTS IN THE PUNJAB, NORTH-WEST FRONTIER PROVINCE, KASHMIR, SIND, AFGHANISTAN AND BALUCHISTAN
H L O GARRETT, IES. (Pubjab Government Printers, 1934)

THE BUILDING OF THE STATION CHURCHES IN THE PUNJAB : THEIR SERVICE TO THE RAJ AND THEIR CONTRIBUTION TO MISSION WORK
David SNOXELL (Al-Munshir, Islamabad, 1876)

THE GOLDEN ORIOLE
Raleigh TREVELYAN (Secker & Warburg, 1987)
ISBN 0 436 53403 7

ACKNOWLEDGEMENTS

The Harley Street Cemetery in Rawalpindi, which forms the major part of the material in this book, was one of the first cemeteries I visited in 1981 on my initial journey to Pakistan. In the fourteen years since then, I couldn't begin to count how many times I have made that fifteen mile journey from Islamabad, especially as it was only recently that I had my own transport. I am particularly grateful, therefore, to everyone who either accompanied or drove me there (or to the churches and other cemeteries) as well as all the unnamed local residents who have been supportive and encouraging, provided food and accommodation, turned up unexpectedly with drinks, or helped clear the undergrowth and turn over fallen headstones as I worked.

I am indebted to Jeremy & Patsy Ainslie, Sir Nicholas Barrington, Sally Foot, Alan Harfield, Rev Peter Koomen, Rev Emmanuel Lorraine, Judy Marshall, David Snoxall, Mary Anne Steggles, Michael Stokes, John & Sally Todd and Tim & Ali Willasey-Wilsey. Special thanks, too, to Frankie Dransfield who has been a meticulous proof-reader, and to my sister-in-law Diana Farrington, who once again has produced so many delightful drawings.

August 1995

S M Farrington
Wiveliscombe
Somerset

"For not in quiet English fields
    Are these, our brothers, laid to rest,
Where we might deck their broken shields
    With all the flowers the dead love best.

"For some are by the Delhi walls,
    And many in the Afghan land,
And many where the Ganges falls
    Through seven mouths of shifting sand."

AVE IMPERATRIX
Oscar Wilde

NOTES

N O T E S

N O T E S